2016 YEARBOOK

OF THE GENERAL ASSEMBLY

CUMBERLAND PRESBYTERIAN CHURCH

Office of the General Assembly

Cumberland Presbyterian Church

April 2016

8207 Traditional Place
Cordova (Memphis), Tennessee 38016

Compiled and edited by Elizabeth A. Vaughn for the Office of the General Assembly of the Cumberland Presbyterian Church.

Published and distributed exclusively by The Discipleship Ministry Team, CPC, Memphis, Tennessee, for the Office of the General Assembly. Additional copies may be acquired through Cumberland Presbyterian Resources.

The Discipleship Ministry Team of the Ministry Council of the Cumberland Presbyterian Church is the successor organization to the Board of Christian Education of the Cumberland Presbyterian Church.

Funded, in part, by your contributions to Our United Outreach.

First Edition 2016 (First Printing)

ISBN-13: 978-0692698921
ISBN-10: 0692698922

OUR UNITED OUTREACH
Made Possible In Part By Your Tithe To Our United Outreach

BOARD OF STEWARDSHIP, FOUNDATION AND BENEFITS
www.cumberland.org/bos

Phone (901)276-4572	FAX (901)272-3913
Robert Heflin, Executive Secretary	
rah@cumberland.org	Ext-207
Mark Duck, Coordinator of Benefits	
rmd@cumberland.org	Ext-204
Kathryn Gilbert Craig, Administrative Assistant	
kgc@cumberland.org	Ext-206

CENTRAL ACCOUNTING

Phone (901)276-4572	FAX (901)272-3913
Dan Scherf, Accounting Supervisor	
dscherf@cumberland.org	Ext-233

CP RESOURCES
resources@cumberland.org   (901)276-4581

GENERAL ASSEMBLY OFFICE
www.cumberland.org/gao

Phone (901)276-4572	FAX (901)272-3913
Michael Sharpe, Stated Clerk	
msharpe@cumberland.org	Ext-225
Elizabeth Vaughn, Assistant to the Stated Clerk	
eav@cumberland.org	Ext-226

HISTORICAL FOUNDATION OF THE CPC & CPCA
www.cumberland.org/hfcpc

Phone (901)276-8602	FAX (901)272-3913
Susan Knight Gore, Archivist	skg@cumberland.org
Missy Rose, Archival Assistant	jmr@cumberland.org

OUR UNITED OUTREACH
www.cumberland.org/ouo
4782 Waverly Court, Ooltewah, TN 37363

Cliff Hudson, Development Director   Phone (901)276-4572 Ext-210
gchudson3@gmail.com

REGIONAL DIRECTORS

Calotta Edsell	cedsell@hotmail.com
Arkansas & West Tennessee Presbyteries	(864)915-6105
Carolyn Harmon	richardharmon09@comcast.net
Presbytery of East Tennessee	(423)639-3037
Jeff McMichael	revmcmichael@outlook.com
Covenant, Cumberland & North Central Presbyteries	(270)617-4016
Susan Parker	(256)247-3877
Grace & Hope Presbyteries	park9301@bellsouth.net

MINISTRY COUNCIL
www.cpcmc.org

Phone (901)276-4572	FAX (901)276-4578
Edith Old, Director of Ministries	
eold@cumberland.org	Ext-228
Executive Assistant to the Director of Ministries	Ext-217

PASTORAL DEVELOPMENT MINISTRY TEAM

Phone (901)276-4572	FAX (901)276-4578
Chuck Brown, Team Leader	
crb@cumberland.org	Ext-235

COMMUNICATIONS MINISTRY TEAM

Phone (901)276-4572	FAX (901)276-4578
Mark J. Davis, Team Leader/Editor	
mdavis@cumberland.org	Ext-216
Sowgand Sheikholeslami, Senior Art Director	
sowgand@cumberland.org	Ext-211

DISCIPLESHIP MINISTRY TEAM

Phone (901)276-4572	FAX (901)276-4578
Elinor Brown, Team Leader	
esb@cumberland.org	Ext-205
Matthew Gore, Resources Development	
& Distribution	
mhg@cumberland.org	Ext-252
Nathan Wheeler, Youth & Young Adult Ministry	
nwheeler@cumberland.org	Ext-218
Cindy Martin, Adult & Third Age Ministry	
chm@cumberland.org	Ext-219
Jodi Rush, Children & Family Ministry	
jhr@cumberland.org	Ext-223
Greg Miller, Part-time Shipping Clerk	Ext-256

MISSIONS MINISTRY TEAM

Phone (901)276-4572	FAX (901)276-4578
Milton Ortiz, Team Leader	
mortiz@cumberland.org	Ext-234
Jinger Ellis, Manager, Finance and Administration	
jellis@cumberland.org	Ext-230
Pam Phillips-Burk, Congregational/Women's Ministry	
pam@cumberland.org	Ext-203
Johan Daza, Cross-Culture Immigrant Ministries USA	
jdaza@cumberland.org	Ext-202
T.J. Malinoski, Evangelism & New Church Development	
tmalinoski@cumberland.org	Ext-232
Lynn Thomas, Global Cross-Culture Missions	
4833 Caldwell Mill Lane, Birmingham, AL 35242	Ext-261
lynndont@gmail.com	(205)601-5770
Julie Min, Bilingual English/Korean Administrative Assistant	Ext-224

OTHER CHURCH OFFICES

BETHEL UNIVERSITY
www.bethelu.edu

325 Cherry Avenue, McKenzie, TN 38201
Phone (731)352-4000   FAX (731)352-6387
Walter Butler, President
Dale Henry, Vice President for Development
Steve Perryman, Vice President for Finance
Nancy Bean, Vice President for College of Arts & Sciences
Roland Colson, Vice President for College of Public Service
Joe Hames, Vice President for College of Health Sciences
Kelly Kelley, Vice President for College of Professional Studies

CHILDREN'S HOME
cpch@cpch.org   www.cpch.org

909 Greenlee Street, Denton, TX 76201	
Mail Address: Drawer G, Denton, TX 76202	
Phone (940)382-5112	FAX (940)387-0821
Richard Brown, President, CEO & General Counsel	(817)360-6874
rbrown@cpch.org	
Jennifer Livings, Vice President of Programs	(469)235-5921
jlivings@cpch.org	
Debbie Garrett, Asst Vice President of Development	(731)446-6241
dgarrett@cpch.org	
Mary Dickerman, Develoopment Operations	(972)765-1180
mdickerman@cpch.org	

MEMPHIS THEOLOGICAL SEMINARY
www.MemphisSeminary.edu

168 East Parkway South, Memphis, TN 38104-4395
Phone (901)458-8232   FAX (901)452-4051
Daniel J. Earheart-Brown, President
Cassandra Price-Perry, Vice-President of Operations/CFO
Stan Wood, Interim Vice-President of Academic Affairs/Dean
Keith Gaskin, Vice President of Advancement
Laurie Sharpe, Executive Assistant to the President

PROGRAM OF ALTERNATE STUDIES
www.MemphisSeminary.edu/program-of-alternate-studies

168 East Parkway South, Memphis, TN 38104-4395
Phone (901)334-5853   FAX (901)452-4051
Michael Qualls, Director
mqualls@MemphisSeminary.edu
Karen Patten, Administrative Assistant
kpatten@MemphisSeminary.edu

2016 YEARBOOK

General Assembly
Cumberland Presbyterian Church

Vision of Ministry

Biblically-based and Christ-centered
  born out of a specific sense of mission,
  the Cumberland Presbyterian Church strives to be true to its heritage:
  to be open to God's reforming spirit,
  to work cooperatively with the larger Body of Christ,
  and to nurture the connectional bonds that make us one.
The Cumberland Presbyterian Church seeks—to be the hands and feet of Christ in
witness and service to the world and, above all, the Cumberland Presbyterian Church
lives out the love of God to the glory of Jesus Christ.

Containing Statistics for the Year 2015

Changes Made to Other Data Through Print Time
(The Yearbook is updated periodically on our website www.cumberland.org/gao)

Cover Artwork by Katie Calvert

Edited by Elizabeth Vaughn

TABLE OF CONTENTS

GENERAL ASSEMBLY OFFICERS

MODERATOR
THE REVEREND MICHELE GENTRY
Urb San Jorge casa 28
Km 8 via a La Tebaida
Armenia, Quindio, COLOMBIA, SA
gentry.andes@yahoo.com
(318)285-1161

VICE MODERATOR
THE REVEREND KIP RUSH
513 Meadowlark Lane
Brentwood, TN 37027
pastor@brenthaven.org
(615)376-4563

STATED CLERK AND TREASURER
THE REVEREND MICHAEL SHARPE
8207 Traditional Place
Cordova, TN 38016
(901)276-4572
FAX (901)272-3913
msharpe@cumberland.org

ENGROSSING CLERK
THE REVEREND VERNON SANSOM
7810 Shiloh Road
Midlothian, TX 76065
(972)825-6887
vernon@sansom.us

THE BOARD OF DIRECTORS OF THE GENERAL ASSEMBLY CORPORATION

(Members whose terms expire in 2016)
(1)MR. TIM GARRETT, 150 Third Avenue South, Suite 2800, Nashville, TN 37201
   tgarrett@bassberry.com
(1)REV. BOBBY COLEMAN, 704 E Webb Street, Mountain View, AR 72560
   bobby.coleman@gmail.com
(Members whose terms expire in 2017)
(1)REV. JOHN BUTLER, PO Box 257, Sacramento, KY 42372
   jbutler@iccable.com
(1)MS. BETTY JACOB, PO Box 158, Broken Bow, OK 74728
   chocpres@pine-net.com
(Members whose terms expire in 2018)
(1)MS. CALOTTA EDSELL, 7044 Woodsong Cove, Germantown, TN 38138
   cedsell@hotmail.com
(1)REV. NORLAN SCRUDDER, 29688 S 534 Road, Park Hill, OK 74451
   ndscrudder@gmail.com

*Ecumenical Partners
+Cumberland Presbyterians in America
Numbers in parenthesis denote number of terms.

MINISTRY COUNCIL

(Members whose terms expire in 2016)
(3)REV. JILL CARR, PO Box 1547, Lebanon, MO 65536
(2)REV. TROY GREEN, 105 Cobb Hollow Lane, Petersburg, TN 37144
(3)MS. ELIZABETH HORSLEY, 1200 Imperial Drive, Denton, TX 76201
(3)MS. GWEN RODDYE, 3728 Wittenham Drive, Knoxville, TN 37921
(3)REV. SAM ROMINES, PO Box 127, Lewisburg, KY 42256
(Members whose terms expire in 2017)
(2)REV. DONNY ACTON, 1413 Oakridge Drive, Birmingham, AL 35242
(3)REV. MICHELE GENTRY DE CORREAL, Urb San Jorge casa 28, Km 8 via a La Tebaida
　　Armenia, Quinido, COLOMBIA, SOUTH AMERICA
(2)REV. LANNY JOHNSON, 120 S Mill Street, Morrison, TN 37357
(1)MR. ADAM MCREYNOLDS, PO Box 162, Bethany, IL 61914
(2)REV. TOM SANDERS, 4201 W Kent Street, Broken Arrow, OK 74012
(Members whose terms expire in 2018)
(2)MR. KENNETH BEAN, 1035 Stonewall Street N, McKenzie, TN 38201
(1)REV. PHILLIP LAYNE, 10699 Griffith Highway, Whitwell, TN 37397
(1)REV. PAULA LOUDER, 98 Gallant Court, Clarksville, TN 37043
(2)REV. RON MCMILLAN, 675 Kimberly Drive, Atoka, TN 38004
(1)MS. PATRICIA SMITH, PO Box 86, Smiths Grove, KY 42171 (deceased)

YOUTH ADVISORY MEMBERS
(1)MR. CALEB DAVIS, 502 S Alley Street, Jefferson, TX 75657
(1)MS. CAROLINA GILLIS, 6243 Sioux Lane, Birmingham, AL 35242
(2)MS. EMILY MAHONEY, 31 Barbara Circle, McMinnville, TN 37110

ADVISORY MEMBERS
REV. MICHELE GENTRY, Urb San Jorge casa 28, Km 8 via a La Tebaida,
　　Armenia, Quindio, Colombia, South America
REV. MICHAEL SHARPE, 8207 Traditional Place, Cordova, TN 38016

COMMUNICATIONS MINISTRY TEAM

(Members whose terms expire in 2016)
(1)REV. NICHOLAS CHAMBERS, 11300 Road 101, Union, MS 39365
(1)REV. STEVEN SHELTON, 7886 Farmhill Cove, Bartlett, TN 38135
(Members whose terms expire in 2017)
(3)MS. B. DENISE ADAMS, 126 Ray, Monticello, AR 71655
(2)MS. DUSTY LUTHY, 400 S Friendship Road Apt G, Paducah, KY 42003
(Members whose terms expire in 2018)
(3)REV. MICHAEL CLARK, 80 Bryan Drive, Winchester, TN 37398
(3)REV. JAMES D. MCGUIRE, 220-2 Southwind Circle, Greeneville, TN 37743

DISCIPLESHIP MINISTRY TEAM

(Members whose terms expire in 2016)
(3)REV. MINDY ACTON, 1413 Oak Ridge Drive, Birmingham, AL 35242
(1)REV. NANCY MCSPADDEN, 120 Roberta Drive, Memphis, TN 38112
(1)REV. JOSEFINA SANCHEZ, 7 Hancock Street, Melrose, MA 02176
(Members whose terms expire in 2017)
(2)MS. LE ILA DIXON, 4406 John Reagan Street, Marshall, TX 75672
(2)REV. DREW GRAY, 8220 Timberland Drive, West Paducah, KY 42086
(3)MS. SAMANTHA HASSELL, 510 N Main Street, Sturgis, KY 42459
(Members whose terms expire in 2018)
(3)MS. JOANNA WILKINSON, 1174 Tanglewood Street, Memphis, TN 38114
(2)MS. RACHEL COOK, 210 Bynum Street, Scottsboro, AL 35768
(2)REV. CHRISTIAN SMITH, 475 State Street, Cookeville, TN 38501

MISSIONS MINISTRY TEAM

(Members whose terms expire in 2016)
(2)REV. MAKIHIKO ARASE, 3-355-4 Kamikitadai Higashiyamato-Shi, Tokyo, 207-0023 JAPAN
(1)REV. VICTOR HASSELL, 510 N Main Street, Sturgis, KY 42459
(1)MR. DOMINIC LAU, 3820 Anza Street, San Francisco, CA
(1)MS. BRITTANY MEEKS, 2664 Morning Sun Road, Cordova, TN 38016
(1)REV. CHRIS WARREN, 906 Prince Lane, Murfreesboro, TN 37129
(Members whose terms expire in 2017)
(2)REV. JAMES BUTTRAM, 103 Golfcrest Lane, Oak Ridge, TN 37830 (resigned)
(3)REV. JIMMY BYRD, 176 E Valley Road, Whitwell, TN 37397
(1)MS. DONNA CHRISTIE, 3221 Whitehall Road, Birmingham, AL 35209
(3)REV. RICARDO FRANCO, 7 Hancock Street, Melrose, MA 02176
(1)MRS. MS. KAREN TOLEN, 6859 A East County Road 000N, Trilla, IL 62469
(Members whose terms expire in 2018)
(3)REV. JIM BARRY, 1405 Anna Street, Hixson, TN 37343
(2)MR. TIM CRAIG, 8958 Carriage Creek Road, Arlington, TN 38002
(2)REV. CARDELIA HOWELL-DIAMOND, 1580 Jeff Road NW, Huntsville, AL 35806
(3)MS. SHERRY POTEET, P.O. Box 313, Gilmer, TX 75644
(2)MS. MELINDA REAMS, 10 W Azalea Lane, Russellville, AR 72802

PASTORAL DEVELOPMENT MINISTRY TEAM

(Members whose terms expire in 2016)
(1)REV. SANDRA SHEPHERD, 525 Summit Oaks Court, Nashville, TN 37221
(1)REV. PATRICK WILKERSON, 7719 S Whispering Oak Circle, Powell, TN 37849
(Members whose terms expire in 2017)
(2)REV. AMBER CLARK, 80 Bryan Drive, Winchester, TN 37398
(2)REV. DREW HAYES, 6322 Labor Lane, Louisville, KY 40291
(Members whose terms expire in 2018)
(2)REV.DUAWN MEARNS, 107 Westoak Place, Hot Springs, AR 71913
(3)REV. LINDA SNELLING, 15791 State Highway W, Ada, OK 74820

*Ecumenical Partners
+Cumberland Presbyterians in America
Numbers in parenthesis denote number of terms.

GENERAL ASSEMBLY BOARD OF:

I. TRUSTEES OF BETHEL UNIVERSITY

(Members whose terms expire in 2016)
(1)MR. JEFF AMREIN, 11711 Paramont Way, Prospect, KY 40059
(3)DR. LARRY A. BLAKEBURN, 790 Emory Valley Road Apt 714, Oak Ridge, TN 37830
(2)*JUDGE BEN CANTRELL, 415 Church Street #2513, Nashville, TN 37219
(2)+DR. ARMY DANIEL, 3125 Searcy Drive, Huntsville, AL 35810
(3)MR. LAWRENCE (LADD) DANIEL, 13023 Taylorcrest, Houston, TX 77079
(1)MR. BILL DOBBINS 5716 Quest Ridge Road, Franklin, TN 37064
(2)DR. ROBERT LOW, c/o New Prime, Inc., 2740 W Mayfair Avenue, Springfield, MO 65803
(3)MR. BEN T. SURBER, 1145 Hico Road, McKenzie, TN 38201
(Members whose terms expire in 2017)
(2)*MS. LISA COLE, PO Box 198615, Nashville, TN 37219
(2)MR. CHESTER (CHET) DICKSON, 24 W Rivercrest Drive, Houston, TX 77042
(1)REV. NANCY MCSPADDEN, 120 Roberta Drive, Memphis, TN 38112
(3)MR. BOBBY OWEN, 1625 Cabot Drive, Franklin, TN 37064
(2)DR. ED PERKINS, 721 Paris Street, McKenzie, TN 38201
(1)MR. KENNETH (KEN) D. QUINTON, 2912 Waller Omer Road, Sturgis, KY 42459
(3)REV. ROBERT (ROB) TRUITT, 1238 Old East Side Road, Burns, TN 37029
(1)REV. ROBERT (BOB) WATKINS, 10950 West Union Hills Drive #1356, Sun City, AZ 85373
(Members whose terms expire in 2018)
(3)MR. CHARLIE GARRETT, 107 Willow Green Drive, Jackson, TN 38305
(2)+REV. ELTON C. HALL, SR., 305 Tiffton Circle, Hewitt, TX 76643
(2)MS. DEWANNA LATIMER, 1077 Jr. Jones Road, Humboldt, TN 38343
(1)MR. LYNDLE MCCURLEY, 198 Rock Creek Drive, Mountain Home, AR 72653
(1)*DR. E. RAY MORRIS, PO Box 924528, Norcross, GA 30010
(1)MR. STEVE PERRYMAN, 535 Ranch Road, Rogersville, MO 65742

Trustee Emeritus – Dr. Vera Low, 3653 Prestwick Court, Springfield, MO 65809 (deceased)

II. TRUSTEES OF CUMBERLAND PRESBYTERIAN CHILDREN'S HOME

(Members whose terms expire in 2016)
(2)*MR. RICHARD DEAN, 2140 Cove Circle North, Gadsden, AL 35903
(2)MS. PATRICIA LONG, 525 E Oak Street, Aledo, TX 76008
(3)REV. ALFONSO MARQUEZ, 389 Bethel Drive, Lenoir City, TN 37772
(3)MR. MICKEY SHELL, 2143 Griderfield-Ladd Road, Pine Bluff, AR 71601
(Members whose terms expire in 2017)
(1)REV. LISA ANDERSON, 1790 Faxon Street, Memphis, TN 38112
(1)MS. CAROLINE BOOTH, 2200 Westview Trail, Denton, TX 76207
(3)+MS. MAMIE HALL, 305 Tiffton Circle, Hewitt, TX 76643
(1)MR. CHARLES HARRIS, 3293 Birch Avenue, Grapevine, TX 76051
(1)MR. KNIGHT MILLER, 1035 Garden Creek Circle, Louisville, KY 40223
(1)MR. JOHN O'CARROLL, 1701 Live Oak Lane, Southlake, TX 76092
(3)REV. DON TABOR, 9611 Mitchell Place, Brentwood, TN 37027
(Members whose terms expire in 2018)
(1)REV. DUANE DOUGHERTY, 212 County Road 4705, Troup, TX 75789
(1)MRS. CAROLYN HARMON, 4435 Newport Highway, Greeneville, TN 37743
(1)DR. ROBIN HENSON, 8220 Westwind Lane, North Richland Hills, TX 76182

*Ecumenical Partners
+Cumberland Presbyterians in America
Numbers in parenthesis denote number of terms.

III. TRUSTEES OF HISTORICAL FOUNDATION

(Members whose terms expire in 2016)

(3)+MS. VANESSA BARNHILL, 819 King Street, Sturgis, KY 42459
(3)MS. PAMELA DAVIS, 5111 County Road 7545, Lubbock, TX 79424
(2)REV. MARY KATHRYN KIRKPATRICK, 401 1/2 Henley-Perry Drive, Marshall, TX 75670
(3)MS. SIDNEY MILTON, 27 Kalee Lane, Calvert City, KY 42029

(Members whose terms expire in 2017)

(3)+MS. EDNA BARNETT, 7 Breezewood Cove, Jackson, TN 38305
(2)MR. MICHAEL FARE, 401 E Deanna Lane, Nixa, MO 65714
(2)*MS. DOROTHY HAYDEN, 3103 Carolina Avenue, Bessemer, AL 35020
(1)+MS. PAT WARD, 2620 Rabbit Lane, Madison, AL 35756
(3)+REV. RICK WHITE, 124 Towne West, Lorena, TX 76655

(Members whose terms expire in 2018)

(1)REV. LISA OLIVER, 110 Allen Drive, Hendersonville, TN 37075
(3)DR. SIDNEY L. SWINDLE, 4407 Swann Avenue, Tampa, FL 33609

IV. TRUSTEES OF MEMPHIS THEOLOGICAL SEMINARY OF THE CUMBERLAND PRESBYTERIAN CHURCH

(Members whose terms expire in 2016)

(2)MR. MICHAEL R. ALLEN, 149 Windwood Circle, Alabaster, AL 35007
(1)*MR. JOHNNIE COOMBS, PO Box 127, Blue Mountain, MS 38610
(2)MS. DIANE DICKSON, 24 West Rivercrest, Houston, TX 77042
(3)*MR. DAN HATZENBUEHLER, 1544 Carr Avenue, Memphis, TN 38104
(1)*DR. RICK KIRCHOFF, 2044 Thorncroft Drive, Germantown, TN 38138
(3)MR. TIM ORR, 1591 Laura Lane, Dyersburg, TN 38024
(2)*DR. INETTA RODGERS, 1824 S Parkway E, Memphis, TN 38114
(3)*MRS. K.C. WARREN, 215 Buena Vista Place, Memphis, TN 38112

(Members whose terms expire in 2017)

(1)*REV. NANCY COLE, 3346 Arcadia Drive, Tuscaloosa, AL 35404
(2)*REV. ROBERT MARBLE, 515 Shamrock Drive, Little Rock, AR 72205
(3)MS. PAT MEEKS, 8540 Edney Ridge Drive, Cordova, TN 38016 (resigned)
(2)REV. JENNIFER NEWELL, 2322 Marco Circle, Chattanooga, TN 37421
(1)REV. SUSAN PARKER, 655 York Drive, Rogersville, AR 35652
(3)REV. ROBERT M. SHELTON, 7128 Lakehurst Avenue, Dallas, TX 75230 (resigned)
(3)+DR. JOE WARD, 2620 Rabbit Lane, Madison, AL 35758
(3)*MS. RUBY WHARTON, 1183 E Parkway South, Memphis, TN 38114

(Members whose terms expire in 2018)

(3)REV. KEVIN BRANTLEY, 729 Old Hodgenville Road, Greensburg, KY 42743
(1)REV. KEVIN HENSON, 8220 Westwind Lane, N Richland Hills, TX 76182
(1)REV. LINDA HOWELL, PO Box 80050, Keller, TX 76244
(3)MR. MARK MADDOX, 225 Oak Drive, Dresden, TN 38225
(2)MS. SONDRA RODDY, 2583 Hedgerow Lane, Clarksville, TN 37043
(3)MR. TAKAYOSHI SHIRAI, 25 Minami Kibogaoka Asahi-ku, Yokohama, Kanagawa-ken 241-0824 JAPAN
(2)*REV. MELVIN CHARLES SMITH, 1263 Haynes Street, Memphis, TN 38114
(2)*MS. LATISHA TOWNS, The Med, 877 Jefferson Avenue, Memphis, TN 38103

V. STEWARDSHIP, FOUNDATION AND BENEFITS

(Members whose terms expire in 2016)

(3)MR. CHARLES G. FLOYD, 1617 Championship Drive, Franklin, TN 37064
(1)REV. CHARLES (BUDDY) POPE, 2391 Fairfield Pike, Shelbyville, TN 37160
(2)MS. SUE RICE, 1301 Brooker Road, Brandon, FL 33511
(2)MS. DEBBIE SHELTON, 1255 MG England Road, Manchester, TN 37355

*Ecumenical Partners
+Cumberland Presbyterians in America
Numbers in parenthesis denote number of terms.

(Members whose terms expire in 2017)
(1)REV. RANDY DAVIDSON, PO Box 880, Ada, OK 74821
(3)MR. CHARLES DAY, 9312 Owensboro Road, Falls of Rough, KY 40119
(3)MS. SYLVIA HALL, 930 Sherry Circle, Hixson, TN 37343
(3)MR. JACKIE SATTERFIELD, 2303 County Road 730, Cullman, AL 35055
(Members whose terms expire in 2018)
(3)MR. ANDREW B. FRAZIER, JR., 107 Doris Street, Camden, TN 38320
(1)MR. JAMES SHANNON, 2307 Littlemore Drive, Cordova, TN 38016
(2)MR. MICHAEL ST. JOHN, 324 Carriage Place, Lebanon, MO 65536

GENERAL ASSEMBLY COMMISSIONS:

I. MILITARY CHAPLAINS AND PERSONNEL

(1) Term Expires in 2016–REV. CASSANDRA THOMAS, 1920 Dancy Street, Fayetteville, NC 28301
(2) Term Expires in 2017–REV. MARY MCCASKEY BENEDICT, 892 Pen Oak Drive, Cookeville, TN 38501
(1) Term Expires in 2018–REV. TONY JANNER, 104 Northwood Drive, McKenzie TN 38201

These three persons and the Stated Clerk represent the denomination as members of the Presbyterian Council for Chaplains and Military Personnel, 4125 Nebraska Avenue NW, Washington, DC 20016

GENERAL ASSEMBLY COMMITTEES

I. JUDICIARY

(Members whose terms expire in 2016)
(3)REV. SHERRY LADD, 4521 Turkey Creek Road, Williamsport, TN 38487
    revsherryladd@gmail.com
(2)REV. ANDY MCCLUNG, 919 Dickinson Street, Memphis, TN 38107
    scubarev@att.net
(3)MS. FELICIA WALKUP, 179 Mary Anne Lane, Manchester, TN 37355
    fbwalkup@gmail.com
(Members whose terms expire in 2017)
(1)REV. HARRY CHAPMAN, 4908 El Picador Court SE, Rio Rancho, NM 87124
    wrightrev2gmail.com
(2)REV. ROBERT D. RUSH, 17822 Deep Brook Drive, Spring, TX 77379
    rushrd74@comcast.net
(3)MR. WENDELL THOMAS, JR., 1200 Paradise Drive, Powell, TN 37849
    volbaby@comcast.net
(Members whose terms expire in 2018)
(2)REV. ANNETTA CAMP, 2263 Mill Creek Road, Halls, TN 38040
    anetta@cumberlandchurch.com
(3)MS. KIMBERLY SILVUS, 1128 Madison Street, Clarksville, TN 37040
    kgsilvus@gmail.com
(1)MR. BILL TALLY, 907 Tipperary Drive, Scottsboro, AL 35768
    wtally@scottsboro.org

*Ecumenical Partners
+Cumberland Presbyterians in America
Numbers in parenthesis denote number of terms.

II. JOINT COMMITTEE ON AMENDMENTS

The committee consists of five members of the Judiciary Committee of the Cumberland Presbyterian Church in America and the Cumberland Presbyterian Church.

III. NOMINATING

(Members whose terms expire in 2016)
(1)MS. NANCY BEAN, 1035 Stonewall Street N, McKenzie, TN 38201
     beann@bethelu.edu
(1)REV. CHARLES MCCASKEY, 679 Canter Lane, Cookeville, TN 38501
     charles@cookevillecpchurch.org
(1)REV. JIMMY PEYTON, 1455 County Road 643, Cullman, AL 35055
     jakjpeyton@att.net
(1)MS. MARJORIE SHANNON, 2307 Littlemore Drive, Cordova, TN 38016
     margieshannon@att.net
(Members whose terms expire in 2017)
(1)REV. TOBY DAVIS, 502 S Alley Street, Jefferson, TX 75657
     pastortobydavis@gmail.com
(1)MS. CAROLYN HARMON, 4435 Newport Highway, Greeneville, TN 37743 (resigned)
     richardharmon09@comcast.net
(1)MS. ELLIE SCRUDDER, 29688 S 535 Road, Park Hill, OK 74451
     escrudder@gmail.com
(1)REV. KEVIN SMALL, 6492 E 400th Road, Martinsville, IL 62442
     revkev61@gmail.com
(Members whose terms expire in 2018)
(1)REV. THOMAS CAMPBELL, PO Box 343, Calico Rock, AR 72519
     tdcampbellar@gmail.com
(1)MS. HEATHER MORGAN, 1468 Williams Cove Road, Winchester, TN 37398
     htmorgan87@gmail.com

IV. OUR UNITED OUTREACH COMMITTEE

(Members whose terms expire in 2016)
(3)MR. RON D. GARDNER, 8668 Wood Mills Drive W, Cordova, TN 38016
(Members whose terms expire in 2017)
(3)MS. SHARON RESCH, PO Box 383, Dongola, IL 62926
(3)REV. WILLIAM RUSTENHAVEN III, PO Box 1303, Marshall, TX 75671
(Members whose terms expire in 2018)
(2)MR. RANDY WEATHERSBY, 1502 Pinecrest Street NW, Cullman, AL 35055
(2)MS. ROBIN WILLS, 4607 E Richmond Shop Road, Lebanon, TN 37090

V. PLACE OF MEETING

THE STATED CLERK OF THE GENERAL ASSEMBLY
THE MODERATOR OF THE GENERAL ASSEMBLY
A REPRESENTATIVE OF WOMEN'S MINISTRIES OF THE MISSIONS MINISTRY TEAM

VI. UNIFIED COMMITTEE ON THEOLOGY AND SOCIAL CONCERNS

(Members whose terms expire in 2016)

(3)MS. LEZLIE P. DANIEL, 13023 Taylorcrest Road, Houston, TX 77079
     lululoop@me.com

(2)+MRS. JIMMIE DODD, c/o Hopewell CPCA, 4100 Millsfield Highway, Dyersburg, TN 38024
     dodd125@gmail.com

(2)REV. BYRON FORESTER, 2376 Eastwood Place, Memphis, TN 38112
     bforester@bellsouth.net; (901)246-1242

(1)REV. JOHN A. SMITH, 916 Allen Road, Nashville, TN 37214
     john.a.smith.81@gmail.com; (573)453-8455

(2)+ELDER JOY WALLACE, 6940 Marvin D Love Freeway, Dallas, TX 75237
     jwallace@wlgllc.net

(Members whose terms expire in 2017)

(1)+MS. SHARON COMBS, PO Box 122, Sturgis, KY 42459
     (270)860-4175

(1)+REV. EDMOND COX, 249 Mimosa Circle, Maryville, TN 37801
     (865)789-6161

(2)+DR. NANCY FUQUA, 1963 County Road 406, Towncreek, AL 35672
     fuq23@bellsouth.net; (256)566-1226

(2)REV. RANDY JACOB, PO Box 158, Broken Bow, OK 74728
     chocpres@pine-net.com; (580)584-3770; (580)236-2469 cell

(1)+REV. LARUTH JEFFERSON, 25757 Primose Lane, Southfield, MI 48033
     (248)945-0349

(1)+DR. PHILLIP REDRICK, 228 Church Street NW, Huntsville, AL 35801
     (256)882-6333

(1)+REV. ROBERT E THOMAS, 1017 N Englewood, Tyler, TX 75702
     (903)592-0238

(Members whose terms expire in 2018)

(2)MR. DAVID PHILLIPS-BURK, 3325 Bailey Creek Cove N, Collierville, TN 38017
     dlphillipsburk@aol.com; (256)520-1380

(2)REV. GEORGE ESTES, 7910 Cloverbrook Lane, Germantown, TN 38138
     geoestes@gmail.com; (901)755-6673

(2)REV. SHELIA O'MARA, 533 Loughton Lane, Arnold, MD 21012
     chaplainshelia@aol.com; (410)757-5713; (443)370-7218 cell

President of Memphis Theological Seminary - Ex-officio Member
     REV. JAY EARHEART-BROWN, 866 N McLean Boulevard, Memphis, TN 38107
     jebrown@memphisseminary.edu; (901)278-0367

OTHER DENOMINATIONAL PERSONNEL

REPRESENTATIVES TO:

American Bible Society: REV. MICHAEL SHARPE, 8207 Traditional Place, Cordova, TN 38016

Caribbean and North American Area Council, World Communion of Reformed Churches:
STATED CLERK MICHAEL SHARPE, 8207 Traditional Place, Cordova, TN 38016

(Member whose terms expire in 2017)

(2)MS. LAURIE SHARPE, 3423 Summerdale Drive, Bartlett, TN 38133

LIVING GENERAL ASSEMBLY MODERATORS

2015—REV. MICHELE GENTRY, Urb San Jorge casa 28, Km 8 via a La Tebaida
    Armenia, Quindio, COLOMBIA, SA

2014—REV. LISA HALL ANDERSON, 1790 Faxon Avenue, Memphis, TN 38112

2013—REV. FOREST PROSSER, 1157 Mountain Creek Road, Chattanooga, TN 37405

2012—REV. ROBERT D. RUSH, 12935 Quail Park Drive, Cypress, TX 77429

2011—REV. DON M. TABOR, 9611 Mitchell Place, Brentwood, TN 37027

2010—REV. BOYCE WALLACE, Cra 101 No 15-93, Cali, Colombia, South America

2009—ELDER SAM SUDDARTH, 206 Ha Le Koa Court, Smyrna, TN 37167

2008—REV. JONATHAN CLARK, 88 Woodcrest Drive, Winchester, TN 37398

2007—REV. FRANK WARD, 8207 Traditional Place, Cordova, TN 38016

2006—REV. DONALD HUBBARD, 2128 Campbell Station Road, Knoxville, TN 37932

2005—REV. LINDA H. GLENN, 49 Mason Road, Threeway, TN 38343

2004—REV. EDWARD G. SIMS, 2161 N. Meadows Drive, Clarksville, TN 37043

2003—REV. CHARLES MCCASKEY, 679 Canter Lane, Cookeville, TN 38501

2001—REV. RANDOLPH JACOB, 610 W. Adams Street, Broken Bow, OK 74728

1999—ELDER GWENDOLYN G. RODDYE, 3728 Wittenham Drive, Knoxville, TN 37921

1998 REV. MASAHARU ASAYAMA, 3-15-9 Higashi, Kunitachi-shi, Tokyo, JAPAN

1996—REV. MERLYN A. ALEXANDER, 80 N. Hampton Lane, Jackson, TN 38305

1995—REV. CLINTON O. BUCK, PO Box 770068, Memphis, TN 38117

1993—REV. ROBERT M. SHELTON, 7128 Lakehurst Avenue, Dallas, TX 75230

1992—REV. JOHN DAVID HALL, 109 Oddo Lane SE, Huntsville, AL 35802

1990—REV. THOMAS D. CAMPBELL, PO Box 315, Calico Rock, AR 72519

1989—REV. WILLIAM RUSTENHAVEN, Jr., 703 W. Burleson, Marshall, TX 75670

1988—ELDER BEVERLY ST. JOHN, 806 Evansdale Drive, Nashville, TN 37220

1982—REV. WILLIAM A. RAWLINS, 3100 Cook Lane, Longview, TX 75604

1981—REV. W. JEAN RICHARDSON, 7533 Lancashire, Powell, TN 37849

*Ecumenical Partners
+Cumberland Presbyterians in America
Numbers in parenthesis denote number of terms.

SYNOD AND PRESBYTERY CLERKS

SYNOD OF GREAT RIVERS

The Reverend Andy McClung
919 Dickinson Street
Memphis, TN 38107
(901)606-6615
scubarev@att.net

Arkansas Presbytery (GRAR)

Janie Stamps
4008 Logan Lane
Fort Smith, AR 72903
(479)478-0161 (Home)
(479)883-5633 (Cell)
(479)782-0454 FAX
bjstamps@msn.com (Home)

Missouri Presbytery (GRMI)

Larry Nottingham
PO Box 281
Stockton, MO 65785
(417)276-3792
mopresbyterycpc2@yahoo.com

West Tennessee Presbytery (GRWT)

The Reverend Andy McClung
919 Dickinson Street
Memphis, TN 38107
(901)606-6615
scubarev@att.net

**SYNOD OF MIDWEST
(MI)**

Debra Shanks
3997 N 100th Street
Casey, IL 62420
(217)932-2995
royndebbie@hotmail.com

Covenant Presbytery (MICO)

Reese Baker
1175 Rowland Cemetery Road
Fredonia, KY 42411
(270)545-3483
rbaker@kynet.biz

Cumberland Presbytery (MICU)

The Reverend Darrell Pickett
113 Woods Drive
Glasgow, KY 42141
(270)834-6102
dpickett@glasgow-ky.com

North Central Presbytery (MINC)

The Reverend Ralph Blevins
1623 County Road 2375 E
Geff, IL 62842
(618)854-2494
statedclerk@ncpwebsite.com

SYNOD AND PRESBYTERY CLERKS

MISSION SYNOD
(MS)

Joseph Owen Smith
119 Pine Island Drive
Marshall, TX 75672
(903)928-9887
otsmith@gmx.com

Andes Presbytery (MSAN)

The Reverend Diana Valdez
Calle 65 #98-45, interior 174
Altos de la Macarena
(Robledo-LaCampina)
Medellin, Antioquia
Colombia, South America
(57)313-826-3153
dianamariavaldezduque@gmail.com

Cauca Valley Presbytery (MSCA)

Jairo Lopez
Paraiso la Morada
5ta Etapa, Casa 36, Jamundi
Colombia, South America
011-5726-615410

Choctaw Presbytery (MSCH)

The Reverend Virginia Espinoza
PO Box 132
Boswell, OK 74727
(580)434-7971
vespinoza@choctawnation.com

Presbytery del Cristo (MSDC)

Karen Avery
9420 Layton Court NE
Albuquerque, NM 87111
(505)821-7668
kavery5@comcast.net

Hong Kong Presbytery (MSHK)

Eliza Yl Chui
2/F Welland Plaza
188 Nam Chong Street
Sham Shui Po, Hong Kong
(011)852-2783-8923
(011)852-2771-2726 FAX
elizaylyau@yahoo.com.hk

Japan Presbytery (MSJA)

Takoyoshi Shirai
25 Minami Kobogaoka
Asahi-ku Yokohama
Kanagawa-ken
241-0824 JAPAN
(011)81-45-361-0059
cpc_japan@ybb.ne.jp

Red River Presbytery (MSRR)

The Reverend Vernon Sansom
7810 Shiloh Road
Midlothian, TX 76065
(972)825-6887
vernon@sansom.us

SYNOD AND PRESBYTERY CLERKS

Trinity Presbytery (MSTR)

Paula Hayes
PO Box 5449
Longview, TX 75608
(903)759-1896 (Home)
(903)759-0092 (Work)
phayes7442@aol.com

SYNOD OF SOUTHEAST
(SE)

The Reverend Forest Prosser
1157 Mountain Creek Road
Chattanooga, TN 37405
(423)877-4114
forestprosser@comcast.net

Cumberland East Coast Presbytery (SEEC)

The Reverend Douglas Park
316 Prospect Avenue Apt 6D
Hackensack, NJ 07601
(201)694-3005
jiwoos@gmail.com

Presbytery of East Tennessee (SEET)

The Reverend Ronald L. Longmire
2041 Eckles Drive
Maryville, TN 37804
(865)984-1647
ronaldlongmire@charter.net

Grace Presbytery (SEGR)

Jessie Dunnaway
New Hope CP Church
5521 Double Oak Lane
Birmingham, AL 35242
(205)991-5252
jessie@newhopecpc.org

Hope Presbytery (SEHO)

Mr. Gerald McGee
9491 Highway 101
Lexington, AL 35648
(256)229-5613
nebo9491@gmail.com

Robert Donnell Presbytery (SERD)

Frances Dawson
PO Box 904, 221 S Market St.
Scottsboro, AL 35768
(256)244-0554 (Cell)
(256)259-0904 (Business)(FAX)
rdpfcd@scottsboro.org

Tennessee-Georgia Presbytery (SETG)

Tracey Gann
475 Sequachee Drive
Whitwell, TN 37397
(423)309-1497
tngastatedclerk@gmail.com

SYNOD AND PRESBYTERY CLERKS

TENNESSEE SYNOD
(TN)

The Reverend Charles McCaskey
565 East Tenth Street
Cookeville, TN 38501
(931)526-6585 (Office)
(931)372-2620 FAX
charles@cookevillecpchurch.org

Columbia Presbytery (TNCO)

The Reverend Charles (Buddy) Pope
2391 Fiarfield Pike
Shelbyville, TN 37160
(931)205-6897
pope6897@yahoo.com

Murfreesboro Presbytery (TNMU)

The Reverend Charles McCaskey
565 East Tenth Street
Cookeville, TN 38501
(931)526-6585 (Office)
(931)528-2273 FAX
charles@cookevillecpchurch.org

Nashville Presbytery (TNNA)

The Reverend Fred Polacek
907 Graham Drive
Old Hickory, TN 37138
(615)754-5328 (Home)
revfredp@gmail.com

MINISTERS GAINED AND LOST IN 2015

MINISTERS RECEIVED BY ORDINATION

NAME	PRESBYTERY	DATE
Attema, Leslie	Trinity	09/25/15
Creamer, Jennifer	East Tennessee	10/03/15
Fortney, Josh	Red River	05/04/15
Harper, Josh	Murfreesboro	04/23/15
Lee, Ho Jin	West Tennessee	07/26/15
Ostrander, Shirley	West Tennessee	10/11/15
Ryu, Si Chun	Cumberland East Coast	03/28/15
Todd, Christopher	West Tennessee	03/22/15
Warren, Glenn	Nashville	01/04/15

MINISTERS REINSTATED OR RECEIVED FROM OTHER DENOMINATIONS

NAME	PRESBYTERY	CHURCH	DATE
Kim, Seong N	Cumberland East Coast	C & MA	03/20/15

MINISTERS WHO HAVE MOVED TO OTHER DENOMINATIONS

NAME	DENOMINATION	DATE
Ferry, Aaron	PCUSA	10/1/2015
Richards, Kenneth	ECO	3/30/2016

MINISTERS DROPPED FROM MINISTRY BY PRESBYTERY

NAME	PRESBYTERY	DATE
Alspaugh, Kevin	Robert Donnell	03/21/2015
Hamilton, Lynn	Trinity	09/25/2015
Winslett, Don	Trinity	02/19/2015
Yi, Woo Young	Tennessee-Georgia	03/21/2015

MILITARY CHAPLAINS

Acuff, David (M8)
4969 Quail Lane
Columbia, SC 29206
david.acuff@us.army.mil
(803)790-9151 TNNA#7300

Baranoski, Timothy (M8)
1205 Tomahawk Drive B
Jber, AK 99505
(615)440-3499
timothy.i.baranoski.mil@mail.mil

Headrick, Anthony (M8)
3327 N Eagle Road Ste 110-132
Meridian, ID 83646
chaps2a@yahoo.com
(619)435-0825 SEGR#0100

LeFavor, David E (M8)
4100 W 3rd Street
Dayton, OH 45428
david.lefavor@med.va.gov
(813)613-4133 SEGR#0100

Logan, Jason B (M8)
212 Saddlebag Court
Rineyville, KY 40162
jason.b.logan.mil@mail.mil
(410)305-8494 TNMU#7200

Nash, Zachary (M8)
(on file in General Assembly Office)
zachary.nash@us.af.mil
( ) GRWT#9100

O'Mara, Shelia (M8)
533 Loughton Lane
Arnold, MD 21012
chaplainshelia@aol.com
(410)757-5713 MSDC#8700

Santillano, Ray Paul (M8)
1270 Polo Road Apt 618
Columbia, SC 29223
ramon.santillano@us.army.mil
(915)500-4928 MSTR#8704

Turner, Glyn (M8)
1660 Chattanooga Valley Road
Flintstone, GA 30725
(585)307-7715
glynturner@outlook.com

NON-MILITARY CHAPLAINS

Aden, Marty (M9)
202 Bennington Place
Wilmington, NC 28412
maden@ec.rr.com
(910)274-8465 MSRR#8400

Anderson, Lisa (M9)
1790 Faxon Avenue
Memphis, TN 38112
anderli60@gmail.com
(901)246-8052 GRWT#9305

Bone, Leslie (M9)
16504 George Franklyn Drive
Independence, MO 64055
lesliebone@comcast.net
(816)373-6625 GRMI#4100

Bowers, Sharon G (M9)
201 Wild Buffalo Drive
Kyle, TX 78640
sharon.bowers@gmail.com
(512)230-7078 MSTR#8100

Brown, Mark (M9)
752 Hawthorne Street
Memphis, TN 38107
dmbrown@utmem.edu
(901)274-1474 GRWT#9100

Carter, Patricia (M9)
2509 Decatur Stratton Road
Decatur, MS 39327
revtree@yahoo.com
(601)635-4120 SEGR#0100

Cook, Lisa (M9)
4101 Dalemere Court
Nashville, TN 37207
tgoose@comcast.net
(615)868-4118 TNNA#7300

Diamond, James (M9)
214 Falmouth Drive
Georgetown, KY 40324
jameswdiamond@yahoo.com
(615)220-2341 TNMU#7200

Ferrol, Ruben (M9)
1823 Straford Court
Allentown, PA 18103
rubeferrol@msn.com
(610)966-7289 MSRR#8400

Gentry, Michele (M9)
Urb San Jorge casa 28
Km 8 via a La Tebaida
Armenia, Quindio, Colombia
South America
gentry.andes@yahoo.com
(318)285-1161 MSAN#8900

Hames, Anne (M9)
118 Paris Street
Mc Kenzie, TN 38201
FAX: (731)352-4069
hamesa@bethel-college.edu
(731)352-4066 GRWT#9100

Hartung, J Thomas (M9)
2291 Americus Boulevard W Apt 1
Clearwater, FL 33763
revtom6@aol.com
(727)797-2882 SEGR#0100

Jackson, Terry (M9)
1461 Mt Pleasant Road
Hernando, MS 38632
tjackson48@comcast.net
(662)429-9741 GRWT#9100

Kelly, Patrick L (M9)
1449 Rainbow Road
Mountain City, TN 37683-2110
(423)727-4067 SEET#2200

Kennemer, Darren (M9)
8828 Highway 119
Alabaster, AL 35007
(205)663-3152
darren.kennemer@va.gov SERD#0107

Knight, Melissa (M9)
5730 Haley Road
Meridian, MS 39305
(530)632-6472
revlissa@gmail.com MSDC#8700

Lain, Judy (M9)
1928 Pine Ridge Drive
Bedford, TX 76021-4650
(817)660-8020 MSRR#8400

Lounsbury-Lombard, Kristi (M9)
902 Clearview
Krum, TX 76249
kristilounsbury@gmail.com
(940)435-5077 MSRR#8400

McCarty, John (M9)
305 W Martindale Drive
Marshall, TX 75672
mtsjohn@gmail.com
(423)650-8788 SETG#2100

McClung, Tiffany (M9)
919 Dickinson Street
Memphis, TN 38107
tmcclung@memphisseminary.edu
(901)606-6604 GRWT#9100

McSpadden, Nancy (M9)
120 Roberta Drive
Memphis, TN 38112
revnancy77@gmail.com
(870)612-0067 GRAR#1100

Melson, Glenda (M9)
331 Tickle Weed Road
Swansea, SC 29160
glendamelson@fidnet.com
(417)588-2758 SEET#2200

Messer, James C (M9)
3653 Old Madisonville Road
Henderson, KY 42420
jcmess@hotmail.com
(270)827-0711 MINC#5304

Mills, David M (M9)
60 Huge Oak Street
Bertram, TX 78605
(512)355-3511 MSTR#8100

Oliver, Lisa (M9)
110 Allen Drive
Hendersonville, TN 37075
( ) TNMU#7200

Pickett, Patricia (M9)
1460 Cheatham Dam Road
Ashland City, TN 37015
tovahtoo@aol.com
(615)792-4973 TNNA#7300

Rice, Keith (M9)
PO Box 100
Itasca, TX 76055
rsvkeith@yahoo.com
(254)087-2418 MSRR#8400

Richards, Carroll (M9)
210 Allison Drive
Lincoln, IL 62656
FAX: (217)732-7894
dr_cr@comcast.net
(217)732-7894 MINC#5200

Ruggia, Mario (Bud) (M9)
603 Rumsey Street
Kiowa, KS 67070
ruggia@aol.com
(620)825-4509 MSRR#8400

Scott, Lisa (M9)
lascott1979@att.net
(816)332-0604 GRMI#4100

Scott, Jerry (M9)
2310 Sentell Drive
Maryville, TN 37803
dmjlscott@yahoo.com
(865)809-2621 SEET#2200

Smith, John Adam (M9)
916 Allen Road
Nashville, TN 37214
john.a.smith.81@gmail.com
(573)453-8455

Sumrall, Phil (M9)
107 Barnhardt Circle
Fort Oglethorpe, GA 30742
phil.sumrall@gmail.com
(423)903-1938 SETG#2100

Travis, Kermit (M9)
3220 Sharon Highway
Dresden, TN 38225
(731)364-2315 GRWT#9415

Truax, Robert Lee, Jr (M9)
2989 Champions Drive Apt 204
Lakeland, TN 38002
revtruax@yahoo.com
(901)266-5927 GRWT#9100

Varner, Susan (M9)
14709 Glisten Lane
Little Rock, AR 72223
smvarner76@yahoo.com
(901)371-1249 GRAR#1100

West, David (M9)
2027 Lucille Street
Lebanon, TN 37087
(217)732-7568 MINC#5405

Wilson, Don <M1 M9>
7300 Calle Montana NE
Albuquerque, NM 87113
(505)823-2594
don-wilson07@comcast.net

MEMORIAL ROLL OF MINISTERS

IN MEMORY OF
MINISTERS LOST BY DEATH

NAME	PRESBYTERY	AGE	DATE
Blakeburn, Roy E	East Tennessee	87	04/14/16
Drylie, James T	West Tennessee	75	02/14/15
Dobson, Howard Wallis "Wally"	East Tennessee	82	09/03/15
Fajardo, Jose	Red River	101	02/21/15
Ferree, Ronald L	Cumberland	69	09/10/15
Gerard, Eugene "Stan"	Covenant	82	04/26/15
Leslie, Eugene	West Tennessee	83	03/10/15
Matlock, Joe	del Cristo	86	02/26/15
Moss, Larry	Covenant	74	11/26/15
Ortiz, Jaime	Andes	83	03/29/16
Phelps, Earl	West Tennessee	87	04/20/16
Powell, Omer Thomas	Cumberland	90	01/30/15
Talley, James E	Cumberland	89	03/15/16
Turpen, Brent	Red River	68	11/27/15

SURVIVING SPOUSES OF MINISTERS BY PRESBYTERY
(Deceased spouse in parenthesis.)

ARKANSAS

Batholomew, Maudline
(Harold Bartholomew)
  13395 Highway 265
  Prairie Grove, AR 72753
  (479)846-2850

DuBose, Sandra
(Paul DuBose)
  207 7th Street
  Cotter, AR 72626
  (870) 373-1021

Elkins, Patsy
(Robert Harold Elkins)
  525 Elkins Road
  Magazine, AR 72943
  (479)637-3723
  robtelkins@cej.net

Faith, Jeannine
(Charles Faith)
  4710 Mount Olive Road
  Melbourne, AR 72556
  (870)368-4069

Hollenbeck, Linda
(Edward B. Hollenbeck)
  409 Carson Drive
  Benton, AR 72015
  (501)315-9737

Kinslow, Jean
(Alfred Kinslow)
  29209 Perdido Beach Blvd
  Vista Bella #701
  Orange Beach, AL 36561
  (251)981-8385

Wynne, Glenna
(W. J. Wynne)
  1501 W Block
  El Dorado, AR 71730
  (870)863-9444

CAUCA VALLEY

Munoz, Aliria Correal de
(Gerardo Munoz)
  5405 Robelene Drive
  Metaire, LA 70003
  gwilson54@cox.net

Yepez, Mrs. (??)
(Juan Yepez)
  Colombia, South America

COLUMBIA

Barker, Nicky
(Jack Barker)
  40 Watson Street
  Savannah, TN 38372
  (731)926-1577

Bates, Betty Ruth
(Harold Bates)
  204 Apache Trail
  Columbia, TN 38401
  (931)381-6737

Burns, Angela C.
(Bobby G. Burns)
  328 Dunnaway Road
  Shelbyville, TN 37160
  (931)294-5105

Denton, Virgie
(Clyde Denton)
  2538 County Club Lane
  Columbia, TN 38401
  (931)388-7154

Gibson, Ernestine
(Charles Gibson)
  33 Hilldale Church Road
  Fayetteville, TN 37334
  (931)433-2666

Green, Marie
(Odis Green)
  18 Oakwood Street NW
  Rome, GA 30165
  (706)291-1738

Nugent, Sue
(Samuel Ellis Nugent)
  2124 Carrie Court
  Columbia, TN 38401
  (931)490-7571
  sue@cadprodinc.com

Sain, Sally
(Edwin Sain)
  27 Hilltop Road
  Fayetteville, TN 37334
  (931)433-8708
  ssain@fayelectric.com

Seaton, Whitney
(Charlie Seaton)
  111 W Hardin Drive
  Columbia, TN 38401
  (931)388-0319

Walker, Lilly Mae
(James Finis Walker)
  704 Woods Drive
  Columbia, TN 38401

Wilkins, Dianne S
(Marvin Edward Wilkins)
  209 Mackey Street
  Rogersville, AL 35652
  (256)247-5557
  marvinwilkins@msn.com

COVENANT

Atchison, Cheryl
(Dean Atchison)
  206 Marsha Drive
  Ledbetter, KY 42058

Cannon, Joyce
(Chester Cannon)
  1026 W Center Street
  Madisonville, KY 42431

Clark, Eileen
(Morris Clark)
  8720 State Route 132 W
  Clay, KY 42404

Dixon, Sonja
(Robert Dixon)
  8550 Lafayette Road
  Hopkinsville, KY 42240
  (270)886-7647
  sonjadixon@earthlink.net

Gerard, Vanda
(Eugene "Stan" Gerard
  615 N 42nd Street
  Paducah, KY 42001
  (270)443-2889

Lively, Louella
(James Lively)
  196 Vicksburg Estate Road
  Benton, KY 42025
  (270)527-3776

Marsiglio, June
(Roger Marsiglio)
  505 Logan
  Providence, KY 42450)

Moss, Lou
(Larry Moss)
  167 Bluegrass Drive
  LaCenter, KY 42056
  (270)292-2000

Murphy, Robbie
(Vernon Murphy)
  128 New Liberty Church Road
  Kevil, KY 42053
  (270)522-3398

Owen, Pat
(Bert Owen)
  7906 Manner Pointe Drive
  Louisville, KY 40220
  (502)749-1940
  bertorpatowen@insightbb.com

SURVIVING SPOUSES OF MINISTERS BY PRESBYTERY CONTINUED
(Deceased spouse in parenthesis.)

Pettit, Jennie
(William H. Pettit)
 248 Skyline Drive
 Princeton, KY 42245
 (270)365-9076

CULLMAN

Kimbrell, Glenda
(Bobby Kimbrell)
 9479 Cumberland Oaks Drive
 Pinson, AL 35126
 (205)680-1743

Weathersby, Dorothy
(E.W. Weathersby)
 1203 2nd Avenue NE
 Cullman, AL 35055
 (256)734-2886

CUMBERLAND

Ferree, Carole
(Ronald Ferree)
 2475 Fallen Timber Road
 Campbellsville, KY 42718
 (270)465-1150

Graham, Mary
(Harold Graham)
 103 Freeman Green Drive
 Elizabethtown, KY 42701
 (270)360-1191

Johnson, Genevie
(Robert Johnson)
 351 Bacon Court
 Harrodsburg, KY 40330
 (859)734-3789

Milam, Dona
(Robert Milam)
 9294 Owensboro Road
 Falls of Rough, KY 40119
 (270)879-8985

Mouser, Wynemia Despain
(Calvin Mouser)
 204 Sunrise Drive
 Greensburg, KY 42743
 (270)932-7377

Phelps, Diann
(John Phelps)
 4743 Happy Hollow Road
 Hawesville, KY 42348
 (270)927-9835
 haor@juno.com

Renner, Wallace
(Patricia Renner)
 1648 Griffith Avenue
 Owensboro, KY 42301
 (270)685-4359
 pwrenner@adelphia.com

Sprague, Rose
(George Sprague)
 101 Clyde Morris Hall #242
 Ormond Beach, FL 32174

DEL CRISTO

Appleby, Judy
(Bob Appleby)
 3265 16th Street
 San Francisco, CA 94103
 (415)703-6090
 gfcc@gum.org

Chang, Grace
(John Chang)
 1753 Castro Drive
 San Jose, CA 95130
 (408)370-0643

Ellis, Ernestine
(John Ellis)
 1432 Cape Verde Place
 Tucson, AZ 85748
 (520)296-9027

Freeman, ??
(Jack Freeman)
 3559 Cody Way
 Sacramento, CA 95864
 (916)489-2567

Kennedy, Louise
(John F Kennedy)
 4916 44th Street
 Lubbock, TX 79414
 (806)796-0738

Matlock, Bettye
(Joe Matlock)
 5905 Hickory Grove Lane
 Bartlett, TN 38134
 (901)937-8457

Moss, Beth
(Greg Moss)

EAST TENNESSEE

Alexander, Carolyn Roberts
(Don Charles Alexander)
 2520 107 Cutoff
 Greeneville, TN 37743
 (423)638-8453
 alexandercda@msn.com

Blakeburn, Wiletta
(Roy E Blakeburn)
 111 Park Place
 Greeneville, TN 37743
 (423)787-9609
 blakeburnr@aol.com

Broyles, Elizabeth
(Lon Broyles)
 753 Snapp Bridge Road
 Limestone, TN 37681
 (865)483-8433

Broyles, Minnie
(Raymond Broyles)
 4944 Kilaminajaro
 Old Hickory, TN 37138-4102
 (615)428-8640

Dobson, Valdean
(Howard Dobson)
 150 Liberty Way
 Greeneville, TN 37645
 (423)798-8947

Johnson, Rebecca
(Scott Johnson)
 512 Rolling Creek Circle
 Knoxville, TN 37922
 (865)966-3699

Scott, Betty
(Lee Scott)
 319 Lavista Drive
 Maryville, TN 37804
 (731)415-2936

GRACE

Baker, Ola
(L. G. Baker)
 7208 12th Street
 Tampa, FL 33604
 (813)5239-3356

Brown, Marye
(Richard C Brown)
 2100 NE 140th Street Apt 510E
 Edmond, OK 73013
 (205)663-5486

Buerhaus, Charity
(Chuck Buerhaus)
 313 S Main Street
 Piedmont, AL 36272
 (256)447-6195

Hegwood, Clara
(James "Pete" Hegwood)
 125 Pinewood Lane
 Montevallo, AL 35115
 (205)665-2134

Mims, Martha Jo
(Howell "Gay" Mims)
 3011 Wolfe Road
 Columbus, MS 39705
 (662)328-3778
 mjmims@muw.edu

SURVIVING SPOUSES OF MINISTERS BY PRESBYTERY CONTINUED
(Deceased spouse in parenthesis.)

Phillips, Edna
(Troy Phillips)
2024 Hilltop Road
Rock Hill, SC 29732
(803)325-1416

Tant, Becky
(Robert H Tant)
516 Davis Drive
Glencoe, AL 35905
(256)494-9450
rtant82091@aol.com

HOPE

Bright, Mildred
(J. P. Bright)
1716 Broadway Boulevard
Florence, AL 35630
(256)766-8361

Copeland, Frances S.
(Bill Copeland)
142 Thornton Terrace Drive
Rogersville, AL 35652
(256)247-1688

Hyden, Mae
(Lee Hyden)
2195 Allsboro Road
Cherokee, AL 35616
(256)360-2896

MISSOURI

Bornert, Paughnee
(Robert D. Bornert)
932 E Snider Street
Springfield, MO 65803
(417)833-2627

Cantrell, Mary
(Ernest Cantrell)
7047 N Garnet Lane
Strafford, MO 65757
(417)736-9017

Cravens, Doris
(Marvin L Cravens)
604 N Hovis Street
Mountain Grove, MO 65711
(417)926-5778

Cravens, Hallie
(Ellis Cravens)
9566 Highway Z
Hartville, MO 65667
(417)668-5954

Cravens, Thelma
(Wilbur Cravens)
2144 Wilbur Road
Mansfield, MO 65704
417-924-8553

Dailey, Sarah
(Larry Dailey)
656 Grand Point Boulevard
Sunrise Beach, MO 65079
(573)374-9537

Gardner, Dossie
(Don Gardner)
26 W Pearl
Aurora, MO 65605
(417)678-3278

Gould, Marjorie
(Robert Gould)
204 W Pleasant
Aurora, MO 65605
(417)678-5422

Hensley, Jean Ann
(Howard Hensley)
537 Piperpoint
Rogersville, MO 65742
(414)753-1108

McCloud, Johnnie
(Theron McCloud)
419 Magnolia Court
Lebanon, MO 65536
(417)532-3388
jmccloud@advertisenet.com

Scobey, Darlis
(James Scobey)
105 Oak Hill Downs Street
Farmington, MO 63640
(573)756-1683

MURFREESBORO

Basham, Earline
(Willard Basham)
335 Myers Road
Winchester, TN 37398

Breeding, Karen
(Gordon Breeding)
1907 Susan Drive
Murfreesboro, TN 37129
(615)867-3660
zanylady1000@yahoo.com

Denman, Susie
(E. H. Denman)
525 Golf Club Drive
Smithville, TN 37166
(615)597-7122

Dickerson, Helen
(Andrew Mizel Dickerson, Jr.)
914 Dogwood Drive
Murfreesboro, TN 37129

Martin, Peggy
(James W Martin)
1922 Battleground Drive
Murfreesboro, TN 37129
(615)896-4442

Martindale, Dana
(J. Craig Martindale)
2913 Pellas Place
Murfreesboro, TN 37127
(615)653-0858
w5bu@hotmail.com

Salisbury, Helen Margaret
(A.D. Salisbury)
1927 Memorial Boulevard
Murfreesboro, TN 37129

Salisbury, Rebecca
(Loyce Estes)
1033 Twin Oaks Drive
Murfreesboro, TN 37130
(615)410-7801
rebsalisbury@yahoo.com

Watson, Mary Leota
(David E Watson)
804 W Main Street
McMinnville, TN 37110
(931)473-7561
leotaw@blomand.net

NASHVILLE

Allen, Hester
(Paul Allen)
300 Bantam Court
LaVerne, TN 37086

Andrews, Jane
(Leonard Andrews)
7390 Cabot Drive
Nashville, TN 37209
(615)352-0145

Burnett, Mary Lee
(Cecil Burnett)
321 Raindrop Lane
Hendersonville, TN 37075

Maxedon, Chris
(Julian Maxedon)
2260 Highway 31
White House, TN 37188

Stiles, Peggy
(John Stiles)
300 Bantam Court
Clarksville, TN 37043

SURVIVING SPOUSES OF MINISTERS BY PRESBYTERY CONTINUED
(Deceased spouse in parenthesis.)

NORTH CENTRAL

McCain, Violet
(Terence McCain)
  15804 Camden Avenue
  Eastpointe, MI 48021
  (586)774-4861

Springer, Eileen
(Robert Springer)
  403 Prairie Ridge Court
  Eureka, IL 61530
  (309)467-5030

RED RIVER

Brown, Beth
(LaRoyce Brown)
  311 S 8th Street
  Marlow, OK 73055
  (580)658-3989

Morgan, Sharon
(Jerome Morgan)
  8420 Baumgarten Drive
  Dallas, TX 75228

Turpen, Mary Lou
(Brent Turpen)
  PO Box 577
  Locust Grove, OK 74352
  (918)479-5613
  mlturpen@hotmail.com

ROBERT DONNELL

Hunter, Jean
(James E. Hunter)
  1905 Delynn
  Hazel Green, AL 35750
  (256)838-3902

TENNESSEE-GEORGIA

Galloway, Katherine
(Cliff Galloway)
  7127 White Oak Valley Road
  McDonald, TN 37353

Kapperman, Linda
(Glenn Kapperman)
  2719 Rio Grande Road
  Chattanooga, TN 37421
  (423)894-7924

Naugher, Catherine
(Doyce Naugher)
  985 Mt Pleasant Road
  Rydal, GA 30171
  (770)382-1982

TRINITY

Allen, Ann M
(Paul Allen)
  311 E Hawkins Parkway Apt 115
  Longview, TX 75605
  (903)759-5508

Johnson, Clyde
(Dave Johnson)
  2801 E Travis Apt 108
  Marshall, TX 75672
  (903)938-9953

Leslie, Jenann
(Marvin E. Leslie)
  300 Henley Perry Drive
  Marshall, TX 75670
  (903)938-6642
  jenann.leslie@gmail.com

Ward, Suzie
(Kevin Ward)
  216 E Caroline
  Marshall, TX 75672

WEST TENNESSEE

Brown, Beverly
(Paul B. Brown)
  406 N McNeil Street
  Memphis, TN 38112
  (901)278-6909

Brown, Phyllis
(David Brown)
  1930 Mignon
  Memphis, TN 38107
  (901)274-1513

Butler, Shirley
(George A Butler)
  306 Flora Circle
  Newbern, TN 38059

Cook, Marcine
(Paul V. Cook)
  144 Big John Drive
  Martin, TN 38237
  (731)587-0787
  marcine175@aol.com

Davis, Willene
(Harold Davis)
  7820 Walking Horse Circle #311
  Germantown, TN 38138
  (901)757-1394

Drylie, Linda
(James Drylie)
  512 JE Blaydes Parkway
  Atoka, TN 38004
  (901)837-1627

Forester, Willie Mae
(J. C. Forester)
  833 Main Street
  McKenzie, TN 38201
  (731)352-3107

Hall, Patsy
(Charles R. Hall)
  4341 Pebble Garden Court
  Birmingham, AL 35235
  (205)538-7993

Hicks, Ruby
(Willam D. Hicks)
  3938 Cardinal Drive
  Union City, TN 38261
  (731)885-5887

Knight, Helen
(James Knight)
  8081 Jills Creek Drive
  Bartlett, TN 38133
  (901)387-0675

Laurence, Brenda
(G. Larry Laurence)
  2823 Nine Mile Road
  Enville, TN 38332
  (731)687-2022
  southernmoma@hotmail.com

Leslie, Cheryl
(Randall Leslie)
  3374 Walnut Grove Road
  Memphis, TN 38111
  (901)458-4413

Leslie, Marilyn
(Eugene Leslie)
  13155 Center Hill Road
  Olive Branch, MS 38654
  (731)613-0425
  eleslie1@bellsouth.net

Lynch, Van
(Jerry Lynch)
  73 Baseline Road
  Dyer, TN 38330

McMahen, Sandra
(Rowe Gene McMahen)
  92 Stonewall Circle
  McKenzie, TN 38201
  (731)352-3067

Stott, Beverly
(Melvin Buddy Stott)
  200 E Main Street
  Dresden, TN 38225
  (731)364-5863
  bevstott@frontiernet.net

CUMBERLAND PRESBYTERIANS
SERVING OUTSIDE THE UNITED STATES

Please e-mail missionaries before mailing anything to them to determine the best way to send them letters or packages. If you want to communicate with missionaries in closed countries, first e-mail the Missions Ministry Team (Lthomas@cumberland.org) and we will forward your e-mail to the missionary.

Boyce & Beth Wallace—Colombia
e-mail: hbwcali@yahoo.com
oovoo and facetime: Boyce Wallace

Anay Ortega—Guatemala
e-mail: anayortegamonroy@hotmail.com
skype: Anay Ortega Monroy
oovoo: Anay Ortega

Fhanor & Socorro Pejendino—Guatemala
email: pastorfhanor@gmail.com
skype: Fhanor Pejendino Arcos
oovoo: pastorestulua

T T G—Kyrgyzstan
email: Lthomas@cumberland.org

D S L—Laos and Cambodia
email: Lthomas@cumberland.org

Carlos & Luz Dary Rivera—Mexico
email: caralrifra@une.lnet.co
oovoo: Carlos Rivera

Daniel & Kay Jang—Philippines
Ilollo Cumberland Mission Church
email: goingup129@hanmail.net

John & Joy Park—Iloilo, Philippines
email: barkmoksa@hanmail.net

Kenneth & Delight Hopson—Uganda
e-mail: ken.hopson@wgm.org
skype: Delight Hopson
oovoo: Kenneth Hopson

Jacob & Lindsey Sims—deputation
e-mail: jacobdsims@gmail.com

Patrick & Jessica Wilkerson—deputation
e-mail: patrickwilkerson3@gmail.com

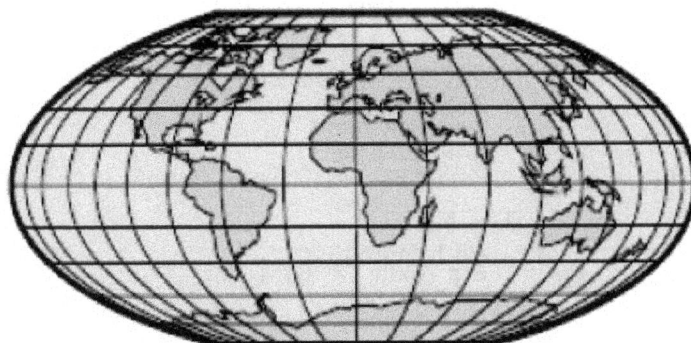

The Cumberland Presbyterian Church
has five families working in closed countries as
humanitarian workers.

NEW CHURCH DEVELOPMENTS & MISSION PROBES

ANDES

Aguadas
Cra 3 #7-14
Aguadas, Caldas
Colombia, SA
(576)851-4773
jeob40@hotmail.com
Pastor: Joaquin Orozco   (M1)
Began: 1996 (as re-development)

Amaga
Cra San Fernando #48-56
Amaga, Antioquia
Colombia, SA
(574)847-3250
rebcaldas@une.net.co
Pastor: Jhon Jairo Arias   (M1)
Began: 1997

Chinchina
Mz 2 Casa 21, Urb. Milan
Dosquebradas, Ris
Colombia, SA
(476)322-2177
oikoninonia@gmail.com
Pastor: Rodrigo Martinez   (M1)

Quimbaya
Cra 6 #25-54
Quimbaya, Quindio
Colombia, SA
(576)752-3570
joenjimu@yahoo.es
Pastor: Jorge Enrique Jimenez
  (M2)
Began: 04/02

ARKANSAS

**Bryant-Benton CP Mission
Fellowship (1102)**
16904 Old Mill Road
Little Rock, AR 72206
(501)888-4190
Pastor: Dwight Shanley   (M1)
Began: 2005

CAUCA VALLEY

Casa de Oracion

Dia de Salvacion
Pastor: Luis Cantor
( )256-2835

Rios de Agua Viva
Pastor: Euripides Moreno   (M1)
( )244-3557

COVENANT

Cadiz
Cadiz, KY
Pastor: Danny York   (M1)
Began: 2008

DEL CRISTO

316 Christian Fellowship
2200 E Dartmouth Circle
Englewood, CO 80113
(720)253-3425
jeanhess@316denver.com
Pastor: Rick & Jean Hess   (M1)
Began: 08/10

Bethesda Korean Fellowship
139 Silverado Drive
Santa Teresa, NM 88008
(915)329-3451
pyongsanyu@hotmail.com
Pastor: Pyong San Yu   (M1)
Began: 03/10

Marantha East
12008 Fred Carter
El Paso, TX 79936
(915)592-6138
yaanaivitaly@yahoo.com
Pastor: Alfredo Rincon   (M1)
Began: 2012

GRACE

Naples Fellowship (0309)
842 Bent Creek Way
Naples, FL 34114
(931)273-0768
revga@hotmail.com
Pastor: Ramon Garcia   (M1

JAPAN

Ichikawa Grace Mission Point (8314)
3-19-5 Sugano
Ichikawa-shi, Chiba-ken
272-0824 JAPAN
(047)326-8675
(047)326-8675 FAX
fwgc6854@mb.infoweb.ne.jp
Pastor: Yasuo Masuda   (M2)

RED RIVER

Church of St. Giles
3500 S Peoria Avenue
Tulsa, OK 74105
(918)760-6145
Pastor: William G. Webb, Jr.   (M1)

Marantha   (8426)
2801 Biway Street
Fort Worth, TX 76114
(817)210-5571
sledadmartinez164@gmail.com
Pastor: Soledad Martinez   (M1)
Began: 2015

TENNESSEE-GEORGIA

Pikeville Mission
530 Sequatchie Road
Pikeville, TN 37367
(423)447-6897
Pastor: Rhonda McGowan   (M1)

WEST TENNESSEE

Cristo Salva Fellowship
3442 Tutwiler
Memphis, TN 38122
diannwhite12@yahoo.com
Pastor: Carlos Solito   (M1)

Grace Fellowship (9323)
9160 Tchulahoma Road
Southaven, MS 38671
(662)393-2552
tthompson393@aol.com
Pastor: Tommy Thompson   (M1)

Iona Community of Faith
1790 Faxon Avenue
Memphis, TN 38112
website: www.iona.gutensite.com
(901)283-8062
wa4mff@aol.com
Pastor: Barry Anderson   (M1)

PROVISIONAL CHURCHES AND PROVISIONAL FELLOWSHIPS

"A provisional fellowship is a pre-existing non-English congregation that is being received into the Cumberland Presbyterian Church through an authorized assimilation process.

ARKANSAS

(2135)
Arkansas Korean Loving Church
8201 Frenchmans Lane
Little Rock, AR 72209
Pastor: Sun Wan Cho   (M1)

CAUCA VALLEY

Bugalagrande
Cra 8 No 7A-12
Bugalagrande, Colombia, SA

Carmelo
Veredo Carmelo
Limones, Cauca, Colombia, SA
Pastor: Juan Ventura   (M3)

Golondrinas
Corregimiento Golondrinas
Montebello, Colombia, SA
vallejo903@hotmail.com
Pastor: Ariel Vallejo

Guachucal
Centro
Guachucal, Colombia, SA
Iflesianuevavida15@gmail.com
Pastor: Martin Termal   (M3)

Ipiales
Cra 2A No 12-54
Ipiales, Colombia, SA
pastoscarealpe@hotmail.com
Pastor: Oscar Realpe   (M1)

Juanico
Vereda Juanico
Guapi, Colombia, SA
Pastor: Bernabe Angulo   (M3)

Limones
Corregimiento Limones
Guapi, Colombia, SA
Pastor: Henry Angulo   (M3)

Los Monos
Vereda Los Monos
Sapuyes, Colombia, SA
Pastor: Mario Paredes   (LS)

Manantial de Vida
Vereda de Brazo Seco
El Charco, Colombia, SA
Pastor: Sofinias Velazco   (M3)

Morales
Morales, Colombia, SA
johnydiana7@hotmail.com
Pastor: John Agredo   (M3)

Rios de Agua Viva
Trav 87 No 2-24
Buenatura, Colombia, SA
euripidesmoreno1@hotmail.com
Pastor: Euripides Moreno   (M2)

Sapuyes
Iglesia Presbiteriana C
Sapuyes, Colombia, SA
walterviteri@gmail.com
Pastor: Oscar Rosero   (M3)

Villa Gorgona
Manzana C Casa 5 Santa Ana
Villa Gorgona, Colombia, SA
daniel.blanco04@hotmail.com
Pastor: Daniel Blanco   (M3)

Villavicencio
Villavicencio, Colombia, SA
german_millanco12@yahoo.com.mx
Pastor: German Millan

COVENANT

(3420)
Zion CP Fellowship
1347 S 6th Street
Paducah, KY 42003
(270)442-6414
zioncpcinfo@gmail.com
Pastor: Steve/Teresa Shauf   (M1)
Began: 10/2012

CUMBERLAND EAST COAST

(2445)
Immanuel Presbyterian Church
67-17 215th
Oakland Gardens, NY 11364
Pastor: Soo Yeol Park
(646)599-4941
shwbpark@naver.com

(2138)
Our Good Presbyterian Church
32132 Huntly Circle
Salisbury, MD 21804
(443)783-3809 (cell)
Pastor: Hyoung Sik Choi   (M1)
Began: 2001

EAST TENNESSEE

Walkertown
6885 Kingsport Highway
Afton, TN 37616
(423)639-1333
Pastor: Kevin McAmis   (M5)

MISSOURI

First CPC Korean Mission
4216 Charleston Avenue
Springfield, MO 65408
(417)888-0442
hesed-park@hanmail.net
Pastor: Sang H Park   (M1)
Began: 10/4/2015

TENNESSEE GEORGIA

Baek Seok Church
3075 Landington Way
Duluth, GA 30096
(404)398-8469
mnb0924@yahoo.co.kr
Pastor: Seung Chon Han   (M1)

(2150)
Divinity Church
3480 Summit Ridge Parkway
Duluth, GA 30096
Pastor: Rev. Frederick Nah
Began: 2013

GJH Ministries
3327 Duluth Highway
Duluth, GA 30096
(770)940-2365
gjhministryatl@gmail.com
Pastor: Duck Hun Lee

(2130)
Korean Livingstone Presbyterian Church
3340 Bentbill xing
Cumming, GA 30041
(770)912-8477
barkmoksa@hanmail.net
Pastor: Rev Young Rae Park   (M1)

New York Chowon Mission Church
254-18 Northern Boulevard
Little Neck, NY 11362
(917)992-5200
lovedasol@gmail.com
Pastor: Si Hoon Park   (M1)

Phillipians Church
2310 His Way
Lawrenceville, GA 30044
(678)462-7526
agatopia@hanmail.net
Pastor: Jin Koo Kang   (M1)

Trinity Church
1050 Grace Drive
Lawrenceville, GA 30043
(678)622-2717
samil2110@yahoo.com
Pastor: Rev. Min Soo Kim   (M1)

(2103)
The Cross Mission
5260 Coacoochee Ter
Alpharetta, GA 30022
(404)421-4262
Pastor: Jea Kwang Lee   (M1)

(2125)
Walking with God Presbyterian Church
3299 Highway 120
Duluth, GA 30096
(678)600-2787
jaeyu117@yahoo.com
Pastor: Jae Hyung Yu   (M1)

We Community Church
302 Satellite Boulevard
Suwanee, GA 30024
(678)908-9191
powerment@hotmail.com
Pastor: Hyang Koo Lee

TRINITY

Ye Rang Korean Church (8602)
12320 Alameda Trail Circle #1309
Austin, TX 78727
(512)474-2646
preacherofgod@gmail.com
Pastor: Sung In Park   (M1)

WEST TENNESSEE

(9436)
ACTS Church
6524 Summer Avenue
Memphis, TN 38134
(901)381-4790
usyoun61@hotmail.com
Pastor: Daniel Youn

Redeemer Evangelical Church
7011 Poplar Avenue
Germantown, TN 38138
(901)737-3370
jimmylatimer@redeemerevangelical.com
Pastor: James M. Latimer

MISSION CHURCHES AND PASTORS
UNDER CARE OF MISSIONS MINISTRY TEAM
(General Assembly Ministry Council)

AUSTRALIA
"Australia CP Council of Churches"

Citinse Mission
(Provisional)
  2142 Swan Avenue
  Strathfield, NSW
  rsk2002@empal.com
  Pastor: Suk Kyn Ryu   (M1)

Darwin Dasom Korean
(Provisional)
  44 Dripstone Road
  Causurina, NT 0820
  hansongwee2@gmail.com
  Pastor: Sun Hee (Sunny) Hwang(M1)

Disciples
(Provisional)
  237 Botany Road
  Waterloo, NSW
  oldrooney@hotmail.com
  Pastor: Sung Yong Cho   (M1)

Hansaesun
(Provisional)
  21 James Street Lidcomb
  Lidcomb
  hansaesunchurch@gmail.com
  Pastor: Young Kwang Kim   (M3)

Melbourne Bang Joo
(Provisional)
  117 Murrumbeena Road
  Murrumbeena, VIC 3163
  min0430446647@gmail.com
  Pastor: Min Huh   (M1)

Sydney Korean
(Provisional)
  458 Burwood Road
  Belmore NSW 2192
  sydneykoreanchurch@gmail.com
  Pastor: Jong One Choi   (M1)

PROVISIONAL PASTORS:

Cho, Sung Yong
  6/58-62 Carnarvon Street
  Silverwater, NSW
  oldrooney@hotmail.com
Choi, Jong One
  458 Burwood Road
  Belmore 2192, NSW
  Phone: 61-414-641-200
  johnillcho@hanmail.net
Huh, Min
  2112 Eunka Street
  Chadstone, VIC 3148
  min0430446647@gmail.com
Hwang, Sun Hee
  1512 Lindsay Street
  Darwin, NT 0800
  hangsongwee@hanmail.net
Ryu, Ouk Kyu
  9155 Manson Road
  Strathfield, NSW 2131
  rsk2002@empal.com

CANDIDATES:

Kim, Jiho
  31 Olga Street
  Chatswood NSW 2067
  lovepresage@naver.com
Kim, Young Kwang
  25 Clemsford Avenue
  Epping, NSW 2121
  basskk77@naver.com

BRAZIL
Hosted by Missions Ministry Team

_____ (8313)
Mata De Sao Joao Church
  Nucleo Colonial JK
  Lote 56 Mata De Sao Joao
  48280-000, Bahia, BRAZIL
  (5571)9641-1307
  Pastor: Keishi Ishitsuka   (M1)
  (5571)9641-1307
  kishitsuka@hotmail.com

LICENTIATES:

Santos, Carlos
  Nucleo Colonial JK
  Lote 56 Mata De Sao Joao
  48280-000, Bahia, BRAZIL
  (5571)3482-3484
  san_coc@hotmail.com

GUATEMALA
"Guatemala CP Council of Churches"

Iglesia Evangelica de Fe y Jubilo
(Provisional)
  6a avenida 3-56 Zona 19
  Colonia La Florida
  Guatemala City, Guatemala
  Pastor: Edgar Buni Avalos   (M1)

Casa de Fe y Oracion
(Provisional)
  31 calle 9-75 Colonia Miralvally
  Zona 6 de Mixco
  Guatemala

Comunidad de Fe
(Provisional)
  29 calle 14-41 Zona 12
  Coonia Santa Rosa II
  Guatemala City, Guatemala

MISSIONARIES:

Reverend Fhanor Pejendino
Reverend Socorro Pejendino
Ms Anay Ortega

PROVISIONAL PASTORS:

Avalos, Edgar Buni
  6a avenida 3-56 Zona 19
  Colonia La Florida
  Guatemala City, Guatemala

HAITI
"Haiti CP Council of Churches"
<u>Hosted by Hope Presbytery</u>

<u>PROVISIONAL CHURCHES:</u>

Eglise Evangelique de Dufour
   Pastor: Jean Joab St Rouis   (M3)

Eglise E U-Chunen Gris de Gris-Gris
   Pastor: Kemson Lundy   (M3)

Eglise Evangelique de Lexi
   Pastor: Smith Fauvelt   (M3)

Eglise Evangelique de Mache Kabrit
   Pastor: Evetuel Theissaint   (M3)

Eglise Evangelique de Nan Akou
   Pastor: Sheslaire Georges   (M3)

Eglise Evangelique de Saint-Jules
   Pastor: Eddy Edouard   (M3)

MEXICO
"Mexico CP Council of Churches"
<u>Hosted by Red River Presbytery</u>

<u>PROVISIONAL CHURCHES:</u>

Casa del Alfarero
   C Norte 12 A Esq OTE 53
   Chalco Edo
   Mexico
   54-4-627-5570
   alaprep28@hotmail.com
   Pastor: Alejandro Alejo   (M1)

Iglesia Marantha
   Arroyo de Miumbre #1749
   Col Felipe Augeles
   Ciudad Juarez
   Mexico
   54-53-67-9103
   jessevega69@gmail.com
   Pastor: Jedidiah Vega   (M1)

Restauration de Vida
   Calle Benito Juarez #35
   Colonia Guadalupe Victoria
   Delegacion Gustavo A Madero
   Mexico
   54-5-318-7622
   castro_dan@hotmail.com
   Pastor: Jose Dan Castro   (M1)

MISSIONS

Fuente de Vida - Ajusco
   Calle Primera Cerrada de Hombres
   Ilustres 2B Colonia Santa Ceilia
   Tepetlapa Delebacion
   Xochimilco CP
   Ciudad Mexico

<u>MISSIONARIES:</u>

Reverend Carlos Rivera
Reverend Luz Dary Rivera

<u>PROVISIONAL PASTORS:</u>

Alejo, Alejandro (Robledo)
   Casa del Alfarero CP Church
   C Norte 12 Esq Ote 53 Col Union
   de GPE
   Chalco Mexico
   Phone: 46-27-5570
   aleprep28@hotmail.com
Castro, Jose Dan (Solis)
   Restauracion de Vida CP Church
   Calle C Col San Marcos
   Azcapotzalco C P 02020 Mexico
   Phone: 55-53-18-7622
   castro_dan@hotmail.com
Gallardo, Gabriel (Uzziel)
   NCD Mission Ajusco 1a Cda
   Hombres Ilustres 20B Sta Cecilia
   Tepetiapa Xochimilco Mexico
   DF CP 16880
   Phone: 55-48-1563
   pastoruzziel@hotmail.com
Mata, Jorge Fernando
   Marantha CP Church Towi 8127 Sta
   Fe Cd C Jaurez
   Chihuahua Mexico
   Phone: 656-62-59-975
   pastormata@hotmail.com

<u>CANDIDATES:</u>

Hernandez, Octavio
   c/o Iglesia Marantha
   Phone: 65-61-939157

PHILIPPINES
"Philippine CP Council of Churches"

_____(2321)
Iloilo Cumberland Presbyterian
(Church)
  PO Box 5
  Aduana Street
  Iloilo City 5000, Philippines
  Pastor: J Sean Saim   (M1)

_____
Mostro Cumberland Presbyterian
(Mission)
  Pastor: Romeo Agana   (M2)

_____
Pavia Cumberland Presbyterian
(Mission)
  Jabonillo Street
  Pavia, Iloilo
  Pastor: Manual Job Baldevia   (M1)

_____
Oton Cumberland Presbyterian
(Church)
  Cabang
  Oton, Iloilo
  Pastor: Alexander Duyac, Jr.   (M1)

MISSIONARIES:

Reverend John Park
Mrs. Joy Park
Reverend Daniel Yang
Mrs Kay Yang

PASTORS:

Baldevia, Manuel Job
Duyac, Alexander, Jr.
  Brgy, Cabang, Oton, Iloilo
Saim, J Sean Espanueva
  c/o Iloilo CP Church

LICENTIATES:

Agana, Romeo G, Jr.
  c/o Iloilo CP Church
Tagurigan, Alpha Faith Singcuenco
  c/o Iloilo CP Church

CANDIDATES:

Bonete, Harold Henry D
  c/o Iloilo CP Church
Dyuac, Aldrandreb D
  c/o Iloilo CP Church
Garnica, Darrel Von
  c/o Iloilo CP Church
Yutig, Lucelle E
  c/o Iloilo CP Church

SOUTH KOREA
"Korean CP Council of Churches"

_____(2221)
First Cumberland Presbyterian Church
of Korea
(Church)
  Hyundai I-park B-02
  Burim-dong 113
  Dongan-gu, Anyang-si
  Gyeonggi-do, Korea 431-787
  Phone: 82-70-8872-8033
  Pastor: Heungsoo Kang   (M1)
  Clerk: Yoon JinSub
  303-101 Raenian Ever heim Apt
  Naeson 2-dong, Uiwangsi
  Gyeonggi-do, Korea 437-761
  jinsyoon@gmail.com

_____
Glory Church
(Mission)
  302 Si-Bum Building
  1342 Seocho 2-dong, Seocho-gu
  Seoul, Korea 137-861
  Phone: 82-2-3474-8405
  Pastor: Geumtaek Lim   (M1)
_____(2323)
New Life Church
(Mission)
  325-1 Donghyeon-dong
  Jecheon-si
  Chungcheongbud-do, Korea 390-
190
  Phone: 82-10-6655-9188
  Pastor: Woonyong Yu   (M1)

_____
Seum Church
(Mission)
  Seobu-ro 2105 beongil 26-6 101 ho
  Jang-gu, Suwan City, South Korea
_____(2324)
Ye-Il Church
(Mission)
  15 Seogyeong-ro, 28beong-gil
  Heungdeok-gu, Cheongiu-si
  Chungcheongbuk-do, Korea 361-
803
  Phone: 82-42-232-6000
  Pastor: Dawie Ahn(M1)

PASTORS:

Ahn, Dawit (David)
  606-304 Gapyeong Jugong Apt
  Jungnim-dong, Heungdeck-gu
  Cheongju-si
  Chungcheongbuk-do
  Korea 361-850
  Phone: 82-10-2421-0219
  ankim91@hanmail.net
Kang, Huengsoo
  Hyundai I-park B-02, Burim-dong 113
  Dongan-gu, Anyang-si
  Gyeonggi-do, Korea 431-787
  Phone: 82-10-8428-0084
  halieus@hanmail.net
Kim, YoungHo (Steve)
  B02 Hyundai I-Space 1608-2
  Burim Dong, Dong An Gu
  AnYang City, Kyunggi Do S Korea
  Phone: 231-348-8033
  paidion4377@naver.com
Lee, Sangdo
  507-1501 Samik Green Apt
  Myeongil 1-dong, Gngdong-gu
  Seoul, Korea 134-782
  Phone: 82-10-3353-2907
  humanolsd@hanmail.net

Lee, Yongrae
  507 Je-Il Officetel, 99-20
  Yulgeon-dong, Jangan-gu
  Suwon-si, gyeonggi-do, Korea
  Phone: 82-10-9928-9012
  path0316@naver.com
Lim, Geumtaek
  302-si-Bum Building
  1342 Seocho 2dong, Seccho-gu
  Seoul, Korea 137-861
  Phone: 82-11-9044-5250
  limkt114@hanmail.net
Park, Bo-Seong
  304-28 Sinlim-Dong, Kwanak-Gu
  Seoul, Korea
  Phone: 002-884-3474
Yu, Woonyong
  325-1 Donghyeon-dong, Jecheon-si
  Chungcheongbuk-do, Korea 390-190
  Phone: 82-10-6655-9188
  lifeyu@hanmail.net

LICENTIATES:

Choi, Justin
  823-4 Naeson 1-dong, Uiwang-si
  Gyeonggi-do, Korea 437-838
  Phone: 82-10-2668-8795
  rev.choi@hotmail.com
Lee, Il-Do (Derek)
  151-2 Ongnyeon-dong
  Yeonsu-gu, Incheon, Korea
  Phone: 82-10-2627-2152
  monya215@naver.com

CAMP GROUNDS

ARKANSAS PRESBYTERY

Camp Peniel
Monte Williams
83 Camp Peniel Drive
Solgohachia, AR 72156
(501)354-5282

CHOCTAW PRESBYTERY

Camp Israel Folsom
Box 158
Broken Bow, OK 74728
(580)584-2099

COLUMBIA PRESBYTERY

Crystal Springs Camp, Inc.
21 Crystal Springs Camp Road
Kelso, TN 37348
(931)937-8621
Medley@cafes.net
Camp Manager: Carol Medley

PRESBYTERY OF EAST TENNESSEE

Camp Chilhowee
c/o Bill & Traci Pressley
1920 Old Chilhowee Loop Road
Maryville, TN 37865
(865)983-7084

Camp John Speer
c/o Dennis Elwell
2154 Viking Mountain Road
Greeneville, TN 37743
(423)636-1366
dpelwell@gmail.com
www.campjohnspeer.com

GRACE PRESBYTERY

Camp Bailey
Route 1 Box 386
Union, MS 39365

Caretaker: Mr. Lynn Frederick
P. O. Box 574
Carthage, MS 39051

MISSOURI PRESBYTERY

Camp Cumberland
South Greenfield, Missouri
(417)637-2059
Renee Rogers, Business Manager

MURFREESBORO PRESBYTERY

Crystal Springs
21 Crystal Springs Camp Road
Kelso, TN 37348
(931)937-8621

NASHVILLE PRESBYTERY

Camp Crystal Springs
21 Crystal Springs Camp Road
Kelso, TN 37348
(931)937-8621
Carol Medley, Director

TENNESSEE-GEORGIA PRESBYTERY

Camp Glancy
1370 Coppinger Cove Road
Sequatchie, TN 37374

TRINITY PRESBYTERY

Camp Gilmont
Rt. 6, Box 254
Gilmer, TX 75644
(903)797-6400

WEST TENNESSEE PRESBYTERY

Camp Clark Williamson
390 Mason Road
Humboldt, TN 38343
(800)655-8204
(731)784-3221
Mike Hannaford, Administrator
www.campclarkwilliamson.com

Explanation of Symbols

MC=
    Abbreviation for name of
    county or state if more
    than one church in the
    presbytery has the same
    name.

4=   The number of Sundays
      each month the church
      engages in worship
M=   Manse
E=   Every Home Plan for The
      Cumberland Presbyterian
W=   Organized women's
      ministry

P = Provisional Church
C = Church
F = Fellowship
U = Union Church

Synod/Presbytery
Abbreviations

Church Name

Church Number

Telephone
Number

Little Brown Church (MC) (4MEWC) GRWT9450
2307 Country Lane
Pleasant Valley, TN 37001
(901)654-0058 <Kingdom>

County

PA: John Doe   <M1>
        1 Church St.
        Pleasant Valley, TN 37001
        (901)654-3210
AP: Mary Smith   <M1>
        20 Serenity Lane
        Pleasant Valley, TN 37001
        (901)654-0123
CL: Jane Doe
        30 Charity Rd.
        Pleasant Valley, TN 37001
        (901)654-2345

CL= Clerk of Session
CO= Chair of commission
       appointed to govern
       church

DE = Denominational Employee
ED = Editor
FM = Former Moderator
IT   = In Transit to another Presbytery
M1 = Ordained Minister
M2 = Licentiate
M3 = Candidate
M4 = Minister of another denomination
         enrolled as a member through
         reciprocal agreement
         (Constitution 5.3)
M5 = Member of another denomination
M6 = Layperson serving church
M7 = Associate or Assistant Pastor
M8 = Military Chaplain
M9 = Non-Military Chaplain
M0 = Mentored Minister
MY = Missionary
OM = Other approved ministry
OP = Member of another presbytery
PR = Professor, Teacher
RT = Retired **or HR (honorably retired)**
ST = Student

AP = Associate/AssistantPastor
IP = Interim Pastor
LS = Layperson serving church
OD= Member of another
      denomination
PA = Installed Pastor
SS = Stated Supply

SUMMARY OF STATISTICS OF PRESBYTERIES BY SYNODS

	GENERAL	MEMBERSHIP			CHANGES				FINANCES				
(Number of Ministers)	1. Church Number	2. Active	3. Total	4. Church School	5. Prof. of Faith	6. Gains	7. Losses	8. Children Baptized	9. OUR UNITED OUTREACH	10. Total Out-Reach Giving	11. All Other Expenses	12. Total Income Received	13. Value Church Prop. 1=1000
	1	2	3	4	5	6	7	8	9	10	11	12	13
GR: SYNOD OF GREAT RIVERS													
Arkansas (53)	53	1,931	3,107	1,185	86	95	190	22	133,062	444,926	1,605,021	2,231,750	21,920
Missouri (16)	21	658	1,068	373	37	53	71	6	53,761	171,467	607,182	720,352	7,609
West Tennessee (105)	95	5,371	9,322	3,219	146	265	434	45	308,888	795,406	4,948,589	5,902,627	54,742
SYNOD TOTALS (174)	169		13,497		269		695		495,711		7,160,792		84,271
		7,960		4,777		413		73		1,411,799		8,854,729	
MI: SYNOD OF THE MIDWEST													
Covenant (43)	43	2,720	5,189	1,799	36	59	204	7	127,977	262,303	1,279,900	1,592,855	24,932
Cumberland (60)	65	2,624	4,326	1,626	38	95	718	24	111,011	283,173	2,260,396	2,376,197	23,438
North Central (33)	31	1,124	1,990	926	8	64	35	3	75,692	282,455	937,482	1,226,449	10,992
SYNOD TOTALS (136)	139		11,505		82		957		314,680		4,477,778		59,362
		6,468		4,351		218		34		827,931		5,195,501	
MS: MISSION SYNOD													
Andes (16)	10	1,861	1,995	743	182	176	93	0	9,436	337,836	688,086	893,600	1,626
Cauca Valley (16)	23	3,134	3,705	2,538	135	310	411	0	8,638	126,789	526,442	699,561	8,546
Choctaw (5)	7	83	133	76	0	6	11	1	1,000	7,312	20,044	30,852	233
del Cristo (52)	11	1,466	3,783	602	10	73	90	6	84,408	407,516	3,138,404	3,578,206	15,191
Hong Kong (10)	10	1,419	2,190	619	65	100	28	35	13,471	328,075	2,556,898	2,930,421	4,384
Japan (18)	13	1,157	2,213	641	18	34	43	6	35,741	228,204	1,551,106	1,464,790	3,103
Red River (61)	24	2,361	4,010	1,389	81	236	213	16	136,193	617,130	4,401,700	5,148,412	36,979
Trinity (46)	22	1,722	2,329	702	28	44	299	19	102,610	547,621	2,615,295	2,939,666	23,570
SYNOD TOTALS (224)	120		20,358		519		1,188		391,497		15,497,975		93,632
		13,203		7,310		979		83		2,600,483		17,685,508	
SE: SYNOD OF THE SOUTHEAST													
Cum East Coast (??)	7	138	167	52	31	25	39	3	1,150	34,494	464,211	348,652	280
East Tennessee (60)	37	2,730	4,677	1,565	38	106	148	21	256,845	621,830	3,417,287	4,105,469	35,298
Grace (104)	35	2,520	3,886	1,454	53	167	120	20	147,968	325,317	2,540,409	2,784,620	30,941
Hope (10)	16	830	1,370	487	16	23	28	8	47,173	143,547	708,956	886,342	9,503
Robert Donnell (27)	16	894	1,537	391	4	13	249	2	55,554	190,653	1,006,222	1,275,216	13,066
Tennessee-Georgia (41)	25	1,774	2,229	679	22	50	173	11	66,296	194,795	1,694,190	1,965,314	18,467
SYNOD TOTALS (242)	136		13,866		164		757		574,986		9,831,275		107,555
		8,886		4,628		384		65		1,510,636		11,365,613	
TN: TENNESSEE SYNOD													
Columbia (30)	38	1,363	2,267	826	79	74	173	9	75,561	263,814	1,751,563	2,034,610	19,890
Murfreesboro (52)	45	3,088	4,519	2,037	46	108	206	19	227,362	436,030	2,543,221	2,890,106	32,761
Nashville (62)	38	2,916	4,798	1,802	68	167	382	31	296,560	576,088	4,041,286	5,903,155	52,074
SYNOD TOTALS (144)	121		11,584		193		761		599,483		8,336,070		104,725
		7,367		4,665		349		59		1,275,932		10,827,871	
GRAND TOTALS (920)	685		70,810		1,227		4,358		2,376,357		45,303,890		449,545
		43,884		25,731		2,343		314		7,626,781		53,929,222	

Andes Presbytery
MISSION SYNOD

	1.Church Number	2.Active	3.Total	4.Church School	5.Prof. of Faith	6.Gains	7.Losses	8.Children Baptized	9. OUR UNITED OUT-REACH	10. Total Out-Reach Giving	11. All Other Expenses	12. Total Income Received	13. Value Church Prop. 1=1000
	1	2	3	4	5	6	7	8	9	10	11	12	13
Armenia	8903	546	546	100	40	29	5	0		52,598	105,779	130,551	450
Cartago	8906	150	190	80	23	28	9	0		6,418	46,550	52,968	100
Dosquebradas*	8907	233	239	125	40	41	21	0		11,014	102,323	95,680	112
El Rebano	8905	259	269	62	0	8	12	0		45,658	17,218	114,442	161
Horeb-Central	8915	104	115	25	15	15	7	0		24,659	63,778	79,098	111
La Rosa*	8911	77	77	60	0	6	4	0		12,090	24,516	42,684	28
La Virginia Mis*	8913	32	34	51	4	7	3	0		4,150	11,673	15,246	21
Manizales*	8914	106	116	60	10	4	17	0		22,282	42,669	63,610	13
Pereira	8916	252	300	130	48	33	15	0		142,991	237,530	346,182	500
Senda de Libertad	8919												
Zamora	8918	102	109	50	2	5	0	0		15,976	36,050	53,139	130
Presbytery	8900								9,436				
TOTALS	11	1,861	1,995	743	182	176	93	0	9,436	337,836	688,086	893,600	1,626

*Math error corrected. **Purged roll..

CHURCHES, PASTORS, AND CLERKS:

Armenia   (4MWC)MSAN8903
Cra 15 #16-39
Armenia, Quindio
Colombia, South America
(574)745-4860   <S America>
FAX: (574)745-4895
ipc-armenia@hotmail.com
PA: John Jairo Correa   <M1>
Calle 2 Norte #16-39
Armenia, Quindio
Colombia, South America
(574)745-0496
jjcedp07@hotmail.com
AP: Esperanza Diaz   <M1>
Calle 2 Norte #16-19
Armenia, Quindio
Colombia, South America
(576)745-0496
CL: Jose Leobardo Castro
Calle 16 #14-43
Armenia, Quindio
Colombia, South America
57(310)-389-2361

Cartago   (4MW C)MSAN8906
Cra 12 #8-47
Cartago, Valle
Colombia, South America
(572)214-5060   <S America>
FAX: (572)214-5060
presbicartago@gmail.com
PA: Alexander Galvis   <M1>
Calle 76 #87-63 Apto 211
Medellin, Antioquia
Colombia, South America
(300)778-4354
alexgt7@hotmail.com

CL: Verney Lopez
Calle 25C #36-15
Cartago, Valle
Colombia, South America
57(314)715-3075

Dosquebradas   (4MWC)MSAN8907
Calle 51 #15-32 (mailing)
Cra 15 A #50-31 (physical)
barrio Los Naranjos
Dosquebradas, Risaralda
Colombia, South America
(574)322-2938   <S America>
PA: Juan Esteban Blandon   <M1>
Calle 51 #15-32
barrio Los Naranjos
Dosquebradas, Risaralda
Colombia, South America
(574)322-2938
juanestebanblandon@yahoo.com
CL: Alba Rodriguez
Cra 15 A #50-31
barrio Los Naranjoa
Dosquebradas, Risaralda
Colombia, South America
(574)322-4899

El Rebano-Caldas   (4WMCF)MSAN8905
Calle 128 Sur #48-13
barrio Central
Caldas, Antioquia
Colombia, South America
(574)278-0787   <S America>
FAX: (574)278-0787
rebcaldas@une.net.co
PA: Juan Alexander Castano   <M1>
Calle 127 sur #42-38 Apto 301
Caldas, Antioquia
Colombia, South America
(574)306-4435
FAX: (574)278-0787
juanalexandercastanovelez@yahoo.com

CL: Consuelo Pena
Calle 130 Sur #57-09, Int 301
Caldas, Antioquia
Colombia, South America
(574)338-6190
FAX: (574)278-0787
chelitopeco@hotmail.com

Horeb-Central   (4WMC)MSAN8915
Carrera 50D #62-69, Prado Centro
Medellin, Antioquia
Colombia, South America
(574)263-2154   <S America>
ipchoreb@hotmail.com
PA: Ricardo Castaneda   <M1>
Calle 65 #98-45 (Interior 174)
Altos de la Macarena-Robledo La Campina
Medellin, Antioquia
Colombia, South America
(574)577-0717
rijcah@gmail.com
AP: Diana Valdez   <M1>
Cra 50 D#62-69
Medellin, Antioquia
Colombia, South America
(574)263-2154
dianamariavaldezduque@gmail.com
CL: Lina Velasquez
Calle 49E #83A91
Recinto de La Arboleda, Calazans
Medellin, Antioquia
Colombia, South America
(574)422-6698
velasquezlina@yahoo.es

La Rosa de Saron   (4C)MSAN8911
Calle 100 #50C-09
Barrio Santa Cruz Sector La Rosa
Medellin, Antioquia
Colombia, South America
(574)236-6509   <S America>

ANDES PRESBYTERY CONTINUED

SS: Andres Giraldo   <M2>
Calle 76 #87-14 Apto 202
Medellin, Antioquia
Colombia, South America
(574)422-6669
andresgiraldo@une.net.co
CL: Claudia Cordoba
Calle 100 #50C-35
Barrio Santa Cruz Sector La Rosa
Medellin, Antioquia
Colombia, South America
57(315)605-0011

_____

La Virginia   (4WMF)MSAN8913
Cra 4 bis #10-35
La Virginia, Risalda
Colombia, South America
(576)368-3589   <S America>
CL: Nora Patricia Diaz
Cra 4 bis #10-35
LaVirginia, Risalda
Colombia, South America
(311)312-2349
noris_1985@hotmail.com

_____

Manizales   (4WMC)MSAN8914
Calle 22 #25-33
Manizales, Caldas
Colombia, South America
(576)883-0383   <S America>
FAX: (576)833-0383
manizales50ipc@hotmail.com
PA: William Diaz   <M1>
Calle 42 #26B-68
Manizales, Caldas
Colombia, South America
(574)890-2972
manizales50ipc@hotmail.com
CL: Luz Dary Herrera
Calle 5 #22-56
Manizales, Caldas
Colombia, South America
(576)889-0994

_____

Pereira   (4MWC)MSAN8916
Cra 12 bis #11-69
Pereira, Risaralda
Colombia, South America
(574)333-9295   <S America>
FAX: (574)324-4110
cumberlandpres@une.net.co
PA: David Montoya   <M1>
Cra 12 bis #11-69
Pereira, Risaralda
Colombia, South America
(574)324-4109
FAX: (574)324-4110
adamonva@gmail.com
AP: Luz Maria Heilbron   <M1>
Cra 12 bis #11-51
Pereira, Risaralda
Colombia, South America
(576)333-9295
pastorapresbi@hotmail.com
AP: Rodrigo Martinez   <M1>
Mz2 Casa 21 Urb Casas De Milan
Dosquebradas, Risaralda
Colombia, South America
(576)322-2177
oikoinonia@gmail.com

CL: Shirley Murillo
Cra 12 bis #11-69
Pereira, Risaralda
Colombia, South America

_____

Senda de Libertad   (C)MSAN8919
Cra 120 #39 F-91
Medellin, Antioquia
Colombia, South America
(574)496-1681
ipcsaladomedellin@gmail.com
PA: Josue Guerrero   <M1>
Calle 76 #88-65
Medellin, Antioquia
Colombia, South America
(574)412-3504
josueggutierrez@yahoo.es
AP: Cruzana Guerrero   <M1>
Cra 120 #39 F-91
Medellin, Antioquia
Colombia, South America
(574)496-1681
ipcsaladomedellin@gmail.com
CL: Session Clerk
Cra 120 #39 F-91
Medellin, Antioquia
Colombia, South America
(574)496-1681
ipcsaladomedellin@gmail.com

_____

Zamora   (4WC)MSAN8918
Calle 20D #42C-56 (physical)
Cra 58 #32A-41 Apt 420 (mailing)
Bello, Antioquia
Colombia, South America
(574)461-0069   <S America>
ipczamora@gmail.com
PA: Alejandro Vasquez   <M1>
Cra 58 #32A-41 Apt 420
Bello, Antioquia
Colombia, South America
(574)451-4816
almaesda@une.net.co
CL: Amparo Hoyos
Calle 120D #42C-56
Bello, Antioquia
Colombia, South America
57(315)424-4547
chilalu1147@hotmail.com

_____

OTHERS ON MINISTERIAL ROLL:

Arias, John Jairo   <M1 WC>
Calle 144 sur #196-08 / Apto 202
Caldas, Antioquia
Colombia, South America
(57)317-693-1162
sajoarias@hotmail.com
Daza, Edilberto   <M1 HR>
Cra 12 #8-47
Cartago, Valle
Colombia, South America
57(314)794-1905
presbicartago@gmail.com
Daza, Johan   <M1 DE>
8148 Yellow Stone Drive
Cordova, TN 38016
(281)793-3869
jdaza@cumberland.org

Gentry, Michele   <M1 M9>
Urb San Jorge casa 28
Km 8 via a La Tebaida
Armenia, Quindio
Colombia, South America
(318)285-1161
gentry.andes@yahoo.com
Guerrero, Luz Dary   <M1 MY>
Calle 22 #25-33
Manizales, Caldas
Colombia, South America
(576)888-4203
clementinajacobo7@hotmail.com
Martinez, Dagoberto   <M1 RT>
Cra 62D #71-113
Bello, Antioquia
Colombia, South America
(574)452-3466
Orozco, Joaquin   <M1 OM>
Cra 3 #7-14
Aguadas, Caldas
Colombia, South America
(576)851-4773
jeob40@hotmail.com
Rivera, Zenobia   <M1 WC>
Cra 12 #8-47
Cartago, Valle
Colombia, South America
57(310)500-1791
zenobiadedaza@yahoo.com.mx
Taborda, Arturo   <M1 RT>
Cra 43 #20D-46
Zamora, Medellin, Antioquia
Colombia, South America
(574)267-1351
chilalu1147@hotmail.com
Valencia, Nulbel   <M1 RT>
Diag 11D Casa 11 urbGemelas
Dosquebradas, Risaralda
Colombia, South America
(576)330-7704
nava1928@hotmail.com
Velez, Gabriel   <M1 RT>
Calle 8A #16A-26, Villa Fanny
Dosquebradas, Risaralda
Colombia, South America
(576)330-1168

_____

OTHER LICENTIATES ON ROLL:

Jimenez, Jorge Enrique   <M2>
Urb Manantiales MzC Casa 6
Armenia, Quindio
Colombia, South America
(321)643-0693
joenjimu@yahoo.es

_____

OTHER CANDIDATES ON ROLL:

Cardona, Nancy   <M3 ST>
Calle 51 #15-32
Dosquebradas, Risaralda
Colombia, South America
(576)322-2938
nancycardona10@yahoo.com
Giraldo, Juan Pablo   <M3>
Calle 51 #15-32
barrio Los Naranjos
Dosquebradas, Risaralda
Colombia, South America
(576)322-2938

ANDES PRESBYTERY CONTINUED

Giraldo, Marcela   \<M3\>
Calle 68 D #40-15
Manizales, Caldas
Colombia, South America
(576)878-5412

Laverde, Alina   \<M3\>
Calle 100 #50C-09
Barrio Santa Cruz Sector La Rosa
Medellin, Antioquia
Colombia, South America
(574)236-6509

Lopez, Carlos Geovanny   \<M3\>
Cra 12 bis #11-69
Pereira, Risaralda
Colombia, South America
(576)333-9295

Morales, Juan Fernando   \<M3\>
Calle 100 #50C-09
Barrio Santa Cruz Sector La Rosa
Medellin, Antioquia
Colombia, South America
(574)236-6509

Ortega, Juan   \<M3\>
Colombia, South America
(574)323-9305

Porras, Rene Wilgen   \<M3\>
Cra 4 bis #10-51
La Virginia, Risalda
(576)367-9529

Vargas, Lida Patricia   \<M3\>
Carrera 50D #62-69, Prado Centro
Medellin, Antioquia
Colombia, South America
(574)263-2154
lidapavargas@hotmail.com

Varilla, Adan Manuel   \<M3\>
Calle 48 D E #96A-30
Medellin, Antioquia
Colombia, South America
(57)313-691-1923

Velez, Gloria Patricia   \<M3\>
Cra 4 bis #10-51
LaVirginia, Risaralda
Colombia, South America
(576)385-4517
renewilgen@hotmail.com

Arkansas Presbytery
GREAT RIVERS SYNOD

GENERAL		MEMBERSHIP		CHANGES				FINANCES				
1.Church Number	2.Active	3.Total	4.Church School	5.Prof. of Faith	6.Gains	7.Losses	8.Children Baptized	9. OUR UNITED OUT-REACH	10. Total Out-Reach Giving	11. All Other Expenses	12. Total Income Received	13. Value Church Prop. 1=1000
1	2	3	4	5	6	7	8	9	10	11	12	13
Appleton* 1202	12	30	27	0	0	0	0	500	2,295	14,531	16,860	40
Arkansas Loving 2135	45	63	2	No Report Received			0	0	0	0	0	700
Barren Fork 1501	98	111	57	4	4	0	0	6,112	15,905	78,038	79,779	400
Ben Lomond 1301	5	7	9	0	0	10	0	0	3,188	11,693	15,859	80
Bethesda 1302	40	62	36	4	5	7	5	0	4,358	79,415	78,235	957
Booneville* 1401	45	45	6	0	0	11	1	6,664	13,597	50,083	69,608	590
Byron 1508	11	11	12	0	0	0	0	300	1,872	4,200	9,618	287
Calico Rock 1503	99	116	55	0	1	2	0	14,000	56,735	86,478	143,213	1,276
Camden** 1303	47	49	38	6	9	40	0	1,019	4,394	67,660	70,016	330
Camp Ground 1101	43	90	16	1	1	3	0	6,622	13,255	48,722	60,302	600
Caulksville* 1402	198	234	70	16	17	23	1	6,478	61,740	72,199	125,906	687
Dilworth 1304	6	12	8	2	0	1	0	0	2,477	20,899	28,999	125
Dover* 1203	21	21	15	1	1	3	2	3,954	13,015	48,508	82,492	275
E. T. Allen 1307	17	17	12	No Report Received			0	0	0	0	0	225
Faith-Hopewell 1502	99	121	87	3	3	4	1	11,983	20,252	109,678	119,848	1,400
Falls Chapel* 1308	37	37	30	14	10	12	0	0	25,272	19,986	60,339	n/a
Fellowship (BC) 1505	88	187	39	0	5	3	1	14,000	25,099	111,985	137,921	1,465
Fellowship (OC) 1309	39	56	49	1	4	0	0	5,287	8,288	22,512	52,866	117
Fomby 1310	7	21	8	0	0	10	0	0	4,960	10,730	16,887	138
Fort Smith 1406	44	172	15	1	1	2	3	1,326	4,007	34,880	25,652	800
Grace 1405	28	28	14	6	6	0	0	4,472	13,202	35,427	47,520	272
Gum Springs (WC) 1205	8	9	10	0	0	0	0	0	750	7,400	8,200	n/a
Gum Springs (YC) 1206				CLOSED 9/12/2015								250
Hector 1207	14	49	12	0	0	1	0	0	2,694	16,325	28,131	93
Lake Hamilton* 1221	68	68	23	0	4	14	1	0	10,246	79,655	68,211	400
Lockesburg 1311	3	3	0	No Report Received			0	0	0	0	0	162
Marietta 1408	47	47	47	0	0	0	0	0	1,843	38,172	32,344	350
Mars Hill* 1211	40	40	25	0	0	0	0	500	1,000	23,950	25,900	225
Mt. Carmel 1212	40	40	15	No Report Received			0	7,359	0	0	0	75
Mt. Olive 1517	22	31	10	0	0	4	0	1,062	24,679	7,439	30,900	230
New Hope 1510	10	10	8	0	0	1	0	2,785	5,809	15,532	28,498	375
Old Union 1409	27	50	28	4	4	5	0	3,699	8,965	26,316	53,360	123
Oxford 1511	26	26	30	0	0	1	0	200	6,649	7,711	13,309	175
Palestine 1103	77	118	53	0	0	3	`	4,200	16,449	123,993	131,411	1,575
Pilot Prairie 1411	8	14	6	No Report Received			0	0	0	0	0	50
Pine Bluff, 1st 1104	13	103	0	No Report Received			0	0	0	0	0	766
Pine Ridge* 1105	15	25	12	0	0	1	0	1,198	1,198	36,633	41,200	402
Pineville 1512	56	73	30	No Report Received			0	8,228	0	0	0	700
Pleasant Grove 1214	5	9	5	No Report Received			0	0	0	0	0	70
Provo 1314	11	38	25	No Report Received			0	0	0	0	0	125
Rodney 1513	15	15	11	15	3	15	1	100	1,200	22,458	26,496	65
Rose Hill 1106	62	62	45	1	7	0	0	7,115	12,405	59,545	71,151	1,000
Russellville 1216	118	228	35	4	9	4	3	2,530	6,709	11,862	163,070	1,700
Salem (FC) 1514	28	29	15	No Report Received			0	1,636	0	0	0	250
Searcy 1218	29	54	20	0	0	2	0	1,200	2,147	15,674	23,685	300
Shaver 1413	1	1	0	No Report Received			0	0	0	0	0	10
Shell Chapel* 1108	7	28	0	0	0	3	0	1,030	1,892	16,625	12,306	500
Sherwood 1220	19	180	5	0	0	3	0	120	1,550	38,400	41,352	777
Sidney 1515	9	18	9	No Report Received			0	0	0	0	0	200
Sulphur Springs 1315	16	48	11	No Report Received			0	0	0	0	0	29
Trimble Camp G 1504	35	20	33	No Report Received			0	4,892	0	0	0	365
Trinity 1219	14	35	0	1	1	0	0	0	6,768	22,124	29,116	220
Walkerville 1317	12	12	21	0	0	14	0	2,491	9,379	20,888	22,981	190
Walnut Grove* 1414	30	60	15	0	1	0	0	0	2,808	33,110	30,353	175
TOTALS 53	1,931	3,107	1,185	86	95	190	22	133,062	444,926	1,605,021	2,231,750	21,920

*Math error corrected. **Purged roll.

ARKANSAS PRESBYTERY CONTINUED

CHURCHES, PASTORS, AND CLERKS:

Appleton (W4C)GRAR1202
171 Tate Street (mailing)
320 Tate Street (physical)
Atkins, AR 72823
( ) <Pope>
CL: Sue Bartlett
171 Tate Street
Atkins, AR 72823
(479)284-4357
msbart@thebartlettpage.com

Arkansas Loving (P)GRAR2135
1603 Coolhurst Avenue
Sherwood, AR 72120
(501)247-5953 <Pulaski>
swcho100491@gmail.com
PA: Sung Wan Cho <M1>
1603 Coolhurst Avenue
Sherwood, AR 72120
(501)247-5953
swcho100491@gmail.com
CL: Eun Hi Lee
110 Beaulieu Court
Maumelle, AR 72113
(501)247-4545

Barren Fork (4MWC)GRAR1501
782 Barren Fork Road
Mount Pleasant, AR 72561
(870)346-5121 <Izard>
PA: Alan Meinzer <M1>
780 Barren Fork Road
Mount Pleasant, AR 72561
(870)612-3936
brotheralan@centurylink.net
CL: Connie Crafton
1275 Barren Fork Road
Mount Pleasant, AR 72561
(870)346-5349

Ben Lomond (4C)GRAR1301
180 LR 39 (mailing)
Ogden, AR 71853
495 N Main Street (physical)
Ben Lomond, AR 71823
( ) <Sevier>
OD: Herman R Welch <M5>
180 LR 39
Ogden, AR 71853
(903)748-2126
herawe@yahoo.com
CL: Kimberly Hatridge
PO Box 53
Ben Lomond, AR 71823
(870)287-4215

Bethesda (4MW C)GRAR1302
395 Ouachita 47
Camden, AR 71701
(870)231-4909 <Ouachita>
CL: Ben Fields
451 Ouachita 47
Camden, AR 71701
(870)231-5080
bfields2011@hotmail.com

Booneville (4MEW C)GRAR1401
PO Box 163 (mailing)
355 Sharp Street (physical)
Booneville, AR 72927
( ) <Logan>
church@boonevillecpc.com
PA: Henry Jenkins <M1>
PO Box 148 (mailing)
90 W Grove (physical)
Magazine, AR 72943
(479)969-8351
henryj@magtel.com
CL: Janet Bedene
PO Box 7 (mailing)
113 Pine Street(physical)
Ratcliff, AR 72951
(479)847-6746
phaparis@magtel.com

Byron (4WC)GRAR1508
PO Box 524 (mailing)
Byron Road, Viola, AR (physical)
Calico Rock, AR 72519
(870)291-8542 <Fulton>
calicowild@hotmail.com
CL: Session Clerk
PO Box 524
Calico Rock, AR 72519
(870)291-8542
calicowild@hotmail.com

Calico Rock (4MEWC)GRAR1503
PO Box 315 (mailing)
692 AR 56 Highway E (physical)
Calico Rock, AR 72519
(870)297-3931 <Izard>
FAX: (870)297-3151
crcpc@centurytel.net
PA: Thomas D Campbell <M1>
PO Box 343
Calico Rock, AR 72519
(870)297-3931
FAX: (870)297-3151
tdcampbellar@gmail.com
CL: Carolyn Jeffery
PO Box 183
Calico Rock, AR 72519
(870)297-8530
cjeffery6@gmail.com

Camden (4MEWC)GRAR1303
1545 California Avenue
Camden, AR 71701
(870)836-8712 <Ouachita>
PA: Michael Suttle <M1>
159 Ouachita 593
Camden, AR 71701
(870)836-0008
m_s_suttle@msn.com
CL: Jimmy Vaughnan
1607 W 3rd Street
Fordyce, AR 71742
(870)818-1512

Camp Ground (4WMC)GRAR1101
1548 E AR 274 Highway
Hampton, AR 71744
(870)798-4302 <Calhoun>

PA: Garland Skidmore <M1>
2083 US Highway 278 E
Hampton, AR 71744
(870)798-4634
CL: Shirley Strickland
1783 E AR 274 Highway
Hampton, AR 71744
(870)918-2344
strick6@sat-co.net

Caulksville (4MWC)GRAR1402
PO Box 2 (mailing)
23 W Main, Caulksville, AR (physical)
Ratcliff, AR 72951
(479)635-4301 <Logan>
PA: Bill Van Meter <M1>
10626 Highway 41
Charleston, AR 72933
(479)965-2998
revbill46@gmail.com
CL: Cherre Nietert
10201 Nietert Lane
Branch, AR 72928
(479)438-0673

Dilworth (4C)GRAR1304
305 N 6th Street (mailing)
De Queen, AR 71832
2517 N Red Bridge Road (physical)
Horatio, AR 71842
(870)642-8051 <Sevier>
mtcarmel2@windstream.net
OD: Byron G Sullivan <M5>
305 N 6th Street
De Queen, AR 71832
(870)642-8051
mtcarmel2@windstream.net
CL: Nita Sue Sullivan
305 N 6th Street
De Queen, AR 71832
(870)642-8051
mtcarmel2@windstream.net

Dover (4MWC)GRAR1203
29 Maple Street (mailing)
Hector, AR 72843
96 Waters Street (physical)
Dover, AR 72837
(479)331-3130 <Pope>
markoe@centurytel.net
OD: Mike Galloway <M5>
2821 Linker Mount Road
Dover, AR 72837
(479)331-0254
markoe@centurytel.net
CL: Beth McAlister
29 Maple Street
Hector, AR 72843
beth.ann56@hotmail.com

E T Allen (4WC)GRAR1307
PO Box 822 (mailing)
153 Highway 71 N
Ashdown, AR 71822
( ) <Little Rive>
CL: Glen Ray Bowman
1050 Oak Place
Ashdown, AR 71822
(903)824-5000
botech64@aol.com

ARKANSAS PRESBYTERY CONTINUED

_____
Faith-Hopewell   (4WC)GRAR1502
  3895 Harrison Street
  Batesville, AR 72501
  (870)612-5949   <Independence>
PA: Rian Puckett   <M1>
  3784 Harrison Street
  Batesville, AR 72501
  (731)288-7742
  rppuckett@memphisseminry.edu
CL: Ionna Hess
  3075 O'Neal Road
  Batesville, AR 72501
  (870)793-5530
  ionnahess@yahoo.com

_____
Falls Chapel   (4MC)GRAR1308
  182 Hunter Falls Loop (mailing)
  127 LW Davis Road (physical)
  Lockesburg, AR 71846
  ( )   <Sevier>
CL: Ann Keith
  182 Hunter Falls Loop
  Lockesburg, AR 71846
  (870)289-6834
  memaplayground@windstream.net

_____
Fellowship (BC)   (4EWC)GRAR1505
  PO Box 866 (mailing)
  1206 E 9th Street (physical)
  Mountain Home, AR 72653
  (870)425-5419   <Baxter>
  info@fellowshipcumberland.org
PA: Gary Robert Tubb   <M1>
  103 Forest Drive
  Mountain Home, AR 72653
  grtubb@yahoo.com
  (870)424-0603
CL: Andy Marts
  393 County Road 1085
  Mountain Home, AR 72653
  (870)481-6092
  amarts@centurytel.net

_____
Fellowship (OC)   (4WC)GRAR1309
  478 Ouachita 54 (mailing)
  2855 Ouachita 3 (physical)
  Camden, AR 71701
  ( )   <Ouachita>
SS: Roberta Smith Johnson   <M1>
  397 Ouachita 54
  Camden, AR 71701
  (870)231-5827
CL: Charles T Jeffus
  478 Ouachita 54
  Camden, AR 71701
  (870)231-9994
  charlesjeffus@yahoo.com

_____
Fomby   (4C)GRAR1310
  704 Highway 317 (mailing)
  1215 Highway 32 E (physical)
  Ashdown, AR 71822
  (870)898-2856   <Little Rive>
  carole4485@att.net
PA: Ann Holley   <M1>
  PO Box 345
  Lockesburg, AR 71846
  (870)289-3421
  ladyrev1115@yahoo.com

CL: Carole C Booth
  704 Highway 317
  Ashdown, AR 71822
  (870)898-2856
  carole4485@att.net

_____
Fort Smith   (4MEWC)GRAR1406
  605 N 47th Street
  Fort Smith, AR 72903
  (479)782-0454   <Sebastian>
  FAX: (479)782-0454
  ksstamps@msn.com
OD: Randall Cross   <M5>
  608 N Crest Drive
  Fayetteville, AR 72701
  (870)917-9303
  rkcross@cox.net
CL: Janie Stamps
  4008 Logan Lane
  Fort Smith, AR 72903
  (479)478-0161
  bjstamps@msn.com

_____
Grace   (4C)GRAR1405
  2451 Wedington Drive
  Fayetteville, AR 72701
  (479)442-6772   <Washington>
CL: Robin Thomas
  1195 N White Rock Lane
  Fayetteville, AR 72704
  (479)521-0371
  rthomas@mman.com

_____
Gum Springs(WC)   (4C)GRAR1205
  1717 W Arch Avenue (mailing)
  Gum Springs Road (physical)
  Searcy, AR 72143
  (501)268-2615   <White>
SS: Jim Bradberry   <M3>
  120 Hummingbird Lane
  Searcy, AR 72143
  (501)278-9750
CL: J C Holleman
  1717 W Arch Avenue
  Searcy, AR 72143
  (501)268-2615

_____
Gum Springs(YC)   (4MC)GRAR1206
  CLOSED 2015
  (membership moved to Mars Hill)

_____
Hector   (4MWC)GRAR1207
  PO Box 53 (mailing)
  29 Maple (physical)
  Hector, AR 72843
  (479)747-7561   <Pope>
CL: Beth McAlister
  PO Box 53
  Hector, AR 72843
  (479)747-7561

_____
Lake Hamilton   (4 C)GRAR1221
  2891 Airport Road
  Hot Springs, AR 71913
  (501)760-3800   <Garland>
  lakehamiltoncpc@yahoo.com
PA: Duawn Mearns   <M1>
  107 Westoak Place
  Hot Springs, AR 71913
  (501)276-1266
  duawn@lakehamiltonchurch.com

CL: Phyllis Pipkin
  197 Cobbleridge Trail
  Hot Springs, AR 71913
  (501)318-3462
  sephpipkin@aol.com

_____
Lockesburg   (1C)GRAR1311
  279 N Park Avenue (mailing)
  114 W Walnut (physical)
  Lockesburg, AR 71846
  ( )   <Sevier>
CL: Joe E Bush
  279 N Park Avenue
  Lockesburg, AR 71846
  (870)289-2433

_____
Marietta   (4C)GRAR1408
  623 Church Street (mailing)
  2604 West Main (physical)
  Charleston, AR 72933
  (479)965-0224   <Franklin>
SS: Vondal Davenport   <M1>
  PO Box 823
  Lavaca, AR 72941
  (479)965-2036
CL: Tim Aldridge
  623 Church Street
  Charleston, AR 72933
  (479)965-7639
  dcotim58@live.com

_____
Mars Hill   (4WC)GRAR1211
  172 Thompson Lane (mailing)
  1224 State Route 363 (physical)
  Pottsville, AR 72858
  ( )   <Pope>
PA: Jo Warren   <M1>
  811 Wall Street
  Morrilton, AR 72110
  (501)354-4139
  pastorjo47@ymail.com
CL: Gary Thompson
  172 Thompson Lane
  Pottsville, AR 72858
  (479)970-4652
  thompgary@gmail.com

_____
Mt Carmel   (4C)GRAR1212
  1470 Mt Carmel Road W
  London, AR 72847
  (479)293-4447   <Pope>
  mtcarmel@centurylink.net
CL: Jennifer Metz
  276 Metz Lane
  London, AR 72847
  (479)293-4229
  jmetz54@hotmail.com

_____
Mt Olive   (4EC)GRAR1517
  214 Bear Trail Hollow (mailing)
  5539 Mt Olive Road (physical)
  Melbourne, AR 72556
  (870)368-4923   <Izard>
  bobeth@centurytel.net
CL: Mary Beth Jeffery
  214 Bear Trail Hollow
  Melbourne, AR 72556
  (870)368-4923
  bobeth@centurytel.net

ARKANSAS PRESBYTERY CONTINUED

New Hope   (2C)GRAR1510
25 Pine Hill Road (mailing)
3655 Bethesda Road (physical)
Batesville, AR 72501
( )   <Independence>
verenaherrin@yahoo.com
PA: Rian Puckett   <M1>
3784 Harrison Street
Batesville, AR 72501
(731)288-7742
rppuckett@memphisseminary.edu
CL: Verena Herrin
25 Pine Hill Road
Batesville, AR 72501
(870)793-6145
verenaherrin@yahoo.com

Old Union   (4C)GRAR1409
PO Box 477 (mailing)
Old Union Road (physical)
Magazine, AR 72943
( )   <Logan>
PA: Henry Jenkins   <M1>
PO Box 148
Magazine, AR 72943
(479)969-8352
henryj@magtel.com
CL: Lee Strickland
PO Box 477
Magazine, AR 72943
(479)849-0198
eljws1@live.com

Oxford   (4U)GRAR1511
618 Camp Ground Road (mailing)
211 Main Street (physical)
Oxford, AR 72565
( )   <Izard>
SS: Bobby D Coleman   <M1>
704 E Webb Street
Mountain View, AR 72560
(870)213-5410
bobbycoleman@gmail.com
CL: Willetta Everett
618 Camp Ground Road
Oxford, AR 72565
(870)258-7798
weverett@centurytel.net

Palestine   (4MEWC)GRAR1103
PO Box 98 (mailing)
223 South Main Street (physical)
Palestine, AR 72372
(870)581-2600   <St. Francis>
FAX: (870)581-2600
PA: Jason Chambers   <M1>
131 E Woods Street
Palestine, AR 72372
(870)807-1930
jmchambers@memphisseminary.edu
CL: Lisa Alldredge
PO Box 803
Palestine, AR 72372
(870)581-2913
lsatmall@yahoo.com

Pilot Prairie   (4MC)GRAR1411
PO Box 1873
Waldron, AR 72958
(479)637-3938   <Scott>

CL: Lee Ann Forest
PO Box 1873
Waldron, AR 72958

Pine Bluff 1st   (4W C)GRAR1104
2401 Camden Road
Pine Bluff, AR 71603
( )   <Jefferson>
PA: Shirley Ostrander   <M1>
210 Glen Park Drive #3
Cordova, TN 38018
(901)827-4830
CL: Catherine Currington
205 Moss Road
White Hall, AR 71602
(870)247-3839

Pine Ridge   (4C)GRAR1105
4890 Grant 14
Grapevine, AR 72057
(870)942-1827   <Grant>
PA: James (Jim) Bradshaw   <M1>
415 S Red Street
Sheridan, AR 72150
(870)942-2525
CL: Buren Walker
336 Grant 748
Sheridan, AR 72150
(870)942-4790

Pineville   (4MWC)GRAR1512
PO Box 256 (mailing)
1229 AR 223 Highway (physical)
Pineville, AR 72566
(870)297-4104   <Izard>
CL: Janie Jenkins
PO Box 504
Calico Rock, AR 72519
(870)297-3991
djjenkins@centurytel.net

Pleasant Grove   (2C)GRAR1214
1083 Highway 305 S
Searcy, AR 72143
(501)796-3466   <White>
CL: Robbie Stroud
1922 Highway 31 N
Beebe, AR 72012
(501)882-3262

Provo   (4C)GRAR1314
131 LR 47 (mailing)
Ashdown, AR 71822
125 Dooley Road (physical)
Lockesburg, AR 71846
( )   <Sevier>
CL: Bonita Ward
166 McHorse Road
Lockesburg, AR 71846
(870)582-4871

Rodney   (2EC)GRAR1513
117 Flint Rock Trail (mailing)
1333 Rodney Road (physical)
Jordan, AR 72519
( )   <Baxter>
PA: Dave Williamson   <M1>
PO Box 67
Dolph, AR 72528
(870)499-7448

CL: Carol Lee
1364 Rodney Road
Jordan, AR 72519
(870)499-3238
txgrany69@yahoo.com

Rose Hill   (4MWC)GRAR1106
1031 Binns Drive (mailing)
2133 Highway 83 N (physical)
Monticello, AR 71655
(870)367-5114   <Drew>
gsaray@att.net
PA: Bruce Hamilton   <M1>
1037 Binns Drive
Monticello, AR 71655
(870)224-5007
bruce@hamiltonnet.org
CL: Stephanie Ray
122 E Shelton Avenue
Monticello, AR 71655
(870)723-3785
gsaray@att.net

Russellville   (4WC)GRAR1216
1200 N Arkansas Avenue
Russellville, AR 72801
(479)968-1061   <Pope>
FAX: (479)880-0071
fcpcrussellville@yahoo.com
PA: Steve Mosley   <M1>
320 N Sherman Circle
Russellville, AR 72801
(479)968-1061
FAX: (479)880-0071
stevemosley@hotmail.com
CL: Deanna Boston
721 Kovel Court
Russellville, AR 72801
(479)890-3880
fcpcrussellville@yahoo.com

Salem (FC)   (4MWC)GRAR1514
1003 Flint Springs Road (mailing)
Viola, AR 72583
Highway 5 S, Salem, AR (physical)
( )   <Fulton>
salemcumberlandchurch@gmail.com
SS: Bobby D Coleman   <M1>
704 E Webb Street
Mountain View, AR 72560
(870)269-6010
bobby.coleman@gmail.com
CL: Bonnie Brown
1003 Flint Springs Road
Viola, AR 72583
(870)458-2657
bbrown325@centurytel.net

Searcy   (4MWC)GRAR1218
100 E Race Street
Searcy, AR 72143
(501)268-8278   <White>
SS: Jim Bradberry   <M3>
120 Hummingbird Lane
Searcy, AR 72143
(501)278-9750
CL:Howard Johnson
2180 Holmes Road
Searcy, AR 72143
(501)268-3071
howardwjohnson@gmail.com

ARKANSAS PRESBYTERY CONTINUED

Shaver (1C)GRAR1413
(no longer has services 10/30/13)
401 Shaver Road (mailing)
1448 Shaver Road (physical)
Paris, AR 72855
( ) <Logan>

Shell Chapel (4WC)GRAR1108
2143 Grider Field Road (mailing)
3110 Highway 425 (physical)
Pine Bluff, AR 71601
(870)535-5408 <Jefferson>
CL: Joyce Shell
2143 Grider Field Road
Pine Bluff, AR 71601
(870)535-5408
mkshell@earthlink.net

Sherwood (4WC)GRAR1220
1402 E Kiehl Avenue
Sherwood, AR 72120
(501)835-8889 <Pulaski>
SS: Elizabeth Terrell <M1>
2073 Vinton Avenue
Memphis, TN 38104
(901)647-2788
CL: Olive Snow
5907 Woodview Drive S
Sherwood, AR 72120
(501)835-7819
ladysnow64@yahoo.com

Sidney (2U)GRAR1515
Batesville, AR 72501
( ) <Sharp>
PA: Alan Meinzer <M1>
780 Barren Fork Road
Mount Pleasant, AR 72561
(870)612-3936
brotheralan@centurylink.net
CL: Jodi Moody
127 Arkansas Highway 58
Sidney, AR 72577
(870)283-6766

Sulphur Springs (4C)GRAR1315
3225 Ouachita 2 (mailing)
3086 Ouachita 2 (physical)
Louann, AR 71751
(870)689-3598 <Ouachita>
mdarden@oeccwildblue.com
CL:Peggy Muckelrath
128 Ouachita 55
Louann, AR 71752
(870)689-3409
pmukelrath@oecc.com

Trimble Camp G (4WC)GRAR1504
PO Box 150 (mailing)
Trimble Camp Ground Road (physical)
Dolph, AR 72528
(870)297-8088 <Izard>
PA: Joel Snyder <M1>
224 Lord Lane
Mountain View, AR 72560
(870)269-9743
synyder.joel@ymail.com

CL: Jana Cowgill
1037 Chriswood Drive
Clarkridge, AR 72623
(870)421-2106

Trinity (4MEWC)GRAR1219
809 W Wall Street
Morrilton, AR 72110
(501)354-4139 <Conway>
PA: Gordon Warren <M1>
811 Wall Street
Morrilton, AR 72110
(501)208-1120
jogordonwarren@suddenlink.net
CL: Jammie Bonds
809 Wall Street
Morrilton, AR 72110
(501)354-4139

Walkerville (4MEWC)GRAR1317
10160 Highway 19 S
Magnolia, AR 71753
( ) <Columbia>
CL: Stella Edwards
10570 S Highway 19
Emerson, AR 71740
(870)696-3973
jse10570@gmail.com

Walnut Grove (4WC)GRAR1414
4724 N State Highway 23 (mailing)
1294 Six Mile Road (physical)
Magazine, AR 72943
( ) <Logan>
danekas@centurytel.net
SS: Don Kennedy <M3>
5335 Dizzy Dean Road
Booneville, AR 72927
(479)675-4418
donkennedy@centurytel.net
CL: Debbie Danekas
4724 N State Highway 23
Booneville, AR 72927
(479)675-5004
danekas@centurytel.net

OTHERS ON MINISTERIAL ROLL:

Blackburn, Samuel N <M1 WC>
6706 S 6th Street
Fort Smith, AR 72908
(479)649-9436
Blanton, D B <M1 RT>
ADDRESS UNKNOWN
Bowling, Andrew <M1 WC>
20945 Highway 16 E
Siloam Springs, AR 72761
(479)524-6576
Brewer, Barbara Jean <M1 WC>
1360 White Oak Bluff Road
Rison, AR 71665
(870)325-6449
Brown, Amy <M1 WC>
679 Freeze Bend Road
Newport, AR 72112
Cadenbach, Mark <M1 OM>
91 Elzadah Lane
Salem, AR 72576
(890)955-9250
cadenbm@nctc.net

Chang, Leo <M1 WC>
819 W Division SE
Springfield, MO 65803
(901)287-9901
Cook, Carl <M1 WC>
475 Western Hills Loop
Mountain Home, AR 72653
(870)425-2570
carlc@suddenlink.net
Deere, Thomas (Tom) <M1 WC>
460 Yukon Drive
Russellville, AR 72811
(479)498-0318
tdeere@suddenlinkmail.com
Fisk, James R <M1 WC>
1 Webb Lane
Bella Vista, AR 72714
jimfisk95@yahoo.com
(479)886-1216
Fleming, Patrick T <M1 WC>
616 N Border Street
Benton, AR 72015
(501)944-4678
ptfleming@live.com
Guthrie, William <M1 WC>
11130 Frenchmen Loop Apt B
Maumelle, AR 72113
(501)584-0019
billybarloe@yahoo.com
Halford, Angela <M1 OM>
PO Box 404
Sebastopol, MS 39359
(501)251-4668
revhalford@gmail.com
Hamelink, Ronald L <M1 WC>
5045 Starlite Court
Las Cruces, NM 88012
(575)640-4341
hamronelink@yahoo.com
Jeffrey, Sarah Ann <M1 WC>
5271 Highway 202 E
Yellville, AR 72687
(870)453-7076
FAX: (870)715-9229
annjeffrey2001@yahoo.com
Jones, Michael <M1 WC>
120 Jennifer Lane
Branson, MO 65616
(417)334-2058
Jones, Victor <M1 WC>
7017 Highway 177 S
Jordan, AR 72519
(870)499-5882
pam.jones@centurytel.net
Mars, Stan <M1 WC>
PO Box 274
Mt Pleasant, AR 72561
(217)254-5120
smars2@liberty.edu
Martin, William E, Jr <M1 WC>
PO Box 98
131 E Wood Avenue
Palestine, AR 72372
(870)581-2530
juniormartin@yahoo.com
McSpadden, Nancy <M1 M9>
120 Roberta Drive
Memphis, TN 38112
(870)612-0067
revnancy77@gmail.com

ARKANSAS PRESBYTERY CONTINUED

Moore, Angela   \<M1 WC\>
3756 Douglass Avenue
Memphis, TN 38111
(870)581-2509

Niswonger, Richard   \<M1 WC\>
20941 Highway 16 E
Siloam Springs, AR 72761
(479)524-4081
rniswonger@cox.net

O'Neal Danhof, Clair   \<M1 WC\>
301 Whispering Hills Street
Hot Springs, AR 71901
acglenn@aol.com

Pedigo, Russell   \<M1 WC\>
1002 Haney Avenue
El Dorado, AR 71730
(870)862-4689
russell_pedigo@hotmail.com

Ryan, Jack   \<M1 WC\>
8806 Kennesaw Mountain Drive
Mabelvale, AR 72103
(501)749-8572

Shanley, Dwight   \<M1 WC\>
16904 Old Mill Road
Little Rock, AR 72206
(501)888-4190
dwightshanley@att.net

Sweigart, John M   \<M1 WC\>
PO Box 876
Dover, AL 72837
(479)229-4041

Treadaway, Kenneth A   \<M1 WC\>
172 Miller County 494
Texarkana, AR 71854
treadaways@ark.net
(870)574-1609

Varner, Susan   \<M1 M9\>
14709 Glisten Lane
Little Rock, AR 72223
(901)371-1249
smvarner76@yahoo.com

Wood, Wayne   \<M1 WC\>
HC 61 Box 600
Calico Rock, AR 72519
(870)297-2205
FAX: (870)297-3151
bexarwood@centurytel.net

Woodliff, George   \<M1 HR\>
310 W Cleveland Street Apt A3
Prairie Grove, AR 72753
(479)410-1933
mwoodliff@kih.net

Wooten, Wallace   \<M1 WC\>
1152 Melrose Road
Lockesburg, AR 71846
(870)289-2224

OTHER LICENTIATES ON ROLL:

Anderson, Christopher   \<M2 ST\>
131 Roberta Drive
Memphis, TN 38112
(870)805-0886
csanderson@memphisseminary.edu

Harbour, Ethan   \<M2\>
77 Burton Road
Booneville, AR 72927
(479)849-6329
ethanharbour@gmail.com

Washburn, Gloria   \<M2\>
PO Box 2484
Jordan, AR 72519
(870)321-3539
grwashburn07@gmail.com

OTHER CANDIDATES ON ROLL:

Anderson, Kyle   \<M3\>
828 E Main Street
Batesville, AR 72501
(870)834-5799
kanderson@memphisseminary.edu

Middleton, Todd   \<M3\>
PO Box 1913
Russellville, AR 72811
(479)748-4613

Walsh, Devin   \<M3\>
801 East "M" Street
Russellville, AR 72801
(479)890-6716

Warren, Elizabeth
811 W Wall Street
Morrilton, AR 72110
(501)354-4139

C a u c a   V a l l e y   P r e s b y t e r y
MISSION SYNOD

GENERAL		MEMBERSHIP			CHANGES				FINANCES			
	1.Church Number	2.Active 3.Total 4.Church School			5.Prof. of Faith 6.Gains 7.Losses 8.Children Baptized				9. OUR UNITED OUT-REACH	10. Total Out-Reach Giving	11. All Other Expenses	12. Total Income Received	13. Value Church Prop. 1=1000
	1	2	3	4	5	6	7	8	9	10	11	12	13
Betania	8204	38	38	30	5	0	0	0		10,592	6,848	16,034	270
Bethel	8205	50	70	65	0	0	93	0		805	23,684	24,506	131
Caleb	8223	110	118	101	0	20	0	0		4,275	17,975	18,000	170
Cali Central	8208	150	238	36	0	0	2	0		10,000	78,000	80,000	1,000
Divino Redentor	8206	202	210	125	0	18	0	0		10,000	46,000	56,000	900
Emaus	8219	56	65	50	0	0	5	0		1,400	2,000	9,000	500
Filipos	8211	85	87	65	0	15	0	0		1,360	13,400	13,000	450
Getsemani	8210	31	34	15	No Report Received			0		0	0	0	90
Guabas		50	58	45	0	0	0	0		720	7,600	8,000	150
Ipiales		95	130	50	0	0	0	0		250	11,500	12,000	300
Maranatha	8220	80	130	110	0	0	7	0		700	3,700	0	200
Nueva Esperanza	8221	100	120	75	0	11	0	0		8,500	9,500	1.000	500
Nueva Jerusalen	8222	52	75	40	0	0	34	0		2,000	10,500	13,000	125
Popayan	8227	950	1,100	900	0	58	0	0		13,000	100,000	162,000	1,000
Principe De Paz	8201	40	55	30	0	0	20	0		0	0	0	150
Renacer	8225	450	490	450	60	52	164	0		45,000	132,574	179,000	900
Rey de Reyes		120	121	55	45	6	0	0		1,800	15,000	18,600	350
Samaria	8217	55	71	0	25	25	10	0		4,348	8,661	13,536	200
San Juan B		80	105	75	0	0	0	0		1,000	3,500	9,000	50
San Lucas*	8215	41	44	36	0	10	22	0		1,209	6,000	26,435	200
San Marcos	8218	55	75	50	0	0	54	0		0	0	0	150
San Pablo	8212	150	165	100	0	5	0	0		9,830	30,000	40,450	350
Tulua Central	8226	80	90	50	0	90	0	0		0	0	0	200
Presbytery	8200								8,638				
TOTALS	23	3,134	3,705	2,538	135	310	411	0	8,638	126,789	526,442	699,561	8,546

*Math error corrected. **Purged roll.

CHURCHES, PASTORS, AND CLERKS:

Betania (4WF)MSCA8204
Av 5 No 29-12
Cali, Colombia, South America
(　)894-0624　　　　<S America>
PA: Mario Gaviria　　　　<M1>
Cra 27 No 7-48
Cali, Colombia, South America
(　)372-3869
mariogaviria50@hotmail.com
CL: Ana Bechara de Montoya
Aereo 851
Cali, Colombia, South America

Bethel (4MWC)MSCA8205
Calle 14 Oeste No 48-17
Cali, Colombia, South America
(　)554-7514　　　　<S America>
SS:Rodrigo Torres　　　　<M2>
Calle 14 Oeste No 48-17
Cali, Colombia, South America
(011)882-8372
rojoana@hotmail.com
CL: Ana Leyda Meneses
Aereo 10701
Cali, Colombia, South America

Caleb (4F)MSCA8223
Av 47 Oeste No 9 A-24
Montebello, Colombia, South America
(　)323-8070　　　　<S America>
PA: Gildardo Agudelo　　　　<M1>
Cra 73C No 1A-54
Cali, Colombia, South America
pastorgildardoaguedelo@outlook.ar
CL: Carmen Rosa
Ave 47 Oe 9-51
Montebello, Colombia, South America

Cali Central (4MWC)MSCA8208
Av De Las Americas 19N-18
Cali, Colombia, South America
(　)668-7109　　　　<S America>
PA: Sergio Betancur　　　　<M1>
Av De Las Americas 19N-18
Cali, Colombia, South America
(　)334-2904
sergiobetancurposada@hotmail.com
CL: Nancy Trejos
Av De Las Americas 19N-18
Cali, Colombia, South America
nantre6@hotmail.com

Divino Redentor (4MWC)MSCA8206
Cra 3 No 36-29
Juan XXIII
Buenaventura, Colombia, South America
(　)242-8399　　　　<S America>
PA: Wilfrido Quinonez　　　　<M1>
Cra 3 No 36-29
Juan XXIII
Buenaventura, Colombia, South America
(310)412-1711
wilqui07@hotmail.com
CL: Marlen Palacios
Cra 3 No 36-29
Juan XXIII
Buenaventura, Colombia, South America

Emaus (4WC)MSCA8219
Diag 1 sur Cra 49-1
Buenaventura, Colombia, South America
(　)244-2624　　　　<S America>
SS: Manuel Medina　　　　<M2>
Diag 1 sur Cra 49-1
Buenaventura, Colombia, South America
(　)244-2624
emauspres@hotmail.com
CL: Omairo Valasco Cosme
Aereo 969
Buenaventura, Colombia, South America

CAUCA VALLEY PRESBYTERY CONTINUED

Filipos　　　(4WF)MSCA8211
　Calle 34 No 24A-36
　Cali, Colombia, South America
　(　)438-2563　　　<S America>
PA: Roberto Fonseca　　　<M1>
　Cra D1 No 46C-22
　Cali, Colombia, South America
　(　)446-7370
　robertoaltafuya@yahoo.com.ar
CL: Nancy Cortez
　Calle 34 No 24A-36
　Cali, Colombia, South America

Getsemani　　　(ARC)MSCA8210
　Cra 15 No 8-43
　El Cerrito, Colombia, South America
　(　)256-4261　　　<S America>
SS: Luis Cantor　　　<M3>
　Cra 15 No 8-43
　El Cerrito, Colombia, South America
　(000)256-4261
　pastoralberto7328@hotmail.com
CL: Amparo Renjifo
　Cra 15 No 8-43
　El Cerrito, Colombia, South America

Guabas
　Corregimiento Guabas
　Guacari, Colombia, South America

Maranatha　　　(4WF)MSCA8220
　Calle 12 No 4-69
　Guapi, Colombia, South America
　(092)840-0940
　FAX (092)840-0120　　　<S America>
LS: Alejandro Madrid　　　<M6>
　Calle 12 No 4-69
　Guapi, Colombia, South America
　ipcmaranatha@yahoo.com
CL: Magali Angulo
　Calle 12 No 4-69
　Guapi, Colombia, South America

Nueva Esperanza　　　(F)MSCA8221
　Cra 89 4C-35
　Cali, Colombia, South America
　(　)332-5849　　　<South America>
　nuevaesperanza1983@hotmail.com
PA: Jorge Valencia　　　<M1>
　Cra 89 4C-35
　Cali, Colombia, South America
　(　)332-5840
CL: Janeth Zuniga
　Cra 89 4C-35
　Cali, Colombia, South America
　tinta_y_papel@hotmail.com

Nueva Jerusalen　　　(4F)MSCA8222
　Cra 73 CN No 1A-54 (Lourdes)
　Cali, Colombia, South America
　(　)323-3009　　　<S America>
SS: Fabian Florez　　　<M3>
　Cra 73 CN No 29-36
　Cali, Colombia, South America
　(　)323-4447
　fabianflorezpastor@yahoo.es
CL: Adriana Montenegro
　Aereo 6365
　Cali, Colombia, South America

Popayan　　　(ARC)MSCA8227
　Cra 9 No 6N-87
　Popayan, Colombia, South America
　(092)823-8988　　　<S America>
PA: Johnny Montano　　　<M1>
　Cra 9 No 6 6N-87
　Popayan, Colombia, South America
　(092)823-8988
　jmonsolis@bmail.com
CL: Irma Cecilia Medina
　Cra 5 No 19N-56
　Popayan, Colombia, South America

Principe De Paz　　　(4WC)MSCA8201
　Cra 27 No 7-48
　Cali, Colombia, South America
　(　)556-6527　　　<S America>
PA: Joel Cuartas　　　<M0>
　Cra 27 No 7-48
　Cali, Colombia, South America
　(000)438-2512
　pastorjoelcuartas@hotmail.com
CL: Holber Molina
　Cra 27 No 7-48
　Cali, Colombia, South America

Renacer　　　(4WF)MSCA8225
　Diag 26M Trv 73A-69
　Cali, Colombia, South America
　(　)422-3940　　　<S America>
PA: Wilson Lopez　　　<M1>
　Cra 100 No 34-65
　Cali, Colombia, South America
　(　)327-2543
　wilsonig7@gmail.com
CL: Maria Onix Lopez
　Diag 26K No 73-A-66
　Cali, Colombia, South America

Rey de Reyes
　Calle 6A No 17-03
　Tulua, Colombia, South America
　presbyreydereyes@hotmail.com
PA: Bertulio Torres
　Calle 5A No 22-03
　Tulua, Colombia, South America
　bertulioevangelista@hotmail.com
CL: Session Clerk
　Calle 6A No 17-03
　Tulua, Colombia, South America

Samaria　　　(4MWC)MSCA8217
　Trans 30 No 17F-122
　Cali, Colombia, South America
　(　)448-5880　　　<S America>
PA: Juan Bautista Reina　　　<M1>
　Trans 30 No 17F-122
　Cali, Colombia, South America
　(　)442-4562
　juanbahu@hotmail.com
CL: Maria Josefa Martinez
　Aereo 4290
　Cali, Colombia, South America

San Juan Bautista
　Corrigimiento Cucurrupi
　Cucurrupi, Colombia, South America
SS: Andres Felipa Lerma　　　<M3>
　Cucurrupi, Colombia, South America

CL: Session Clerk
　Cucurrupi, Colombia, South America

San Lucas　　　(4WC)MSCA8215
　Calle 26 No 29-53
　Palmira, Colombia, South America
　(　)272-7584　　　<S America>
　sanlucaspalmira@hotmail.com
SS: Alexander Quintero　　　<M2>
　Calle 26 No 29-53
　Palmira, Colombia, South America
　(　)272-7584
　maalgo75@hotmail.com
CL: Janneth Naranto
　Aereo 329
　Palmira, Colombia, South America

San Marcos　　　(4MWC)MSCA8218
　Calle 46 A No 4N-25
　Cali, Colombia, South America
　(　)446-3311　　　<S America>
SS: Diego Palomino
　Calle 46 A No 4N-25
　Cali, Colombia, South America
　diegofer323@gmail.com
CL: Luz Dazy Ceballos
　Calle 46 A No 4N-25
　Cali, Colombia, South America

San Pablo　　　(4MWC)MSCA8212
　Cra 8 No 5-27
　Guacari, Colombia, South America
　(　)253-2751　　　<S America>
PA: Aldrin Calero　　　<M1>
　Cra 8 No 5-27
　Guacari, Colombia, South America
　(　)253-0453
　aldrin_calero@hotmail.com
CL: Luis Mayorga
　Carrera 13 # 3-81
　Guacari, Colombia, South America

Tulua Central　　　(4WF)MSCA8226
　Calle 41A No 26-26
　Tulua, Colombia, South America
　(　)224-5004　　　<S America>
　iglesiacentral@hotmail.com
PA: Orlando Mendez　　　<M3>
　Calle 41A No 26-26
　Tulua, Colombia, South America
　orlandomendezf@hotmail.com
CL: Arnaldo Tajama
　Cra 26 #36-40
　Tulua, Colombia, South America

OTHERS ON MINISTERIAL ROLL:

Aguirre, Luciria　　　<M1 WC>
　Calle 3B No 97-05
　Cali, Colombia, South America
　(300)686-9161
　pastorluciana50@yahoo.com.co
Ariza, Fabiola　　　<M1 WC>
　Calle 1A No 62A-130 Apto 124
　Cali, Colombia, South America
　fatvioleta@hotmail.com
　(316)419-8414
Caicedo, Efrain　　　<M1 WC>
　Calle 29 No 29A-03
　Cali, Colombia, South America

CAUCA VALLEY PRESBYTERY CONTINUED

Camacho, Blanca   <M9>
Calle 4D 89-26 Apto 205
Cali, Colombia, South America
blancanidiacamacho@yahoo.com

Diaz, William   <M1 WC>
Calle 5 Con Cra 89
Cali, Colombia, South America
( )332-5849
nuevaesperanza1983@hotmail.com PA:

Fonseca, Roberto   <M1 WC>
Cll 46 A No 4N 25
Cali, Colombia, South America
( )446-7370

Gaviria, Mario   <M1 WC>
Cra 27 No 7-48
Cali, Colombia, South America
( )372-3869
pastormariogaviria@hotmail.com

Giraldo, William   <M1 WC>
Calle 62 No 1B-15
Cali, Colombia, South America
( )439-5436
giraldo_william@yahoo.co

Gonzalez, Rito   <M1 MY>
Cali, Colombia, South America

Jimenez, Raul   <M9>
Calle 3B No 97A-05 Apto 102C
Cali, Colombia, South America

Madrid, Alejandro   <M1 WC>
Calle 12 No 4-69
Guapi, Colombia, South America

Pejendino, Fhanor   <M1 MY>
Cll 41 A No 26-26
Tulua, Colombia, South America
(317)654-5750
ph_apear@hotmail.com

Pejendino, Socorro   <M1 MY>
Cll 41 A No 26-26
Tulua, Colombia, South America
(317)654-5750
pastorasocorrod@hotmail.com

Racines, Jairo   <M1 WC>
Calle 39 No 13-40
Cali, Colombia, South America
(311)385-6546
senicartheos@live.com

Rodriguez, Jairo   <M1 WC>
Cra 1D 2 53 41
Cali, Colombia, South America
jairo.hrodriguez@hotmail.com
(572)377-8741

Sanchez, Sol Maria   <M9>
Av Americas 19N - 18
Cali, Colombia, South America
sol.marias@hotmail.com

Solis, Arcadio   <M1 WC>
Cra 42 D1 No 55-69
Cali, Colombia, South America
( )328-5486

Torres, Mariano
Cra 34 No 4-34A 34
Buenaventura, Colombia, South America

Wallace, Boyce   <M1 MY>
Cra 101 No 15-93
Cali, Colombia, South America
( )339-1579
hbwcali@yahoo.com

OTHER LICENTIATES ON ROLL:

Orozeo Ariza, Juan Carlos   <M2>
Aereo 6365
Cali, Colombia, South America

Paredes, Flavio   <M2>
Cra 7 No 1-76
Ipiales, Colombia, South America
fepa5308@hotmail.com

OTHER CANDIDATES ON ROLL:

Arteaga, Gilberto   <M3>
Aereo 794
Buenaventura, Colombia, South America
(000)256-4261
pastorgilbertoa@hotmail.com

Artega, Jose Felix   <M3>
Ipiales, Colombia, South America

Caicedo, Jose Urier   <M3>
Cra 4 sur 9C-15
Jamundi, Colombia, South America
joscuricr@hotmail.com

Gonzalez, Patricia   <M3>
Tulua, Colombia, South America
adriapatriciag@gmail.com

Guanaquillo, Samuel   <M3>
Aereo 10701
Cali, Colombia, South America
FAX: (408)255-5938
samijg@hotmail.com

Gutierrez, Consuelo   <M3>
Calle 18N No 4N-49
Cali, Colombia, South America
consuelogutierrezrico@hotmail.com

Gutierrez, Diana   <M3>
Cra 100 No 34-65
Cali, Colombia, South America
gutierrezdp21@hotmail.com

Gutierrez, Gloria   <M3>
Valle 18N No 4rN-49
Cali, Colombia, South America
gloritabondadosa@hotmail.com

Guyara, Elizabeth   <M3>
Ave 3 No 19-18
Cali, Colombia, South America
bethgu00@hotmail.com

Hoyos, Javier   <M3>
Calle 34 24A-36
Cali, Colombia, South America

Lubo, Jaime   <M3>
AA 6365
Montebello, Colombia, South America

Madrid, Alejandro   <M3>
Popayan
Cali, Colombia South America
ale.madrid@yahool.com

Madrid, Jorge Alexis   <M3>
Popayan
Cali, Colombia South America
sacrydea@hotmail.com

Micolta, Ruby Mabely   <M3>
Calle 51N No 11-85
Popayan, Colombia, South America
rumami@gmail.com

Munoz, Arles   <M3>
Ave 3N No 19-18
Cali, Colombia, South America
armisport2@gmail.com

Osorio, Fernando   <M3>
Cll 26 No 29 53
Palmira, Colombia, South America
( )272-7584
sanlucaspalmira@hotmail.com

Paz, Ivan   <M3>
Pasto, Colombia, South America
ivanpaz1234@hotmail.com

Piamba, Juan Carlos   <M3>
Cra 7 #21N-35
Popayan, Colombia, South America

Ponce, Dennis Adrian   <M3>
Buenaventura, Colombia, South America

Ramirez, Oscar   <M3>
Piendamo, Colombia, South America
oscarramiezbenitez@hotmail.com

Restrepo, Johanna   <M3>
Calle 14 Oe No 48-17
Cali, Colombia, South America
rojo_nana@hotmail.es

Rizo, Yency   <M3>
Diag 26 H 2 83-35
Cali, Colombia, South America

Urrutia, Julio Cesar   <M3>
Cra 10 No 9N-04
Popayan, Colombia, South America
julioc.urrutia52@hotmailk.com

Valencia, Ana Dolly   <M3>
Cra 27 No 7 48
Cali, Colombia, South America
anadollycuartas@hotmail.com

Vargas, Guido   <M3>
Calle 73N 7B-07
Popayan, Colombia, South America
g_var9@yahoo.com

Choctaw Presbytery
MISSION SYNOD

	1.Church Number	2.Active	3.Total	4.Church School	5.Prof. of Faith	6.Gains	7.Losses	8.Children Baptized	9. OUR UNITED OUT-REACH	10. Total Out-Reach Giving	11. All Other Expenses	12. Total Income Received	13. Value Church Prop. 1=1000
	1	2	3	4	5	6	7	8	9	10	11	12	13
Coal Creek	6102	5	26	10	0	0	1	0		290	6,353	6,560	11
Lone Star	6105	9	22	11	0	0	0	0		418	2,802	6,492	68
McGee Chapel	6106	35	35	10	0	1	2	0		1,659	6,000	9,000	100
Panki Bok	6108	2	4	2	No Report Received			0		0	0	0	6
Pigeon Roost*	6109	7	21	7	0	0	4	0		465	4,535	5,000	20
Rock Creek*	6111	16	16	16	0	5	4	1		4,480	354	3,800	25
Round Lake	6112	9	9	20	No Report Received			0		0	0	0	3
Presbytery									1,000				
TOTALS	7	83	133	76	0	6	11	1	1,000	7,312	20,044	30,852	233

CHURCHES, PASTORS, AND CLERKS:

Coal Creek   (4WC)MSCH6102
  Route 1 Box 1215
  Coalgate, OK 74538
  ( )   <Atoka>
PA: Nathan Scott   <M1>
  960 S Katy Road
  Atoka, OK 74525
  (580)364-6155
CL: Lola John
  Route 1 Box 1215
  Coalgate, OK 74538
  (580)258-8244

Lone Star   (2WC)MSCH6105
  PO Box 44 (mailing)
  206 S Newell Street (physical)
  Coalgate, OK 74538
  ( )   <Atoka>
SS: Hannah Bryan   <M1>
  32 Trenton Lane
  Mead, OK 73449
  (580)775-4955
  hbryan@choctawnation.com
CL: Evangeline Robinson
  PO Box 44
  Boswell, OK 74727
  (580)513-0170
  erobinson@choctawarchiving.com

McGee Chapel   (2EW C)MSCH6106
  PO Box 158 (mailing)
  99 Chapel Circle (physical)
  Broken Bow, OK 74728
  (580)584-2099   <McCurtain>
  FAX: (580)584-2099
  chocpres@pine-net.com
PA: Randy Jacob   <M1>
  PO Box 158
  Broken Bow, OK 74728
  (580)236-2374
  FAX: (580)584-2099
  chocpres@pine-net.com

CL: Betty Jacob
  PO Box 158
  Broken Bow, OK 74728
  (580)584-2099
  FAX: (580)584-2099
  chocpres@pine-net.com

Panki Bok   (2C)MSCH6108
  PO Box 375
  Eagletown, OK 74734
  ( )   <McCurtain>
PA: Randy Jacob   <M1>
  610 W Adams Street
  Broken Bow, OK 74728
  (580)584-2099
  FAX: (580)584-2099
  chocpres@pine-net.com
CL: Mildred Ashalintubbi
  PO Box 375
  Eagletown, OK 74734
  (580)835-7336

Pigeon Roost   (2C)MSCH6109
  960 S Katy Road
  Atoka, OK 74525
  (580)889-2292
PA: Virginia Espinoza   <Choctaw>
  PO Box 132   <M1>
  Boswell, OK 74727
  (580)775-4138
  vespinoza@choctawnation.com
CL: Virginia Espinoza
  960 S Katy Road
  Atoka, OK 74525
  (580)889-2292

Rock Creek   (2WC)MSCH6111
  c/o Betty Walton (mailing)
  PO Box 126
  Talihina, OK 74571
  Honobia, OK (physical)
  (918)567-2370   <LeFlore>
PA: Nathan Scott   <M1>
  960 S Katy Road
  Atoka, OK 74525
  (580)364-6155

CL: Betty Walton
  PO Box 126
  Talihina, OK 74571
  (918)567-2370

Round Lake   (1WC)MSCH6112
  Box 127
  Tupelo, OK 74572
  (580)317-7427   <Coal>
PA: Hannah Bryan   <M1>
  32 Trenton Lane
  Mead, OK 73449
  (580)775-4955
  hbryan@choctawnation.com
CL: Vickie McClure
  Box 127
  Tupelo, OK 74572
  (580)317-7427

OTHERS ON MINISTERIAL ROLL:

OTHER CANDIDATES ON ROLL:

Crosby, Ronald   <M3>
  407 N "A" Street
  Calera, OK 74730
Scott, Linda   <M3>
  960 S Katy Road
  Atoka, OK 74525
  (580)889-2292

Columbia Presbytery
TENNESSEE SYNOD

	GENERAL		MEMBERSHIP			CHANGES				FINANCES			
	1.Church Number	2.Active	3.Total	4.Church School	5.Prof. of Faith	6.Gains	7.Losses	8.Children Baptized	9. OUR UNITED OUT-REACH	10. Total Out-Reach Giving	11. All Other Expenses	12. Total Income Received	13. Value Church Prop. 1=1000
	1	2	3	4	5	6	7	8	9	10	11	12	13
Ash Hill	7101	37	66	29	1	4	4	0	3,033	7,767	28,734	30,550	275
Belleview	7104	14	25	0	0	1	0	0	350	9,315	22,354	28,917	375
Boonshill	7106	26	64	24	2	2	1	0	800	7,900	21,575	29,950	321
Champ	7108	9	9	5	0	0	2	0	0	500	15,173	13,633	40
Chapel Hill	7109	33	33	20	3	6	1	3	1,000	3,800	49,000	52,500	410
Columbia*	7110	88	88	28	0	2	18	1	400	7,520	143,219	147,164	1,500
Elora	7111	5	5	6	0	0	0	0	0	100	9,294	7,860	150
Fayetteville	7112	111	273	65	3	11	13	1	14,400	24,759	166,484	205,574	2,300
Fiducia*	7113	11	11	11	0	0	15	0	0	1,448	15,555	14,965	80
Flintville	7115	7	7	13	0	0	0	0	0	1,383	8,755	10,626	25
Franklin	7116	28	28	10	No Report Received			0		0	0	0	800
Grace	7145	12	12	0	No Report Received			0		0	0	0	10
Green Hill	7118	16	16	19	3	3	0	0	1,605	3,869	23,684	32,101	86
Harpeth Lick	7119	29	38	13	1	1	1	0	1,400	6,199	31,358	42,162	200
Hohenwald	7120	13	13	0	0	0	2	0	0	0	26,935	38,048	250
Howell	7121	50	124	71	1	1	1	1	3,000	26,627	58,903	77,232	750
Jenkins**	7144	87	185	42	1	1	30	0	15,883	28,361	183,899	212,876	3,623
Kelso*	7122	28	86	19	0	0	8	0	750	5,750	55,383	75,091	180
Kingdom	7123	10	10	5	0	0	0	0	520	3,138	10,585	16,961	175
Lawrenceburg*	7124	19	19	12	1	1	9	0	118	0	42,053	22,172	1,230
Lewisburg, 1st	7125	69	176	68	3	9	5	2	0	9,023	122,800	118,800	500
McCains**	7126	49	49	22	0	0	28	0	4,500	9,925	52,187	64,778	464
Mt. Carmel	7127	71	98	20	0	0	15	0	1,000	3,150	76,305	82,894	900
Mt. Hebron	7128	4	5	4	0	0	0	0	0	0	8,654	7,772	141
Mt. Joy	7129	58	105	20	3	5	2	0	1,164	1,164	71,315	72,479	300
Mt. Lebanon	7130	44	44	25	0	0	10	0	717	7,838	30,858	40,920	125
Mt. Moriah	7131	51	116	30	0	0	2	0	0	16,900	36,000	51,000	250
Mt. Nebo	7132	7	7	7	0	0	0	0	0	1,890	18,638	19,107	90
Mt. Pleasant	7133	46	97	22	0	0	0	1	2,904	7,046	42,867	51,921	1,000
New Bethel	7134	10	10	10	0	2	0	0	455	405	3,774	7,482	100
Petersburg	7135	41	51	35	5	4	0	0	9,750	27,254	44,524	71,778	232
Pleasant Mount	7136	31	80	29	0	0	3	0	2,200	5,000	58,000	65,000	500
Richland	7137	57	125	49	0	5	1	0	1,500	7,809	67,673	73,809	150
Santa Fe*	7138	22	22	18	0	0	5	0	0	905	21,989	29,228	0
Swan	7140	13	13	10	1	1	0	0	100	878	22,896	27,973	300
Union Grove	7141	10	10	0	0	0	0	0	0	754	14,004	13,284	100
Waynesboro	7142	63	63	15	1	2	5	0	7,012	18,974	65,445	81,011	618
West Point	7143	67	67	40	1	2	7	0	1,000	6,463	80,741	96,902	1,000
TOTALS	38	1,363	2,267	826	79	74	173	9	75,561	263,814	1,751,563	2,034,610	19,890

*Math error corrected. **Purged roll.

CHURCHES, PASTORS, AND CLERKS:

Ash Hill   (4WC)TNCO7101
4930 Ash Hill Road
Spring Hill, TN 37174
(931)381-3367   <Williamson>
PA: James R Miller   <M1>
1214 Whitney Drive
Columbia, TN 38401
(931)215-2108
rev.james.miller@charter.net
CL: Helen Logue
1603 Emerald Court
Franklin, 37064
(615)599-6764

Belleview   (4WC)TNCO7104
1752 Burke Hollow Road (mailing)
Nolensville, TN 37135
4724 Murfreesboro Road (physical)
Franklin, TN 37064
( )   <Williamson>
PA: James R Miller   <M1>
1214 Whitney Drive
Columbia, TN 38401
(931)381-3367
rev.james.miller@charter.net
CL: David C Hughes
1752 Burke Hollow Road
Nolensville, TN 37135
(615)395-4935

Boonshill   (4C)TNCO7106
91 Red Oak Road (mailing)
Petersburg, TN 37144
Rt 2 (physical)
Boonshill, TN
( )   <Lincoln>
OD: Thomas Smith   <M5>
467 Gunter Hollow Drive
Fayetteville, TN 37334
(931)732-5426
tomandbobbie@ardmore.net
CL: Sammy Luna
91 Red Oak Road
Petersburg, TN 37144
(931)703-0536
srluna@ardmore.net

COLUMBIA PRESBYTERY CONTINUED

Champ (2C)TNCO7108
290 Sullenger Bend Road (mailing)
Belvidere, TN 37306
61 Tucker Creek Road (physical)
Mulberry, TN
( ) <Lincoln>
PA: Elmer L Alverson <M1 HR OP>
354 Roy Davis Road
New Market, AL 35761
(256)828-4503
bud@alscomputers.com
CL: Diann Adams
2800 Hillsboro Road
Huntsville, AL 35805
(256)534-6076

Chapel Hill (4MWC)TNCO7109
4801 Eagleville Pike (mailing)
302 N Horton Parkway (physical)
Chapel Hill, TN 37034
(931)364-7819 <Marshall>
PA: Joe Wiggins <M1>
2734 US Highway 41A S
Eagleville, TN 37060
(615)274-2011
jwigginz@aol.com
CL: Spence Walls
4521 Polaris Drive
Chapel Hill, TN 37034
(931)364-2573
walls.family95@yahoo.com

Columbia (4MWC)TNCO7110
1106 Nashville Highway
Columbia, TN 38401
(931)388-9177 <Maury>
pastor@fcpccolumbia.com
PA: Calvin Lunn <M1>
859 Cranford Hollow Road
Columbia, TN 38401
(931)381-2397
pastor@fcpccolumbia.com
CL: Brian Keith Tilghman
1036 Theta Pike
Columbia, TN 38401
(931)698-0141
tilghmanphoto@aol.com

Elora (2C)TNCO7111
69 Bear Wallow Road (mailing)
Flintville, TN 37335
Elora, TN 37328 (physical)
( ) <Lincoln>
SS: John Blair <M1>
108 Cliff Drive
Lawrenceburg, TN 38464
(931)762-2480
jnbblair@charter.net
CL: Jim Ramsey
69 Bear Wallow Road
Flintville, TN 37335
(931)937-8765
jim.brenda.ramsey710@gmail.com

Fayetteville (4WC)TNCO7112
1015 Lewisburg Highway
Fayetteville, TN 37334
(931)433-5441 <Lincoln>
FAX: (931)433-0056
cpc@fpunet.com

PA: Timothy Smith <M1>
712 Morningside Drive
Fayetteville, TN 37334
(931)438-2820
FAX: (931)433-0056
tims38@hotmail.com
CL: Larry Ventress
1003 First Avenue
Fayetteville, TN 37334
(931)433-5053
FAX: (931)433-0056
dooda49@fpunet.com

Fiducia (2EW C)TNCO7113
1342 Bethel Road (mailing)
Pulaski, TN 38478
1695 Fiducia Road (physical)
Prospect, TN 38477
( ) <Giles>
PA: John Blair <M1>
108 W Cliff Drive
Lawrenceburg, TN 38464
(931)766-2480
jnbblair@charter.net
CL: Ewing Brooks
1429 Crooked Hill Road
Pulaski, TN 38478
(931)363-5985

Flintville (2C)TNCO7115
35 Well Lee Road (mailing)
9 Flintville School Road (physical)
Flintville, TN 37335
( ) <Lincoln>
PA: John Blair <M1>
108 W Cliff Drive
Lawrenceburg, TN 38464
(931)766-2480
jnbblair@charter.net
CL: Jimmie D Wicks
35 Wells Lee Road
Flintville, TN 37335
(931)937-8562
bfwicks@bellsouth.net

Franklin (4MC)TNCO7116
PO Box 1134 (mailing)
615 West Main Street (physical)
Franklin, TN 37065
(615)599-0029 <Williamson>
FAX: (615)807-2959
cp1876@hotmail.com
PA: John Hyden <M1>
6525 Peytonsville Arno Road
College Grove, TN 37046
(615)975-9584
cp1876@hotmail.com
CL: Dorris Douglass
724 Fair Street
Franklin, TN 37064
(615)790-7914
FAX: (615)595-1247
ansercher@aol.com

Grace (4C)TNCO7145
PO Box 682462 (mailing)
1153 Lewisburg Pike (physical)
Franklin, TN 37068
(615)794-0370 <Williamson>
gracecpchurchpastor@gmail.com

PA: Fonda Blair <M1>
2911 Kedzie Drive
Murfreesboro, TN 37130
(615)491-2432
blairfonda2010@comcast.net
CL: Lee Bagby
311 E Chownings Court
Franklin, TN 37064
(615)794-9532
bagbyl@bellsouth.net

Green Hill (3WC)TNCO7118
1900 Unionville-Deason Road
Bell Buckle, TN 37020
(931)294-2040 <Bedford>
CL: Angela Burns
328 Dunnaway Road
Shelbyville, TN 37160
(931)294-5105

Harpeth Lick (4C)TNCO7119
6981 Arno Allisona Road
College Grove, TN 37046
( ) <Williamson>
SS: Larry Guin <M1>
125 Glider Loop
Eagleville, TN 37060
(615)668-5236
lguin43@hotmail.com
CL: Virginia Lou Rogers
8876 Horton Highway
College Grove, TN 37046
(615)368-2202
mudpuddle42@gmail.com

Hohenwald (4MWC)TNCO7120
PO Box 456 (mailing)
201 Park Avenue S (physical)
Hohenwald, TN 38462
(931)796-3657 <Lewis>
CL: Byrne Dunn
617 Oakdale Drive
Hohenwald, TN 38462
(931)796-2806
FAX: (931)796-2153
marvinwilkins@msn.com

Howell (4MWC)TNCO7121
43 Brown Teal Road
Fayetteville, TN 37334
(931)433-0818 <Lincoln>
PA: Todd Gaskill <M1>
430 Haysland Road
Petersburg, TN 37144
(931)580-2708
tgaskill@pens.com
CL: Tim Porter
85 Icy Bank Road
Fayetteville, TN 37334
(931)433-8306

Jenkins (4MWC)TNCO7144
PO Box 518 (mailing)
2501 York Road (physical)
Nolensville, TN 37135
(615)776-2339 <Williamson>
FAX: (615)776-3520
jenkinspastor@gmail.com
CL: Joyce A Allemore
2442 Fly Road
Nolensville, TN 37135
(615)776-2985
jallemore@yahoo.com

COLUMBIA PRESBYTERY CONTINUED

Kelso   (4MWC)TNCO7122
PO Box 28 (mailing)
16 Teal Hollow Road (physical)
Kelso, TN 37348
( )   <Lincoln>
CL: Bill Dickey
1501 Swanson Boulevard
Fayetteville, TN 37334
(931)433-2462

Kingdom   (4C)TNCO7123
4532 Barfield Crescent Road (mailing)
Murfreesboro, TN 37128
800 Kingdom Road (physical)
Unionville, TN 37180
( )   <Bedford>
SS: Larry Guin   <M1>
125 Glider Loop
Eagleville, TN 37060
(615)668-5236
lguin43@hotmail.com
CL: Thelma Shockey
4532 Barfield Crescent Road
Murfreesboro, TN 37128
(615)896-1890

Lawrenceburg   (4MWC)TNCO7124
228 S Military Avenue
Lawrenceburg, TN 38464
(931)762-4343   <Lawrence>
cumberlandpresby@bellsouth.net
CL: Kaye Luffman
5 Powell Circle
Five Points, TN 38457
(931)556-2252
kluffman@hotmail.com

Lewisburg 1st   (4MWC)TNCO7125
210 Haynes Street (mailing)
402 2nd Avenue N (physical)
Lewisburg, TN 37091
(931)359-3857   <Marshall>
FAX: (931)270-8624
fcpclewisburg@bellsouth.net
PA: Roger Reid   <M1>
1505 Experiment Farm Road
Lewisburg, TN 37091
(931)422-5257
drrtr@yahoo.com
CL: Tammy Caneer-Carter
1400 Green Valley Road
Pulaski, TN 38478
(931)637-7374
FAX: (931)270-8624
cantam@bellsouth.net

McCains   (4MWC)TNCO7126
PO Box 29 (mailing)
3532 McCains Lane (physical)
Columbia, TN 38401
(931)540-0160   <Maury>
PA: Tommy Clark   <M1>
124 Roberta Drive
Memphis, TN 38112
(615)430-9158
fattire77@gmail.com
CL: Gary Weatherford
3926 Campbellsville Pike
Columbia, TN 38401
(931)388-0599
gmweatherford@cs.com

Mt Carmel   (4C)TNCO7127
4810 Ash Hill Road (mailing)
Spring Hill, TN 37174
2300 Lewisburg Pike (physical)
Franklin, TN 37064
(615)591-3930   <Williamson>
PA: John Eatherly   <M1>
1377 Moss Road
Chapel Hill, TN 37034
(931)364-2087
jrev@united.net
CL: Peggy S Fisher
4810 Ash Hill Road
Spring Hill, TN 37174
(615)944-9300
fishpest@ymail.com

Mt Hebron   (4C)TNCO7128
59 Giles Hollow Road (mailing)
927 Shelbyville Highway (physical)
Fayetteville, TN 37334
( )   <Lincoln>
PA: Todd Gaskill   <M1>
430 Haysland Road
Petersburg, TN 37144
(931)580-2708
tgaskill@pens.com
CL: Jimmy Buchanan
59 Giles Hollow Road
Fayetteville, TN 37334
(931)433-6446

Mt Joy   (4MWC)TNCO7129
8364 Mt Joy Road
Mount Pleasant, TN 38474
( )   <Maury>
CL: Evelyn Luckett
8432 Mount Joy Road
Mount Pleasant, TN 38474
(931)379-4600

Mt Lebanon   (4EC)TNCO7130
4497 Kedron Road
Spring Hill, TN 37174
( )   <Maury>
mortonco@bellsouth.net
PA: Patric Fife   <M1>
73 Jordan Road
Lawrenceburg, TN 38464
(931)629-8146
pnlfifernak@gmail.com
CL: Judy L Morton
1272 John Sharp Road
Columbia, TN 38401
(931)381-1140
mortonco@bellsouth.net

Mt Moriah   (4C)TNCO7131
485 Agnew Road (mailing)
463 Big Dry Creek Road (physical)
Pulaski, TN 38478
( )   <Giles>
PA: Steve Nave   <M1>
5172 Fall River Road
Leoma, TN 38468
(931)424-0020
thenaves@wildblue.net
CL: Dickson Marks
485 Agnew Road
Pulaski, TN 38478
(931)363-2432
jmarks0912@mindspring.com

Mt Nebo   (4C)TNCO7132
84 S Old Military Road (mailing)
Saint Joseph, TN 38481
473 Mt Nebo Road (physical)
Iron City, TN 38463
( )   <Lawrence>
LS: Sean Richardson   <M6>
4227 Highway 43 N
Ethridge, TN 38456
(931)829-2094
sean@misterrichardson.com
CL: William B Gabel
104 Spring Street
Saint Joseph, TN 38481
(931)845-4203
stjoemerry@gmail.com

Mt Pleasant   (4EWC)TNCO7133
PO Box 689 (mailing)
504 Florida Avenue (physical)
Mount Pleasant, TN 38474
(931)379-3662   <Maury>
PA: Robert Mullenix   <M1>
1408 Azalee Lane
Chapel Hill, TN 37034
(931)364-4611
glonix@live.com
CL: Rickey Massey
609 Circle Drive
Mount Pleasant, TN 38474
(931)379-3617
rickeymassey@bellsouth.net

New Bethel   (2C)TNCO7134
5060 Reynolds Road
Columbia, TN 38401
(931)364-2378   <Marshall>
SS: John Eatherly   <M1>
1377 Moss Road
Chapel Hill, TN 37034
(931)364-2087
jrev@united.net
CL: James W Hood
1532 Lewisburg Pike
Franklin, TN 37064
(615)591-8689

Petersburg   (4MWC)TNCO7135
PO Box 82 (mailing)
303 Russell Street (physical)
Petersburg, TN 37144
(931)607-1859   <Lincoln>
petersburgpreacher@att.net
PA: Troy Green   <M1>
105 Cobb Hollow Lane
Petersburg, TN 37144
(931)659-6627
thegreens101@att.net
CL: Ann Hemphill
803 Washington Street W Apt B
Fayetteville, TN 37334
(931)433-8380
ahemphill@fpunet.com

Pleasant Mount   (4WC)TNCO7136
609 Woods Drive (mailing)
1620 Fountain Heights Road (physical)
Columbia, TN 38401
( )   <Maury>

COLUMBIA PRESBYTERY CONTINUED

PA: William L Rolman, Jr   <M1>
602 Canyon Drive
Columbia, TN 38401
(931)388-2611
wmrolmanjr@att.net

CL: James H Rochell, Jr
609 Woods Drive
Columbia, TN 38401
(931)388-1947
tnpappy53@yahoo.com

Richland   (4C)TNCO7137
3452 Spring Place Road
Lewisburg, TN 37091
(931)270-6135   <Marshall>

PA: Charles (Buddy) Pope   <M1>
2391 Fairfield Pike
Shelbyville, TN 37160
(931)205-6897
pope6897@yahoo.com

CL: Douglas A Looney
3045 Monte Murrey Road
Lewisburg, TN 37091
(931)359-3781
ld.looney@yahoo.com

Santa Fe   (4WC)TNCO7138
PO Box 58 (mailing)
2630 Santa Fe Pike (physical)
Santa Fe, TN 38482
(931)682-3555   <Maury>

SS: Sherry Ladd   <M1>
4521 Turkey Creek Road
Williamsport, TN 38487
(931)682-2263
revsherryladd@gmail.com

CL: Whitney Seaton
111 W Hardin Drive
Columbia, TN 38401
(931)388-9319

Swan   (4C)TNCO7140
4521 Turkey Creek Road (mailing)
Williamsport, TN 38487
Swan Creek Road (physical)
Centerville, TN 37033
(931)682-2263   <Hickman>
revsherryladd@gmail.com

PA: Sherry Ladd   <M1>
4521 Turkey Creek Road
Williamsport, TN 38487
(931)682-2263
revsherryladd@gmail.com

CL: George C Ladd
4521 Turkey Creek Road
Williamsport, TN 38487
(931)682-2263
gladd@hughes.net

Union Grove   (4C)TNCO7141
2409 Green Mills Road Lot 30 (mailing)
1452 Cliff White Road (physical)
Columbia, TN 38401
(931)486-2799   <Maury>
patricia.cates@att.net

PA: Scott Yates   <M1>
8818 New Town Road
Rockvale, TN 37153
(615)274-3000
scott@scottyates.net

CL: Patricia Cates
2409 Green Mills Road Lot 30
Columbia, TN 38401
(931)486-2799
patricia.cates@att.net

Waynesboro   (4MEWC)TNCO7142
PO Box 234 (mailing)
110 North High Street (physical)
Waynesboro, TN 38485
(931)722-5621   <Wayne>

CL: Susan Myers
PO Box 234
Waynesboro, TN 38485
(931)722-5621
warden02@tds.net

West Point   (4MC)TNCO7143
1431 Spainwood Street (mailing)
1533 Theta Pike (physical)
Columbia, TN 38401
(931)388-7268   <Maury>

PA: Terry Peery   <M1>
1431 Spainwood Street
Columbia, TN 38401
(931)381-6871
coppreacher@gmail.com

CL: Mike McCord
4543 Snow Creek Road
Santa Fe, TN 38482
(931)682-2500
mmccord59@bellsouth.net

OTHERS ON MINISTERIAL ROLL:

Cole, Dwayne   <M1 HR>
6460 Village Parkway
Anchorage, AK 99504
(907)854-5793
tadpolejr@aol.com

Gaskin, Tony   <M1 WC>
1414 Saint Joseph Street NW
Cullman, AL 35055
(256)338-7893
tgaskin46@hotmail.com

Heflin, Robert   <M1 DE>
4144 Meadow Court Drive
Bartlett, TN 38135
(901)382-8198
rdheflin@bellsouth.net

Kelly, Lawrence (Larry)   <M1 HR>
77 Stonewall Court
Mount Juliet, TN 37122
(615)934-1517

Kinnaman, Richard Terry   <M1 WC>
2018 Spring Meadow Circle
Spring Hill, TN 37174
(615)302-3321
kinnaman91@att.net

Liles, Dwight   <M1 WC>
8467 Joy Road
Mount Pleasant, TN 38474
(931)379-0326
dwightliles@att.net

Smith, Kirk   <M1 WC>
813 1st Avenue
Fayetteville, TN 37334
(931)438-8649
kirks37334@att.net

Trotter, Wendell   <M1 HR>
1516 Fell Avenue NE
Huntsville, AL 35811
(256)519-6571
wendelltrotter@knology.net

Watson, Jonathan   <M1 WC>
4017 Claude Drive
Smyrna, TN 37167
watsonjonathan@bellsouth.net
(615)630-9153

OTHER LICENTIATES ON ROLL:

OTHER CANDIDATES ON ROLL:

King, Mark   <M3>
717 Big Swan Creek Road
Hampshire, TN 38461
(931)626-6915

Covenant Presbytery
MIDWEST SYNOD

GENERAL	1.Church Number	2.Active	3.Total	4.Church School	5.Prof. of Faith	6.Gains	7.Losses	8.Children Baptized	9. OUR UNITED OUTREACH	10. Total Out-Reach Giving	11. All Other Expenses	12. Total Income Received	13. Value Church Prop. 1=1000
	1	2	3	4	5	6	7	8	9	10	11	12	13
Bayou de Chien	3401	40	77	28	No Report Received			0	0	0	0	0	516
Benton	3403	15	40	15	No Report Received			0	0	0	0	0	215
Bethel	3404	182	363	101	No Report Received			0	11,600	0	0	0	2,500
Calvary	3405	23	52	25	No Report Received			0	0	0	0	0	0332
Camp Ground	5103	21	51	27	0	0	1	0	2,486	7,812	28,344	31,741	695
Chandler	5302	110	387	97	3	3	3	1	15,485	37,502	154,694	182,525	1,399
Ebenezer	5105	20	25	15	No Report Received			0	74	0	0	0	50
Ebenezer Hall	5106	1	11	5	No Report Received			0	874	0	0	0	57
Flat Lick	3606	45	96	30	No Report Received			0	5,566	0	0	0	350
Fredonia	3608	102	240	78	No Report Received			0	17,620	0	0	0	1,015
Gilead	5110	50	155	31	No Report Received			0	1,845	0	0	0	375
Good Spring	3609	50	50	14	0	0	1	0	2,400	20,320	25,315	47,016	140
Highland	3414	90	200	69	1	3	6	0	8,200	34,905	129,632	167,674	1,000
Hopewell	3610	60	103	30	0	2	2	0	720	1,860	49,358	62,211	120
Hopkinsville	3611	44	73	41	0	7	4	0	2,458	5,455	100,344	40,085	1,181
Liberty*	3406	97	107	55	0	0	5	0	0	12,236	89,977	105,664	720
Lisman	3613	27	45	22	No Report Received			0	1,488	0	0	0	225
Macedonia	3614	22	22	15	No Report Received			0	0	0	0	0	300
Madisonville	3615	40	150	25	No Report Received			0	1,198	0	0	0	356
Margaret Hank	3415	70	107	35	No Report Received			0	0	0	0	0	750
Marion First	3616	44	137	20	No Report Received			0	3,868	0	0	0	698
Milburn Chapel**	3416	87	131	50	5	0	131	0	0	13,314	145,691	172,571	1,800
Mt. Carmel	3617	75	135	10	0	3	0	1	0	2,463	52,493	35,609	600
Mt. Pleasant	3618	23	27	18	0	0	0	0	0	2,336	17,777	30,865	35
Mt. Sterling*	5117	180	270	80	17	25	7	1	0	11,390	115,495	140,000	340
Mt. Zion*	5118	12	12	0	0	2	0	0	2,425	7,065	27,241	22,427	35
New Hope	3410	165	236	159	No Report Received			0	14,319	0	0	0	1,550
No. Pleasant Gr	3411	23	53	31	No Report Received			0	0	0	0	0	200
Oak Grove	3412	60	98	40	No Report Received			0	0	0	0	0	400
Oak Grove Union**	3619	30	30	30	0	0	26	0	0	14,268	45,572	52,590	200
Oakland	3413	45	132	32	No Report Received			0	0	0	0	0	1,250
Piney Fork	3620	37	77	30	0	2	2	0	1,467	11,602	34,006	48,898	250
Pleasant Valley	3418	5	7	5	No Report Received			0	0	0	0	0	150
Providence	5122	2	28	8	CLOSED 2015			0	0	0	0	0	70
Providence 1st	3621	8	51	0	No Report Received			0	0	0	0	0	80
Rose Creek	3622	27	60	10	3	3	10	1	4,648	17,770	56,031	85,532	900
Rozzell Chapel	3419	62	102	57	6	6	1	0	3,500	14,498	57,447	110,612	380
Sturgis	3625	107	213	78	1	3	5	2	14,694	47,507	150,483	256,835	2,100
Sugar Grove	3626	71	145	39	No Report Received			0	3,000	0	0	0	700
Union Chapel	5123	33	54	19	No Report Received			0	0	0	0	0	150
Unity	3422	115	193	65	No Report Received			0	2,200	0	0	0	350
Vaughn's Chapel	3423	48	63	12	No Report Received			0	3,283	0	0	0	400
Village	5125	10	10	11	No Report Received			0	1,000	0	0	0	10
Wheatcroft	3627	32	57	10	No Report Received			0	2,559	0	0	0	110
Woodlawn	3417	72	303	47	No Report Received			0	0	0	0	0	1,744
TOTALS	43	2,720	5,189	1,799	36	59	204	7	127,977	262,303	1,279,900	1,592,855	24,932

*Math error corrected. **Purged roll.

COVENANT PRESBYTERY CONTINUED

CHURCHES, PASTORS, AND CLERKS:

Bayou de Chine   (4MWC)MICO3401
   2 Kingston Road
   Water Valley, KY 42085
   (270)355-2089   <Graves>
CL: Mark Crass
   1990 Kingston Road
   Water Valley, KY 42085
   (270)355-2381
   jimcrassauto10@bellsouth.net

Benton   (4WC)MICO3403
   2968 Aurora Highway (mailing)
   Hardin, KY 40248
   Kentucky Highway 58 (physical)
   Benton, KY 42025
   ( )   <Marshall>
CL: Michele Shearer
   2969 Aurora Highway
   Hardin, KY 42048
   (270)354-8656
   mshearer92858@hotmail.com

Bethel   (4WC)MICO3404
   12304 Wickliffe Road
   Kevil, KY 42053
   (270)876-7239   <Ballard>
   FAX: (270)876-7513
   bethelcpchurch@gmail.com
PA: Drew Gray   <M1>
   8220 Timberland Drive
   West Paducah, KY 42086
   (270)331-5569
   drewgray01@gmail.com
CL: Teresa Higdon
   230 Lake Point Drive
   Paducah, KY 42003
   (270)554-5003
   teresa@qservicesco.com

Calvary   (4MC)MICO3405
   98 Calvary Church Road
   Mayfield, KY 42066
   (270)376-5525   <Graves>
CL: Darla Jo Tucker
   665 McNutt Road
   Wingo, KY 42088
   (270)376-2065

Camp Ground   (4C)MICO5103
   2645 Lick Creek Road (mailing)
   70 Tunnel Lane (physical)
   Anna, IL 62906
   (618)833-9000   <Union>
OD: Dwight Kaylor   <M5>
   9393 Hamlettsburg Road
   Brookport, IL 62910
   (270)366-6881
   dkaylor70@gmail.com
CL: Sandra Boaz
   2645 Lick Creek Road
   Anna, IL 62906
   (618)833-8216
   skboaz@yahoo.com

Chandler   (4MWC)MICO5302
   338 S State Street
   Chandler, IN 47610
   (812)925-6175   <Warrick>
   FAX: (812)925-3628
   chandlercpc2@hotmail.com
PA: Jesse Thornton   <M1>
   122 E Cherry Street
   Chandler, IN 47610
   (812)925-6475
   FAX: (812)925-3628
   jessthornton@msn.com
CL: Robert Hooper
   PO Box 351
   Chandler, IN 47610
   (812)925-6965
   rwhooper@yahoo.com

Ebenezer   (C)MICO5105
   Thompsonville, IL 62890
   ( )   <Saline>
CL: Pat Fletcher
   24535 Kaskaskia Road
   Thompsonville, IL 62890
   (618)627-2288

Ebenezer Hall   (4WC)MICO5106
   9850 Lick Creek Road (mailing)
   750 Grand View (physical)
   Buncombe, IL 62912
   (618)833-8280   <Union>
CL: Carolyn Hammon
   9850 Lick Creek Road
   Buncombe, IL 62912
   (618)833-8280

Flat Lick   (4WC)MICO3606
   415 Bennetttown Street (mailing)
   Herndon, KY 42236
   9355 Lafayette Road (physical))
   Herndon, KY 42236
   (270)885-1350   <Christian>
   pastorsteve88@yahoo.com
CL: Mike Barbee
   415 Bennetttown Street
   Herndon, KY 42236
   (270)498-3664

Fredonia   (4MEWC)MICO3608
   204 West Pierson Street (mailing)
   303 Cassidy Avenue (physical)
   Fredonia, KY 42411
   (270)545-3481   <Caldwell>
SS: Larry Buchanan   <M1>
   730 Shelby Road
   Salem, KY 42078
   (270)988-1880
   lbuchanan.tse@gmail.com
CL: Cindy Cruce
   46 Penn Drive
   Marion, KY 42064
   (270)965-4520
   ccruce@fredoniavalleybank.com

Gilead   (4EC)MICO5110
   3470 Gilead Church Road (mailing)
   4385 Gilead Church Road (physical)
   Simpson, IL 62985
   (618)695-2653   <Johnson>
   tim-arm@live.com

CL: Tim Armstrong
   745 Webb Town Road
   Tunnel Hill, IL 62972
   (618)559-7021
   tim-arm@live.com

Good Spring   (2WC)MICO3609
   1800 Old Fredonia Road (mailing)
   Princeton, KY 42445
   4142 Good Spring Road (physical)
   Fredonia, KY 42411
   ( )   <Caldwell>
CL: Mike Stephens
   1800 Old Fredonia Road
   Princeton, KY 42445
   (270)559-6032
   mwstephens1800@gmail.com

Highland   (4MWC)MICO3414
   3950 Lovelaceville Road
   Paducah, KY 42001
   (270)554-3572   <McCracken>
   hcpsec@bellsouth.net
PA: Olen (Bud) Russell   <M1>
   9595 Wickliffe Road
   Wickliffe, KY 42087
   olen552@aol.com
   (270)562-1096
CL: Elaine S Overton
   3915 Lovelaceville Road
   Paducah, KY 42001
   (270)554-1259
   jred3915@bellsouth.net

Hopewell   (4C)MICO3610
   768 Lola Road (mailing)
   1235 Lola Road (physical)
   Salem, KY 42078
   (270)988-3859   <Livingston>
SS: Troy Newcomb   <M3>
   PO Box 858
   Salem, KY 42078
SS: Larry Buchanan   <M1>
   730 Shelby Road
   Salem, KY 42078
   (270)988-1880
   lbuchanan.tse@gmail.com
CL: Michael Heneisen
   1162 Hampton Road
   Salem, KY 42078
   (270)988-4856
   heneisen@tds.net

Hopkinsville   (4MWC)MICO3611
   2701 Faircourt
   Hopkinsville, KY 42240
   (270)886-1464   <Christian>
   FAX: (270)885-1531
   cumberland1@bellsouth.net
PA: Robert T Spurling Jr   <M1>
   305 Wayne Drive
   Hopkinsville, KY 42240
   (865)803-8582
CL: Marcia Ballard
   306 Lucky Debonair
   Hopkinsville, KY 42240
   (270)839-5482

COVENANT PRESBYTERY CONTINUED

Liberty   (4C)MICO3406
510 Richardson Street (mailing)
150 Liberty Road (physical)
Murray, KY 42071
( )   <Calloway>
PA: Gary Vacca   <M1>
2203 Creekwood Drive
Murray, KY 42071
(270)978-0818
garyvacca@spiritualliving.com
CL: Brenda Lawson
441 Old Shiloh Road
Murray, KY 42071
(270)227-5872
bsnip10@hotmail.com

Lisman   (4EC)MICO3613
153 Woodland Acres (mailing)
Dixon, KY 42409
2085 State Route 270 W (physical)
Clay, KY 42404
( )   <Webster>
PA: John R Shoulta   <M1>
1154 Mt Carmel Road
White Plains, KY 42464
(270)676-3563
johnshoulta@bellsouth.net
CL: Nancy Burnett
451 Jim Villines Road
Dixon, KY 42409
(270)639-6204

Macedonia   (4WC)MICO3614
18030 Beulah Road (mailing)
Princeton, KY 42445
Highway 291 (physical)
Dalton, KY
( )   <Hopkins>
SS: Dennis Weaver   <M1>
1750 Government Road
Princeton, KY 42245
(731)592-9054
dsweaver@memphisseminary.edu
CL: Narvin Darnall
18030 Beulah Road
Princeton, KY 42445
(279)836-7089
narvin-d@yahoo.com

Madisonville   (4MWC)MICO3615
PO Box 392 (mailing)
1540 Anton Road (physical)
Madisonville, KY 42431
(270)821-5970   <Hopkins>
SS: Shelley Hunt   <M2 ST>
6035 State Route 506
Marion, KY 42064
sheljean@kynet.biz
(270)704-2189
CL: Jean Duncan
330 S Daves Street
Madisonville, KY 42431
(270)821-5138
jduncan42431@att.net

Margaret Hank   (4WC)MICO3415
1526 Park Avenue
Paducah, KY 42001
(270)443-3689   <McCracken>
holyday@vci.net

PA: Christopher Fleming   <M1>
133 Minerva Place
Paducah, KY 42001
(615)424-8561
holyday@vci.net
CL: Amy Fleming
133 Minerva Place
Paducah, KY 42001
(270)443-3689
holyday@vci.net

Marion First   (4MEWC)MICO3616
PO Box 323 (mailing)
224 W Bellville Street (physical)
Marion, KY 42064
(270)965-4746   <Crittenden>
firstcpchurch@mchsi.com
PA: Dee Ann Thompson   <M1>
226 W Bellville Street
Marion, KY 42064
(270)445-0310
deethomp5@hotmail.com
CL: Jo Ann McClure
PO Box 92
Marion, KY 42064
(270)965-3323

Milburn Chapel   (4EC)MICO3416
3760 Metropolis Lake Road
West Paducah, KY 42086
(270)488-2588   <McCracken>
milburnchapel@gmail.com
CL: Joe Neal Neftzger
903 E 6th Street
Metropolis, IL 62960
(618)524-5349
milburnchapel@gmail.com

Mt Carmel   (4MW C)MICO3617
11504 Mt Carmel Road (mailing)
11410 Mt Carmel Road (physical)
White Plains, KY 42464
(270)676-3563   <Hopkins>
bshoulta@bellsouth.net
PA: John R Shoulta   <M1>
11504 Mt Carmel Road
White Plains, KY 42464
(270)676-3563
johnshoulta@bellsouth.net
CL: Larry Putman
1319 Mt Carmel Pond River Road
White Plains, KY 42464
(270)676-3628

Mt Pleasant   (4 C)MICO3618
16647 State Route 109
Sullivan, KY 42460
( )   <Union>
PA: Dale Williams   <M1>
3156 State Route 2837
Clay, KY 42404
(270)664-2044
CL: Richard White
2465 State Route 270 E
Sturgis, KY 42459
(270)333-6109
whitefarms1@att.net

Mt Sterling   (4MWC)MICO5117
1780 Mt Sterling Road
Brookport, IL 62910
(618)564-2616   <Massac>
FAX: (618)564-2616
mscpchurch@yahoo.com
PA: David LeNeave   <M1>
8725 Hamletsburg Road
Brookport, IL 62910
(618)564-2437
mscpchurch_bd@yahoo.com
CL: Gary N Angelly
8646 Independence Road
Brookport, IL 62910
(618)564-2874
FAX: (618)564-2874
angelly@djklink.net

Mt Zion   (4WC)MICO5118
PO Box 383 (mailing)
1159 Mt Zion Road (physical)
Dongola, IL 62926
(618)827-4463   <Union>
jsr487@frontier.com
SS: Donna Davenport   <M1>
PO Box 234
Wingo, KY 42088
chamberdonna@yahoo.com
(270)376-5488
SS: Philip Brown   <M1>
540 Mt Pisgah Road
Dongola, IL 62926
(618)697-0972
brownlp75@yahoo.com
CL: Sharon R. Resch
PO Box 383
Dongola, IL 62926
(618)827-4463
jsr487@frontier.com

New Hope   (4MWC)MICO3410
7620 Cross Mill Road
Paducah, KY 42001
(270)554-0473   <McCracken>
newhopecpchurch@hotmail.com
PA: Curtis Franklin   <M1>
7620 Cross Mill Road
Paducah, KY 42001
(270)625-1898
brocurtis@fredonia.biz
CL: Leslie Wright
6575 New Hope Church Road
Paducah, KY 42001
(270)534-1699
leslie.wright@mccracken.kyschools.us

North Pleasant Grove   (4WC)MICO3411
Murray, KY 42071
( )   <Calloway>
PA: April Watson   <M1>
529 W Bellville
Marion, KY 42064
(270)965-2850
aprilwatson@hotmail.com
CL: Fred Kemp
276 Airport Road
Murray, KY 42071

COVENANT PRESBYTERY CONTINUED

Oak Grove   (4MWC)MICO3412
2465 Magness Road
Benton, KY 42025
(270)437-4606   <Calloway>
PA: Randy Lowe   <M1>
222 McDougal Drive
Murray, KY 42071
(270)753-8255
loweshodle@aol.com
CL: Jeff Gordon
2465 Magness Road
Benton, KY 42025
(270)437-4613
jgordon@wk.net

Oak Grove Union   (4C)MICO3619
Highway 132
Clay, KY 42404
(270)664-0008   <Webster>
jvfulton@wk.net
SS: James V Fulton   <M1>
1520 Oak Grove Road
Benton, KY 42025
(270)437-4320
CL: Daniel M Heady
2564 State Route 132 W
Dixon, KY 42409
(270)748-6848
danielheady@kycourts.net

Oakland   (4MWC)MICO3413
9104 US Highway 68 W
Calvert City, KY 42029
(270)898-2630   <Marshall>
PA: Danny York   <M1>
5420 State Routh 902 W
Fredonia, KY 42411
(270)350-7262
nonnieyork@yahoo.com
CL: John Jenkins
1265 Elva Loop Road
Symsonia, KY 42082
(270)705-3229

Piney Fork   (4WC)MICO3620
4294 Coppers Spring Road
Marion, KY 42064
( )   <Crittenden>
PA: William E Martin, Jr   <M1>
741 Chapel Hill Road
Marion, KY 42064
(870)270-3344
juniormartin@yahoo.com
CL: Sarah Ford
220 S Weldon Street
Marion, KY 42064
(270)965-3833

Pleasant Valley   (4C)MICO3418
111 College Drive
Kevil, KY 42053
(270)224-2497   <Ballard>
SS: April Watson   <M1>
529 W Bellville
Marion, KY 42064
(270)965-2850
aprilwatson@hotmail.com

CL: William E Kilby
PO Box 413
La Center, KY 42056
(270)665-5405

Providence   (4WC)MICO5122
CLOSED 4/11/2015
(membership transferred to Union Chapel)

Providence 1st   (4MEWC)MICO3621
305 Locust Street (mailing)
119 Locust Street (physical)
Providence, KY 42450
(270)667-2485   <Webster>
chalit@apex.net
SS: Paul Stone   <M1>
3490 State Route 2837
Clay, Kentucky 42404
(270)664-6244
stonepstc@aol.com
CL: Paul Northern
317 N Broadway
Providence, KY 42450
(270)667-2636

Rose Creek   (4WC)MICO3622
7650 Island Ford Road (mailing)
Hanson, KY 42413
7220 Rose Creek Road (physical)
Nebo, KY 42441
( )   <Hopkins>
PA: Paul Stone   <M1>
3490 State Route 2837
Clay, KY 42404
(270)664-6244
CL: Joseph E Peyton
7650 Island Ford Road
Hanson, KY 42413
(270)619-0636
jepeyton@madisonville.com

Rozzell Chapel   (4C)MICO3419
1258 Rozzell Church Road
Mayfield, KY 42066
(270)623-6866   <Graves>
PA: D Frederick (Fred) Fahl   <M1>
500 3rd Street
Fulton, KY 42041
(270)472-1476
dffahl@gmail.com
CL: Donna Davenport   <M1>
PO Box 234
Wingo, KY 42088
(270)804-3526
chamberdonna@yahoo.com

Sturgis   (4MWC)MICO3625
504 N Main Street
Sturgis, KY 42459
(270)333-2851   <Union>
FAX: (270)333-3118
sturgiscpc@att.net
PA: Victor Hassell   <M1>
510 N Main Street
Sturgis, KY 42459
(270)333-9170
FAX: (270)333-3118
hassellvictor@hotmail.com

CL: Barbara B Sutton
849 State Route 950
Morganfield, KY 42437
(270)333-4385

Sugar Grove   (4MWC)MICO3626
585 Sugar Grove Church Road
Marion, KY 42064
(270)965-4435   <Crittenden>
CL: Gladys Brown
6781 State Route 120
Marion, KY 42064
(270)965-2969
gbrown6781@live.com

Union Chapel   (4C)MICO5123
PO Box 100 (mailing)
2210 Droit Road (physical)
Galatia, IL 62935
( )   <Saline>
CL: Jennifer Romonosky
PO Box 100
Galatia, IL 62935
realtorjlr@yahoo.com

Unity   (4MWC)MICO3422
1503 Story Avenue (mailing)
Murray, KY 42071
1929 E Unity Church Road (physical)
Hardin, KY 42048
(270)354-8216   <Marshall>
cprevbhayes@gmail.com
PA: Brian Hayes   <M1>
69 Cactus Drive
Benton, KY 42025
(270)210-8165
cprevbhayes@gmail.com
CL: Jonathan Whisman
5352 Murray Highway
Hardin, KY 42048
(270)437-3949
jwhisman@wk.net

Vaughn's Chapel   (4MWC)MICO3423
4775 Calvert City Road
Calvert City, KY 42029
(270)395-7318   <Marshall>
PA: Wendell Ordway   <M1>
4775 Calvert City Road
Calvert City, KY 42029
(270)395-7318
CL: John P Case
93 W Second Avenue
Calvert City, KY 42029
(270)395-4203

Village   (4C)MICO5125
324 County Road 250 N
Norris City, IL 62869
(618)962-3256   <White>
SS: Rudolph Barnett   <M1>
RR 5 Box 267
McLeansboro, IL 62859
(618)643-3253
CL: Charles F Edwards
324 County Road 250 N
Norris City, IL 62869
(618)962-3256
(618)962-3256

<White>

COVENANT PRESBYTERY CONTINUED

_____
Wheatcroft (4WC)MICO3627
PO Box 7 (mailing)
47 Hammock Street E (physical)
Wheatcroft, KY 42463
( ) <Webster>
PA: Dale Williams <M1>
3156 State Route 2837
Clay, KY 42404
(270)664-2802
dalewilliams@roadrunner.com
CL: Jackie Gass
147 Blackford-Sullivan Road
Clay, KY 42404
(270)664-9310

_____
Woodlawn (4MWC)MICO3417
3402 Old Benton Road
Paducah, KY 42002
(270)442-7713 <McCracken>
woodlawnchurch@live.com
PA: David Fackler <M1>
3409 Benton Road
Paducah, KY 42003
(270)442-7713
woodlawnpastor@live.com
CL: Todd Belt
3402 Old Benton Road
Paducah, KY 42002
(270)442-7713
woodlawnyouth@msn.com

_____
OTHERS ON MINISTERIAL ROLL:

Aden, Dare <M1 WC>
1280 Kimber Road
Dongola, IL 62926
(618)827-3625
FAX: (618)827-4612
dare_aden@hotmail.com
Ballow, Brent <M1 WC>
715 Highland Church Road
Paducah, KY 42001
(270)564-8891
hcppastor@bellsouth.net
Board, N Ray <M1 WC>
267 State Route 293 N
Princeton, KY 42445
(270)365-3850
rayboard@att.net
French, Jeff <M1 WC>
5 Rose Petal Lane
Dawson Springs, KY 42408
(270)993-0855
brojeff7@bellsouth.net
Gerard, Eugene S <M1 OM>
615 N 42nd Street
Paducah, KY 42001
(270)443-2889
Guarneros, Stephen H <M1 WC>
506 Clifton Court
Hopkinsville, KY 42240
(270)869-7544
pastorsteve88@yahoo.com
Heidel, Jason <M1 WC>
218 Morningside Drive
Hopkinsville, KY 42240
(270)498-7380
heidelj@hotmail.com

Hughes, Douglas <M1 WC>
5545 Hocker Road
Paducah, KY 42001
(270)488-2588
milburnchapel@gmail.com
Lawson, James <M1 OM>
1003 West 3rd Street
Fulton, KY 42041
(270)472-5272
ridgepointefarm@bellsouth.net
Lively, Louella <M1 WC>
196 Vicksburg Estate Road
Benton, KY 42025
(270)527-3776
Mays, Ronald B <M1 PR>
1100 Cindy Lane
Mayfield, KY 42066
(270)247-0070
rbmays@wk.net
Moore, Hillman C <M1 RT>
300 Medical Parkway Ste 2320
Lakeway, TX 78738
(731)437-9561
hillmancm@att.net
Murrie, Willard <M1 RT>
506 11th Street
Vienna, IL 62995
(618)658-2430
Potts, Danny <M1 WC>
418 Eddings Street Apt 2
Fulton, KY 42041
(270)376-2901
Rudolph, Allie D <M1 WC>
855 Old Rosebower Church Road
Paducah, KY 42003
(270)898-4903
rallie307@aol.com
Shauf, Steve <M1 WC>
3032 Monroe Street
Paducah, KY 42001
(870)346-5021
sshauf@hotmail.com
Shauf, Teresa <M1 WC>
3032 Monroe Street
Paducah, KY 42001
(870)291-2938
theshaufs@hotmail.com
Shirey, John <M1 RT>
10181 State Route 56 W
Sturgis, KY 42459
(270)389-3562
amshirey7@ips.com
Vasseur, Terry <M1 WC>
121 Crossland Road
Murray, KY 42071
(270)554-2468
tvasseur@bellsouth.net
Westfall, Charles K <M1 RT>
94 Honeysuckle Drive
Gilbertsville, KY 42044
(270)362-0816
Williams, David J <M1 WC>
20 Acorn Drive
Harrisburg, IL 62946
(618)252-1851

_____
OTHER LICENTIATES ON ROLL:

Cain, Greg <M2 ST>
2500 Vernon Street Ext B-3
Union City, TN 38261
(731)445-4446
greg.cain07@gmail.com
Hopkins, Daniel <M2 ST>
1608 Oak Park Boulevard
Calvert City, KY 42029
(270)205-1847
danielhopkins2469@yahoo.com
Kerner, Leanne <M2 ST>
156 State Route 348
W Symsonia, KY 42082
(270)851-9709
cooldoll@bellsouth.net

_____
OTHER CANDIDATES ON ROLL:

Alderson, Cameron <M3 ST>
122 E Cherry Street
Chandler, IN 47610
(812)925-6475
Ashley, Jack (Nick) <M3 ST>
2625A Raleigh Drive
Evansville, IN 47715
(812)204-1422
edencateringusa@aol.com
Hassell, Samantha <M3 ST>
510 N Main Street
Sturgis, KY 42459
(270)333-9170
hassell_samantha@hotmail.com
Hopkins, Wayne <M3 ST>
1413 E Unity Church Road
Hardin, KY 42048
(270)437-4481
Impastato, Paulino <M3>
1547 Mt Zion Church Road
Marion, KY 42064
(270)965-9528
Luthy, Dusty
400 S Friendship Road Apt G
Paducah, KY 42003
(270)933-2722
dustyluthy@gmail.com

Cumberland Presbytery
MIDWEST SYNOD

	GENERAL	MEMBERSHIP			CHANGES				FINANCES				
	1.Church Number	2.Active	3.Total	4.Church School	5.Prof. of Faith	6.Gains	7.Losses	8.Children Baptized	9. OUR UNITED OUT-REACH	10. Total Out-Reach Giving	11. All Other Expenses	12. Total Income Received	13. Value Church Prop. 1=1000
	1	2	3	4	5	6	7	8	9	10	11	12	13
Antioch	3101	30	30	16	No Report Received			0	0	0	0	0	300
Auburn	3301	57	100	30	No Report Received			0	0	0	0	0	405
Bald Knob	3302	40	143	32	No Report Received			0	0	0	0	0	250
Bethel	3102	62	62	28	0	1	1	1	2,000	3,956	49,569	31,649	0
Bethel #1	3103	14	71	11	0	2	0	1	1,000	1,984	21,645	16,789	200
Beulah*	3501	22	26	44	0	0	13	0	2,528	4,209	45,845	26,777	123
Boiling Springs	3303	16	19	14	No Report Received			0	0	0	0	0	27
Bowling Green**	3304	150	230	73	3	6	209	2	11,088	28,627	225,615	252,742	1,100
Bridgeport 1st	3131	108	108	23	No Report Received			0	0	0	0	0	651
Brier Creek	3503	85	159	65	0	1	2	0	9,828	15,670	72,316	87,986	300
Campbellsville	3104	84	92	38	4	0	94	0	0	11,597	141,502	139,261	1,700
Caneyville	3201	3	5	27	0	0	0	0	0	800	14,165	14,661	157
Casey's Fork	3105	14	19	14	No Report Received			0	1,151	0	0	0	37
Cedar Flat*	3106	18	58	25	0	0	5	0	0	1,200	20,093	23,366	90
Clear Point*	3107	26	48	18	0	0	19	0	1,496	1,459	29,704	14,962	175
Clifton Mills	3202	12	35	48	0	0	3	0	0	3,989	18,082	20,583	274
Coyle**	3203	26	31	24	0	0	112	0	0	2,024	36,136	38,160	200
Dukes	3204	12	49	7	No Report Received			0	0	0	0	0	300
Ephesus	3205	12	24	12	0	0	41	0	0	1,000	8,689	10,770	150
Fairview	3504	7	28	0	No Report Received			0	1,286	0	0	0	20
Freedom	3207	63	89	52	0	1	3	0	1,472	10,367	85,022	88,323	450
Garfield*	3208	60	112	51	10	4	1	1	0	12,555	86,632	98,924	495
Gasper River	3306	36	49	20	No Report Received			0	0	0	0	0	105
Gill's Chapel	3307	7	23	0	0	0	1	0	0	1,607	12,388	13,302	34
Glasgow	3108	177	229	103	4	25	2	2	0	4,672	127,672	168,157	2,600
Good Hope	3109	25	25	25	No Report Received			0	352	0	0	0	50
Green Ridge	3308	36	58	17	No Report Received			0	5,717	0	0	0	450
Greensburg*	3110	133	133	52	1	1	48	1	11,168	17,006	101,271	103,652	1,000
Greenville	3505	18	49	0	0	0	0	4	1,000	3,848	38,297	48,370	535
Harrodsburg*	3111	18	136	12	2	7	0	0	1,117	3,869	0	21,850	383
Heartsong	3222	25	25	0	No Report Received			0	0	0	0	0	1,650
High Point	3314	20	20	8	0	0	3	0	0	850	15,916	11,732	500
Hopewell	3112	14	25	14	No Report Received			0	0	0	0	0	60
Irvington*	3210	24	26	10	0	1	0	0	0	980	21,100	23,226	86
Leitchfield	3211	50	77	25	5	5	2	2	2,750	7,009	62,589	68,486	550
Lewisburg	3309	28	70	29	0	0	3	0	1,250	6,036	66,848	83,195	300
Liberty	3116	30	58	12	No Report Received			0	0	0	0	0	750
Lick Branch	3117	64	191	38	No Report Received			0	0	0	0	0	90
Little Muddy	3310	19	19	15	0	0	0	0	2,783	6,836	23,171	41,168	119
Louisville 1st	3212	64	126	38	No Report Received			0	0	0	0	0	1,000
Magnolia**	3214	65	73	35	0	0	103	1	0	14,132	60,997	70,456	550
Monroe Chapel	3119	35	56	24	1	3	1	2	2,114	3,614	27,963	30,117	150
Morgantown	3311	21	21	6	No Report Received			0	0	0	0	0	80
Mt. Moriah	3120	16	32	12	2	2	0	0	0	708	15,376	22,667	62
Mt. Olive*	3216	17	17	9	0	4	0	0	0	1,878	18,588	21,226	70
Mt. Olivet	3312	35	42	20	2	3	0	0	500	1,050	41,502	39,095	1,121
Mt. Pleasant	3217	50	68	40	0	0	0	0	4,211	6,467	74,263	42,079	175
Mt. Vernon	3218	24	32	14	0	0	2	1	0	875	19,492	25,991	70
Mt. Zion (AC)	3121	5	18	8	No Report Received			0	0	0	0	0	0
Mt. Zion (DC)	3507	30	62	25	0	0	0	0	3,114	8,688	39,127	44,971	255
Neal's Chapel	3122	25	43	9	0	0	3	0	0	2,368	18,435	19,843	150
Needham	3219	16	16	8	0	1	8	0	0	1,092	30,047	16,072	6
New Cypress	3508	11	27	6	0	0	14	0	1,003	1,330	12,062	10,897	122
Oak Forest	3123	102	216	88	0	4	10	0	7,925	16,600	64,800	76,700	115
Owensboro	3509	123	123	63	0	15	10	4	6,763	21,180	280,483	227,852	1,646
Pleasant Hill	3510	4	5	4	No Report Received			0	0	0	0	0	230
Point Pleasant	3313	5	5	0	No Report Received			0	0	0	0	0	0

Cumberland Presbytery   (Continued)
MIDWEST SYNOD

	GENERAL	2.Active 3.Total 4.Church School	MEMBERSHIP		5.Prof. of Faith 6.Gains 7.Losses 8.Children Baptized	CHANGES			9. OUR UNITED OUT-REACH	10. Total Out-Reach Giving	11. All Other Expenses	12. Total Income Received	FINANCES 13. Value Church Prop. 1=1000
	1.Church Number												
	1	2	3	4	5	6	7	8	9	10	11	12	13
Poplar Grove	3511	8	41	6	0	0	0	0	1,789	1,789	22,406	17,882	90
Radcliff	3220	28	28	14	No Report Received			0	0	0	0	0	237
Sacramento	3512	107	210	85	2	4	3	2	12,249	24,549	95,949	122,498	134
Salem	3127	9	32	0	No Report Received			0	0	0	0	0	35
Seven Springs	3128	16	35	18	No Report Received			0	0	0	0	0	267
Shiloh	3129	40	86	26	2	2	1	0	7,440	14,028	67,010	60,190	400
Short Creek	3221	21	54	19	0	0	0	0	2,917	7,937	16,922	29,174	95
Wisdom*	3130	30	30	10	0	3	0	0	0	840	7,391	0	75
TOTALS	65	2,624	4,326	1,626	38	95	718	24	111,011	283,173	2,260,396	2,376,197	23,438

*Math error corrected. **Purged roll.

CHURCHES, PASTORS, AND CLERKS:

Antioch   (4C)MICU3101
103 Clarksdale Circle (mailing)
Glasgow, KY 42141
68 Antioch Church Road (physical)
Knob Lick, KY 42154
( )   <Metcalfe>
SS: Michael E Fancher   <M3>
356 Breeding Road
Edmonton, KY 42129
(270)432-3138
princo1975@live.com
CL: Kathy B Nason
103 Clarksdale Circle
Glasgow, KY 42141
(270)670-4796

Auburn   (4MWC)MICU3301
Box 6
Auburn, KY 42206
(270)542-4304   <Logan>
PA: Grant Minton   <M1>
PO Box 270
Auburn, KY 42206
(270)542-7991
FAX: (270)271-4603
gminton@logantele.com
CL: Ashley Engler
695 Howlett Road
Auburn, KY 42206
(270)542-6730

Bald Knob   (4C)MICU3302
102 Bald Knob Church Road
Russellville, KY 42276
( )   <Logan>
PA: Byron Dumas   <M1 OP>
1775 Theresa Drive
Clarksville, TN 37043
(931)358-3348
lodumas7346@aol.com

CL: Kathleen Tynes
3175 Caney Fork Road
Lewisburg, KY 42256
(270)755-4218

Bethel   (2WC)MICU3102
454 Iron Mountain Road (mailing)
Center, KY 42214
( )   <Metcalfe>
SS: Keith G Atwell   <M1>
7688 Hardyville Road
Hardyville, KY 42746
(270)528-3667
CL: Steven McMullen
454 Iron Mountain Road
Center, KY 42214
(270)565-5440
mcmfarm@yahoo.com

Bethel #1   (4MWC)MICU3103
1259 Perryville Road (mailing)
2586 Perryville Road (physical)
Harrodsburg, KY 40330
( )   <Mercer>
PA: John Contini   <M1>
4344 Poor Ridge Pike
Lancaster, KY 40444
(859)339-0747
john@hillsideheritagefarm.com
CL: James L Wheeler
1259 Perryville Road
Harrodsburg, KY 40330
(859)734-2045
jlwheeler@roadrunner.com

Beulah   (4WC)MICU3501
PO Box 233 (mailing)
320 Beulah Church Road (physical)
Hartford, KY 42347
(270)298-3352   <Ohio>
FAX: (270)298-7007
cmwsaw2@bellsouth.net

PA: Michael Justice   <M1>
250 W 5th Street #B
Russellville, KY 42276
(270)726-6673
CL: Chuck Westerfield
PO Box 233
Hartford, KY 42347
(270)298-3352
FAX: (270)298-7007
smwsaw@connectgradd.net

Boiling Springs   (4C)MICU3303
3360 Highway 259 (mailing)
2412 Highway 259 (physical)
Portland, TN 37148
(615)325-2618   <Sumner>
PA: Chris Darland   <M1>
582 Ada Drive
Harrodsburg, KY 40330
(859)734-2254
CL: Pearl Kepley
3380 Highway 259
Portland, TN 37148
(615)325-3645

Bowling Green   (4MWC)MICU3304
807 Campbell Lane
Bowling Green, KY 42104
(270)781-3295   <Warren>
FAX: (270)781-2368
bgcpc@insightbb.com
PA: Steve Delashmit   <M1>
2705 Garrett Drive
Bowling Green, KY 42104
(270)796-8822
FAX: (270)781-2368
CL: Hoy Hodges
295 Carver Lane
Alvaton, KY 42122
(270)843-4008
hhlaw319@aol.com

CUMBERLAND PRESBYTERY CONTINUED

Bridgeport 1st   (4C)MICU3131
515 DeKalb Street
Bridgeport, PA 19405
(610)275-6942   <Philadelphi>
PA: Donald Grey Barnhouse, Jr   <M1>
51 Harristown Road
Paradise, PA 17562
(717)768-0048
donaldbarnhouse@gmail.com
CL: William McLay
9 E Brown Street
Norristown, PA 19401
(610)277-8295

Brier Creek   (4MWC)MICU3503
3467 State Route 175 N
Bremen, KY 42325
(270)525-3611   <Muhlenberg>
PA: Marc Bell   <M1>
3467 State Route 175 N
Bremen, KY 42325
(270)846-4203
marcbell@insightbb.com
CL: Sherry Skimehorn
59 Whitmer Street
Central City, KY 42330
(270)525-3472
skimehor@bellsouth.net

Campbellsville   (4MWC)MICU3104
500 Cumberland Way
Campbellsville, KY 42718
(270)465-4091   <Taylor>
FAX: (270)469-9651
firstcpchurch@windstream.net
PA: Wayne E Brooks   <M1>
1505 Parkview Drive
Campbellsville, KY 42718
(270)465-9235
webrooks@windstream.net
CL: Faye Adams
902 Rosecrest Avenue
Campbellsville, KY 42718
(270)789-1791
newlifeblessed@yahoo.com

Caneyville   (4EWC)MICU3201
PO Box 334 (mailing)
203 River Park Drive (physical)
Caneyville, KY 42721
( )   <Grayson>
PS: Steven Smith   <M3 ST>
100 Valleyview Drive
Leitchfield, KY 42754
CL: Mary Alice Woosley-Logsdon
PO Box 334
Leitchfield, KY 42721
(270)230-2818
FAX: (270)879-9211
alicewoosley71@yahoo.com

Casey's Fork   (1C)MICU3105
PO Box 186 (mailing)
Highway 90 (physical)
Marrowbone, KY 42759
(502)864-3129   <Cumberland>
CL: Jimmy Mosby
210 Bombshell Creek Road
Burkesville, KY 42717

Cedar Flat   (C)MICU3106
1444 Milam Clark Road (mailing)
Summer Shade, KY 42166
Cedar Flat - Curtis Road (physical)
Edmonton, KY 42129
( )   <Metcalfe>
CL: Janet A Proffitt
1444 Milam Clark Road
Summer Shade, KY 42166
(270)428-4379

Clear Point   (4MWEC)MICU3107
7895 S Jackson Highway
Horse Cave, KY 42749
( )   <Hart>
PA: Darrell Pickett   <M1>
113 Woods Drive
Glasgow, KY 42141
(270)834-6102
dpickett@glasgow-ky.com
CL: Barbara Ogden
7895 S Jackson Highway
Horse Cave, KY 42749
(270)786-2695

Clifton Mills   (4WC)MICU3202
521 Butler Hobbs Road (mailing)
Hardinsburg, KY 40143
6406 W Highway 86 (physical)
Irvington, KY 40146
(270)547-5717   <Breckinridge>
PA: Don Bruington   <M1>
PO Box 105
Falls of Rough, KY 40119
(270)257-2228
CL: Edna M Hobbs
521 Butler Hobbs Road
Hardinsburg, KY 40143
(270)756-2592
tejthbs@att.net

Coyle   (4C)MICU3203
1285 Centerview Rough River Lane
Hudson, KY 40145
(270)257-0851   <Breckinridge>
tucker_rd@bellsouth.net
PA: Billy Ray Carter   <M1>
33 Mockingbird Drive
Leitchfield, KY 42754
(270)259-3897
cartercbc@windstream.net
CL: Ralph D Tucker
1285 Centerview Rough River Lane
Hudson, KY 40145
(270)257-0851
tucker_rd@bellsouth.net

Dukes   (4C)MICU3204
4743 Happy Hollow Road (mailing)
7814 State Route 144 E (physical)
Hawesville, KY 42348
(270)927-9577   <Hancock>
kimwilborn@yahoo.com
SS: Kimberley Wilborn   <M3>
4743 Happy Hollow Road
Hawesville, KY 42348
(270)927-9577
kimwilborn@yahoo.com

CL: Joe Wilborn
4743 Happy Hollow Road
Hawesville, KY 42348
(270)927-9577
joeandkimwilborn@bellsouth.net

Ephesus   (4EC)MICU3205
2300 Ephesus Church Road (mailing)
30 Ephesus Church Loop (physical)
Harned, KY 40144
( )   <Breckinridge>
bridget.keesee@ky.gov
CL: Bridget Keesee
2300 Ephesus Church Road
Harned, KY 40144
(270)756-9278
bridget.keesee@ky.gov

Fairview   (4C)MICU3504
PO Box 195 (mailing)
Sacramento, KY 42372
Fairview Road (physical)
Bremen, KY
(270)736-5189   <Muhlenberg>
CL: Ottis E Markwell
PO Box 195
Sacramento, KY 42372
(270)736-5189

Freedom   (4MWC)MICU3207
224 John Drane Lane (mailing)
394 John Drane Lane (physical)
Harned, KY 40144
(270)617-4016   <Breckinridge>
PA: Jeff McMichael   <M1>
224 John Drane Lane
Harned, KY 40144
(270)617-4016
revmcmichael@outlook.com
CL: Larry Collard
4634 Highway 261 N
Hardinsburg, KY 40143
(270)617-0609

Garfield   (4MWC)MICU3208
PO Box 39 (mailing)
90 W Highway 86 (physical)
Garfield, KY 40140
(270)580-4796   <Breckinridge>
mccallum@bbtel.com
PA: Frank McCallum   <M1>
PO Box 56
Garfield, KY 40140
(270)580-4796
mccallum@bbtel.com
CL: Stephen J Tabor
PO Box 39
Garfield, KY 40140
(270)536-3297
btabor@bbtel.com

Gasper River   (4C)MICU3306
3201 Bucksville Road (mailing)
3005 Bucksville Road (physical)
Auburn, KY 42206
(270)542-8998   <Logan>
SS: Byron Dumas   <M1 OP>
1775 Theresa Drive
Clarksville, TN 37043
(931)358-3348

CUMBERLAND PRESBYTERY CONTINUED

CL: Sandy Tinsley
3201 Bucksville Road
Auburn, KY 42206
(270)542-7900
tinsley@logantele.com

_____

Gill's Chapel   (4EC)MICU3307
PO Box 127 (mailing)
Lewisburg, KY 42256
955 Hermon Road (physical)
Guthrie, KY 42234
(270)755-4282   <Todd>
sam60romines@hotmail.com
PA: Sam Romines   <M1>
PO Box 127
Lewisburg, KY 42256
(270)755-4282
sam60romines@hotmail.com
CL: Sam Romines
PO Box 127
Lewisburg, KY 42256
(270)755-4282
sam60romines@hotmail.com

_____

Glasgow   (4MWC)MICU3108
101 Cumberland Street
Glasgow, KY 42141
(270)651-3308   <Barren>
gcpc@glasgow-ky.com
CL: Buelon R (Pete) Moss
101 Cumberland Street
Glasgow, KY 42141
(270)646-0305
mossbue@auburn.edu

_____

Good Hope   (2C)MICU3109
700 Dutton Creek Road (mailing)
Lemon Bend Road (physical)
Campbellsville, KY 42718
(270)789-1482   <Taylor>
glwgaw@windstream.net
PA: Earl West   <M1>
246 Maple Avenue
Greensburg, KY 42743
(207)932-5010
west5010@windstream.net
CL: Gayle Whitley
700 Dutton Creek Road
Campbellsville, KY 42718
(270)789-1482
glwgaw@windstream.net

_____

Green Ridge   (4MWC)MICU3308
7424 Highland Lick Road
Lewisburg, KY 42256
(270)726-8497   <Logan>
brojoe2@logantele.com
PA: Joseph R Vaught   <M1>
7424 Highland Lick Road
Lewisburg, KY 42256
(270)726-8497
brojoe2@logantele.com
CL: Shannon Wells
1720 Crawford Road
Lewisburg, KY 42256
(270)277-9977
chps@bellsouth.net

_____

Greensburg   (4MEWC)MICU3110
699 Old Hodgenville Road
Greensburg, KY 42743
(270)932-4864   <Green>
greensburgcpc@windstream.net
PA: Kevin T Brantley   <M1>
729 Old Hodgenville Road
Greensburg, KY 42743
(270)932-3780
kbrantley1971@windstream.net
CL: Amy Beard
699 Old Hodgenville Road
Greensburg, KY 42743
(270)932-4864
greensburgcpc@windstream.net

_____

Greenville   (4WC)MICU3505
234 Sunset Park (mailing)
108 S Cherry Street (physical)
Greenville, KY 42345
(270)338-0882   <Muhlenberg>
PA: Arthur L Burrows, Jr   <M1>
PO Box 511
Hopkinsville, KY 42241
(270)886-1301
CL: Joseph Harris
234 Sunset Park
Greenville, KY 42345
(270)338-6555
josephharris234@yahoo.com

_____

Harrodsburg   (4MWC)MICU3111
1113 Louisville Road
Harrodsburg, KY 40330
( )   <Mercer>
PA: Geoff Barrett   <M1>
155 Maude Lane
Harrodsburg, KY 40330
(859)748-0450
glbarrett@live.com
CL: Nancy R Tatum
4955 Louisville Road
Salvisa, KY 40372
(859)865-4482

_____

Heartsong   (4C)MICU3222
6322 Labor Lane (mailing)
6800 S Hurstbourne Parkway (physical)
Louisville, KY 40291
(502)635-8587   <Jefferson>
PA: Drew Gray   <M1>
8220 Timberland Drive
West Paducah, KY 42086
(270)331-5569
drewgray01@gmail.com
CL: Susan Lawson
6322 Labor Lane
Louisville, KY 40291
(502)968-0006

_____

High Point Community   (C)MICU3314
610 Walnut Street (mailing)
Somerset, KY 42501
190 Longview Drive (physical)
West Somerset, KY 42503
(606)271-0842   <Pulaski>
highpointcpc@gmail.com

PA: Fred Michael (Mike) Adams   <M1>
42 Julies Way
Somerset, KY 42503
(606)451-9155
fma46@twc.com
CL: Betty Huffman
610 Walnut Street
Somerset, KY 42501
(606)561-3645
betty.huffman@hotmail.com

_____

Hopewell   (4C)MICU3112
1012 N Jackson Highway (mailing)
Hardyville, KY 42746
Hopewell Church Road (physical)
Canmer, KY 42722
( )   <Hart>
CL: Kaye Atwell
1012 N Jackson Highway
Hardyville, KY 42746
(270)528-5341
mkatwell@yahoo.com

_____

Irvington   (4MWC)MICU3210
4108 Highway 477 (mailing)
Webster, KY 40176
111 W Walnut Street (physical)
Irvington, KY 40146
( )   <Breckinridge>
PA: Charles Meredith   <M1>
144 Barbara Circle
Elizabethtown, KY 42701
(270)307-0607
CL: Ruby Bell
4108 Highway 477
Webster, KY 40176
(270)547-7455
rrbells@bbtel.com

_____

Leitchfield   (4MC)MICU3211
501 W Chestnut Street
Leitchfield, KY 42754
(270)259-3835   <Grayson>
PA: Jim Butler   <M1>
507 W Chestnut Street
Leitchfield, KY 42754
(502)635-8587
jbutler54@insightbb.com
CL: Arita French
245 Embry Road
Leitchfield, KY 42754
(270)259-4457
kenarita@windstream.net

_____

Lewisburg   (4MWC)MICU3309
PO Box 127 (mailing)
101 Church Street (physical)
Lewisburg, KY 42256
(270)755-4282   <Logan>
PA: Sam Romines   <M1>
PO Box 127
Lewisburg, KY 42256
(270)755-4282
sam60romines@hotmail.com
CL: Ralph Cropper
178 Cardinal Street
Lewisburg, KY 42256
(270)755-2357
ralph.cropper@novelis.com

CUMBERLAND PRESBYTERY CONTINUED

Liberty   (4WC)MICU3116
PO Box 4105 (mailing)
4139 Old Columbia Road (physical)
Campbellsville, KY 42718
(270)849-7377   <Taylor>
PA: Earl West   <M1>
246 Maple Avenue
Greensburg, KY 42743
(207)932-5010
west5010@windstream.net
CL: Barbara Davenport
216 Happy Hill Drive
Campbellsville, KY 42718
(270)465-3633
teebdee@windstream.net

Lick Branch   (4C)MICU3117
50 B Jones Road (mailing)
7318 Lecta Kino Road (physical)
Glasgow, KY 42141
(270)670-6698   <Barren>
doncynem@gmail.com
OD: Jerry D Martin   <M5>
292 Bristletown Road
Glasgow, KY 42141
(270)678-2476
doncynem@glasgow-ky.com
CL: Nancy Jolly
2979 Kino Road
Glasgow, KY 42141
(270)428-5722
jollyfarms@scrtc.com

Little Muddy   (4MC)MICU3310
1061 Sugar Grove Road (mailing)
170 Little Muddy Church Road (physical)
Morgantown, KY 42261
( )   <Butler>
CL: William Gabe Keen
822 Sugar Grove Road
Morgantown, KY 42261
(270)526-5895

Louisville 1st   (4MWC)MICU3212
4610 Manslick Road
Louisville, KY 40216
(502)368-4709   <Jefferson>
FAX: (502)368-4709
firstcumberland@att.net
PA: Rodney E Harris   <M1>
7420 Conjar Court
Louisville, KY 40214
(502)368-5501
rodneypat@insightbb.com
CL: Carrie Roth
4610 Manslick Road
Louisville, KY 40216
(502)368-4709
firstcumberland@att.net

Louisville Japanese   (4C)MICU3223
8710 Hickory Falls Lane
Pewee Valley, KY 40056
(502)657-9643
PA: Iwao Satoh
8710 Hickory Falls Lane
Pewee Valley, KY 40056
(502)657-9643
iwaosatoh@gmail.com

CL: Session Clerk
8710 Hickory Falls Lane
Pewee Valley, KY 40056
(502)657-9643

Magnolia   (4MWC)MICU3214
PO Box 1 (mailing)
235 Old L and N Turkpike (physical)
Magnolia, KY 42757
(270)324-3472   <LaRue>
magnoliacpchurch@gmail.com
SS: Anthony Harris   <M2>
1604 Parkview Drive
Campbellsville, KY 42718
(270)403-1126
aharris044@gmail.com
CL: Charlotte Tucker
1080 Greensburg Road
Hodgenville, KY 42748
(270)358-3090
charlotte.tucker@larue.kyschools.ust

Monroe Chapel   (4C)MICU3119
7688 Hardyville Road (mailing)
Rt 2 Highway 88 (physical)
Hardyville, KY 42746
(270)528-3667   <Hart>
jbuggforbis@hotmail.com
SS: Richard Harrison   <M3>
93 Earl Jones Road
Hodgenville, KY 42748
CL: Janie B Forbis
2465 Possum Trot Road
Hardyville, KY 42746
(270)528-3873
jbuggforbis@hotmail.com

Morgantown   (4MWC)MICU3311
308 Helm Lane (mailing)
118 W Ohio Street (physical)
Morgantown, KY 42261
( )   <Butler>
SS: David Hocker   <M3>
309 N Taylor Street
Morgantown, KY 42261
(270)526-6027
dhocker@hocker.com
CL: Carolyn Henderson
308 Helm Lane
Morgantown, KY 42261
(270)526-3439

Mt Moriah   (2C)MICU3120
107 James Street (mailing)
Edmonton, KY 42129
2038 Mt Moriah Road (physical)
Summer Shade, KY 42166
( )   <Metcalfe>
CL: Sandy England
107 James Street
Edmonton, KY 42129
(270)432-3778
englandsim@scrtc.com

Mt Olive   (4WC)MICU3216
1295 Solway Meeting Road (mailing)
Mt Olive Church Road (physical)
Big Clifty, KY 42712
( )   <Hardin>

CL: Gayle Johnson
1295 Solway Meeting Road
Big Clifty, KY 42712
(270)862-4313
vonnie.g0000@yahoo.com

Mt Olivet   (4MEWC)MICU3312
2640 Mt Olivet Road
Bowling Green, KY 42101
(270)843-0223   <Warren>
SS: Robert (Bob) Bunnell   <M1>
329 Lexington Drive
Glasgow, KY 42141
(270)629-6209
bob_bunnell@yahoo.com
CL: Betty Grammer
180 Sir Wilburn Way
Alvaton, KY 42122
(270)781-4435
thememaw02@walmartconnect.com

Mt Pleasant   (4C)MICU3217
364 E Big Reedy Road (mailing)
E Big Reedy Road (physical)
Caneyville, KY 42721
( )   <Edmonson>
PS: Greg Bowen   <M3 ST>
3241 South Fork Road
Glasgow, KY 42141
CL: Gloria Slaughter
364 E Big Reedy Road
Caneyville, KY 42721
(270)286-9372
gslaughter@mtownbank.com

Mt Vernon   (4WC)MICU3218
1870 Brandenburg Road (mailing)
2373 Brandenburg Road (physical)
Leitchfield, KY 42754
( )   <Grayson>
PA: William M Macy   <M1>
1358 Ephesus Church Road
Harned, KY 40144
(270)756-2775
CL: Marcella Lucas
1870 Brandenburg Road
Leitchfield, KY 42754
(270)259-9215

Mt. Zion (AC)   (1C)MICU3121
c/o Lena Bryson
1925 Loren Collins Road
Glens Fork, KY 42741
( )   <Adair>
CL: Lena Bryson
214 Buell Collins Road
Glens Fork, KY 42741
(502)378-6172

Mt Zion (DC)   (4MWC)MICU3507
7447 Knottsville Mt Zion Rd (mailing)
8001 Knottsville Mt Zion Rd (physical)
Philpot, KY 42366
( )   <Daviess>
PA: Dennis J Preston   <M1>
7447 Knottsville Mount Zion Road
Philpot, KY 42366
(270)925-8144
dennis.preston@daviess.kyschools.us

CUMBERLAND PRESBYTERY CONTINUED

CL: Shirley L Bratcher
3815 Locust Hill Drive
Owensboro, KY 42303
(270)993-4056
slbratcher24@yahoo.com

Neal's Chapel   (4C)MICU3122
62 Oscar Gilpin Road (mailing)
860 Lecta Kino Road (physical)
Glasgow, KY 42141
( )   <Barren>
CL: Pam H Browning
62 Oscar Gilpin Road
Glasgow, KY 42141
(270)670-1047
pshbrowning@hotmail.com

Needham   (4WC)MICU3219
3179 Meeting Creek Road (mailing)
State Route 84 (physical)
Eastview, KY 42732
( )   <Hardin>
PA: Shelby O Haire   <M1>
3179 Meeting Creek Road
Eastview, KY 42732
(270)862-3887
CL: Odelia Dewall
2548 Meeting Creek Road
Eastview, KY 42732
(270)862-4362

New Cypress   (4C)MICU3508
127 W 23rd Street (mailing)
Owensboro, KY 42303
4814 Highway 81 S (physical)
Rumsey, KY 42371
( )   <McLean>
PA: Terry Fortner   <M1>
1079 Luzerne Depoy Road
Greenville, KY 42345
(270)836-3635
terryfortner@att.net
CL: Phyllis Davis
127 W 23rd Street
Owensboro, KY 42303
(270)926-6033
phyllisdavis966@hotmail.com

Oak Forest   (4MWC)MICU3123
170 Milby Rattliff Road
Summersville, KY 42782
(270)932-4685   <Green>
OD: Robert Knight   <M5>
1360 Free Union Road
Columbia, KY 42728
(270)384-0677
CL: Mike Durrett
170 Milby Rattliff Road
Summersville, KY 42782
(270)932-4685
thedurretts@windstream.net

Owensboro   (4C)MICU3509
910 Booth Avenue
Owensboro, KY 42301
(270)683-4479   <Daviess>
brotim.cpc@gmail.net

PA: Timothy McGuire   <M1>
PO Box 42
Mt Sherman, KY 42764
(270)766-9027
brotim.cpc@gmail.com
CL: Becky Pedigo
2508 Duke Drive Apt 10
Owensboro, KY 42301
(270)999-8301
becky_pdg@yahoo.com

Pleasant Hill   (4MEC)MICU3510
10851 Highway 593
Owensboro, KY 42301
(386)689-9340   <Daviess>
CL: Carole Robertson
4709 Forrest Drive
Owensboro, KY 42303
(270)315-5288

Point Pleasant   (1C)MICU3313
7030 State Route 269
Beaver Dam, KY 42320
( )   <Butler>
SS: David Hocker   <M3>
309 N Taylor Street
Morgantown, KY 42261
(270)526-6027
CL: Kathy Pharris
7030 State Route 269
Beaver Dam, KY 42320
(270)274-7418
kathyspharris@yahoo.com

Poplar Grove   (4WC)MICU3511
2929 Kentucky 254 W (mailing)
5112 State Highway 1155 (physical)
Sacramento, KY 42372
( )   <McLean>
PA: James E Talley   <M1>
203 Browning Place
Hopkinsville, KY 42240
(270)886-4184
CL: Gibson H Riggs
PO Box 224
Calhoun, KY 42327
(270)273-3280
FAX: (270)273-3280
riggsg@bellsouth.net

Radcliff   (4U)MICU3220
1751 S Logsdon Parkway
Radcliff, KY 40159
(270)351-6199   <Hardin>
radpres@bbtel.com
OD: John Lentz   <M5>
1876 Highway 44 E
Shepherdsville, KY 40165
(502)543-2659
lentzhome@aol.com
CL: Patricia T. Crosby
851 S Archer Street
Radcliff, KY 40160
(270)351-8548
ptcrosby@bbtel.com

Sacramento   (4MWC)MICU3512
PO Box 257 (mailing)
40 Lyons Lane (physical)
Sacramento, KY 42372
(270)736-5176   <McLean>
jbutler@iccable.com
PA: John Butler   <M1>
PO Box 257
Sacramento, KY 42372
(270)736-2268
jbutler@iccable.com
CL: Brenda Lee
386 Dillahay Dame Loop
Island, KY 42350
(270)736-5160

Salem   (2C)MICU3127
1570 Old Salem Church Road (mailing)
291 Clay Wright Road (physical)
Greensburg, KY 42743
( )   <Green>
CL: Joan Cook
1570 Old Salem Church Road
Greensburg, KY 42743
(502)932-5717

Seven Springs   (2C)MICU3128
1607 Seven Springs Church Road
Center, KY 42214
(270)565-4865   <Metcalfe>
PA: Randall Gray   <M1>
1230 New Liberty Big Meadow Road
Knob Lick, KY 42154
(270)432-5322
CL: Louise London
2466 Highway 1048
Center, KY 42214
(270)565-3015

Shiloh   (4MEWC)MICU3129
252 Tabernacle Road (mailing)
1186 Shiloh Road (physical)
Campbellsville, KY 42718
(270)789-2346   <Taylor>
CL: Sue Campbell
333 Campbell Road
Campbellsville, KY 42718
(270)465-5492

Short Creek   (4WC)MICU3221
9312 Owensboro Road (mailing)
Hollow Church Road (physical)
Falls of Rough, KY 40119
( )   <Grayson>
PS: Steven Smith   <M3 ST>
100 Valleyview Drive
Leitchfield, KY 42754
CL: George Fentress
11680 Owensboro Road
Falls of Rough, KY 40119
(270)879-8883

Wisdom   (2C)MICU3130
254 Echo Road (mailing)
State Route 640 (physical)
Knob Lick, KY 42129
( )   <Metcalfe>

CUMBERLAND PRESBYTERY CONTINUED

CL: Frances Royse
491 Cave Ridge Road
Knob Lick, KY 42154
(270)432-0112
froyse@scrtc.com

OTHERS ON MINISTERIAL ROLL:

Akai, Anum   <M1 WC>
458 Dean Taylor Court
Simpsonville, KY 40067
(502)405-3120

Barton, Robert   <M1 RT>
22460 Klines Resort Road #290
Three Rivers, MI 49093
(859)613-2686
csm2ndinfbde2002@yahoo.com

Blevins, Tom   <M1 WC>
50 Blevins Road
Center, KY 42214
(270)565-1792

Boggs, Robert   <M1 WC>
89 Maple Leaf Lane
Leitchfield, KY 42754
(270)259-5546

Byrd, James F   <M1 WC>
1158 Cornishville Road
Harrodsburg, KY 40330
(859)734-0534
jfbyrd@bluezoomwifi.com

Cottingim, Tom   <M1 WC>
353 Atwood Drive
Lexington, KY 40515
(859)273-3800
FAX: (859)272-4315
t.cottingim@insightbb.com

Diamond, James   <M1 M9>
214 Falmouth Drive
Georgetown, KY 40324
(615)220-2341
james.diamond007@comcast.net

Ferree, Carole   <M1 WC>
2475 Fallen Timber Road
Campbellsville, KY 42718
(270)465-1150
ferree047@wildblue.net

Gary, Brian   <M1 WC>
105 Wilma Avenue
Radcliff, KY 40160
(502)351-6938

Jones, Joseph M   <M1 RT>
405 Lakeview Drive
Campbellsville, KY 42718
joepegjones@windstream.net

Love, James R   <M1 WC>
14382 Sonora Hardin Springs Road
Eastview, KY 42732
(502)862-4119

Milby, Elizabeth L   <M1 WC>
207 Summersville Road
Greensburg, KY 42743
(270)932-5659

Neafus, Kenneth R   <M1 WC>
237 Richland Church Road
Morgantown, KY 42261
(270)526-6835

Norris, Freddie   <M1 WC>
330 Lexington Drive
Glasgow, KY 42141
(270)651-7932

Perkins, William H   <M1 WC>
PO Box 632
Central City, KY 42330
(270)754-5333

Ranson, Doris   <M1 WC>
9440 Fenwick Road
Owensboro, KY 42301
(270)229-2875
dorisranson@bellsouth.net

Renner, Wallace   <M1 WC>
1648 Griffith Avenue
Owensboro, KY 42303
(270)685-4359
pwrenner@adelphia.net

Ricketts, Roger   <M1 WC>
205 Contantz Drive
Canton, MO 63435

Thompson, Eugene   <M1 WC>
2825 Albatross Road
Del Ray Beach, FL 33444

Thompson, W Fay   <M1 RT>
210 Macbeth Lane
Glasgow, KY 42141
(270)646-2218

Tucker, James D   <M1 WC>
PO Box 34
Mc Daniels, KY 40152
(270)257-8971

Underwood, Jerrell M   <M1 RT>
PO Box 9
Garfield, KY 40140
(270)536-3706

Wilson, Brenda   <M1 WC>
35 Collins Drive
Elizabethtown, KY 42701
(270)249-3835
susieq2007@windstream.net

OTHER LICENTIATES ON ROLL:

Smith, Nicholas   <M2>
101 Cumberland Street
Glasgow, KY 42141
(270)651-3308
pastornic@gcpchurch.tv

Watts, Glenn David   <M2 ST>
7400 Willowbend Drive
Crestwood, KY 40014
(502)241-0436
hongkongbrother@hotmail.com

OTHER CANDIDATES ON ROLL:

Craddock, Barry   <M3>
147 Moss Way
Glasgow, KY 42141

Cumberland East Coast Presbytery
SOUTHEAST SYNOD

	GENERAL	MEMBERSHIP			CHANGES				FINANCES				
	1.Church Number	2.Active	3.Total	4.Church School	5.Prof. of Faith	6.Gains	7.Losses	8.Children Baptized	9. OUR UNITED OUT-REACH	10. Total Out-Reach Giving	11. All Other Expenses	12. Total Income Received	13. Value Church Prop. 1=1000
	1	2	3	4	5	6	7	8	9	10	11	12	13
Comeback	2446	14	15	0	2	3	1	0	100	3,905	51,926	58,003	0
Gil	2444	4	4	0	0	0	0	0	100	2,600	8,223	10,823	0
Hope Korean	2131	12	14	0	0	0	5	0	600	23,189	64,952	70,909	0
One Way	2137	75	101	48	9	18	21	3	100	4,500	138,000	125,000	255
Outreach	2143								100				
Sharing	2141	20	20	4	20	0	8	0	100	100	63,110	68,617	0
Sunnyside			2										
True Love	2443	13	13	0	0	4	4	0	50	200	138,000	15,300	25
TOTALS	7	138	167	52	31	25	39	3	1,150	34,494	464,211	348,652	280

*Math error corrected. **Purged roll.

CHURCHES, PASTORS, AND CLERKS:

Comeback   (C)SECE2446
  316 Prospect Avenue Apt 6D
  Hackensack, NJ 07601
PA: Ji Woo Park
  316 Prospect Avenue Apt 6D
  Hackensack, NJ 07601
  (201)694-3005
  jiwoos@gmail.com
CL: Session Clerk
  316 Prospect Avenue Apt 6D
  Hackensack, NJ 07601

Gil   (C)SECE2444
  139 A Grove Street
  Tenafly, NJ 07670
PA: Si Chun Ryu
  139 A Grove Street
  Tenafly, NJ 07670
  (201)410-3445
  isaac9191@hotmail.com
CL: Session Clerk
  139 A Grove Street
  Tenafly, NJ 07670

Hope Korean   (C)SECE2131
  1189 Hope Road
  Tinton Falls, NJ 07724
  (   )   <Monmouth>
PA: Buhwan Yang   <M1>
  19 Taylors Run
  Tinton Falls, NJ 07712
  (732)918-0011
  yangmoksa@gmail.com
CL: Session Clerk
  1189 Hope Road
  Tinton Falls, NJ 07724

One Way   (C)SECE2137
  9 Carlton Avenue
  Port Washington, NY 11050
  (516)815-1164   <Queens>
  FAX: (516)921-2821

PA: Jin Soo Park   <M1>
  21155 45th Drive
  Bayside, NY 11361
  (516)558-7298
  jpkorea@daum.net
AP: Si Hoon Park   <M1>
  511 4th Street #B
  Palisades Park, NJ 07650
  (201)944-7913
CL: Session Clerk
  21155 45th Drive
  Bayside, NY 11361
  (516)558-7298
  jpkorea@daum.net

Outreach   (C)SECE2143
  800 Silver Lane Room 205
  East Hartford, CT 06118
  (860)830-6808
  lovejcamen@yahoo.com
PA: Sansook Cho   <M1>
  7 Falmouth Court
  Middletown, CT
  lovejcamen@yahoo.com
  (860)830-6808
CL: Session Clerk
  800 Silver Lane Room 205
  East Hartford, CT 06118
  (860)830-6808
  lovejcamen@yahoo.com

Sharing   (C)SECE2141
  35-24 Union Street 1C
  Flushing, NY 11354
  (718)460-1118   <Queens>
  spcko1188@gmail.com
PA: John Jae Ko   <M1 RT>
  13955 35th Avenue #5A
  Flushing, NY 11354
  (718)460-1118
  spcko@hanmail.net
CL: Session Clerk
  35-24 Union Street 1C
  Flushing, NY 11354
  spcko1188@gmail.com

Sunnyside   (C)SECE0000
  27-27 Bayside Lane
  Flushing, NY 11354
  (718)809-5191
PA: Kio Seob Kim   <M1>
  14430 35th Avenue Apt A62
  Flushing, NY 11354
  (718)539-3476
  imkioseob@hotmail.com
CL: Session Clerk
  14430 35th Avenue Apt A62
  Flushing, NY 11354
  (718)539-3476
  imkioseob@hotmail.com

True Love   (C)SECE2443
  42-40 208th Street
  Bayside, NY 11361
  (347)308-4333
  ingodswill@gmail.com
PA: Taeho Oh   <M1>
  42-40 208th Street
  Bayside, NY 11361
CL: Session Clerk
  42-40 208th Street
  Bayside, NY 11361

OTHERS ON MINISTERIAL ROLL:

Craig, Peggy Jean   <M1 WC>
  825 S 13th Street Floor 2
  Philadelphia, PA 19147
  (256)277-1147
  pjfpeggy@gmail.com
Ma, Choil   <M1 WC>
  40 Conger Street #1404A
  Bloomfield, NJ 07003
Lee, Choongmin   <M1 WC>
Lee, Paul   <M1 WC>
Park, Sooyeol   <M1 WC>

CUMBERLAND EAST COAST PRESBYTERY CONTINUED

Ryoo, Hwa Chang   <M1 WC>
450 Island Road Unit 146
Ramsey, NJ 07446
(404)512-9147

Son, Woosuk   <M1 WC>

___

OTHER LICENTIATES ON ROLL:

Chin, Kwang Sik   <M2>
1168 Palisade Avenue
Fort Lee, NJ 07024
(201)220-3390

Sung, John   <M2>
26 Old Orchard Road
Cherry Hill, NJ 08003
(856)751-0227

___

OTHER CANDIDATES ON ROLL:

Kang, Eun Hee   <M3>
14715 46th Avenue
Flushing, NY 11355
(718)762-0778

Presbytery del Cristo
MISSION SYNOD

GENERAL		MEMBERSHIP			CHANGES				FINANCES				
	1.Church Number	2.Active	3.Total	4.Church School	5.Prof. of Faith	6.Gains	7.Losses	8.Children Baptized	9. OUR UNITED OUT-REACH	10. Total Out-Reach Giving	11. All Other Expenses	12. Total Income Received	13. Value Church Prop. 1=1000
	1	2	3	4	5	6	7	8	9	10	11	12	13
Chinese	8501	587	587	205	0	33	16	0	30,936	69,801	912,420	984,030	3,500
Desert Gardens	8705	16	23	10	0	0	1	0	2,000	7,084	37,630	55,894	180
El Paso First*	8704	12	25	0	0	2	7	0	1,583	4,656	63,229	61,019	1,000
Grace Fellowship	8510	146	146	81	0	0	1	0	36,667	136,181	512,184	669,372	2,000
Heights	8701	317	2,483	80	0	14	18	4	0	112,856	695,644	853,151	2,604
Lubbock First	8702	80	80	35	2	5	33	0	0	6,289	224,562	231,965	4,332
Maranatha	8706	100	100	60	0	0	0	0	0	3,705	66,000	43,654	0
Redeemer	8512	45	48	64	3	4	0	0	5,000	21,651	217,322	222,971	0
St. Andrew	8703	106	203	40	2	2	9	0	7,350	32,753	290,221	322,974	1,200
Trona	8503	6	34	15	0	1	0	0	272	1,243	11,866	14,975	125
Westside	8709	51	65	37	3	12	5	2	600	11,297	107,326	119,101	250
TOTALS	11	1,466	3,783	602	10	73	90	6	84,408	407,516	3,138,404	3,578,206	15,191

*Math error corrected. **Purged roll.

___

CHURCHES, PASTORS, AND CLERKS:

___

Chinese   (4C)MSDC8501
865 Jackson Street
San Francisco, CA 94133
(415)421-1624   <San Francisco>
FAX: (415)421-1874
church@cumberlandsf.org
PA: Walter Lau   <M1>
865 Jackson Street
San Francisco, CA 94133
(415)421-1624
FAX: (415)421-1874
walter@cumberlandsf.org
AP: Steven Chen   <M1>
865 Jackson Street
San Francisco, CA 94133
(415)421-1624
psalm1305@yahoo.com
AP: Sonny Wan   <M1>
13 Wexford Place
Aladema, CA 94502
(415)421-1624
sonny@cumberlandsf.org

AP: Alexis Yu   <M1>
1761 Willow Way
San Bruno, CA 94066
(415)421-1624
alexis.yu.k@gmail.com
CL: John Fang
2362 - 39th Avenue
San Francisco, CA 94116
(415)665-3721
johnfang@pacbell.net

___

Desert Gardens   (4C)MSDC8705
10851 E Old Spanish Trail
Tucson, AZ 85748
(520)296-0703   <Pima>
PA: Gerald (Jerry) Hagelin   <M1>
10851 E Old Spanish Trail
Tucson, AZ 85712
(520)275-8110
azcef@cs.com
CL: Bonnie Kopke
10851 E Old Spanish Trail
Tucson, AZ 85748
(520)647-4700
bkopke@cox.net

___

El Paso First   (4WC)MSDC8704
11299 Pebble Hills Boulevard
El Paso, TX 79936
(915)592-6138   <El Paso>
FAX: (915)592-3538
fcpcelp@sbcglobal.net
PA: Alfredo Rincon   <M1>
12008 Fred Carter
El Paso, TX 79936
(915)857-1343
yaanaivitaly@yahoo.com
CL: Norma Frye
3317 Funston Place
El Paso, TX 79936
(915)633-6877
cherokee80@sbcglobal.net

___

Grace Fellowship   (4C)MSDC8510
3265 16th Street
San Francisco, CA 94103
(415)703-6090   <San Francisco>
FAX: (415)864-1543

PRESBYTERY DEL CRISTO CONTINUED

PA: Sharon Huey   <M1>
3265 16th Street
San Francisco, CA 94103
(415)703-6090
sharon_huey@yahoo.com

AP: Douglas Lee   <M1>
3265 16th Street
San Francisco, CA 94103
(415)703-6090
dlee@gum.org

CL: Mike Peterson
3265 16th Street
San Francisco, CA 94103
(415)247-9421 ext 17
FAX: (415)864-5830
sfmikepeterson@gmail.com

Heights   (4WC)MSDC8701
8600 Academy Road NE
Albuquerque, NM 87111
(505)821-1993   <Bernalillo>
FAX: (505)797-8599

AP: Jerry Smyrl   <M1>
3421 Montreal Street NE
Albuquerque, NM 87111
(505)293-0108
jwsmyrl@hotmail.com

AP: Marty Goehring   <M1>
8600 Academy NE
Albuquerque, NM 87111
(505)821-3628
FAX: (505)797-8599
mgoehring@heightscpc.org

AP: Justin Richter   <M1>
8600 Academy Road NE
Albuquerque, NM 87111
(505)363-8738
richteryp@gmail.com

CL: Barbara J Cok
8600 Academy Road NE
Albuquerque, NM 87112
(505)275-0108
FAX: (866)280-0731
barbara@lobo.net

Lubbock First   (4WC)MSDC8702
7702 Indiana Avenue
Lubbock, TX 79423
(806)792-3553   <Lubbock>
joy@cpclubbock.com

PA: Steve Doles   <M1>
7702 Indiana Avenue
Lubbock, TX 79423
(806)787-7551
steve@cpclubbock.com

CL: Diana K Akins
4712 63rd Street
Lubbock, TX 79414
(806)797-5246
FAX: (806)744-0640
dkakins48@yahoo.com

Maranatha   (4C)MSDC8706
PO Box 1040 (mailing)
San Elizario, TX 79849
11497 Socorro Road (physical)
Socorro, TX 79927
(915)851-8349   <El Paso>
hectoryliz@att.net

PA: Hector Mata   <M1>
PO Box 1040
San Elizario, TX 79849
(915)851-5354
hectoryliz@att.net

AP: Elizabeth Mata   <M1>
PO Box 1040
San Elizaro, TX 79849
(915)851-5354
hectoryliz@att.net

AP: Isaac Mata   <M1>
PO Box 1040
San Elizaro, TX 79849
(915)851-5354
isaacmata96@yahoo.com

AP: Lyvia Rincon   <M1>
12008 Fred Carter
El Paso, TX 79936
(915)857-1343
yaanaivitaly@yahoo.com

AP: Manuel (Alex) Saldana   <M1>
536 Telop
El Paso, TX 79927
(915)317-9349
campe13@yahoo.com

CL: Miguel Flores
PO Box 1040
San Elizario, TX 79849
(915)346-2071
mr_titof@yahoo.com

Redeemer   (4C)MSDC8512
1224 Fairfax Avenue
San Francisco, CA 94124
(415)671-2194   <San Francisco>
info@redeemersf.org

PA: Danny Fong   <M1>
1224 Fairfax Avenue
San Francisco, CA 94124
(415)671-2194
dfong@redeemersf.org

CL: Daniel Kim
1224 Fairfax Avenue
San Francisco, CA 94124
(415)596-6400
dannydhkim@gmail.com

St Andrew   (4MEWC)MSDC8703
1415 N Grandview
Odessa, TX 79761
(432)367-8603   <Ector>
FAX: (432)367-8605
standrewcp@sbcglobal.net

PA: Jimmy Braswell   <M1>
1514 E 10th Street
Odessa, TX 79761
(432)335-9346
jjcgbraz@cableone.net

AP: Sharon Notley   <M1>
16500 S Grey Wolf Apt 5
Odessa, TX 79766
(432)210-9059
sharon_standrewcp@sbcglobal.net

CL: Linda Anglley
309 E 89th Street
Odessa, TX 79765
(432)550-8569
anglley@yahoo.com

Trona   (4C)MSDC8503
83456 Argus Avenue
Trona, CA 93592
(760)382-8636   <San Bernardino>

PA: Dennis Benadom   <M1>
13314 Sage Street
Trona, CA 93562
(760)372-4536
galerose91@msn.com

CL: Cindy Barton
83426 Argus Avenue
Trona, CA 93562
(760)372-4033
cbarton53@hotmail.com

Westside   (4C)MSDC8709
PO Box 15209 (mailing)
4110 Sabana Grande Avenue (physical)
Rio Rancho, NM 87174
(505)620-2427   <Sandoval>
nancye320@aol.com

PA: Harry W Chapman   <M1>
4908 El Picador Court
Rio Rancho, NM 87124
(505)620-2427
wrightrev@gmail.com

CL: Sherry Meier
7113 Hartford Hills Drive NE
Rio Rancho, NM 87144
(505)771-0418
sjmeier53@aol.com

OTHERS ON MINISTERIAL ROLL:

Bondurant, Lee   <M1 WC>
1453 Paseo Del Sur Court
El Paso, TX 79928
(915)309-7269
leebondurant@yahoo.com

Bower, Clay   <M1 WC>
221 Waterlemon Way
Monroe, NC 28110
(704)575-9497
cblower@lzbsoutheast.com

Collins, Paul   <M1 RT>
915 Warm Sands Drive SE
Albuquerque, NM 87123
(505)294-3842
FAX: (505)254-7707
chapp3@comcast.net

Estes, George R   <M1 RT>
7910 Cloverbrook Lane
Germantown, TN 38138
(901)755-6673
geoestes@gmail.com

Estes, Sam R, Jr   <M1 RT>
3026 54th Street Apt 311
Lubbock, TX 79413
(806)748-6116

Freund, Henry O   <M1 RT>
913 Sam Houston Drive
Dyersburg, TN 38024
(731)285-1744
freundly@att.net

Fung, David   <M1 WC>
1846 Gunston Way
San Jose, CA 95124
(408)266-3398
revfung@gmail.com

PRESBYTERY DEL CRISTO CONTINUED

Fung, Lawrence <M1 WC>
2/F Weeland Plaza
188 Nam Cheong Street
Sham Shui Po Kowloon, HONG KONG
(852)2783-8923
FAX: (852)2771-2726
revfung@yahoo.com

Giron, Francisco <M1 OM>
3451 Los Mochis Way
Oceanside, CA 92056
(760)203-0381
FAX: (760)414-1236
thegirons@cox.net

Gonzales, Homer <M1 WC>
8924 Armistice NE
Albuquerque, NM 87109
(505)821-4376
FAX: (505)841-4267
hgabq1985@gmail.com

Green, Paul <M1 RT>
5228 Anchorage Avenue
El Paso, TX 79924
(915)751-7960

Hess, Jean <M1 WC>
2200 E Dartmouth Circle
Englewood, CO 80113
(303)504-0275
jeanhess@316denver.com

Hess, Rick <M1 WC>
2200 E Dartmouth Circle
Englewood, CO 80113
(303)504-0275
rick@densem.edu

Hom, Paul <M1 RT>
722 24th Avenue
San Franciso, CA 94121
(415)751-9766

Kim, Byong Sam <M1 RT>
6290 Dawnridge Court
Paradise, CA 95969
(530)877-4651

Knight, Melissa <M1 M9>
5730 Haley Road
Meridian, MS 39305
(530)632-6472
revlissa@gmail.com

Lui, Stephen <M1 RT>
512 16th Avenue
San Francisco, CA 94118
(415)386-2302
FAX: (415)386-2302

Luo, Tian-en <M1 WC>
87 Berta Circle
Daly City, CA 94015
(650)754-9885
FAX: (650)754-9885
tianenyang555@gmail.comt

Maddux, Cynthia <M1 WC>
5735 Timber Creek Place Drive Apt 212
Houston, TX 77084
(832)343-8867
cmaddux1962@gmail.com

Mata, Pablo <M1 WC>
PO Box 1040
San Elizaro, TX 79849
(915)851-8348
pablomata@yahoo.com

McMillan, Lloyd Aaron <M1 WC>
8600 Academy Road NE
Albuquerque, NM 87111
(505)503-0714
FAX: (505)797-8599
mcmillanaaron@hotmail.com

McNeese, Michael C <M1 WC>
16410 Wesley Evans Road
Prairieville, LA 70769
(520)722-1350
mcneesemc@cox.net

O'Mara, Shelia <M1 M8>
533 Loughton Lane
Arnold, MD 21012
(410)757-5713
chaplainshelia@aol.com

Patterson, Jerry <M1 WC>
7007 Whitaker Avenue
Van Nuys, CA 91406
(818)994-5828

Shin, Kyung I <M1 WC>
1805 Gallinas Road NE
Rio Rancho, NM 87144
(505)453-5461
pastorkshin@gmail.com

Sze, Joseph <M1 WC>
Rau Sao Joaquim, 382
Liberdale, Sao Paulo, SP
CEP 015068-000 Brazil
pastorsze@yahoo.com

Tan, Pek Hua <M1 WC>
7 Belhaven Avenue
Daly City, CA 94015
(415)515-0076
ptan27@yahoo.com

Tsujimoto, Mark <M1 WC>
88 S Broadway Unit 3210
Millbrae, CA 94030
(650)697-6901
mltsujimoto@gmail.com

Wilson, Don <M1 M9 RT>
7300 Calle Montana NE
Albuquerque, NM 87113
(505)823-2594
don-wilson07@comcast.net

Wong, Bruce <M1 WC>
716 Duncanville Court
Campbell, CA 95008
(408)628-1723
revbwong@gmail.com

Yu, Pyong San (Sonny) <M1 WC>
139 Silverado Drive
Santa Teresa, NM 88008
(915)329-3451
pyongsanyu@hotmail.com

OTHER LICENTIATES ON ROLL:

Barton, Cindy <M2>
83426 Argus Avenue
Trona, CA 93562
(760)372-4033
cbarton53@hotmail.com

Bell, Michelle <M2>
8643 Dry Creek Road Unit 1226
Centennial, CO 80112
(720)344-4040
mabbell@comcast.net

George, Thomas <M2>
908 N Brown Avenue
Casa Grande, AZ 85222
(640)447-2676
tgeorge@aerogram.net

Okala, Achile <M2>
5887 Newcombe Court
Arvada, CO 80004
(720)880-8511
achileok@me.com

Ralph, Brian <M2>
6419 S Vinewood Street Apt 205
Littleton, CO 80120
(312)315-6915
ralph1970@gmail.com

Wang, Huiling <M2>
5562 S Yank Court
Littleton, CO 80127
(303)330-3929
whuiling88@yhoo.com

OTHER CANDIDATES ON ROLL:

Hom, Patti <M3>
811 Faxon Avenue
San Francisco, CA 94112
(415)586-5998
phom@gfccsf.org

Jimenez, Jacqueline <M3>
11161 San Ysidro
Socorro, TX 79927
(915)252-8395
jjimenez22282gmail.com

Presbytery of East Tennessee
SOUTHEAST SYNOD

GENERAL		MEMBERSHIP		CHANGES				FINANCES				
	1.Church Number	2.Active	3.Total / 4.Church School		5.Prof. of Faith / 6.Gains		7.Losses / 8.Children Baptized	9. OUR UNITED OUT-REACH	10. Total Out-Reach Giving	11. All Other Expenses	12. Total Income Received	13. Value Church Prop. 1=1000
	1	2	3	4	5	6	7	8	9	10	11	12	13
Beaver Creek	2301	500	790	275	3	12	12	6	51,181	79,847	448,955	511,810	3,600
Bethesda	2201	46	49	40	0	0	3	0	3,631	11,232	43,952	59,368	170
Casa De Fe#	2220	40	40	20	2	4	64	3	500	2,840	65,500	54,402	0
Cedar Hill*	2202	56	173	40	0	1	6	1	9,031	19,348	49,171	96,826	850
Clark's Grove	2302	42	116	22	1	0	8	0	5,975	9,858	40,147	50,005	500
Corntassel	2304	16	36	16	0	0	2	0	2,789	3,858	29,389	28,987	200
Dover	2203	40	40	15	No Report Received			0	2,387	0	0	0	1,250
Fairview	2204	48	101	53	0	0	3	0	4,835	21,394	119,767	107,677	602
FaithFellowship	2319	60	141	35	0	0	1	1	0	6,112	205,421	232,984	1,930
Gass Memorial	2205	3	7	5	0	0	0	0	741	1,882	7,541	9,423	160
Greeneville	2206	401	565	96	3	15	13	2	44,800	85,913	405,202	502,829	4,200
Heartland	2306	69	123	34	9	9	0	0	3,544	7,657	88,777	133,127	550
Knoxville	2305	109	282	68	2	4	3	0	1,200	12,273	239,798	241,631	2,500
Lebanon	2207	16	21	10	0	0	0	0	3,387	9,010	23,596	36,224	300
Loudon	2307	124	210	105	2	6	6	3	0	11,740	200,773	202,743	3,744
Marietta	2308	70	201	60	0	0	1	0	20,807	41,004	163,195	202,411	600
Maryville 1st	2309	85	228	71	0	0	5	0	2,400	7,333	110,646	112,600	1,561
Mercy	2320	16	26	27	No Report Received			0	0	0	0	0	5
Mohawk*	2208	22	49	16	1	0	13	0	1,955	2,455	16,474	19,549	300
Mt. Carmel	2310	58	96	20	3	7	1	0	4,329	13,910	31,007	48,510	450
Mt. Pleasant	2209	26	64	33	0	0	2	0	2,692	5,649	10,352	28,191	100
New Bethel	2210	13	29	25	0	0	3	0	1,357	4,002	17,739	15,242	333
New Hope*	2311	36	36	13	0	0	0	0	2,812	6,738	18,807	35,975	800
Oak Ridge**	2313	124	124	28	2	4	13	1	12,508	31,150	150,555	181,705	1,650
Oakland*	2211	15	29	0	0	4	0	2	0	45,584	0	80,918	100
Oliver Springs	2314	7	9	6	No Report Received			0	609	0	0	0	180
Philadelphia	2212	25	25	25	0	0	1	0	550	600	17,579	14,450	300
Pilot Knob	2213	9	9	27	No Report Received			0	973	0	0	0	100
Pleasant Hill	2214	22	28	20	0	0	3	0	3,075	7,800	23,446	31,048	400
Pleasant Vale	2215	11	11	26	No Report Received			0	196	0	0	0	250
Salem	2216	31	36	31	0	0	1	0	0	1,242	15,223	29,947	104
Shiloh	2217	107	203	77	1	4	17	0	10,762	25,697	109,652	127,263	1,150
Talbott*	2218	54	91	31	0	0	2	0	10,343	25,852	45,437	124,735	1,125
Union	2315	221	399	86	6	30	6	1	14,136	65,165	403,155	436,005	2,343
Virtue	2316	53	80	25	1	1	4	0	15,798	15,852	156,131	153,334	1,616
Willoughby	2219	11	11	13	0	0	1	0	1,608	1,608	13,866	16,068	250
Young's Chapel	2317	93	140	52	2	5	14	0	15,934	37,225	146,033	179,482	1,000
Presbytery of East Tennessee									3,998				
TOTALS	37	2,730	4,677	1,565	38	106	148	21	256,845	621,830	3,417,287	4,105,469	35,298

*Math error corrected. **Purged roll. #Correction to last year's report.

PRESBYTERY OF EAST TENNESSEE CONTINUED

CHURCHES, PASTORS, AND CLERKS:

Beaver Creek   (4WC)SEET2301
7225 Old Clinton Pike
Knoxville, TN 37921
(865)938-7245   <Knox>
FAX: (865)938-1465
tsweet1@comcast.net
PA: Thomas Sweet   <M1>
7225 Old Clinton Pike
Powell, TN 37849
(865)938-7245
tsweet1@comcast.net
AP: Fran Vickers   <M1>
7225 Old Clinton Pike
Knoxville, TN 37921
(865)859-0805
franv3@comcast.net
AP: Patrick Wilkerson   <M1>
7719 S Whispering Oak Circle
Powell, TN 37849
(865)617-9126
patrickwilkerson3@gmail.com
CL: John Todd
4912 Montmorency Drive
Powell, TN 37849
(865)938-7211
jtodd4912@comcast.net

Bethesda   (4C)SEET2201
155 Old Shiloh Road (mailing)
Greeneville, TN 37745
16340 Kingsport Highway (physical)
Fall Branch, TN 37656
(423)620-7753   <Greene>
FAX: (423)798-2042
kcor_98@yahoo.com
CL: Jeff H Hayes
155 Old Shiloh Road
Greeneville, TN 37745
(423)639-8404
mdlpilot@yahoo.com

Casa De Fe   (PRESC)SEET2220
493 Main Street, 2nd Floor
Malden, MA 02148
(781)322-2685   <Middlesex>
casadefepastores@verizon.net
PA: Josefina Sanchez   <M1>
7 Hancock Street
Melrose, MA 02176
(479)970-8654
fsfamily64@gmail.com
CL: Myriam Santizo
125 Pennsylvania Avenue
Somerville, MA 02145
(617)666-6763

Cedar Hill   (4EWC)SEET2202
4170 Newport Highway
Greeneville, TN 37743
(423)639-0268   <Greene>
cedarhill@centurylink.net
CL: Carolyn Harmon
4435 Newport Highway
Greeneville, TN 37743
(423)639-3037
richardharmon09@comcast.net

Clark's Grove   (4WC)SEET2302
1662 Peppertree Drive (mailing)
Alcoa, TN 37701
3137 Old Knoxville Highway (physical)
Maryville, TN 37802
(865)982-5280   <Blount>
FAX: (865)273-8726
lwaters111@aol.com
CL: Lynn Waters
1662 Peppertree Drive
Alcoa, TN 37701
(865)982-9083
FAX: (865)379-0654
lwaters111@aol.com

Corntassel   (4C)SEET2304
933 Kahite Trail (mailing)
Vonore, TN 37885
2100 Povo Road (physical)
Madisonville, TN 37354
(423)884-3909   <Monroe>
miriamf23@tds.net
PA: Bill S Middleton   <M1 RT>
12826 Union Road
Knoxville, TN 37922
(865)966-1706
revbill@charter.net
CL: Carolyn Swabe
2203 Povo Road
Madisonville, TN 37354
(423)442-4377
swabec@aol.com

Dover   (4MEWC)SEET2203
1550 Dover Road
Morristown, TN 37813
(423)581-4719   <Hamblen>
dovercp@comcast.net
CL: John Ayers
4371 Danbury Drive
Morristown, TN 37813
(423)586-6883
bigorange@charter.net

Fairview   (4MWC)SEET2204
4720 Snapps Ferry Road
Afton, TN 37616
(423)639-9011   <Greene>
PA: Ronnie Duncan   <M1>
146 Deseree Broyles Road
Chuckey, TN 37641
(423)552-0321
ronkduncan@icloud.com
CL: Rick Taylor
175 Stone Dam Road
Chuckey, TN 37641
(423)470-0216

Faith Fellowship   (4EWC)SEET2319
PO Box 24162 (mailing)
Knoxville, TN 37934
14025 Highway 70 E (physical)
Lenoir City, TN 37772
(865)988-8522   <Knox>
info@faithfellowshipcp.org

PA: Greg Tucker   <M1>
612A Idlewood Lane
Knoxville, TN 37923
(865)242-4086
greg.tucker311@outlook.com
CL: Regina Stinnett
508 Windham Hill Road
Knoxville, TN 37934
(865)898-3001
reginastinnett@tds.net

Gass Memorial   (4C)SEET2205
PO Box 1767 (mailing)
815 Gass Memorial Road (physical)
Greeneville, TN 37744
(423)278-7610   <Greene>
FAX: (423)638-3452
gassch@comcast.net
PA: Rex Brown   <M1>
134 Everhart Drive
Greeneville, TN 37745
(423)639-4298
CL: George C Mays
PO Box 1767
Greeneville, TN 37744
(423)638-8624
FAX: (423)638-3452
g.mays@comcast.net

Greeneville   (4MEWC)SEET2206
201 N Main Street
Greeneville, TN 37745
(423)638-4119   <Greene>
FAX: (423)636-1017
office@gcpchurch.org
PA: James W Lively   <M1>
906 Lyle Circle
Greeneville, TN 37745
(423)798-1959
FAX: (423)636-1017
jlively@gcpchurch.org
AP: Abby Cole Keller   <M1>
4415 Fieldstone Drive
Kingsport, TN 37664
(423)863-6565
colekeller@yahoo.com
CL: Dick Parrack
201 N Main Street
Greeneville, TN 37745
(423)638-4119
FAX: (423)636-1017
parrackd@embarqmail.com

Heartland   (4MWC)SEET2306
160 Harrison Road
Lenoir City, TN 37772
(865)986-3018   <Loudon>
lccpc@icx.net
PA: Kenneth P Phillips   <M1>
6419 Town Creek Road East
Lenoir City, TN 37772
(865)986-7344
CL: Jennifer L Smith
1085 Crestview Circle
Lenoir City, TN 37772
(865)986-5099
jlleslie@chartertn.net

PRESBYTERY OF EAST TENNESSEE CONTINUED

Knoxville   (4WC)SEET2305
6900 Nubbin Ridge Drive
Knoxville, TN 37919
(865)588-8581   <Knox>
FAX: (865)588-8581
firstcpc@earthlink.net
PA: Michael Wilkinson   <M1>
1174 Tanglewood Street
Memphis, TN 38114
(334)517-6568
pastormike@kfcpc.comcastbiz.net
CL: Dianne Pipkin
1725 Covey Rise Trail
Knoxville, TN 37922
(865)675-2872
pndpip@aol.com

Lebanon   (4MEC)SEET2207
2117 Murray Street (mailing)
Morristown, TN 37814
714 Lebanon Road (physical)
Jefferson City, TN 37760
( )   <Jefferson>
PA: Howard E Shipley   <M1>
3800 Dan Drive
Morristown, TN 37814
(423)581-1092
hshipley@charter.net
CL: Frances McCarter
2117 Murray Street
Morristown, TN 37814
(423)586-6292
lofmcar@aol.com

Loudon   (4MWC)SEET2307
PO Box 373 (mailing)
503 College Avenue (physical)
Loudon, TN 37774
(865)458-2270   <Loudon>
FAX: (865)458-5360
loudoncpc@bellsouth.net
PA: Robert N Coker   <M1>
721 Lakeview Drive
Loudon, TN 37774
(865)458-8791
FAX: (865)458-5360
nickcoker@bellsouth.net
AP: Rebecca Prenshaw   <M1>
1100 Albemarie Lane
Knoxville, TN 37923
(865)531-1954
bprenshaw@yahoo.com
CL: Russ Newman
623 Mulberry Street
Loudon, TN 37773
(865)282-1977
mulberry623@yahoo.com

Marietta   (4MC)SEET2308
11402 Hardin Valley Road (mailing)
1922 Marietta Church Road (physical)
Knoxville, TN 37932
(865)693-0080   <Knox>
mariettacpc@comcast.net
PA: Randall Mayfield   <M1>
12470 Daisywood Drive
Knoxville, TN 37932
(865)769-4756
FAX: (865)769-4756
mayfield07@comcast.net

CL: Virgil R Hubbard
2122 Campbell Station Road
Knoxville, TN 37932
(865)740-4863
vrhubbard@comcast.net

Maryville First   (4MWC)SEET2309
1301 E Broadway
Maryville, TN 37804
(865)982-7860   <Blount>
firstcumberland@gmail.com
PA: Ronald L Longmire   <M1>
2041 Eckles Drive
Maryville, TN 37804
(865)984-1647
ronaldlongmire@charter.net
CL: Tom Longmire
630 Garfield Street
Alcoa, TN 37701
(865)983-3604

Mercy   (4C)SEET2320
634 Martel Road
Lenoir City, TN 37772
(865)660-7579   <Knox>
iglesiapcmisericordia@gmail.com
PA: Alfonso Oscar Marquez   <M1>
389 Bethel Drive
Lenoir City, TN 37772
(865)660-7579
amarquez61@bellsouth.net
AP: Martha Marquez   <M1>
389 Bethel Drive
Lenoir City, TN 37772
(865)660-7579
amarquez61@bellsouth.net
AP: Miguel Gonzales   <M1>
200 Bethel Drive
Lenoir City, TN 37772
(865)988-4238
CL: Miguel Angel Gonzalez
200 Bethel Drive
Lenor City, TN 37772
(865)227-2710
mgonzalez865@bellsouth.net

Mohawk   (4MWC)SEET2208
PO Box 7 (mailing)
50 Soville Loop (physical)
Mohawk, TN 37810
( )   <Greene>
SS: Chris Franklin   <M2>
310 Yellow Springs Road
Midway, TN 37809
(423)972-3609
chrisfranklin104@comcast.net
CL: Velta Rhea Riley
2149 Phillipe Road
Mohawk, TN 37810
(423)235-6179

Mt Carmel   (4EC)SEET2310
PO Box 4 (mailing)
Coalfield, TN 37719
5515 Knoxville Highway (physical)
Oliver Springs, TN 37840
(865)435-9247   <Morgan>
PA: Donald W Acton   <M1>
1186 Jenkins Lane
Knoxville, TN 37922
(865)966-5132

CL: Lisa Layne
714 Back Valley Road
Oliver Springs, TN 37840
(865)382-8817
lalayne64@yahoo.com

Mt Pleasant   (4MWC)SEET2209
3945 Babbs Mill Road
Afton, TN 37616
( )   <Greene>
PA: James L Carter   <M1>
6155 Hummingbird Lane
Whitesburg, TN 37891
(423)587-8423
jandjmt@comcast.net
CL: Louise Gass
701 Franklin Street
Greeneville, TN 37745
(423)639-3731

New Bethel   (3WC)SEET2210
2820 Blue Springs Parkway (mailing)
90 Cox Road (physical)
Greeneville, TN 37743
( )   <Greene>
PA: Rex Brown   <M1>
134 Everhart Drive
Greeneville, TN 37745
(423)639-4298
firstcumberland@gmail.com
CL: Coriece Baxter
2820 Blue Springs Parkway
Greeneville, TN 37743
(423)638-4089

New Hope   (4C)SEET2311
904 Acorn Gap Road
Madisonville, TN 37354
( )   <Monroe>
PA: David L Koopman   <M1>
5606 Brandon Park Drive
Maryville, TN 37804
(865)660-2440
racewthrev@aol.com
CL: Yvonne Wolfe
139 Old Loudon Road
Sweetwater, TN 37874
(423)442-3045

Oak Ridge   (4EWC)SEET2313
PO Box 4836 (mailing)
127 Lafayette (physical)
Oak Ridge, TN 37831
(865)483-8433   <Anderson>
FAX: (865)483-8445
1stcpc@comcast.net
PA: Larry A Blakeburn   <M1>
790 Emory Valley Road Apt 714
Oak Ridge, TN 37830
(731)676-2978
larry@1stcpc.org
CL: Linda Diggs
315 Laurel Hollow Road
Clinton, TN 37716
(865)457-5355
ldiggs06@comcast.net

PRESBYTERY OF EAST TENNESSEE CONTINUED

————————
Oakland   (4C)SEET2211
694 Oakland Road
Telford, TN 37690
(423)257-2258   <Washington>
OD: Sam Smith   <M5>
114 College View Drive
Greeneville, TN 37743
(423)639-8551
CL: Freda Graham
959 Bowmantown Road
Limestone, TN 37681
(423)257-5050

————————
Oliver Springs   (4C)SEET2314
PO Box 175 (mailing)
400 Spring Street (physical)
Oliver Springs, TN 37840
firstcumberland@gmail.com
( )   <Roane>
PA: Ken Johnson   <M1>
122 Ridge Lane
Clinton, TN 37716
(865)463-7090
kenjoxav122@bellsouth.net
CL: Sid Thurmer
PO Box 175
Oliver Springs, TN 37840
(865)435-5438

————————
Philadelphia   (4MWC)SEET2212
509 Snapp Bridge Road (mailing)
757 Snapp Bridge Road (physical)
Limestone, TN 37681
( )   <Washington>
SS: Byrd Broyles   <M2>
295 Davy Crockett Road
Limestone, TN 37681
(423)257-4578
b3broyles@outlook.com
CL: Greg Stafford
509 Snapp Bridge Road
Limestone, TN 37681
(423)257-3796
gregandlesa509@comcast.net

————————
Pilot Knob   (2C)SEET2213
515 Marvin Mountain Road (mailing)
445 Gap Creek Road (physical)
Bulls Gap, TN 37711
( )   <Greene>
LS: Richard Snowden   <M6>
PO Box 6004
Morristown, TN 37815
(423)235-5914
FAX: (423)254-3206
richard.snowden@wallacehardware.com
CL: Joyce Lamb
4185 Gap Creek Road
Bulls Gap, TN 37711
(423)235-6858

————————
Pleasant Hill   (4WC)SEET2214
13385 Kingsport Highway
Chuckey, TN 37641
( )   <Greene>
PA: Rex Brown   <M1>
134 Everhart Drive
Greeneville, TN 37745
(423)639-4298
firstcumberland@gmail.com

CL: Genevieve M Bolton
15440 Kingsport Highway
Chuckey, TN 37641
(423)234-7942

————————
Pleasant Vale   (4C)SEET2215
525 Pleasant Vale Road
Chuckey, TN 37641
( )   <Greene>
OD: Chris Bains   <M5>
155 Pelican Lane
Greeneville, TN 37743
(423)525-7497
CL: Howard Collins
3750 Rheatown Road
Chuckey, TN 37641
(423)278-6072

————————
Salem   (4C)SEET2216
695 West Pines Road (mailing)
Afton, TN 37616
1927 Lost Mountain Pike (physical)
Greeneville, TN 37745
( )   <Greene>
OD: Billy Moore   <M5>
880 Black Bear Road
Greeneville, TN 37745
(423)552-1594
CL: Helen Starnes
695 West Pines Road
Afton, TN 37616
(423)234-0281
cehwstarnes@comcast.net

————————
Shiloh   (4WC)SEET2217
1121 Shiloh Road
Greeneville, TN 37745
(423)639-3763   <Greene>
shilohcpc@embarqmail.com
PA: Tammy L Greene   <M1>
109 Armitage Drive
Greeneville, TN 37745
(423)972-5525
tg6386@aol.com
CL: Tara Thompson
1121 Shiloh Road
Greeneville, TN 37745
(423)639-3763
shilohcpc@embarqmail.com

————————
Talbott   (4C)SEET2218
PO Box 116 (mailing)
7410 W Andrew Johnson Hwy (physical)
Talbott, TN 37877
(865)475-1221   <Hamblen>
FAX: (865)475-1221
talbottchurch@bellsouth.net
LS: Richard Snowden   <M6>
PO Box 6004
Morristown, TN 37815
(423)235-5914
FAX: (423)254-3206
richard.snowden@wallacehardware.com
CL: Lon Barry Knight
950 Rocktown Road
Jefferson City, TN 37760
(865)548-8449
lonknight1@hughes.net

————————
Union   (4WC)SEET2315
400 Everett Road
Knoxville, TN 37934
(865)966-9040   <Knox>
FAX: (865)675-3787
union@unioncpchurch.com
PA: Leonard E Turner, Jr   <M1>
12651 Wagon Wheel Circle
Knoxville, TN 37934
(865)966-9040
FAX: (865)675-3787
pastor@unioncpchurch.com
CL: Hugh Turpin
101 E Passmore Lane
Oak Ridge, TN 37830
(865)272-5116
FAX: (865)675-3787
turpinhk@cs.com

————————
Virtue   (4MWC)SEET2316
725 Virtue Road
Knoxville, TN 37934
(865)966-1491   <Knox>
FAX: (865)966-0558
virtuecpchurch@tds.net
PA: Steve Graham   <M1>
11108 Thornton Drive
Knoxville, TN 37934
(865)206-0012
CL: Jack A Watson
12309 Turkey Creek Road
Knoxville, TN 37934
(865)966-5998
jwatson423@aol.com

————————
Willoughby   (4C)SEET2219
240 Wheeler Road (mailing)
220 Willoughby Road (physical)
Bulls Gap, TN 37711
( )   <Greene>
SS: Chris Franklin   <M2>
310 Yellow Springs Road
Midway, TN 37809
(423)638-5600
chrisfranklin104@comcast.net
CL: Charles Clowers
240 Wheeler Road
Bulls Gap, TN 37711
(423)235-5249

————————
Young's Chapel   (4WC)SEET2317
1705 Lawnville Road
Kingston, TN 37763
(865)376-2192   <Roane>
FAX: (865)376-2196
info@youngschapel.net
PA: Dale Watson   <M1>
1705 Lawnville Road
Kingston, TN 37763
(865)376-2192
revdwatson@comcast.net
CL: Paul McCallie
3340 Kingston Highway
Kingston, TN 37763
(865)376-9199
pt57466@bellsouth.net

PRESBYTERY OF EAST TENNESSEE CONTINUED

OTHERS ON MINISTERIAL ROLL:

Choi, Ezra   <M1 WC>
605 Arbor Hollow Circle #203
Cordova, TN 38018
(901)236-82635

Creamer, Jennifer   <M1 WC>
22 Oakhurst Avenue
Ipswich, MA 01938
(831)809-9890
jencreamer@gmail.com

Harper, Carlton   <M1 WC>
255 Glenview Circle
Lenoir City, TN 37771
(865)317-1296
carltonharperone@gmail.com

Fly, William   <M1 OM>
3002 Trowbridge Drive
Paragould, AR 72450
(865)938-6273
billyfly3@gmail.com

Franco, Ricardo   <M1 WC>
7 Hancock Street
Melrose, MA 02176
(781)662-0267
casadefericardo@verizon.net

Freeman, A Daniel   <M1 WC>
210 Dogwood Drive
Greeneville, TN 37743
(423)638-5925

Gillis, Ernest H   <M1 WC>
3273 Bruckner Boulevard
Snellville, GA 30078
(770)982-6587
professorgil64@hotmail.com

Greenwell, James C   <M1 WC>
7165 Wind Whisper Boulevard
Knoxville, TN 37924
(865)742-1653
FAX: (865)742-1653
greenwelljc@comcast.net

Hartman, Gary   <M1 WC>
3001 Hines Valley Road
Lenoir City, TN 37771
(865)986-4949
g37771@att.net

Hester, Mark S   <M1 WC>
763 Finn Long Road
Friendsville, TN 37737
(865)995-1541
markshester@att.net

Hubbard, Donald   <M1 RT>
2128 N Campbell Station Road
Knoxville, TN 37932
(865)693-0264
djhubbard@mindspring.com

Ivey, Billy F   <M1 RT>
409 Rodeo Drive
Knoxville, TN 37922
(865)966-5946
iveybe@tds.net

Johnson, Beverly B   <M1 RT>
801 Riverhill Drive Apt 308
Athens, GA 30606
(865)977-0405
bevloujohnson@aol.com

Kelly, Patrick L   <M1 M9>
1449 Rainbow Road
Mountain City, TN 37681
(423)727-4067

Keown, Gale J   <M1 RT>
2130 Cason Lane
Murfreesboro, TN 37128
(865)805-5451

Malinoski, T J   <M1 DE>
9087 Fenmore Cove
Cordova, TN 38016
(423)972-1239
mlmalinoski@comcast.net

McConnell, Donald R   <M1 RT>
147 Confederacy Circle
Knoxville, TN 37934
(865)288-0230
donjoyce515@hotmail.com

McGuire, James D   <M1 WC>
220 Southwind Circle #2
Greenville, TN 37745
(423)638-6380
jmcguire915@comcast.net

Melson, Glenda   <M1 M9>
331 Tickle Weed Road
Swansea, SC 29160
(417)588-2758
gmelson@fidnet.com

Nicholson, Casey   <M1 WC>
1020 Tusculum Boulevard
Greeneville, TN 37745
(423)639-0268
caseynicholson@mac.com

Ortiz, Milton   <M1 DE>
8846 N Cortona Circle
Cordova, TN 38018
(901)486-6679
mortiz@cumberland.org

Peterson, Lisa   <M1 WC>
7778 Cedar Creek Road
Townsend, TN 37882
(901)604-0737
petersonli@aol.com

Pickard, Ronald   <M1 WC>
6292 Golden Drive
Morristown, TN 37814
(423)587-9735

Richardson, W Jean   <M1 RT>
7533 Lancashire Boulevard
Powell, TN 37849
(865)947-3111
jeanandregena@frontier.com

Scott, Jerry   <M1 M9>
2310 Sentell Drive
Maryville, TN 37803
(865)803-3669
dmjlscott@yahoo.com

Sledge, Jeff   <M1 WC>
241 Long Bow Road
Knoxville, TN 37934
(865)318-5565
jeffsledge@charter.net

Sweet, Don   <M1 RT>
3008 Shropshire Boulevard
Powell, TN 37849
(865)938-7435
mariondon77@netscape.com

West, Fred E, Jr   <M1 WC>
510 Cedaredge Drive
New Smyrna, FL 32168
(206)409-8321
jwest616@earthlink.net

Winn, Don   <M1 WC>
375 Cumberland Mountain Circle
Sunbright, TN 37872
(615)478-9910
dwinn_ky@yahoo.com

OTHER LICENTIATES ON ROLL:

Choi, Sean   <M2 ST>
7565 Macon Road
Cordova, TN 38016
(901)826-2993
esloveh2@hotmail.com

Craig, Aaron   <M2>
325 Cherry Avenue
McKenzie, TN 38201
(731)352-6718

Sweet-Brockman, Anna   <M2>
210 E Main Street Apt B
Greenfield, TN 38230
(865)803-8582
amsweet@memphisseminary.edu

OTHER CANDIDATES ON ROLL:

Brown, Whitney   <M3 ST>
137 Roberta Drive
Memphis, TN 38112
(865)387-0002
whitneymbrown@gmail.com

Peach, John
221 Geronimo Road
Knoxville, TN 37934
(865)675-5956
peachroot@aol.com

Grace Presbytery
SOUTHEAST SYNOD

GENERAL		MEMBERSHIP			CHANGES				FINANCES				
	1.Church Number	2.Active	3.Total	4.Church School	5.Prof. of Faith	6.Gains	7.Losses	8.Children Baptized	9. OUR UNITED OUT-REACH	10. Total Out-Reach Giving	11. All Other Expenses	12. Total Income Received	13. Value Church Prop. 1=1000
	1	2	3	4	5	6	7	8	9	10	11	12	13
Antioch	0701	31	38	24	0	0	0	0	1,593	4,601	9,814	15,933	150
Beersheba	0702	164	202	90	0	7	2	2	17,796	44,463	175,320	219,783	1,200
Branchville	0106	153	219	40	22	67	14	2	0	13,500	111,500	135,000	1,650
Cairo	0704	9	23	9	0	0	1	0	0	2,515	13,914	20,858	145
Christ	0303	60	96	25	0	0	3	0	1,780	2,100	92,008	24,510	1,300
Coker	0705	52	99	25	2	6	8	0	326	2,452	67,886	59,577	1,936
Columbus	0706	133	133	30	3	13	29	1	700	560	167,367	168,895	1,500
Crestline	0102	30	30	18	0	0	2	0	6,000	13,158	69,956	71,075	1,500
El Camino	0310	65	76	28	5	6	1	2	1,000	3,020	75,326	73,166	530
Enon	0707	148	261	143	2	5	5	2	1,200	13,623	235,447	250,436	1,050
Erin	0601	64	106	42	1	8	1	1	0	7,049	55,647	65,108	218
First Hispanic+*	0307	76	76	39	2	39	11	0	0	1,024	96,046	94,051	175
Forrest Avenue	0403	20	115	8	0	0	0	0	2,146	5,401	18,251	23,652	240
Gadsden	0402	91	158	43	No Report Received			0	10,992	0	0	0	800
Glencoe	0404	85	247	70	No Report Received			0	0	0	0	0	2,000
Grace Commun	0407	80	129	40	1	3	3	0	7,473	15,688	82,002	115,044	1,200
Greens Chapel	0208	40	71	25	No Report Received			0	6,925	0	0	0	819
Groverton	0602	28	42	14	0	0	0	0	0	613	5,153	5,766	0
Helena	0108	56	59	40	2	9	0	0	1,625	11,218	98,166	109,384	700
Homewood*	0111	78	115	45	No Report Received			0	12,600	0	0	0	2,025
Hope	0308	78	127	20	1	3	2	1	6,141	12,219	141,875	152,190	1,985
Hopewell	0101	20	22	13	0	0	1	0	3,400	6,400	47,746	44,854	1,310
House of Prayer	0214	180	180	180	No Report Received			0	0	0	0	0	450
Hueytown 1st	0109	20	102	6	No Report Received			0	0	0	0	0	385
Immanuel	0311	20	23	9	4	11	8	0	2,226	0	2,200	22,459	0
McLeod Chapel	0708	15	20	10	No Report Received			0	0	0	0	0	350
Mt. Zion*	0709	23	23	12	3	1		0	5,604	9,193	37,704	55,547	650
New Hope	0104	195	233	75	4	13	3	1	32,505	69,868	251,422	321,290	2,400
Oldham Chapel	0405	14	14	10	CLOSED 2015			0	0	0	0	0	325
Piedmont	0406	59	76	71	0	3	7	1	1,800	4,910	77,548	81,787	1,101
Pleasant Hill	0710	14	32	5	No Report Received			0	0	0	0	0	160
Roca DeSalvacion	0115	29	65	9	No Report Received			0	0	0	0	0	41
Rocky Ridge	0105	65	214	30	0	2	13	2	18,087	27,049	204,052	230,004	1,200
Salem	0607	35	55	16	0	0	3	0	1,200	10,447	30,092	31,178	150
Spring Creek	0113	125	163	94	1	1	2	1	3,650	31,500	201,018	279,000	1,000
Steam Mill	0608	49	67	60	0	0	1	2	0	12,746	131,730	114,073	400
Union	0114	45	63	35	No Report Received			0	1,199	0	0	0	500
TOTALS	35	2,520	3,886	1,454	53	167	120	20	147,968	323,517	2,540,409	2,784,620	30,941

*Math error corrected. **Purged roll (x)Closed 2013 +Union church

GRACE PRESBYTERY CONTINUED

CHURCHES, PASTORS, AND CLERKS:

Antioch (2C)SEGR0701
2994 Antioch Church Road
Reform, AL 35481
( ) <Pickens>
PA: William L Benson <M1>
137 W Lowndes Drive
Columbus, MS 39701
(662)386-3433
willardb715@gmail.com
CL: Reba Carpenter
3951 County Road 45
Reform, AL 35481
(205)375-6042
rebcar0228@gmail.com

Beersheba (4MEWC)SEGR0702
1736 Beersheba Road
Columbus, MS 39702
(662)327-9615 <Lowndes>
FAX: (662)324-8320
officebeersheba@att.net
PA: Timothy Daniel Lee <M1>
186 Blasingame Drive
Columbus, MS 39702
(601)433-3714
eelmit@bellsouth.net
CL: Charles Studdard
95 Studdard Drive
Columbus, MS 39702
(662)328-8844
FAX: (662)327-8773
clstuddard@cableone.net

Branchville (4MWC)SEGR0106
80 Hurst Road
Odenville, AL 35120
(205)629-3258 <St Clair>
FAX: (205)629-3258
session@branchvillechurch.org
PA: Keith L. Mariott <M1>
155 Ridgewood Lane
Odenville, AL 35120
(205)903-5251
kjmariott@windstream.net
CL: Steve Smith
80 Hurst Road
Odenville, AL 35120
session@branchvillechurch.org

Cairo (4MC)SEGR0704
3836 Highway 50 W (mailing)
West Point, MS 39773
Cairo Road (physical)
Cedar Bluff, MS 39741
( ) <Clay>
CL: Judy Chrismond
3836 Highway 50 W
West Point, MS 39773
(662)494-7290
tjchrismond@gmail.com

Christ (4EWC)SEGR0303
19501 Holly Lane
Lutz, FL 33548
(813)909-9789 <Hillsborough>
ccpclutz@verizon.net

PA: Joshua Murray <M1>
3714 Landings Way Drive Apt 305
Tampa, FL 33624
(870)723-3286
jdm4428@yahoo.com
CL: Jeannie Vaughn
16107 Carden Drive
Odessa, FL 33556
(813)926-6631
jvaughn1@tampabay.rr.com

Coker (4MEWC)SEGR0705
PO Box 262 (mailing)
14705 Romulus Road (physical)
Coker, AL 35452
(205)339-1178 <Tuscaloosa>
cokercpgreg@att.net
SS: Greg Tucker <M2>
PO Box 262
Coker, AL 35452
(205)541-7484
cokercpgreg@att.net
CL: Retha Channell
15535 Lisenba Drive
Coker, AL 35452
(205)339-8125

Columbus (4EWC)SEGR0706
2698 Ridge Road
Columbus, MS 39705
(662)328-2692 <Lowndes>
fcpcsecretary@att.net
PA: Luke Lawson <M1>
270 N Ridgeland Circle
Columbus, MS 39705
(662)295-9322
luke_lawson03@hotmail.com
CL: Carol Carley
71 Little Tom Road
Columbus, MS 39705
(662)328-4589
carleyr@bellsouth.net

Crestline (4MWC)SEGR0102
605 Hagood Street
Birmingham, AL 35213
(205)879-6001 <Jefferson>
FAX: (205)968-8105
jan@crestlinechurch.org
PA: Janice M Overton <M1>
3320 Pipeline Road
Birmingham, AL 35243
(205)281-6819
FAX: (205)968-8105
jan@crestlinechurch.org
CL: Birki Cvacho
1214 Regal Avenue
Birmingham, AL 35213
(205)592-3023
blcvacho@bellsouth.net

El Camino (C)SEGR0310
6248 SW 14th Street (mailing)
6790 SW 12th Street (physical)
West Miami, FL 33144
(305)261-6200 <Dade>
lucatha@aol.com
PA: Luciano Jaramillo <M1>
6249 SW 14th Street
West Miami, FL 33144
(305)264-1074
ljara@aol.com

CL: Hedemarrie Dussan
6248 SW 14th Street
Miami, FL 33144
(054)812-0613

Enon (4MWC)SEGR0707
PO Box 294 (mailing)
9000 Highway 12 (physical)
Ackerman, MS 39735
(662)285-3303 <Choctaw>
enoncpchurch@dtcweb.net
PA: Jerry L Lawson <M1>
6039 MS Highway 415
Ackerman, MS 39735
(662)285-8295
lawson@dtcweb.net
CL: Raymond D Gillon Jr
PO Box 294
Ackerman, MS 39735
(601)916-3589
rgillon@dtcweb.net

Erin (4WC)SEGR0601
PO Box 574, Carthage, MS (mailing)
590 Pete Freeman Road (physical)
Union, MS 39051
( ) <Newton>
OD: Scott Engle <M5>
PO Box 1023
Decatur, MS 39327
(601)683-9586
CL: Lynn Federick
PO Box 574
Carthage, MS 39051
(601)267-4954

First Hispanic (4MWU)SEGR0307
2828 W Kirby Street
Tampa, FL 33614
(813)932-9684 <Hillsborough>
FAX: (813)932-9700
fhpctampafla@aol.com
PA: Alexandri Sosa <M1>
2828 W Kirby Street
Tampa, FL 33614
(813)960-1473
FAX: (813)932-9700
sosapcus@gmail.com
CL: Martha Lezama
8510 Kings Rail Way
Tampa, FL 33647

Forrest Avenue (4MWC)SEGR0403
2316 Forrest Avenue
Gadsden, AL 35904
(256)547-2833 <Etowah>
SS: Lem Lockmiller Jr <M1>
PO Box 348
Leesburg, AL 35983
(256)490-3021
CL: Joe Neal
1110 Cabot Avenue
Gadsden, AL 35904
(256)547-2833
jnwr996@gmail.com

GRACE PRESBYTERY CONTINUED

Gadsden (4MWC)SEGR0402
PO Box 2055 (mailing)
1200 Piedmont Cutoff (physical)
Gadsden, AL 35903
(256)492-2556 <Etowah>
FAX: (256)492-2525
office@gadsdencp.com
PA: Daniel Barkley <M1>
2732 Rexford Street
Hokes Bluff, AL 35903
daniel@gadsdencp.com
(256)478-0397
CL: Joe Neal
1110 Cabot Avenue
Gadsden, AL 35904
(256)547-2833
jnwr996@gmail.com

Glencoe (4WC)SEGR0404
200 N College Street
Glencoe, AL 35905
(256)492-1584 <Etowah>
FAX: (256)492-1584
glencoecpchurch@yahoo.com
PA: Rodney McInnis <M1>
6589 Harbor Place
Gadsden, AL 35907
(256)454-2399
mcinnisrodneyand@bellsouth.net
CL: Scott Stewart
200 N College Street
Gadsden, AL 35905
(256)492-1584
stewie242@hotmail.com

Grace Community (4C)SEGR0407
3515 Highway 14
Millbrook, AL 36054
(334)285-4655 < >
millbrookgcc@gmail.com
SS: Albert Russell <M2>
375 Ashton Park Drive
Millbrook, AL 36054
(334)290-0399
chemistry.russell@gmail.com
CL: Debbie Silva
3515 Highway 14
Millbrook, AL 36054
(334)290-3884
quilter.deb@gmx.com

Greens Chapel (4WC)SEGR0208
PO Box 729 (mailing)
81 Greens Chapel Road (physical)
Cleveland, AL 35049
(205)559-7671 <Blount>
CL: Ben Royal
148 Truman Drive
Cleveland, AL 35049
(205)274-7503
broyal@otelco.net

Groverton (2C)SEGR0602
222 Leon Harrell Road
Morton, MS 39117
( ) <Scott>
OD: Ronnie Spears <M5>
101 Shirley Drive
Pelahatchie, MS 39145

CL: Joel Lingle
6266 Highway 481 N
Morton, MS 39117
(601)942-1927

Helena (4MC)SEGR0108
PO Box 418 (mailing)
3396 Helena Road (physical)
Helena, AL 35080
(205)663-2174 <Shelby>
helenacpchurch@bellsouth.net
SS: Mike Emsinger <M3>
4910 Cox Cove
Helena, AL 35080-3424
(205)620-4699
me0573@att.com
CL: Betty Barron
1263 Siskin Drive
Alabaster, AL 35007
205-664-9251
barron1263@asi-web.com

Homewood (4WC)SEGR0111
513 Columbiana Road
Homewood, AL 35209
(205)942-3051 <Jefferson>
FAX: (205)945-0677
hcpc@homewoodcpc.com
PA: Mathew Derek Jacks <M1>
341 Shadeswood Drive
Hoover, AL 35226
(205)903-8469
pastorderek@homewoodcpc.com
CL: Melissa Dameron-Vines
1517 Astre Circle
Hoover, AL 35226
(205)422-1253
mdvines73@hotmail.com

Hope (4WC)SEGR0308
826 S Miller Road
Valrico, FL 33594
(813)684-4689 <Hillsborough>
FAX: (813)655-7919
hopecpc@verizon.net
PA: William E (Eddie) Jenkins <M1>
1836 S Ridge Drive
Valrico, FL 33594
(813)651-3802
hopechurch4@aol.com
CL: Donna Cachia
4122 Helene Place
Valrico, FL 33594
(813)684-8391
djc1948@msn.com

Hopewell (4MWC)SEGR0101
2139 Cumberland Drive SE
Bessemer, AL 35023
(205)425-2126 <Jefferson>
SS: James Scott Edwards <M3>
226 Jasmine Drive
Alabaster, AL 35007
(205)837-4069
jedwards53163@bellsouth.net
CL: Beverly Edwards
226 Jasmine Drive
Alabaster, AL 35007
(205)529-4507
bedwards@primehydraulic.net

House of Prayer (4C)SEGR0214
405 E Moulton Street (mailing)
Decatur, AL 35601
170 County Road 730 (physical)
Decatur, AL 35601
(256)355-0947 <Cullman>
FAX: (256)355-0947
nlajap@yahoo.com
PA: Neil Aguiar <M1>
405 E Moulton Street
Decatur, AL 35601
(256)616-1318
nlajap@yahoo.com
AP: Antonio Mena Rojas <M1>
1421 1st Street NW
Cullman, AL 35055
(256)531-8193
antonio.mena.7@facebook.com
CL: Andres Esteban
405 E Moulton Street
Decatur, AL 35601
(256)355-0947
FAX: (256)355-0947

Hueytown First (4MWC)SEGR0109
2711 Clyburne Street (mailing)
4846 15th Street Road (physical)
Hueytown, AL 35023
( ) <Jefferson>
CL: Thomas S Neel
2711 Clyburne Street
Hueytown, AL 35023
(205)491-6772
tardistom@hotmail.com

Immanuel (4MC)SEGR0311
10235 US Highway 301
Dade City, FL 33525
(352)567-7427 <Pasco>
PA: Charles Reed <M1>
10235 US Highway 301
Dade City, FL 33525
instchuck12@centurylink.net
(352)567-7427
CL: Chad Reed
36821 Indian Lake Cemetary Road
Dade City, FL 33523
(352)567-8755
chadrreed@embarqmail.com

McLeod Chapel (4MC)SEGR0708
305 E Minor Street (mailing)
Macon-Lynn Creek Road (physical)
Macon, MS 39341
(662)726-4609 <Noxubee>
CL: James B Moore III
305 E Minor Street
Macon, MS 39341
(662)726-4609

Mt Zion (4C)SEGR0709
3044 Wolfe Road
Columbus, MS 39705
(662)328-3778 <Lowndes>
mjmims@muw.edu
CL: Martha Jo Mims
3011 Wolfe Road
Columbus, MS 39705
(662)328-3778
mjmims@muw.edu

GRACE PRESBYTERY CONTINUED

_____
New Hope　　　　(4EWC)SEGR0104
5521 Double Oak Lane
Birmingham, AL 35242
(205)937-3684　　　　<Shelby>
FAX: (205)991-5159
jessie@newhopecpc.org
PA: Donny Acton　　　　<M1>
5521 Double Oak Lane
Birmingham, AL 35242
(205)991-5252
FAX: (205)991-5259
donny@newhopecpc.org
AP: Mindy Acton　　　　<M1>
1413 Oak Ridge Drive
Birmingham, AL 35242
(205)991-3204
FAX: (205)991-5259
mindy@newhopecpc.org
AP: Sherrlyn Frost　　　　<M1>
5557 Surrey Lane
Birmingham, AL 35242
(205)408-0729
FAX: (205)991-5259
sherrlyn@newhopecpc.org
CL: Jessie R Dunnaway
120 Virginia Way
Birmingham, AL 35242
(205)991-7434
FAX: (205)991-5259
jessie@newhopecpc.org

_____
Oldham Chapel　　　　(4EC)SEGR0405
CLOSED 3/13/2015

_____
Piedmont　　　　(4MWC)SEGR0406
23746 AL Highway 9 N
Piedmont, AL 36272
(256)447-7275　　　　<Calhoun>
PA: Jacob Sims　　　　<M1>
23716 Alabamaa Highway 9 N
Piedmont, AL 36272
(205)907-8273
jacobdsims@gmail.com
CL: Tinley Kirby
714 Reynolds Circle
Gadsden, AL 35901
(256)490-4159
tinleykirby@gmail.com

_____
Pleasant Hill　　　　(4MC)SEGR0710
115 Westwood Drive SW (mailing)
7782 CR 181, Eutaw, AL (physical)
Bessemer, AL 35022
(205)425-9659　　　　<Greene>
williambetts7177@gmail.com
LS: William H Betts　　　　<M6>
115 Westwood Drive SW
Bessemer, AL 35022
(205)425-9659
CL: Greg Espey
12034 County Road 60
Eutaw, AL 35462
(205)372-2260
gregandmichel@bellsouth.net

_____
Roca De Salvacion　　　　(C)SEGR0115
2404 Altadena Road
Birmingham, AL 35243
(205)705-3145　　　　<Jefferson>
cpcrocadesalvacion@gmail.com

PA: William Alas　　　　<M1>
612 King Valley Circle
Pelham, AL 35124
(205)966-9411
alas3542085@yahoo.es
CL: Arely Torres
1902 Chandalar Court
Pelham, AL 35124
(205)994-1978
arelymartinez07@live.com

_____
Rocky Ridge　　　　(4WC)SEGR0105
2404 Altadena Road
Birmingham, AL 35243
(205)823-2719　　　　<Jefferson>
rockyridgechurch@bellsouth.net
PA: James DuWayne Pounds　　　　<M1>
364 Vincent Street
Alabaster, AL 35007
(205)540-4284
duwaynelbs50@gmail.com
AP: Don H Thomas　　　　<M1 RT>
4829 Caldwell Mill Road
Birmingham, AL 35242
(256)742-0785
dhtatn4ybc@cs.com
CL: Jaclyn Tow
1913 Creek Trace
Hoover, AL 35244
(205)910-3758
jackietow13@gmail.com

_____
Salem　　　　(4WC)SEGR0607
PO Box 121 (mailing)
Sebastopol, MS 39359
1220 Highway 487 E (physical)
Walnut Grove, MS 39189
(601)253-2678　　　　<Leake>
sondragould@att.net
PA: Halford, Angela　　　　<M1 OP>
PO Box 404
Sebastopol, MS 39359
(501)251-4668
revhalford@gmail.com
CL: Virginia Gould
1220 Highway 487 E
Walnut Grove, MS 39189
(601)253-2678
sondragould@att.net

_____
Spring Creek　　　　(4MWC)SEGR0113
3411 Spring Creek Road (mailing)
3455 Spring Creek Road (physical)
Montevallo, AL 35115
(205)665-4184　　　　<Shelby>
springcreekcp@aol.com
PA: Scott Fowler　　　　<M1>
1900 Alex Mill Road
Montevallo, AL 35115
(205)901-8478
springcreekcp@aol.com
CL: Ben Ingram
15 Quincy Lane
Montevallo, AL 35115
(205)665-4145
ben_ingram@msn.com

_____
Steam Mill　　　　(4WC)SEGR0608
593 Pine Grove Road (mailing)
Walnut Grove, MS 39189
11551 Road 101 (physical)
Union, MS 39365
(　)　　　　<Neshoba>
nchambers@hughes.net
PA: Nicholas Chambers　　　　<M1>
11300 Road 101
Union, MS 39365
(601)697-4470
nachambrs@hotmail.com
CL: Myra Bankston
593 Pine Grove Road
Walnut Grove, MS 39189
(601)616-0436
mbankston@ecmhci.com

_____
Union　　　　(4MWC)SEGR0114
PO Box 64 (mailing)
11633 Bama Rock Garden Road (physical)
Vance, AL 35490
(　)　　　　<Tuscaloosa>
LS: Herbie Gray　　　　<M6>
2554 A Rocky Ridge
Birmingham, AL 35226
CL: Clifford Odell
11491 Bama Rock Garden Road
Vance, AL 35490
wjsrabbit@aol.com

_____
OTHERS ON MINISTERIAL ROLL:

Acton, Wade　　　　<M1 RT>
1615 Estes Drive
Glencoe, AL 35905
(256)492-8542
ginnyacton@juno.com
Black, Gary G　　　　<M1 WC>
503 S Main Street
Piedmont, AL 36272
(205)447-7142
Brasher, Karen　　　　<M1 WC>
2931 Barker Cypress Road, Apt 415
Houston, TX 77084
(205)777-2420
ekb077@gmail.com
Carter, Patricia　　　　<M1 M9>
2509 Decatur Stratton Road
Decatur, MS 39327
(601)604-3813
revtree@yahoo.com
Chuquimia, Walter　　　　<M1 OM>
18240 S US Highway 301
Winauma, FL 33598
(813)399-4050
walter@beth-el.info
Clark, J Don　　　　<M1 RT>
1601 Lake Ridge Circle
Birmingham, AL 35216
(205)942-4054
jdsjcl@charter.net
Crawford, Roger B　　　　<M1 RT>
541 Highway 25 N
Carthage, MS 39051
(601)298-1899

GRACE PRESBYTERY CONTINUED

Davis, C Timothy　　　　　　　<M1 WC>
8880 Childress Road
West Paducah, KY 42086
(850)995-8383
FAX: (904)994-6003
charles0828@earthlink.net

Edmonds, Wayne　　　　　　　<M1 RT>
112 Dogwood Trail
Eclectic, AL 36024
(334)857-2202
sweetpea@comlinkinc.net

English, Don W　　　　　　　<M1 WC>
4311 Guys Court
Bessemer, AL 35022
(205)428-4790

Foreman, Samuel L　　　　　　<M1 WC>
2811 Laredo Drive
Hattiesburg, MS 39402
(601)562-1415
slfcpc@yahoo.com

Gaither, Randy　　　　　　　<M1 WC>
No 3 Pacific Street
Belmopan City
Belize, Central America
rgaither@valuelinx.net

Garcia, Ramon　　　　　　　<M1 OM>
2714 Callista Court Apt 104
Naples, FL 34114
(239)200-5714
revga@hotmail.com

Hartung, J Thomas　　　　<M1 M9 ST>
2291 Americus Boulevard W Apt 1
Clearwater, FL 33763
(727)797-2882
revtom6@aol.com

Headrick, Anthony　　　　　　<M1 M8>
3327 N Eagle Road Ste 110-132
Meridian, ID 83646
(619)524-8821
chaps2a@yahoo.com

Headrick, Christopher　　　　　<M1 WC>
1913 Vestavia Court Apt B
Vestavia Hills, AL 35216
(205)240-0979
bravespop@gmail.com

Headrick, Jerry　　　　　　　<M1 RT>
9950 Old Stage Road
Stockton, AL 36579
(251)377-9744
willjheadrick@gmail.com

Hunley, Jearl　　　　　　　<M1 RT>
2618 Canterbury Road
Columbus, MS 39705
(662)329-1516
jdhunley@cableone.net

Johnson, Thomas (Tommy) C　<M1 RT>
PO Box 566
Helena, AL 35080
(205)936-1350
revtomjohnson@aol.com

Laperche, Michael　　　　　　<M1 WC>
9317 Moondancer Circle
Roseville, CA 95747
(813)948-8016
pastor-mike@earthlink.net

Lathem, W Ray　　　　　　　<M1 WC>
452 County Road 1462
Cullman, AL 35055
(256)708-1247
lathemray@bellsouth.net

Lefavor, David　　　　　　　<M1 M8>
414 S Monroe Siding Road
Xenia, OH 45385
(813)613-4133
david.lefavor@med.va.gov

Maynard, Terrell D　　　　　　<M1 RT>
3 Nelson Cove
Milan, TN 38358
(731)437-0056
terrellmaynard@bellsouth.net

Moore, James R, Sr　　　　　　<M1 RT>
2778 Marguerite Street S
Hokes Bluff, AL 35903
(256)494-9030
jmoore@microxl.com

Mora, Wilfredo　　　　　　　<M1 WC>
17512 SW 153rd Court
Miami, FL 33187
(786)554-1478
moraw68@gmail.com

Morrow, Charles　　　　　　<M1 RT>
5032 Pine Grove Road
Union, MS 39365
(601)479-0288
morrowp7@yahoo.com

Payne, Robert (Bob)　　　　　<M1 WC>
1660 3rd Street NW
Birmingham, AL 35215
(205)856-2427
payne.bob.emmet@gmail.com

Ros, Ramiro　　　　　　　<M1 WC>
107 Bracken Lane
Brandon, FL 33511
(813)633-1548
bethel@gte.net

Rowlett, Ron　　　　　　　<M1 WC>
22 Diana Drive
Savannah, GA 31406
(912)351-0736

Schultz, Don　　　　　　　<M1 RT>
708 Gateway Lane
Tampa, FL 33613
(813)960-1473

Talley, Ed　　　　　　　<M1 WC>
404 Serenity Circle
Walland, TN 37886
(205)854-1886

Thomas, Lynn　　　　　　　<M1 DE>
4833 Caldwell Mill Lane
Birmingham, AL 35242
(205)601-5770
lynndont@gmail.com

Tobler, Garth　　　　　　　<M1 WC>
136 Boat Landing Road
Oneonta, AL 35121
(205)683-0298
gatobler@gmail.com

Travieso, Julio　　　　　　　<M1 WC>
15910 Countrybrook Street
Tampa, FL 33624
(813)963-3727
jutra98@aol.com

Weldon, Mark　　　　　　　<M1 WC>
1515 Chambliss Drive
Birmingham, AL 35226
(205)330-8580
weldonm@bellsouth.net

Yarce, Omar　　　　　　　<M1 WC>
10925 Neptune Drive
Cooper City, FL 33026
alphavida@gmail.com
(205)919-9685

OTHER LICENTIATES ON ROLL:

Diego, Aida Melendez　　　　　<M2>
412 SW 87 Place
Miami, FL 33174
(305)815-1197
revaidamd@yahoo.com

Ferguson, David　　　　　　　<M2>
1841 Pebble Lake Drive
Birmingham, AL 35232
(205)200-9205
fergusondavid15@yahoo.com

Linski, David　　　　　　　<M2>
1060 Alpine Way
Indian Springs, AL 35124
(205)677-8163
david.linski@gmail.com

Sumerlin, Larkin　　　　　　　<M2>
174 Brookgreen Lane
Indian Springs, AL 35124
(334)357-00007
larkin_sumerlin72@hotmail.com

Tanck, Brian　　　　　　　<M2>
64 Mercer Street
Princeton, NJ 08540
(630)730-1577
brian.tanck@gmail.com

OTHER CANDIDATES ON ROLL:

Barrios, Janina　　　　　　　<M3>
10090 NW 80th Court
Hialeah Gardens, FL 33016
(786)757-0369
janina83@hotmail.com

Byford, Ken　　　　　　　<M3>
58 Quincy Lane
Montevallo, AL 35115
(205)665-5753
kenabyford@gmail.com

Hernandez, Jhonathan　　　　　<M3>
10090 NW 80th Court
Hialeah Gardens, FL 33016
jhoto2006@hotmail.com

Ingram, Matthew　　　　　　<M3>
29 Quincy Lane
Montevallo, AL 35115
(205)914-0829
mbingram80@gmail.com

Marquez, Jose Ignacio　　　　　<M3>
8976 W Flagler Street
Miami, FL 33174
jimarquez.aviation@gmail.com

Prevost, Abigail　　　　　　<M3>
4731 Lafayette Road
Hopkinsville, KY 42240
(731)343-5386
abbyprevost@gmail.com

Seva, Judith　　　　　　　<M3>
7685 Tara Circle Apt 204
Naples, FL 34104
(239)269-3917
jclthgirl12@gmail.com

Solito, Carlos　　　　　　　<M3>
106 Highway 63
Calera, AL 35040
(205)329-8514
fcg9700@gmail.com

Yarce, Virginia　　　　　　　<M3>
10925 Neptune Drive
Cooper City, Fl 33026
(954)850-7111
ginnyyarce@gmail.com

Hong Kong Presbytery
MISSION SYNOD

	GENERAL		MEMBERSHIP			CHANGES				FINANCES			
	1.Church Number	2.Active	3.Total	4.Church School	5.Prof. of Faith	6.Gains	7.Losses	8.Children Baptized	9. OUR UNITED OUT-REACH	10. Total Out-Reach Giving	11. All Other Expenses	12. Total Income Received	13. Value Church Prop. 1=1000
	1	2	3	4	5	6	7	8	9	10	11	12	13
Cheung Chau	8801	39	39	21	0	1	0	1	64	2,338	41,380	49,499	128
Kowloon	8803	104	292	137	6	7	4	4	1,545	39,100	213,880	188,000	154
Macau	8804	77	145	17	3	5	8	1	1,427	13,954	97,015	160,009	761
Mu Min	8810	200	315	58	26	35	3	12	773	19,103	388,205	488,846	0
North Point	8805	47	117	37	1	1	2	0	2,350	34,857	121,285	157,920	100
Po Lam	8808	78	136	20	4	4	0	1	386	6,760	131,650	166,370	0
Shatin	8807	220	239	50	11	13	0	4	229	8,053	370,117	362,735	385
Tao Hsien	8806	400	548	200	0	12	7	6	2,576	152,545	740,444	838,903	2,856
Xi Lin	8809	110	166	54	3	6	2	6	1,932	31,723	239,212	277,997	0
Yao Dao	8811	144	193	25	11	16	2	0	2,189	19,642	213,710	240,142	0
TOTALS	10	1,419	2,190	619	65	100	28	35	13,471	328,075	2,556,898	2,930,421	4,384

CHURCHES, PASTORS, AND CLERKS:

Cheung Chau   (4C)MSHK8801
11 On Wing Centre 2/F
Pak She Back Street
Cheung Chau, HONG KONG
(852)2981-4933   <Hong Kong>
cccpcmail@yahoo.com.hk
SS: Kelvin Ho   <M2>
11 On Wing Centre 2/F
Pak She Back Street
Cheung Chau, HONG KONG
(852)2981-4933
kelvinskho@gmail.com
CL: Kelvin Ho
11 On Wing Centre 2/F
Pak She Back Street
Cheung Chau, HONG KONG
(852)2981-4933
kelvinskho@gmail.com

Kowloon   (4WC)MSHK8803
338-340 Castle Peak Road
Flat D 2/FL
Kowloon, HONG KONG
(852)2386-6563   <Hong Kong>
FAX: (852)3020-0365
kcumber@biznetvigator.com
SS: Ting Bong Ha   <M2>
338-340 Castle Peak Road
Flat D 2/FL
Kowloon, HONG KONG
(852)2386-6563
FAX: (852)3020-0365
kcumber@biznetvigator.com
CL: Lai Seung AU
338-340 Castle Peak Road
Flat D 2/FL
Kowloon, HONG KONG
(852)2386-6563
FAX: (852)3020-0365
kcumber@biznetvigator.com

Macau   (4WC)MSHK8804
258 Carlos D'Assumpcao
Ed Kin Heng Long 4 Andar LMN
MACAU
(853)2892-1702   <Macau>
cpc_macau@yahoo.com.hk
SS: Eva Watt   <M3>
258 Carlos D'Assumpcao
Ed Kin Heng Long 4 Andar LMN
MACAU
(853)2892-1702
eva6e@hotmail.com
CL: Mei Teng Lio
258 Carlos D'Assumpcao
Ed Kin Heng Long 4 Andar LMN
MACAU
(853)2892-1702
cpc_macau@yahoo.com.hk

Mu Min   (C)MSHK8810
2/F Fu Tung Shopping Center
Tung Chung
Lantau Island, HONG KONG
(852)2109-1738   <Hong Kong>
FAX: (852)2109-1737
mmcpc@cumberland.org.hk
PA: Patrick Tat Wing So   <M1>
2/F Fu Tung Shopping Center
Tung Chung
Lantau Island, HONG KONG
(852)2109-1738
FAX: (852)2109-1737
pattwso1@gmail.com
CL: Lai Yuet Liu   <M2>
2/F Fu Tung Shopping Center
Tung Chung
Lantau Island, HONG KONG
(852)2109-1738
FAX: (852)2109-1737
lyliu0914@gmail.com

North Point   (4WC)MSHK8805
14-16 Tsat Tsz Mui Road
1/Fl Block B
North Point, HONG KONG
(852)2562-2148   <Hong Kong>
FAX: (852)2564-2898
northpointcpc@yahoo.com.hk
SS: Eliza Yuk Lan Yau   <M2>
14-16 TsatTsz Mui Road
1/Fl Block B
North Point, HONG KONG
(852)2562-2148
FAX: (852)2564-2898
elizaylyau@yahoo.com.hk
CL: Queenie Tang
14-16 Tsat Tsz Mui Road
1/Fl Block B
North Point, HONG KONG
(852)2562-2148
FAX: (852)2564-2898
northpointcpc@yahoo.com.hk

Po Lam   (ARC)MSHK8808
Wing B&C, G/F, Ming Wik House
Kin Ming Estate
Tseung Kwan O NT, HONG KONG
(852)2706-0111   <Hong Kong>
FAX: (852)2706-0114
polamcpc@yahoo.com.hk
SS: Yim Ngar Wong   <M2>
Wing B&C G/F Ming Wik House
Kin Ming Estate
Tseung Kwan O NT, HONG KONG
(852)2706-0111
FAX: (852)2706-0114
yimngar@yahoo.com.hk
CL: Yim Ngar Wong
Wing B&C G/F Ming Wik House
Kin Ming Estate
Tseung Kwan O NT, HONG KONG
(852)2706-0111
FAX: (852)2706-0114
yimngar@yahoo.com.hk

HONG KONG PRESBYTERY CONTINUED

Shatin   (ARC)MSHK8807
G/1F 251 Tin Sam Village
Shatin NT, HONG KONG
(852)2693-3444   <Hong Kong>
FAX: (852)2607-2245
cpcshatin@yahoo.com.hk
PA: Jonathan Chor K Siu   <M1>
G/1F 251 Tin Sam Village
Shatin NT, HONG KONG
(852)2693-3444
FAX: (852)2607-2245
cpccksiu@yahoo.com.hk
CL: Angelo Chui
G/1F 251 Tin Sam Village
Shatin NT, HONG KONG
(852)2693-3444
FAX: (852)2607-2245
cpcshatin@yahoo.com.hk

Tao Hsien   (4F)MSHK8806
2/F Welland Plaza
188 Nam Cheong Street
Sham Shui Po, Kowloon, HONG KONG
(852)2783-8923   <Hong Kong>
FAX: (852)2771-2726
thchurch@taohsien.org.hk
PA: Amos Pui Chung Yuen   <M1>
2/F Welland Plaza
188 Nam Cheong Street
Sham Shui Po, Kowloon, HONG KONG
(852)2783-8923
FAX: (852)2771-2726
revyuen@taohsien.org.hk
CL: Adays Lee
2/F Welland Plaza
188 Nam Cheong Street
Sham Shui Po, Kowloon, HONG KONG
(852)2783-8923
FAX: (852)2771-2726
thchurch@taohsien.org.hk

Xi Lin   (4C)MSHK8809
28 Hong Yip Street
Yuen Long, HONG KONG
(852)2639-9176   <Hong Kong>
FAX: (853)2639-5620
info@yuenlongchurch.org
PA: William Kin Keung Yeung   <M1>
28 Hong Yip Street
Yuen Long, HONG KONG
(852)2639-9176
FAX: (852)2639-5620
william@xilincpc.org.hk
CL: Loarinne Tang
28 Hong Yip Street
Yuen Long, HONG KONG
(852)2639-9176
FAX: (852)2639-5620
loarinne@yuenlongchurch.org

Yao Dao   (4C)MSHK8811
CPC Yao Dao Primary School
Tin Yuet Estate
Tin Shui Wai, NT, HONG KONG
(852)2617-7872   <Hong Kong>
FAX: (852)2617-0287
ydgrowth@yaodaocpc.org

SS: Antony Cheng   <M3>
CPC Yao Dao Primary School
Tin Yuet Estate
Tin Shui Wai, NT, HONG KONG
(852)2617-7872
FAX: (852)2617-0287
antonycycheng@yahoo.com.hk
CL: Kwong Lung Leung
CPC Yao Dao Primary School
Tin Yuet Estate
Tin Shui Wai, NT, HONG KONG
(852)2617-7872
FAX: (852)2617-0287
ydgrowth@yaodaocpc.org

OTHERS ON MINISTERIAL ROLL:

Cheung, Luke   <M1 WC>
2/F Welland Plaza
188 Nam Cheong Street
Sham Shui Po Kowloon, HONG KONG
(852)2783-8923
FAX: (852)2771-2726
luke.cheung@cgst.edu
Hung, Ella Siu Kei   <M1 WC>
2/F Welland Plaza
188 Nam Cheong Street
Sham Shui Po, Kowloon, HONG KONG
(852)2783-8923
FAX: (852)2771-2726
siukee@taohsien.org.hk
Lee, Ted Shu Tak   <M1 WC>
2/F Welland Plaza
188 Nam Cheong Street
Sham Shui Po, Kowloon, HONG KONG
(852)2783-8923
FAX: (852)2771-2726
tedlee@taohsien.org.hk
Leung, Grace Siu Tim Yu   <M1 WC>
2/F Welland Plaza
188 Nam Cheong Street
Sham Shui Po, Kowloon, HONG KONG
(852)2783-8923
FAX: (852)2771-2726
yuleungsiutim@netvigator.com
Wong, So Li   <M1 WC>
2/F Fu Tung Shopping Center
Tung Chung
Lantau Island, HONG KONG
(852)2109-1738
FAX: (852)2109-1737
soliwong@gmail.com
Yu, Carver Tat Sum   <M1 WC>
2/F Welland Plaza
188 Nam Cheong Street
Sham Shui Po, Kowloon, HONG KONG
(852)2783-8923
FAX: (852)2771-2726
carver.yu@cgst.edu

OTHER LICENTIATES ON ROLL:

Ho, Carmen   <M2>
Tin Yuet Estate
Tin Shui Wai NT, HONG KONG
(852)2617-7872
FAX: (852)2617-0287
ho_carcar@yahoo.com.hk

Lam, Janice   <M2>
G/F & 1/F 251 Tin Sum Village
Tai Wai, Shatin NT, HONG KONG
(852)2693-3444
FAX: (852)2607-2245
janiceyeung929@gmail.com
Lee, Priscilla   <M2>
Tin Yuet Estate
Tin Shui Wai NT, HONG KONG
(852)2617-7872
FAX: (852)2617-0287
wai_yung_lee@yahoo.com.hk
Leung, Paulus   <M2>
Wing B & C
G/F Ming Wik House
Kin Ming Es
Tseung Kwan O, HONG KONG
(852)2706-0111
FAX: (852)2706-0114
pineapple0207@yahoo.com.hk
Li, Chun Wai   <M2>
1/Fl Block B
14 TsatTsz Mui Road
North Point, HONG KONG
(852)2562-2148
FAX: (852)2564-2898
cwli2000hk@yahoo.com.hk
Liu, Lai Yuet   <M2>
2/F Fu Tung Shopping Centre
Tung Chung
Lantau Island NT, HONG KONG
(852)2109-1738
FAX: (852)2109-1737
laiyuet0914@gmail.com
Mak, Daphne Suet Chung   <M2>
2/F Welland Plaza
188 Nam Cheong Street
Sham Shui Po, Kowloon, HONG KONG
(852)2783-8923
FAX: (852)2771-2726
daphne@taohsien.org.hk
Wong, Samson Chi   <M2>
2/F Fu Tung Shopping Centre
Tung Chung
Lantau Island NT, HONG KONG
(852)2109-1738
FAX: (852)2109-1737
wongchishui@yahoo.com.hk
Yau, Chat Ming   <M2>
G/F 251 Tin Sum Village
Shatin NT, HONG KONG
(852)2693-3444
FAX: (852)2607-2245
summerycm@yahoo.com.hk
Yuen, Susanna   <M2>
28 Hong Yip Street
Yuen Long, NT, HONG KONG
(522)639-9176
FAX: (522)639-5620
susanna@yuenlongchurch.org
Yung, Karen Wing Man   <M2>
Flat D 2/F
338-340 Castle Peak Road
Kowloon, HONG KONG
(852)2386-6563
FAX: (852)3020-0365
yungyungmiss@yahoo.com.hk

OTHER CANDIDATES ON ROLL:

Cheung, Agnes <M3>
2/F Welland Plaza
188 Nam Cheong Street
Sam Shui Po
Kowloon, HONG KONG
(852)2783-8923
FAX: (852)2771-2726
agnes@taoshien.org.hk

Ho, Jessie <M3>
2/F Welland Plaza
188 Nam Cheong Street
Sam Shui Po
Kowloon, HONG KONG
(852)2783-8923
FAX: (852)2771-2726
agnes@taoshien.org.hk

Hung, Kevin <M3>
28 Hong Yip Street
Yuen Long NT, HONG KONG
(852)2639-9176
FAX: (852)5620
kevinhk0627@gmail.com

Lam, Mercy <M3>
28 Hong Yip Street
Yuen Long NT, HONG KONG
(852)2639-9176
FAX: (852)5620
thlammercy@gmail.com

Sze, Yat Sung <M3>
Tin Yuet Estate
Tin Shui Wai NT, HONG KONG
(852)2617-7872
FAX: (852)2617-0287
yatsungs@yahoo.com.hk

Tsui, Sukie <M3>
Wing B & C
G/F Ming Wik House
Kin Ming Es
(852)2706-0111
FAX: (852)2706-0114
sukiecpc@yahoo.com.hk

Hope Presbytery
SOUTHEAST SYNOD

GENERAL		MEMBERSHIP		CHANGES				FINANCES				
1.Church Number	2.Active	3.Total	4.Church School	5.Prof. of Faith	6.Gains	7.Losses	8.Children Baptized	9. OUR UNITED OUT- REACH	10. Total Out- Reach Giving	11. All Other Expenses	12. Total Income Received	13. Value Church Prop. 1=1000
1	2	3	4	5	6	7	8	9	10	11	12	13
Allsboro*	0501	45	84	24	0	6	0	1	0	8,750	67,680	87,654	300
Baldwin Chapel	0202	40	65	17	0	0	0	1	0	858	29,720	35,406	200
Faith	0213	49	107	31	No Report Received			0	0	0	0	0	600
Florence 1st	0506	87	125	51	0	3	2	2	14,354	62,630	109,687	172,612	1,200
Hickory Grove	0507	26	37	16	No Report Received			0	0	0	0	0	150
Hurricane	0508	60	92	30	No Report Received			0	0	0	0	0	300
Maud	0509	10	4	0	No Report Received			0	0	0	0	0	90
Mt. Hester	0510	10	10	5	0	0	0	0	0	200	10,316	17,910	200
Mt. Pleasant	0511	7	7	6	0	0	0	0	0	0	18,985	8,114	280
Nebo	0512	32	32	22	0	0	2	0	200	1,575	63,280	66,496	1,225
Old Mt Bethel*	0513	28	36	24	0	0	2	1	0	3,322	20,396	25,959	55
Park Terrace	0514	34	34	25	3	3	2	1	0	4,475	76,000	76,830	671
Rogersville 1st	0517	122	274	87	No Report Received			0	15,019	0	0	0	1,025
Springfield	0515	89	171	52	0	0	1	0	0	11,040	94,168	113,511	1,000
Union Hill	0516	82	120	37	12	10	2	0	0	9,136	95,075	101,473	1,500
Welti	0212	124	201	69	1	1	17	2	17,600	41,561	123,249	180,369	925
TOTALS	16	830	1,370	487	16	23	28	8	47,173	143,547	708,956	886,342	9,503

*Math error corrected. **Purged roll.

CHURCHES, PASTORS, AND CLERKS:

Allsboro (4MEWC)SEHO0501
515 Iuka Road (mailing)
1925 Allsboro Road (physical)
Cherokee, AL 35616
(256)360-2919 <Colbert>
SS: Don F Thomas <M1 OP>
400 Park Hill Road
Collierville, TN 38017
(901)861-6398
thomas63981@comcast.net
CL: Dale Johnson
515 Iuka Road
Cherokee, AL 35616
(256)360-2973
djohnson@bibank.com

Baldwin Chapel (4MEWC)SEHO0202
381 County Road 404 (mailing)
126 County Road 1153 (physical)
Cullman, AL 35057
(256)737-1850 <Cullman>
PA: Gary Carter <M1>
8311 County Road 1082
Vinemont, AL 35179
(256)443-8389
garycarter51@gmail.com
CL: Bonnie Marty
381 County Road 404
Cullman, AL 35057
(256)734-6399
brmarty45@yahoo.com

Faith (4WC)SEHO0213
5821 County Road 1114 (mailing)
Vinemont, AL 35179
6880 AL Highway 157 (physical)
Cullman, AL 35057
(256)734-0893 <Cullman>
PA: Dudley Brock <M1>
490 County Road 1184
Cullman, AL 35057
(256)734-0893
preacherbrock@att.net
CL: Philip Nickles
5821 County Road 1114
Vinemont, AL 35179
(256)620-1977
nickles.phil@yahoo.com

Florence First (4WC)SEHO0506
2422 Darby Drive
Florence, AL 35630
(256)766-0471 <Lauderdale>
FAX: (256)766-0736
fcpoffice@comcast.net
PA: Dwayne McDuff <M1>
9770 County Road 5
Florence, AL 35633
(256)764-6354
FAX: (256)766-0736
fcpdmcduff@comcast.net
CL: Philip Gambrell
1045 Piedmont Street
Florence, AL 35630
(256)443-8924
pgambrell@ffcuonline.com

Hickory Grove (4MC)SECU0507
75 County Road 59
Moulton, AL 35650
(256)306-0025 <Lawrence>
dhtatn4ybc@cs.com
CL: Noah Williamson
655 County Road 38
Mount Hope, AL 35651
(256)974-9413
mwilliamson@lawrenceal.org

Hurricane (4EWC)SEHO0508
1331 County Road 86 (mailing)
1000 County Road 156 (physical)
Rogersville, AL 35652
(256)247-7483 <Lauderdale>
PA: Jimmy R Cox <M1>
2250 County Road 156
Anderson, AL 35610
(256)710-1702
dcox01@msn.com
CL: Bryan Belue
1331 County Road 86
Rogersville, AL 35652
(256)247-7175
rbeluebigboy@aol.com

Maud (4MWC)SEHO0509
2280 Maud Road (mailing)
Gypsy Loop (physical)
Cherokee, AL 35616
(256)360-2811 <Colbert>

HOPE PRESBYTERY CONTINUED

CL: Paula Pardue
2280 Maud Road
Cherokee, AL 35616
(256)360-2811

Mt Hester   (4MEWC)SEHO0510
PO Box 174 (mailing)
14720 Mount Hester Road (physical)
Cherokee, AL 35616
( )   <Colbert>
CL: Leigh Ann Malone
2625 Sutton Hill Road
Cherokee, AL 35616
(256)359-6134
leighmalone05@yahoo.com

Mt Pleasant   (4MC)SEHO0511
30 Carolyn Road (mailing)
13575 County Line Road (physical)
Muscle Shoals, AL 35661
(256)446-5397   <Colbert>
CL: James Letsinger
8285 2nd Street
Leighton, AL 35646
(256)446-9367

Nebo   (4MEWC)SEHO0512
9491 Highway 101
Lexington, AL 35648
(256)577-5952   <Lauderdale>
nebo9491@gmail.com
PA: Terry Herston   <M1>
390 County Road 95
Rogersville, AL 35652
(256)247-3004
tpaw51@gmail.com
CL: Steve Littrell
9491 Highway 101
Lexington, AL 35648
(256)577-5952
nebo9491@gmail.com

Old Mt Bethel   (4C)SEHO0513
County Road 51
Rogersville, AL 35652
( )   <Lauderdale>
PA: Terry Herston   <M1>
390 County Road 95
Rogersville, AL 35652
(256)247-3004
tpaw51@gmail.com
CL: Tommy Word
620 County Road 521
Lexington, AL 35648
(256)247-3182
tword1956@gmail.com

Park Terrace   (4MEWC)SEHO0514
100 E Wheeler Avenue
Sheffield, AL 35660
(256)383-8052   <Colbert>
pastor@parkterracechurch.org
PA: George Lee   <M1>
104 Parc Circle
Florence, AL 35630
(256)740-0809
butchleeautos@yahoo.com
CL: Peggy Vickers
112 Pasadena Avenue
Muscle Shoals, AL 35661
(256)383-1992

Rogersville First   (4WC)SEHO0517
16751 Highway 72
Rogersville, AL 35652
(256)247-3339   <Lauderdale>
fcprogersville@yahoo.com
PA: James P Driskell   <M1>
154 Mountain Way
Anderson, AL 35610
(256)648-6758
FAX: (256)247-3339
patprespax@yahoo.com
CL: Kathy W Ezell
275 McGraw Circle
Anderson, AL 35610
(256)247-3625
kwhiteheadezell@aol.com

Springfield   (4MWC)SEHO0515
5400 Highway 101
Rogersville, AL 35652
(256)247-1424   <Lauderdale>
FAX: (256)247-1424
kennymorgan330@hotmail.com
PA: Kenneth P Morgan   <M1>
5400 Highway 101
Rogersville, AL 35652
(256)247-3890
FAX: (256)247-1424
kennymorgan330@hotmail.com
CL: Charles G Lash
170 Meadow Ridge Lane
Rogersville, AL 35652
(256)247-0040

Union Hill   (4MEWC)SEHO0516
6535 Bailey Road
Anderson, AL 35610
(256)233-1841   <Limestone>
PA: Charles Hood   <M1>
1200 County Road 519
Anderson, AL 35610
(256)229-6251
hooddad11@gmail.com
CL: Curtis Usery
28341 Easter Ferry Road
Lester, AL 35647
(256)232-9237

Welti   (4MWC)SEHO0212
8817 County Road 747
Cullman, AL 35055
(256)737-9138   <Cullman>
weltipastor@welticpchurch.com
PA: James L Peyton   <M1>
1455 County Road 643
Cullman, AL 35055
(256)735-3620
jakjpeyton@att.net
CL: Lee Holder
6589 County Road 747
Cullman, AL 35055
(256)739-5136
lholder@tvpinc.com

OTHERS ON MINISTERIAL ROLL:

Deaton, John   <M1 WC>
277 School Lane
Springfield, PA 19064
(215)906-7067
deatonjr11@gmail.com
Malone, John W   <M1 RT>
3693 Highway 67 South
Sommerville, AL 35670
(256)778-8237
Parker, Susan   <M1 WC>
655 York Drive
Rogersville, AL 35652
(256)247-3877
park9301@bellsouth.net
Rodgers, Howard   <M1 RT>
336 County Road 1216
Vinemont, AL 35179
(256)739-6296
djbr421@yahoo.com
Yaple, George H   <M1 RT>
2051 Lost Creek Road
Carbon Hill, AL 35549
(205)924-9921

OTHER LICENTIATES ON ROLL:

OTHER CANDIDATES ON ROLL:

Japan Presbytery
MISSION SYNOD

| GENERAL | MEMBERSHIP | | | CHANGES | | | | FINANCES | | | | |
| 1.Church Number | 2.Active | 3.Total | 4.Church School | 5.Prof. of Faith | 6.Gains | 7.Losses | 8.Children Baptized | 9. OUR UNITED OUT-REACH | 10. Total Out-Reach Giving | 11. All Other Expenses | 12. Total Income Received | 13. Value Church Prop. 1=1000 |
1	2	3	4	5	6	7	8	9	10	11	12	13
Asahi Mission 8315	28	28	10	1	1	0	2	979	2,591	34,649	37,240	9
Den-en Mission 8310	14	37	15	0	0	3	0	300	973	47,243	30,406	70
EbinaShionNoOka 8311	118	171	30	1	9	2	1	2,725	22,047	17,744	97,444	74
Higashi Koganei 8301	30	36	6	0	1	1	0	1,069	5,787	55,141	49,965	130
Ichikawa Grace 8314	18	23	11	0	2	0	0	413	1,038	47,270	33,072	45
Izumi 8312	30	42	6	4	4	1	0	572	2,589	37,507	40,097	36
Kibougaoka 8302	171	328	60	1	1	5	0	4,796	33,243	123,808	160,820	171
Koza 8303	528	1,122	404	7	12	25	2	16,302	124,960	560,813	685,375	1,512
KunitachiNozomi 8306	59	104	60	0	0	0	0	2,120	10,811	75,720	81,952	170
Megumi 8309	41	49	5	2	2	1	0	1,585	7,039	55,148	60,716	71
Naruse 8305	53	116	14	2	2	4	0	1,915	10,310	67,565	72,373	96
Sagamino 8304	29	56	9	0	0	0	1	1,269	2,709	36,694	38,673	174
Shibusawa 8307	38	101	11	0	0	1	0	1,696	4,107	61,804	67,647	245
TOTALS 13	1,157	2,213	641	18	34	43	6	35,741	228,204	1,551,106	1,464,790	3,103

*Math error corrected. **Purged roll.

CHURCHES, PASTORS, AND CLERKS:

Asahi Mission   (4F)MSJA8315
 1F Miyabi-Bldg
 1-19-21 Honcho Tsurugamine
 Asahi-ku Yokohama, Kanagawa-Ken
 241-0021 JAPAN
 (045)489-3720   <Japan>
 FAX: (045)953-2588
 info@asahi-ch.com
PA: Atsushi Suzuki   <M1>
 53-17 Higashi Kibogaoka Asahi-ku
 Yokohama, Kanagawa-ken
 241-0826 JAPAN
 (045)362-2603
 FAX: (045)362-2603
 asyuwa98@m10.alpha-net.ne.jp
CL: Session Clerk Asahi Mission Point
 1F Miyabi-Bldg
 1-19-21 Honcho Tsurugamine
 Asahi-ku Yokohama, Kanagawa-Ken
 241-0021 JAPAN
 (045)489-3720
 FAX: (045)953-2588
 info@asahi-ch.com

Den-en Mission   (4MC)MSJA8310
 9-41-2 Kamitsuruma-honcho
 Sagamihara-Shi, Kanagawa-Ken
 228-0818 JAPAN
 (042)744-6804   <Japan>
 FAX: (042)744-6804
 den-en.church@pc5.so-net.ne.jp

PA: Kazuhiko Furuhata   <M1>
 #310, 9-41-15 Kamitsurumahoncho
 Sagamihara-shi, Kanagawa-ken
 252-0318 JAPAN
 (042)814-7802
 FAX: (042)814-7802
 cpc.furuhata@gmail.com
CL: Takashi Kanazashi
 3-6-406 Shimoyuzuki
 Hachiouji-shi, Tokyo
 197-0732 JAPAN
 (042)675-6895
 fredericfchopin@gmail.com

Ebina Shion No Oka (4MWC)MSJA8311
 3-17-57 Nakashinden
 Ebina-shi, Kanagawa-ken
 243-0422 JAPAN
 (046)234-3426   <Japan>
 ebinazion@gmail.com
PA: Yukio Tamai   <M1>
 3-17-57 Nakashinden
 Ebina-shi, Kanagawa-ken
 243-0422 JAPAN
 (046)234-3426
 yukiotamai@icloud.com
CL: Hiroko Fushimi
 2-4-7 Rinkan Yamato-shi
 Kanagawa-ken
 242-0003 JAPAN
 (046)275-3801
 FAX: (046)725-3801
 hrkfsm@hotmail.com

Higashi Koganei   (4MWC)MSJA8301
 2-14-16 Higashi-cho
 Koganei-shi, Tokyo
 184-0011 JAPAN
 (042)231-1279   <Japan>
 FAX: (042)231-1279
PA: Shigeru Katsuki   <M1>
 2-14-16 Higashi-cho
 Koganei-shi, Tokyo
 184-0011 JAPAN
 (042)232-3640
 FAX: (042)231-1279
 shigeru.katsuki@nifty.com
CL: Eiko Imai
 3-4-19 Higashi-cho
 Koganei-shi, Tokyo
 184-0011 JAPAN
 (042)232-1417
 FAX: (042)231-1279

Ichikawa Grace Mission (4MF)MSJA8314
 1-11-20 Kokubu
 Ichikawa-shi, Chiba-ken
 272-0834 JAPAN
 (047)369-7540   <Japan>
 FAX: (047)369-7540
 ichikawa-grace@mbi.nifty.com
PA: Yasuo Masuda   <M1>
 1-11-20 Kokubu
 Ichikawa-shi, Chiba-ken
 272-0834 JAPAN
 (047)369-7540
 FAX: (047)369-7540
 fwgc6854@mb.infoweb.ne.jp

JAPAN PRESBYTERY CONTINUED

CL: Session Clerk Ichikawa Grace Mission
1-11-20 Kokubu
Ichikawa-shi, Chiba-ken
272-0834 JAPAN
(047)369-7540
FAX: (047)369-7540
ichikawa-grace@mbi.nifty.com

Izumi   (4WC)MSJA8312
4194-13 Izumi-cho Izumi-ku
Yokohama, Kanagawa-ken
245-0016 JAPAN
(045)803-1749   \<Japan\>
FAX: (045)361-4351
izumi@kyokai.org
PA: Kenji Ushioda   \<M1\>
2-47-3 Akuwa-higashi Seya-ku
Yokohama, Kanagawa-ken
243-0023 JAPAN
(046)361-4351
ushioda@jc.ejnet.ne.jp
CL: Kenji Ushioda
2-47-3 Akuwa-higashi Seya-ku
Yokohama, Kanagawa-ken
246-0023 JAPAN
(046)361-4351
FAX: (045)361-4351
ushioda@jc.ejet.ne.jp

Kibougaoka   (4WMC)MSJA8302
72-2 Naka Kibogaoka
Asahi-ku Yokohama, Kanagawa-ken
241-0825 JAPAN
(045)391-6038   \<Japan\>
FAX: (045)391-6653
PA: Ryuzo Matsuya   \<M1\>
72-2 Naka Kibogaoka Asahi-ku
Yokohama, Kanagawa-ken
241-0825 JAPAN
(045)364-8297
matsuya.r@woody.ocn.ne.jp
CL: Kazuhiro Ohashi
2-50-16 Akuwa-Higashi
Seya-ku Yokohama, Kanagawa-ken
246-0023 JAPAN
(045)363-4923
k_0084@nifty.com

Koza   (4MWC)MSJA8303
2-14-1 Minami Rinkan
Yamato-shi, Kanagawa-ken
242-0006 JAPAN
(046)724-1370   \<Japan\>
FAX: (046)276-9685
cpckoza@koza-church.jp
PA: Masahiro Matsumoto   \<M1\>
2-14-1 Minami Rinkan
Yamato-shi, Kanagawa-ken
242-0006 JAPAN
(046)275-2767
matsumoto@koza-church.jp
AP: Nobuko Seki   \<M1\>
4-12-42-403 Shimorenjyaku
Mitaka-shi
242-0004 JAPAN
(042)248-5379
seki@koza-church.jp

CL: Yutaka Shibata
1-18-3 Rinkan Yamato-shi
Kanagawa-ken
241-0003 JAPAN
(046)272-0579
shibata@koza-church.jp

Kunitachi Nozomi   (4MWC)MSJA8306
3-15-9 Higashi
Kunitachi-shi, Tokyo
186-0002 JAPAN
(042)572-7616   \<Japan\>
FAX: (042)572-7616
nozomi-ch@ceres.ocn.ne.jp
PA: Kenta Karasawa   \<M1\>
3-15-10 Higashi
Kunitachi-shi, Tokyo
186-0002 JAPAN
(042)575-5549
FAX: (042)575-5549
smbno6@gmail.com
CL: Keita Komine
3-26-16 Higashi
Kunitachi-shi, Tokyo
186-0002 JAPAN
(042)507-9971
bgmgb65@gmail.com

Megumi   (4MWC)MSJA8309
3-355-4 Kami Kitadai Higashi
Yamato-shi, Tokyo
207-0023 JAPAN
(042)564-0593   \<Japan\>
megumikyokai@gmail.com
PA: Makihiko Arase   \<M1\>
3-355-4 Kamikitadai Higashi
Yamato-shi, Tokyo
207-0023 JAPAN
(080)6636-1960
viator@cb3.so-net.ne.jp
CL: Takao Uchida
4-1505-2 Imokubo
Higashiyamato-shi, Tokyo
2074-0033 JAPAN
(042)567-0145
u-tko47@m3.dion.ne.jp

Naruse   (4WC)MSJA8305
7-20-12 Tamagawa Gakuen
Machida-shi, Tokyo
194-0041 JAPAN
(042)725-9909   \<Japan\>
FAX: (042)725-9909
cpc-naruse@nifty.com
PA: Yoshimasa Niwa   \<M1\>
15-402 Narakita Danchi
2913 Naramachi Aoba-ku
Kanagawa-ken, Yokohama
227-0036 JAPAN
(045)961-1540
FAX: (045)961-1540
rsb09335@nifty.com
CL:Toru Abe
5-18-14 Nara Aboba-ku
Yokohama-shi, Kanagawa-ken
227-0038 JAPAN
(045)961-8620
FAX: (045)961-8620
abe.tooru@rouge.plala.or.jp

Sagamino   (4MWC)MSJA8304
4-13-24 Higashihara
Zama-shi, Kanagawa-ken
228-0004 JAPAN
(046)255-6441   \<Japan\>
FAX: (046)255-6441
kyokai@sagamino.org
PA: Takehiko Miyai   \<M1\>
A-201 2-2-48 Higashihara Zama-shi
Kanagawa-ken
228-0004 JAPAN
(046)207-6558
FAX: (046)207-6558
tacke.m@gmail.com
CL: Akimasa Nakano
1-105 Sagaminosakura 5-1
Higashihara Zama-shi
Kanagawa-ken
228-0004 JAPAN
(046)254-8564
nakano.a.ipt@gmail.com

Shibusawa   (4MWC)MSJA8307
1-8-50 Magarimatsu
Hadano-shi, Kanagawa-ken
259-1321 JAPAN
(046)387-1203   \<Japan\>
FAX: (046)387-1203
keitaro_o@hotmail.com
PA: Keitaro Ohi   \<M1\>
1-8-50 Magarimatsu
Hadano-shi, Kanagawa-ken
259-1321 JAPAN
(046)387-1203
FAX: (046)387-1203
keitaro_o@hotmail.com
CL: Kiyoshi Kumon
3-26-5 Shibusawa
Hadano-shi, Kanagawa-ken
259-1322 JAPAN
(046)388-3609
kiyokumon@yahoo.co.jp

OTHERS ON MINISTERIAL ROLL:

Asayama, Masaharu   \<M1 RT\>
6-3-2-308 Toyogaoka
Tama-shi, Tokyo
206-0031 JAPAN
(042)373-2710
asa@ipcc-21.com
Hamazaki, Takashi   \<M1 RT\>
1551-1-202 Inokuchi
Nakai-cho Ashigarakami-gun
Kanagawa-ken
259-0151 JAPAN
(046)541-8550
gen22-14@qf7.so-net.ne.jp
Ikushima, Michinobu   \<M1 RT\>
2074 Nakashinden
Ebina-Shi, Kanagawa-Ken
243-0422 JAPAN
(046)232-9888
m.ikushima@tbz.t-com.ne.jp
Satoh, Iwao   \<M1 OM\>
8710 Hickory Falls Lane
Pewee Valley, KY 40056
iwaosatoh@gmail.com
(502)210-0852

JAPAN PRESBYTERY CONTINUED

Yano, Fumitsuta   <M1 WC>
424-4 Kamide, Fjinomiya-shi
Shuizuika-ken JAPAN
(054)454-0313

OTHER LICENTIATES ON ROLL:

Suzuki, Temote   <M2>
9-41-15-310 Honcho Kamitsuruma
Sagamihara-shi, Kanagawa-ken
228-0818 JAPAN
timocsuzuki@gmail.com
Miyajima, Atsushi   <M2>
Rua Araja
58 Paraiso Sao Joa
48280-000, Bahia, BRAZIL
(5571)3664-1037
ariel.atsushi@gmail.com

OTHER CANDIDATES ON ROLL:

Inoh, Yuki   <M3>
Tokyo Christian University
3-301-5 Uchino Inzai-shi, Chiba
270-1347 JAPAN
(047)646-1141
yuki_inoh0615@yahoo.co.jp
Miyagi, Ken
Tokyo Christian University
3-301-5 Uchino Inzai-shi, Chiba
270-1347 JAPAN

Taira, Masanori
Japan Biblical Theological Seminary
2-14-1 Minami Rinkan
Yamoto-shi, Kanagawa-ken
242-0006 JAPAN
Wada, Ichiro   <M3>
Tokyo Christian University
3-301-5 Uchino Inzai-shi, Chiba
270-1347 JAPAN
(047)646-1141
ichirowada@gmail.com

Missouri Presbytery
GREAT RIVERS SYNOD

	GENERAL	MEMBERSHIP			CHANGES				FINANCES			
	1. Church Number	2. Active	3. Total	4. Church School	5. Prof. of Faith	6. Gains	7. Losses	8. Children Baptized	9. OUR UNITED OUT-REACH	10. Total Out-Reach Giving	11. All Other Expenses	12. Total Income Received	13. Value Church Prop. 1=1000
	1	2	3	4	5	6	7	8	9	10	11	12	13
Bethel	4102	6	6	6	0	0	0	0	0	1,483	3,901	10,445	10
Elk Creek	4304	19	19	16	0	0	1	0	0	500	39,339	28,704	75
God's Grace*	4104	34	34	5	22	20	0	0	0	1,790	29,308	12,889	120
Happy Home	4306	20	23	0	0	0	1	0	2,000	4,419	15,858	23,441	175
Harmony	4203	25	42	8	6	0	0	0	3,042	6,986	23,966	35,030	80
Hopewell	4105	37	37	23	1	6	3	0	4,644	13,982	37,903	42,340	310
Lobb	4209	13	13	14	No Report Received			0	0	0	0	0	170
Mansfield	4308	54	73	30	No Report Received			0	0	0	0	0	75
Marshall	4210	98	201	33	0	1	6	1	11,907	46,939	84,635	119,073	1,000
Montrose	4107	2	17	0	CLOSED 2015			0	0	0	0	0	32
New Hope (DeC)	4309	17	17	9	No Report Received			0	0	0	0	0	60
Orange	4108	45	45	45	0	7	1	0	3,000	29,889	62,028	76,405	780
Phillipsburg	4311	9	13	6	No Report Received			0	0	0	0	0	150
Pierson*	4312	7	7	4	0	0	5	0	356	9,462	4,415	15,002	125
Pleasant Grove	4109	7	59	0	0	0	0	0	0	0	2,499	2,390	30
Salem	4216	10	10	0	0	1	0	0	0	176	8,829	5,939	150
Seymour	4313	15	29	6	No Report Received			0	0	0	0	0	50
Shawnee Mound	4111	4	38	6	0	0	1	0	680	1,221	4,658	6,811	60
Spring Creek*	4113	40	47	15	0	11	0	4	4,274	5,992	27,001	31,298	182
Springfield 1st**	4314	41	69	50	3	1	47	0	5,823	18,287	80,850	95,472	1,500
Warrensburg	4115	58	72	20	2	3	2	0	1,875	4,225	46,639	42,806	300
White Oak Pond	4315	108	201	84	3	3	4	0	16,160	27,061	120,001	161,601	2,150
TOTALS	21	658	1,068	373	37	53	71	6	53,761	171,467	607,182	720,352	7,609

*Math error corrected. **Purged roll.

CHURCHES, PASTORS, AND CLERKS:

Bethel   (2C)GRMI4102
14621 Lawrence 1032 (mailing)
Sarcoxie, MO 64862
Crossroads Lawrence 1030 & Lawrence 2170 (physical)
Wentworth, MO
(417)285-6571   <Lawrence>
SS: Tim Steeley   <M3>
PO Box 281
Mt Vernon, MO 65712
(417)466-4345
tsteeley@swr5.k12.mo.us
CL: Lana Moore
14621 Lawrence 1032
Sarcoxie, MO 64862
(417)285-6571
lanajeanmoore@hotmail.com

Elk Creek   (4MEC)GRMI4304
7423 County Road 3730 (mailing)
Peace Valley, MO 65788
US Highway 160 E (physical)
West Plains, MO 65775
(417)257-0983   <Howell>
pastorbrown44@yahoo.com

PA: Dale M Brown   <M1 HR>
HC 61 Box 4740
West Plains, MO 65775
(417)257-0983
pastorbrown44@yahoo.com
CL: Cindy Rasor
7423 County Road 3730
Peace Valley, MO 65788
(417)256-7353
rrasor@centurytel.net

God's Grace   (4MC)GRMI4104
423 Water Street (mailing)
417 W Water Street (physical)
Greenfield, MO 65661
( )   <Dade>
CL: Debra Kay Bartlett
423 Water Street
Greenfield, MO 65661
(417)637-5678
debrakaybartlett@gmail.com

Happy Home   (4C)GRMI4306
510 S Newport Avenue (mailing)
5604 State Highway ZZ (physical)
Conway, MO 65632
( )   <Webster>
CL: Rex Luallin
510 S Newport Avenue
Conway, MO 65632
(417)589-3804

Harmony   (4WC)GRMI4203
3508 Scott Street (mailing)
Saint Joseph, MO 64507
SE State Road Z (physical)
San Antonio, MO 64443
(816)279-0733   <Buchanan>
orvalschafer@aol.com
OD: Marion Cannon   <M5>
4248 SW State Route N
Stewartsville, MO 64490
(816)449-2437
orvalschafer@aol.com
CL: Viola Schafer
3508 Scott Street
Saint Joseph, MO 64507
(816)279-0733
orvalschafer@aol.com

Hopewell   (4EWC)GRMI4105
248 NE 50th Road (mailing)
273 NE 50th Road (physical)
Lamar, MO 64759
(417)682-2396   <Barton>
FAX: (417)682-3514
parrishron@att.net
OD: George Haag   <M5>
301 Gulf Street
Lamar, MO 64759
(417)682-3876

MISSOURI PRESBYTERY CONTINUED

CL: Reba Simmons
63 E Highway C
Lamar, MO 64759
(417)884-2810

Lobb   (4MC)GRMI4209
1410 W Walnut Street(mailing)
Flynn Road & 7-Highway (physical)
Independence, MO 64050
(   )   <Jackson>
OD: Paul J Petralie   <M5>
1409 Granite Creek Drive
Blue Springs, MO 64015
(816)229-2804
CL: Pamela Markey
1419 W Walnut Street
Independence, MO 64050
(816)254-1130
pammarkey@sbcglobal.net

Mansfield   (4MEC)GRMI4308
PO Box 673 (mailing)
307 S Phelps Avenue (physical)
Mansfield, MO 65704
(   )   <Wright>
OD: S Larry Scott   <M5>
2211 Airport Road
Mansfield, MO 65704
(417)924-4390
revslscott@gmail.com
CL: Leon Veenstra
4680 Highway F
Hartville, MO 65667
(417)741-7408
veenstra@getgoin.net

Marshall   (4MWC)GRMI4210
1000 S Miami
Marshall, MO 65340
(660)886-2402   <Saline>
pastor_randy_shannon@yahoo.com
PA: Randy Shannon   <M1>
30282 Highway H
Marshall, MO 65340
(660)886-9454
pastor_randy.shannon@yahoo.com
CL: Brenda Guthrie
28 Cattle Drive
Slater, MO 65349
(660)529-2420
blguthrie1949@hotmail.com

Montrose   (4MWC)GRMI4107
CLOSED 2015

New Hope (DeC)   (4WC)GRMI4309
230 County Road 2630 (mailing)
Dent County Road 6200 (physical)
Salem, MO 65560
(   )   <Dent>
SS: Michael Reno   <M2>
52 Rolla Gardens
Rolla, MO 65401
(573)578-5321
rollarenomike@gmail.com
CL: Fay J Haxton
230 County Road 2630
Salem, MO 65560
(573)729-5524
rafay@embarkmail.com

Orange   (4WC)GRMI4108
109 Agnes (mailing)
Crane, MO 65633
15743 Highway K (physical)
Aurora, MO 65605
(417)678-5220   <Lawrence>
PA: D Kevin Vanderlaan   <M1>
17246 Highway K
Aurora, MO 65605
(217)620-2723
pastorkevin2@gmail.com
CL: Leah Estes
109 Agnes
Crane, MO 65633
(417)723-8033
lestesx5@centurytel.net

Phillipsburg   (4WC)GRMI4311
11187 Cuba Road (mailing)
Grovespring, MO 65662
Grover Street (physical)
Phillipsburg, MO 65722
(   )   <Laclede>
OD: Chris Wilson   <M5>
745 Birchwood
Marshfield, MO 65706
(417)425-0863
chris@springfieldbsu.org
CL: Cheryl Brown
11187 Cuba Drive
Grovespring, MO 65662
(417)462-0813
brownc@hartville.k12.mo.us

Pierson   (4C)GRMI4312
12754 State Highway M (mailing)
Billings, MO 65610
45129 State Highway 413 (physical)
Billings, MO 65610
(417)369-2104   <Stone>
OD: Jon White   <M5>
12754 State Highway M
Billings, MO 65610
(417)890-1533
CL: Kary Crumpley
1513 Crumpley Drive
Marionville, MO 65705
(417)839-3552
karycrumpley@gmail.com

Pleasant Grove   (4C)GRMI4109
PO Box 97 (mailing)
891 SE Y Highway (physical)
Knob Noster, MO 65336
(   )   <Johnson>
CL: Dana Smith
836 Southeast Y Highway
Knob Noster, MO 65536
(660)563-9739
dsmith@knobnoster.k12.mo.us

Salem   (4WC)GRMI4216
211 NW County Road OO (mailing)
382 NW County Road H (physical)
Warrensburg, MO 64093
(   )   <Johnson>

CL: Anne Patrick
211 NW County Road OO
Warrensburg, MO 64093
(660)747-8902
apatrick52@hotmail.com

Seymour   (4C)GRMI4313
PO Box 40 (mailing)
222 Main Street (physical)
Seymour, MO 65746
(417)935-2235   <Webster>
OD: Sam Burt   <M5>
102 E Summit Avenue
Seymour, MO 65746
(417)735-2759
CL: Denise Burt
102 E Summit Avenue
Seymour, MO 65746
(417)300-6451
gerrydburt@gmail.com

Shawnee Mound   (4WC)GRMI4111
72 NW 1150 Road
Chilhowee, MO 64733
(   )   <Henry>
SS: Mary Anna Townsend   <M3>
1123 Tyler Avenue
Warrensburg, MO 64093
(660)909-5966
wrenhse1123@gmail.com
CL: Doris Hunter
62 NW 1150 Road
Chilhowee, MO 64733
(660)885-3709
dfhunter@embarqmail.com

Spring Creek   (4EWC)GRMI4113
307 E 365th Road (mailing)
Hwy 123 & Hwy A Junction (physical)
Dunnegan, MO 65640
(417)754-8498   <Polk>
OD: Scott Garner   <M5>
1403 E Primrose Lane
Republic, MO 65738
(417)732-4218
CL: Gary M Roetto
307 E 365th Road
Dunnegan, MO 65640
(417)754-8498

Springfield First   (4MWC)GRMI4314
4216 S Charleston Avenue
Springfield, MO 65804
(417)862-6434
reformedminister@yahoo.com
PA: Andrew (Andy) Eppard
1427 W McGee Street
Springfield, MO 65807
(417)862-6434
reformedminister@yahoo.com
CL: Carol Fare
302 N Market Street
Nixa, MO 65714
(417)725-2775
cjfare52@sbcglobal.net

Warrensburg   (4WC)GRMI4115
201 Grover Street
Warrensburg, MO 64093
(660)747-3021   <Johnson>

MISSOURI PRESBYTERY CONTINUED

PA: Randy Crawshaw   <M1>
136 NE 1271 Road
Knob Noster, MO 65336
(660)563-5149
randy_crawshaw@yahoo.com

CL: Dana Moore
113 Larkin Street
Warrensburg, MO 64093
(660)747-8777
dmoore@ucmo.edu

White Oak Pond   (4MWC)GRMI4315
16549 Highway 5 (mailing)
16551 Highway 5 (physical)
Lebanon, MO 65536
(417)532-5049   <Laclede>
wopcpc@whiteoakpond.org

PA: Terry Hansen   <M1>
16549 Highway 5
Lebanon, MO 65536
(417)533-8106
thansen@whiteoakpond.org

CL: Janie Lewis
1931 King James Drive
Lebanon, MO 65536
(417)664-6357

OTHERS ON MINISTERIAL ROLL:

Ang, John   <M1 HR>
5843 S Farm Road 157
Springfield, MO 65810
(417)886-3487
pastorcares@yahoo.com

Appling, John   <M1 WC>
1722 S Fairway Avenue
Springfield, MO 65804
(417)877-4643
pegblessings@sbcglobal.net

Appling, Peggy   <M1 WC>
1722 S Fairway
Springfield, MO 65804
(417)877-4643
pegblessings@sbcglobal.net

Bone, Leslie   <M1 M9>
16504 E George Franklin Drive
Independence, MO 64055
(816)373-6625
lesliebone@comcast.net

Campbell, Gordon C   <M1 WC>
1469 E Wayland Street
Springfield, MO 65804
(417)823-9567
gofor12@gmail.com

Carr, Jill   <M1 OM>
PO Box 1547
Lebanon, MO 65536
(417)532-6760
dig.micah.6.8@gmail.com

Harris, Edward   <M1 HR>
10000 Wornall Road Apt 2315
Kansas City, MO 64114
(816)214-8977
ed121@kcrr.com

Park, Sang Hoon   <M1 WC>
3504 W Shawnee Drive
Springfield, MO 65810
(417)888-0442

Plachte, Richard   <M1 HR>
615 Grover Street
Warrensburg, MO 64093
(660)441-4427
rap@aerobiz.org

Rodden, Linda   <M1 WC>
363 Cornelison Street
Lebanon, MO 65536
(417)588-2207
linda.rodden@mercy.net

Roedder, Unhui Grace   <M1 WC>
419 S Jonathan Avenue
Springfield, MO 65802
(417)494-6491
kimroedder@hotmail.com

Wieland, Jack G, Jr   <M1 WC>
PO Box 116
Napoleon, MO 64074
(217)823-4331
jgwieland@hotmail.com

OTHER LICENTIATES ON ROLL:

OTHER CANDIDATES ON ROLL:

Griffin, Adam   <M3>
23502 Clinton Road
Lebanon, MO 65536
(417)588-2522
plowboy3500@hotmail.com

Hudson, Jennifer   <M3>
716 Apache Drive
Marshall, MO 65340
(660)631-3893

Wolf, Matthew   <M3>
1178 S Salt Pond
Marshall, MO 65340
(660)202-3762
cleanwolf77@yahoo.com

Murfreesboro Presbytery
TENNESSEE SYNOD

GENERAL		MEMBERSHIP			CHANGES				FINANCES				
	1.Church Number	2.Active	3.Total	4.Church School	5.Prof. of Faith	6.Gains	7.Losses	8.Children Baptized	9. OUR UNITED OUT-REACH	10. Total Out-Reach Giving	11. All Other Expenses	12. Total Income Received	13. Value Church Prop. 1=1000
	1	2	3	4	5	6	7	8	9	10	11	12	13
Algood	7201	21	29	6	No Report Received			0	0	0	0	0	180
Banks	7202	15	17	13	2	3	0	0	1,002	4,488	30,282	36,675	344
Bates Hill	7203	66	103	37	No Report Received			0	11,127	0	0	0	325
Beech Grove	7204	20	20	10	No Report Received			0	0	0	0	0	423
Belvidere	7205	7	40	6	0	0	7	0	0	200	7,088	7,234	60
Blues Hill	7207	19	31	13	0	2	4	0	3,559	8,167	27,406	35,573	120
Cloyd's	7208	97	97	45	No Report Received			0	5,100	0	0	0	2,500
Commerce	7209	61	61	39	0	2	3	1	3,000	4,549	49,835	54,384	425
Cookeville 1st	7210	564	635	250	6	12	6	4	48,251	98,000	411,575	509,575	4,600
Cowan	7211	71	71	44	0	1	2	0	11,293	18,173	103,735	113,739	1,880
Dibrell	7212	8	9	9	1	1	1	0	0	0	10,225	14,469	35
Dry Valley	7213	8	10	10	No Report Received			0	250	0	0	0	10
Goshen	7214	95	95	45	No Report Received			0	3,500	0	0	0	874
Gum Creek	7215	23	23	12	0	0	0	0	0	1,414	15,999	27,430	130
Harmony	7216	62	99	55	2	5	6	2	10,359	23,087	83,916	113,045	1,041
Hickory Valley	7251	9	9	21	No Report Received			0	0	0	0	0	0
Hillsboro	7217	16	18	6	No Report Received			0	0	0	0	0	250
Jerusalem	7218	49	49	26	2	2	84	0	9,631	18,317	95,973	90,056	275
Joywood	7250	25	36	12	No Report Received			0	0	0	0	0	375
LaGuardo	7219	25	25	3	No Report Received			0	0	0	0	0	150
Lebanon	7220	313	491	230	No Report Received			0	24,000	0	0	0	4,000
Liberty	7222	96	146	52	2	3	4	0	12,939	31,542	99,527	129,212	989
Livingston 1st	7223	10	42	3	No Report Received			0	0	0	0	0	250
LuzD.L.Naciones	7252	9	20	23	No Report Received			0	0	0	0	0	0
Manchester	7224	90	219	68	0	1	3	0	19,281	28,380	162,596	192,812	1,300
McMinnville*	7225	6	6	6	0	0	8	0	485	641	19,699	18,430	200
Monteagle	7227	5	5	0	0	0	0	0	0	0	7,225	7,305	70
Mt. Carmel	7228	11	23	0	0	0	0	0	0	950	13,200	15,500	350
Mt. Hermon	7229	9	18	10	No Report Received			0	0	0	0	0	200
Mt. Tabor	7230	30	37	12	2	2	2	0	3,437	5,899	34,733	36,383	138
Mt. Vernon	7231	32	37	26	No Report Received			0	0	0	0	0	410
Murfreesboro	7232	165	401	95	4	13	27	4	13,453	26,421	253,832	279,870	3,245
New Hope	7233	60	68	40	No Report Received			0	0	0	0	0	1,022
Old Zion	7234	9	9	8	0	0	1	0	400	3,378	19,540	22,918	300
Owens Chapel	7235	55	72	14	1	1	2	0	500	5,670	89,129	108,244	210
Providence	7238	14	14	38	No Report Received			0	0	0	0	0	150
Rockvale	7239	82	153	34	4	6	1	0	2,400	5,081	83,154	88,235	1,307
Rocky Glade	7240	63	75	59	2	2	1	2	3,500	11,400	43,258	63,014	375
Ruth Chapel	7241	2	5	0	No Report Received			0	0	0	0	0	3
Sewanee	7242	22	28	12	No Report Received			0	1,857	0	0	0	225
Smithville*	7243	151	151	100	6	18	34	0	24,000	24,000	224,899	248,239	1,700
Suggs Creek	7244	8	8	0	1	0	0	0	2,223	0	21,269	22,224	120
Union Hill	7246	49	71	41	0	2	1	0	1,164	17,007	45,712	58,223	250
Watertown	7247	12	12	9	0	0	0	0	500	1,118	14,355	16,786	443
Winchester 1st	7249	509	939	450	11	32	8	0	58,402	98,148	582,284	587,836	3,500
TOTALS	45	3,088	4,519	2,037	46	108	206	19	227,362	436,030	2,543,221	2,890,106	32,761

*Math error corrected. **Purged roll.

MURFREESBORO PRESBYTERY CONTINUED

CHURCHES, PASTORS, AND CLERKS:

Algood (4WC)TNMU7201
3617 Burton Cove Road (mailing)
Cookeville, TN 38506
Corner Harp & Main Street (physical)
Algood, TN 38506
( ) <Putnam>
PA: Richard Bond <M1>
2425 Fisk Road, Lot 0
Cookeville, TN 38506
(931)526-7610
erbond@frontier.net
CL: Elaine Burton
3617 Burton Cove Road
Cookeville, TN 38506
(931)537-6661
e_burton@frontier.com

Banks (4MWC)TNMU7202
846 Luttrell Avenue (mailing)
2933 Banks Pisgah Road (physical)
Smithville, TN 37166
( ) <DeKalb>
SS: Greg Whaley <M2>
4970 Comstock Road
Chapel Hill, TN 37034
(931)364-7637
grewha@mail.com
CL: Robert Joins
846 Lutrell Avenue
Smithville, TN 37166
(615)597-6366
b_joins@hotmail.com

Bates Hill (4MEWC)TNMU7203
9957 Nashville Highway (mailing)
6111 Old Nashville Highway (physical)
Mc Minnville, TN 37110
(931)939-3235 <Warren>
cavecrew1979@gmail.com
CL: William R Black
205 Ben Lomond Drive
Mc Minnville, TN 37110
(931)743-9809
cavecrew1979@gmail.com

Beech Grove (4MC)TNMU7204
PO Box 26 (mailing)
471 Oscar Crowell Road (physical)
Beechgrove, TN 37018
(931)394-2387 <Coffee>
CL: Crystal B Brandon
269 French Brantley Road
Wartrace, TN 37183
(931)394-2387
no_tenn@hotmail.com

Belvidere (4WC)TNMU7205
Walnut Hill Road
Belvidere, TN 37306
( ) <Franklin>
PA: Joseph H Butler <M1>
56 Cline Ridge Road
Winchester, TN 37398
(931)224-8423
jhbu737@bellsouth.net
CL: Alton Smith
123 Post Oak Road
Belvidere, TN 37306
starsmith53@hotmail.com

Blues Hill (4MWC)TNMU7207
7292 Short Mountain Road
Mc Minnville, TN 37110
( ) <Warren>
SS: Lyon Walkup <M1>
225 Bertha Owen Road
Morrison, TN 37357
(931)607-3233
dirtroad@blomand.net
CL: Naomi Smith
522 Smith Town Road
Mc Minnville, TN 37110
(931)939-2435
memesmith@blomand.net

Cloyd's (4WC)TNMU7208
PO Box 277 (mailing)
595 West Division (physical)
Mt Juliet, TN 37121
(615)758-7434 <Wilson>
PA: Michael Reese <M1>
404 Five Oaks Boulevard
Lebanon, TN 37087
(615)443-0457
michaelhreese@bellsouth.net
CL: Vickie Hibdon
7141 Lebanon Road
Mount Juliet, TN 37122
(615)444-6498

Commerce (4WC)TNMU7209
351 Borum Road (mailing)
4260 S Commerce Road (physical)
Watertown, TN 37184
(615)237-9409 <Wilson>
crutchmckinwater@aol.com
SS: Denny C Shepard <M1>
8514 Newsom Station Road
Nashville, TN 37221
(615)662-1114
CL: Jacki Crutcher
351 Borum Road
Watertown, TN 37184
(615)237-3310
crutchmckinwater@aol.com

Cookeville First (4WC)TNMU7210
565 E 10th Street
Cookeville, TN 38501
(931)526-6585 <Putnam>
FAX: (931)528-2270
charles@cookevillecpchurch.org
PA: Charles McCaskey <M1>
679 Canter Lane
Cookeville, TN 38501
(931)526-4885
charles@cookevillecpchurch.org
AP: Christian Smith <M1>
2017 Grademere Drive
Cookeville, TN 38501
(931)265-8896
csmith2490@gmail.com
CL: Lanny Knight
521 Chad Lane
Cookeville, TN 38501
(931)528-7800
alknight2@msn.com

Cowan (4MC)TNMU7211
PO Box 277 (mailing)
206 Cowan Street W (physical)
Cowan, TN 37318
(931)967-7431 <Franklin>
cowancpchurch@bellsouth.net
PA: Ronnie M Pittenger <M1>
207 Cowan Street W
Cowan, TN 37318
(615)832-8832
CL: Cindy Henn
PO Box 277
Cowan, TN 37318
(931)967-7431
cowancpchurch@bellsouth.net

Dibrell (4C)TNMU7212
128 Mitchell Road (mailing)
Mike Muncey Road (physical)
McMinnville, TN 37110
( ) <Warren>
CL: Jacqulyn S Boyd
128 Mitchell Road
McMinnville, TN 37110
(931)934-2088

Dry Valley (4C)TNMU7213
5196 Shady Lane (mailing)
4415 Highway 70 N (physical)
Cookeville, TN 38506
( ) <Putnam>
PA: Richard Bond <M1>
2425 Fisk Road Lot 0
Cookeville, TN 38506
(931)854-0979
CL: Janice F Bohannon
5196 Shady Lane
Cookeville, TN 38506
(931)528-7894
jandan80@gmail.com

Goshen (4MWC)TNMU7214
PO Box 881 (mailing)
1262 Williams Cove Road (physical)
Winchester, TN 37398
(931)967-0245 <Franklin>
goshenchurch@cafes.net
PA: Richard Morgan <M1>
1468 Williams Cove Road
Winchester, TN 37398
(931)349-4474
icthuse3@gmail.com
CL: Frances Hanger
251 Whipperwill Lane
Winchester, TN 37398
(931)967-7730
FAX: (931)967-7730
bhanger@bellsouth.net

Gum Creek (4C)TNMU7215
1063 Franklin Heights Drive
Winchester, TN 37398
(931)967-6539 <Franklin>
PA: Coyle Campbell <M1>
186 Old Limestone Road
New Market, AL 35761
(256)379-4392

MURFREESBORO PRESBYTERY CONTINUED

CL: Molly Perry
1063 Franklin Heights Drive
Winchester, TN 37398
(931)967-6539

_____

Harmony   (4MWC)TNMU7216
8891 Lynchburg Road
Winchester, TN 37398
(931)962-0842   <Franklin>
PA: Joseph H Butler, Jr   <M1>
261 Ridgefield Drive
Winchester, TN 37398
(931)224-8423
jhbu737@live.com
CL: Clare Wiseman
8555 Lynchburg Road
Winchester, TN 37398
(931)967-3932
wisrc9802@gmail.com

_____

Hickory Valley   (4U)TNMU7251
Sparta, TN 38583
(931)738-5812   <White>
PA: Richard Bond   <M1>
1528 Eastlake Drive
Cookeville, TN 38506
(931)526-7610
CL: Kathryn Adcock
1450 Oak Grove Road
Sparta, TN 38583
(931)761-5858
kadcock@blomand.net

_____

Hillsboro   (4EC)TNMU7217
PO Box 4
Hillsboro, TN 37342
(931)394-2415   <Coffee>
CL: Robert L Jenkins
68 Hillsboro Viola Road
Hillsboro, TN 37342
(931)596-2745

_____

Jerusalem   (4MWC)TNMU7218
7192 Mona Road
Murfreesboro, TN 37129
(615)895-8118   <Rutherford>
PA: Brent Wills   <M1>
4607 E Richmond Shop Road
Lebanon, TN 37090
(615)449-3258
bwills9185@yahoo.com
CL: Jimmy C Francis
4657 W Jefferson Pike
Murfreesboro, TN 37129
(615)893-8311
jcfjimmy@aol.com

_____

Joywood   (4MWC)TNMU7250
7120 Old Nashville Highway
Murfreesboro, TN 37129
(615)459-6518   <Rutherford>
joywoodchurch@yahoo.com
PA: Jeff Clark   <M1>
327 Haynes Haven Lane
Murfreesboro, TN 37129
(615)896-7733
jclark7733@aol.com

CL: Mark Tharp
5018 Willowbend Drive
Murfreesboro, TN 37128
(615)895-4772
markat52@comcast.net

_____

LaGuardo   (4WC)TNMU7219
7320 Highway 109 N
Lebanon, TN 37087
(615)444-0419   <Wilson>
OD: Gary Mraz   <M5>
8630 Highway 109 N
Lebanon, TN 37087
CL: Nancy Voight
500 Woods Ferry Pike
Lebanon, TN 37087

_____

Lebanon   (4MWC)TNMU7220
522 Castle Heights Avenue
Lebanon, TN 37087
(615)444-7453   <Wilson>
FAX: (615)444-6671
lcpsecretary@hotmail.com
PA: Kevin Medlin   <M1>
316 Dandelion Drive
Lebanon, TN 37087
(615)444-7453
FAX: (615)444-6671
kmedlin12@hotmail.com
CL: Kelly Hendricks
464 Locust Grove Road
Watertown, TN 37184
(615)443-0226
FAX: (615)444-6671

_____

Liberty   (4MWC)TNMU7222
317 Liberty Lane
McMinnville, TN 37110
(931)473-3813   <Warren>
libertycpc@gmail.com
PA: Marcus Hayes   <M1>
102 River Drive
McMinnville, TN 37110
(270)841-7576
marcus.hayes@att.net
AP: Jennifer Hayes   <M1>
102 River Drive
McMinnville, TN 37110
(205)533-1018
hayesj712@gmail.com
CL: Patty Boyd
35 Lonsvale Drive
McMinnville, TN 37110
(931)473-8059
pattyboyd@blomand.net

_____

Livingston First   (4WC)TNMU7223
PO Box 393 (mailing)
110 Byrdstown Highway (physical)
Livingston, TN 38570
(931)823-5115   <Overton>
SS: Donald Ray Fossey, II   <M3>
328 Waterloo Road
Cookeville, TN 38506
(931)498-2149
dfossey@twlakes.net
CL: Helen Fossey
611 W 4th Street
Livingston, TN 38570
(931)823-9884

Luz D L Naciones   (4F)TNMU7252
114 Northwood Lane
Mc Minnville, TN 37110
(   )   <Warren>
PA: Jose Perez   <M1>
89 Northwood Lane Apt A102
Mc Minnville, TN 37110
(931)743-5585
CL: Session Clerk
114 Northwood Lane
Mc Minnville, TN 37110
(931)815-9502

_____

Manchester   (4MWEC)TNMU7224
838 McArthur Street
Manchester, TN 37355
(931)728-2975   <Coffee>
FAX: (931)728-2975
mancp@cafes.net
PA: Mark Barron   <M1>
836 McArthur Street
Manchester, TN 37355
(931)728-2975
FAX: (931)728-2975
mbarron@cafes.net
CL: Debbie Shelton
1255 M G England Road
Manchester, TN 37355
(931)728-9422
debbiebl@cafes.net

_____

McMinnville   (4MWC)TNMU7225
115 Peers Street
McMinnville, TN 37110
(931)474-4255   <Warren>
dwalhart@aol.com
PA: Daryl Alhart   <M1>
2187 Rutledge Ford Road
Decherd, TN 37324
(931)349-7104
dwalhart@aol.com
CL: Leota Watson
804 W Main Street
Mc Minnville, TN 37110
(931)473-7561
leotaw@blomand.net

_____

Monteagle   (4C)TNMU7227
PO Bos 243 (mailing)
343 College Street (physical)
Monteagle, TN 37356
(   )   <Grundy>
CL: Billie Faye Terrill
PO Box 243
Monteagle, TN 37356
(931)924-2787

_____

Mt Carmel   (4MEWC)TNMU7228
1484 Elora Road
Huntland, TN 37345
(931)469-7394   <Franklin>
PA: Richard, "Rocky" Whray   <M1>
201 8th Avenue SE
Winchester, TN 37398
(931)636-4844
rocklex1017@att.net

MURFREESBORO PRESBYTERY CONTINUED

CL: Tina M Morrow
714 Baxter Hollow Road
Belvidere, TN 37306
(931)967-3853
ramtmm@netzero.net

——————————
Mt Hermon   (4MEWC)TNMU7229
5544 Mt Hermon Road
Cookeville, TN 38506
( )   <Putnam>
SS: Maury A Norman   <M1 OP>
1750 Shipley Road
Cookeville, TN 38501
(931)526-1644
maurynorman@yahoo.com
CL: Ruth Shubert
6799 Cherry Creek Road
Cookeville, TN 38506
(931)526-5109

——————————
Mt Tabor   (4EC)TNMU7230
3122 Donard Court (mailing)
6000 Manchester Highway (physical)
Murfreesboro, TN 37127
(615)545-4695   <Rutherford>
sheila.mcclain4695@gmail.com
PA: Brent Wills   <M1>
4607 E Richmond Shop Road
Lebanon, TN 37090
(615)449-3258
bwills9185@yahoo.com
CL: Sheila McClain
3122 Donard Court
Murfreesboro, TN 37128
(615)545-4695
sheila.mcclain4695@gmail.com

——————————
Mt Vernon   (4C)TNMU7231
131 Hickory Hills Drive (mailing)
Murfreesboro, TN 37128)
11915 Mt Vernon Road (physical)
Rockvale, TN 37153
(615)890-9125   <Rutherford>
PA: Judy Taylor Sides   <M1>
534 Bethany Circle
Murfreesboro, TN 37128
(615)895-1627
CL: Gregory L Sides
534 Bethany Circle
Murfreesboro, TN 37128
(615)895-1627

——————————
Murfreesboro   (4MEWC)TNMU7232
907 E Main Street
Murfreesboro, TN 37130
(615)893-6755   <Rutherford>
FAX: (615)893-4553
firstcp@comcast.net
PA: Christopher Warren   <M1>
906 Prince Lane
Murfreesboro, TN 37129
(615)828-8719
chris@murfreesborocpc.org
AP: Joy Warren   <M1>
907 W Main Street
Murfreesboro, TN 37129
(615)828-8719
revjoywarren@gmail.com

CL: Margaret Barlow
4965 Steeplechase Road
Christiana, TN 37037
(615)895-4918
mbarlow@viammfg.com

——————————
New Hope   (4EWC)TNMU7233
PO Box 1215 (mailing)
7845 Coles Ferry Pike (physical)
Lebanon, TN 37087
(615)449-7020   <Wilson>
PA: Paul Hancock   <M1>
107 Highland Ridge
Hendersonville, TN 37075
(615)429-4331
paul.hancock6@comcast.net
CL: Mary Ann Smith
423 Stonegate Drive
Lebanon, TN 37090
(615)444-0102
nwhpchrch0@gmail.com

——————————
Old Zion   (4C)TNMU7234
395 Coventry Drive (mailing)
Nashville, TN 37211
7489 Old Kentucky Road (physical)
Sparta, TN 38583
( )   <White>
PA: James A McGill   <M1>
433 S Walnut Avenue
Cookeville, TN 38501
(931)526-6936
jam7235@frontiernet.net
CL: Kay Armstrong
268 Tulip Drive
Sparta, TN 38583
(931)406-3976

——————————
Owens Chapel   (4C)TNMU7235
PO Box 839 (mailing)
Sewanee, TN 37375
3058 Liberty Road (physical)
Winchester, TN 37398
(931)636-8076   <Franklin>
ferguea9@gmail.com
PA: Blake Stephens   <M1>
2559 Holders Cove Road
Winchester, TN 37398
(931)939-2628
blsteph@edge.net
CL: Jimmy McKinney
1310 Liberty Road
Winchester, TN 37398
(931)967-3679
bigmacj37@comcast.net

——————————
Providence   (3C)TNMU7238
c/o Pierce Dodson(mailing)
106 Bartonwood Drive
Lebanon, TN 37087
Providence Road (physical)
Hartsville, TN 37074
( )   <Trousdale>
CL: Session Clerk
c/o Pierce Dodson(mailing)
106 Bartonwood Drive
Lebanon, TN 37087

Rockvale   (4MEWC)TNMU7239
PO Box 67 (mailing)
8769 Rockvale Road (physical)
Rockvale, TN 37153
(615)274-3143   <Rutherford>
CL: Martha A Lannom
903 Sunset Avenue
Murfreesboro, TN 37129
(615)896-1348
malannom@bellsouth.net

——————————
Rocky Glade   (4C)TNMU7240
PO Box 8 (mailing)
2017 Rocky Glade Road (physical)
Eagleville, TN 37060
( )   <Rutherford>
PA: J. Tommy Jobe   <M1>
PO Box 8
Eagleville, TN 37060
(615)776-7755
cppreacher@united.net
CL: Bill Lamb
425 River Eagleville Road
Eagleville, TN 37060
(615)274-2275
billlamb1@bellsouth.net

——————————
Ruth Chapel   (2C)TNMU7241
347 Windle Community Road (mailing)
146 Windle Community Road (physical)
Livingston, TN 38570
( )   <Overton>
SS: Donald Fossey II   <M3>
328 Waterloo Road
Cookeville, TN 38506
(931)498-2149
dfossey@twlakes.net
CL: Jo K Smith
347 Windle Community Road
Livingston, TN 38570
(931)823-5916

——————————
Sewanee   (4WC)TNMU7242
Box 11
Sewanee, TN 37375
(931)598-0766   <Franklin>
smdiam@hotmail.com
CL: Paul E Mooney
Box 11
Sewanee, TN 37375
(931)598-0766

——————————
Smithville   (4MWC)TNMU7243
201 S College Street
Smithville, TN 37166
(615)597-4197   <DeKalb>
FAX: (615)597-4397
office@smithvillecpc.com
PA: Isaac Gray   <M1>
512 Ed Taft Drive
Smithville, TN 37166
(870)373-4731
revgray08@gmail.com
CL: Wesley A Rogers
305 S College Street
Smithville, TN 37166
(615)597-5549
wesrogers305@gmail.com

MURFREESBORO PRESBYTERY CONTINUED

Suggs Creek   (4MWC)TNMU7244
405 Corinth Road
Mount Juliet, TN 37122
( )   <Wilson>
IP: Larry Green   <M1>
525 Dearman Street
Smithville, TN 37166
(615)597-5832
larrylgreen24@aol.com
CL: Dianna Huff
167 Eakes Thompson Road
Mount Juliet, TN 37122
dhuff1983@bellsouth.net

Union Hill   (4MWC)TNMU7246
235 Sykes Road
Brush Creek, TN 38547
(615)683-8327   <Smith>
brotherperry@msn.com
SS: Dennis Croslin   <M3>
165 Maple Street
Gordonsville, TN 38563
(615)934-2383
CL: Robin L Nixon
237 Temperance Hall Highway
Hickman, TN 38567
(615)418-5074
robinlpn@hotmail.com

Watertown   (4WC)TNMU7247
510 W Main Street
Watertown, TN 37184
( )   <Wilson>
OD: Rodger McCann   <M5>
352 Winding River Lane
Sparta, TN 38563
(931)738-0352
CL: Emily Nix
305 Cornwell Avenue
Watertown, TN 37184
(615)237-3488
emilymckin_1@juno.com

Winchester First   (4WC)TNMU7249
PO Box 176 (mailing)
200 2nd Avenue NW (physical)
Winchester, TN 37398
(931)967-2121   <Franklin>
FAX: (931)967-8444
wintncp@bellsouth.net
PA: Michael Clark   <M1>
80 Bryan Drive
Winchester, TN 37398
(931)967-2121
book_worm35@comcast.net
AP: Amber Clark   <M1>
80 Bryan Drive
Winchester, TN 37398
(931)967-2121
revamber@comcast.net
CL: Karen Zarecor
260 Harris Chapel Road
Estill Springs, TN 37330
(931)962-4465
zarecor@bellsouth.net

OTHERS ON MINISTERIAL ROLL:

Benedict, Mary McCaskey   <M1 WC>
892 Pen Oak Drive
Cookeville, TN 38501
(931)260-1422
marykat_61@hotmail.com
Boggs, Barry   <M1 WC>
1039 Johnnie Bud Lane
Cookeville, TN 38501
(931)979-1701
boggsone@hotmail.com
Burrow, Vernon   <M1 RT>
603 Saratoga Drive
Murfreesboro, TN 37130
(615)406-6385
vernonburrow@comcast.net
Clark, Jonathan   <M1 RT>
88 Woodcrest Drive
Winchester, TN 37398
(931)967-9613
FAX: (931)967-8444
clark3568@bellsouth.net
Estep, William   <M1 RT>
239 Skyline Drive
Harriman, TN 37748
(865)882-5114
Ferguson, Elizabeth   <M1 WC>
PO Box 839
Sewanee, TN 37375
(931)636-8076
ferguea9@gmail.com
Green, Harry   <M1 WC>
45 Wood Way
McMinnville, TN 37110
(931)815-9190
Hackman-Truhan, Deborah   <M1 WC>
7314 N Miramar Drive
Peoria, IL 61614
(931)537-9040
cprevdeb@hotmail.com
Hancock, B. J.   <M1 RT>
103 W Cowan Street
Cowan, TN 37318
(931)967-8491
Harper, Josh   <M1 WC>
227 LaCroix Drive #1
Collierville, TN 38017
(615)934-7940
jdharperministry@hotmail.com
Jeffrey, Peter   <M1 WC>
61 Northwood Drive
McKenzie, TN 38201
(731)352-0792
jeffreyp@bethelu.edu
Johnson, Lanny   <M1 RT>
120 S Mill Street
Morrison, TN 37357
(931)212-1658
ljohnson37357@gmail.com
Labrada, Hector   <M1 WC>
74 Cumberland Drive
McMinnville, TN 37110
Logan, Jason   <M1 M8>
212 Saddlebag Court
Rineyville, KY 40162
(502)626-0722
jason.b.logan.mil@mail.mil

Malone, Michael   <M1 WC>
1229 Farrish Drive
Fredericksburg, VA 22401
(865)692-2415
Matlock, Robert   <M1 RT>
156 Dovenshire Drive
Fairfield Glade, TN 38558
(931)210-0614
revbobm@msn.com
Merritt, Joyce   <M1 WC>
3929 Snail Shell Cave Road
Rockvale, TN 37153
(615)574-3047
Oliver, Lisa   <M1 M9 OM>
110 Allen Drive
Hendersonville, TN 37075
(615)319-6466
lisa.oliver316@gmail.com
Parks, Sam   <M1 WC>
10 Lila Way
Cartersville, GA 60120
(615)529 2165
wsamparks@aol.com
Salisbury, Rebecca   <M1 WC>
1033 Twin Oaks Drive
Murfreesboro, TN 37130
(615)410-7801
rebsalisbury@yahoo.com

OTHER LICENTIATES ON ROLL:

White, Mack   <M2>
408 W Main Street
Smithville, TN 37166
(615)318-9863
wmax408@yahoo.com

OTHER CANDIDATES ON ROLL:

Quevedo, Mariano   <M3>
289 Golf Club Lane
McMinnville, TN 37110
Ramiriz, Araceli   <M3>
234 Vinewood Road Apt DG
McMinnville, TN 37110
Twilla, Kevin   <M3>
287 Owl Cirle
Lebanon,TN 37087
Watson, Micah   <M3>
2529 Middle Tennessee Boulevard
Murfreesboro, TN 37130
(615)692-2742
mwatson4289@gmail.com
Wills, Robin   <M3>
4607 E Richmond Shop Road
Lebanon, TN 37090
(615)870-4773
robinrush24@aol.com
Wright, John   <M3>

Nashville Presbytery
TENNESSEE SYNOD

GENERAL		MEMBERSHIP			CHANGES				FINANCES				
	1.Church Number	2.Active	3.Total	4.Church School	5.Prof. of Faith	6.Gains	7.Losses	8.Children Baptized	9. OUR UNITED OUT-REACH	10. Total Out-Reach Giving	11. All Other Expenses	12. Total Income Received	13. Value Church Prop. 1=1000
	1	2	3	4	5	6	7	8	9	10	11	12	13
Arlington	7311	19	39	23	0	0	1	0	146	11,719	30,591	50,871	403
Beech	7301	177	177	100	2	5	3	1	12,527	26,789	269,692	407,606	2,998
Bethel	7302	58	73	44	6	8	30	1	1,200	3,022	123,365	127,933	576
Brenthaven	7331	296	484	160	4	11	13	1	31,166	87,000	356,938	418,258	7,000
Brush Hill+	7325	141	209	63	1	9	18	1	11,548	20,994	195,782	231,161	5,600
Calvary	7342	15	10	10	0	0	5	0	214	300	44,771	47,328	500
Camp Ground*	7312	17	19	10	0	0	1	0	0	3,500	62,180	45,977	450
Cane Ridge	7326	18	18	5	0	0	1	0	0	0	21,532	27,350	275
Charlotte+	7303	26	56	17	0	0	1	0	3,145	4,667	31,010	32,173	527
Clarksville	7304	281	281	250	6	22	5	0	38,317	51,746	387,127	411,550	4,600
Concord*	7306	31	31	35	6	6	2	0	1,000	2,441	31,045	35,613	125
Cristo Vive	7314				No Report Received			0	0	0	0	0	0
Cumberland Valle	7307	27	43	20	0	0	0	1	3,006	5,797	30,473	30,062	250
Dickson	7308	330	407	115	5	7	0	7	11,000	37,691	172,454	218,518	1,500
Donelson	7327	52	117	65	3	4	2	2	1,000	13,208	66,732	91,439	1,650
Dry Fork	7309	12	25	0	1	3	2	0	1,000	2,770	15,230	21,055	100
Erin*	7310	13	13	0	0	0	3	0	0	579	20,733	22,913	350
Goodlettsville	7328	299	299	221	11	26	81	2	0	29,380	529,068	522,087	3,500
Halls Creek*	7313	50	56	45	0	4	1	0	0	6,021	29,044	40,760	505
Hendersonville*	7340	19	19	17	0	2	0	0	0	430	33,233	35,616	500
Liberty	7315	52	52	51	12	12	7	0	2,404	21,190	87,404	108,594	600
Locust Grove*	7316	10	39	5	0	0	4	0	0	1,672	22,731	39,415	313
Madison 1st	7329	28	51	28	0	2	3	1	4,764	5,187	57,625	62,812	340
Mariah	7317	40	40	25	0	11	3	0	0	3,012	38,880	44,326	150
McAdoo	7318	38	38	14	0	0	14	0	4,989	8,623	82,702	94,611	646
Mt. Denson	7319	50	171	28	No Report Received			0	8,623	0	0	0	730
Mt. Liberty	7320	98	164	48	2	4	0	4	3,900	11,118	105,054	121,311	1,300
Mt. Sharon	7321	76	206	51	0	6	8	0	8,750	15,597	169,251	178,630	1,750
Mt. Sinai	7330	15	15	8	6	6	1	0	0	480	13,094	14,289	300
Mt. View*	7322	40	90	20	2	5	0	0	0	3,525	4,600	74,435	450
New Hope	7337	7	7	12	No Report Received			0	0	0	0	0	52
New Providence	7305	28	28	10	1	2	2	2	0	1,490	36,201	27,608	998
Shiloh	7338	35	67	18	No Report Received			0	200	0	0	0	900
St. Luke	7332	117	305	51	0	0	0	0	20,371	33,600	172,331	205,931	3,525
Sudanese	7341	38	38	0	0	4	0	0	0	0	0	0	24
Tusculum	7333	178	687	125	0	7	5	6	106,974	130,530	443,145	1,769,915	3,405
Waverly**	7339	25	25	6	0	0	162	0	0	2,973	68,580	73,768	768
West Nashville	7334	116	399	105	1	1	4	1	20,316	29,037	288,688	269,540	3,894
TOTALS	38	2,916	4,798	1,802	68	167	382	31	296,560	576,088	4,041,286	5,903,155	52,074

*Math error corrected. **Purged roll.

NASHVILLE PRESBYTERY CONTINUED

CHURCHES, PASTORS, AND CLERKS:

Arlington (4WC)TNNA7311
PO Box 624 (mailing)
7 Knight Street (physical)
Erin, TN 37061
(931)289-3597 <Houston>
OD: Paul S Moody
600 Hurricane Loop
Tennessee Ridge, TN 37178
(931)721-3953
CL: Andrea Dillard
85 Victor Lane
Erin, TN 37061
(931)289-4004
adillard@workforceessentials.com

Beech (4MWC)TNNA7301
3216 Long Hollow Pike
Hendersonville, TN 37075
(615)824-3990 <Sumner>
FAX: (615)824-6507
office@beechcp.com
PA: Jeff DeWees <M1>
116 Lancaster Court
Gallatin, TN 37066
(931)209-3331
pastorjeff@beechcp.com
CL: Sarah Ezell
787 New Shackle Island Road
Hendersonville, TN 37075
(615)824-6815
sarahezell2@att.net

Bethel (4MC)TNNA7302
3375 Sango Road
Clarksville, TN 37043
(931)358-3295 <Montgomery>
PA: Stewart Salyer <M1>
2211 Foxfire Road
Clarksville, TN 37043
(931)980-2829
stewart.salyer@gmail.com
CL: Chris Davis
632 Eastwood Court
Clarksville, TN 37043
(931)624-9449
cdavis@cemc.org

Brenthaven (4C)TNNA7331
516 Franklin Road
Brentwood, TN 37027
(615)373-4826 <Williamson>
FAX: (615)373-4869
secretary@brenthaven.org
PA: Kip J Rush <M1>
513 Meadowlark Lane
Brentwood, TN 37027
(615)376-4563
pastor@brenthaven.org
AP: Sandra Shepherd <M1>
525 Summit Oaks Court
Nashville, TN 37221
(615)772-5358
woolywagon@gmail.com
CL: Christi Peppers
5008 Woodland Hills Drive
Brentwood, TN 37027
(615)376-9977
christi.peppers@gmail.com

Brush Hill (4MEWC)TNNA7325
3705 Brush Hill Road
Nashville, TN 37216
(615)227-2504 <Davidson>
FAX: (615)227-0039
bhcpc@birch.net
PA: Kenny Butcher <M1>
4608 Cather Court
Nashville, TN 37214
(615)719-1887
bhpastor@birch.net
AP: Paul Tucker <M1>
3801 Brush Hill Pike
Nashville, TN 37216
(615)430-9158
paultucker@gmail.com
CL: Terri Peltier
403 Cunniff Parkway
Goodlettsville, TN 37072
(615)227-2504
tp1260@aol.com

Calvary (4C)TNNA7342
340 Ringgold Road
Clarksville, TN 37042
(931)645-9200 <Montgomery>
2ourchurch@gmail.com
SS: Choil Ma <M1>
300 Ringgold Road Apt 503
Clarksville, TN 37042
(931)824-2443
choilma@yahoo.com
CL: Huisuk Snitker
436 Victory Road
Clarksville, TN 37042
(931)552-5813

Camp Ground (4MWC)TNNA7312
88 Campground Road
Erin, TN 37061
(931)289-4605 <Houston>
LS: Terry Mathis <M6>
88 Campground Road
Erin, TN 37061
(931)289-3602
ttmathis@peoplestel.net
CL: Tammy Simmons
5970 Highway 13
Erin, TN 37061
(931)289-3727
tsimmons3658@yahoo.com

Cane Ridge (4EC)TNNA7326
6867 Burkitt Road (mailing)
13412 Old Hickory Boulevard (physical)
Cane Ridge, TN 37013
(615)941-8317 <Davidson>
FAX: (615)941-2985
gdunn6867@comcast.net
LS: Gregory (Greg) Dunn <M6>
6867 Burkitt Road
Cane Ridge, TN 37013
(615)941-8317
FAX: (615)941-2985
gdunn6867@comast.net
CL: Eleanor Willett
145 Greenwood Drive
La Vergne, TN 37086
(615)793-5016
tuffyw9@comcast.net

Charlotte (4WC)TNNA7303
515 Mt Hebron Road (mailing)
3 Court Square (physical)
Charlotte, TN 37036
( ) <Dickson>
SS: Dean Guye <M1>
2759 Highway 70 E
Dickson, TN 37055
(615)446-7687
deanjoy@att.net
CL: Eloise Jones
515 Mount Hebron Road
Charlotte, TN 37036
(615)789-5353
joneseloise515@bellsouth.net

Clarksville (4WC)TNNA7304
1410 Golf Club Lane
Clarksville, TN 37040
(931)648-0817 <Montgomery>
office@clarksvillecpc.com
PA: Stephen L Louder <M1>
98 Gallant Court
Clarksville, TN 37043
(931)217-0369
pastorsteve@clarksvillecpc.com
AP: Paula Louder <M1>
98 Gallant Court
Clarksville, TN 37043
(615)804-4809
paula@clarksvillecpc.com
CL: Ashley Kettle
205 Bullock Drive
Clarksville, TN 37040
(931)624-8769
ashleykettle@gmail.com

Concord (4MC)TNNA7306
63 Gander Branch Road
Waverly, TN 37185
( ) <Humphreys>
CL: Phyllis Webb
3571 Fire Tower Road
Erin, TN 37061
(931)289-4601

Cristo Vive (4C)TNNA7314
611 Cheron Road
Madison, TN 37115
( ) <Davidson>
PA: Carlos Cinco <M1>
611 Cheron Road
Madison, TN 37115
(615)586-1269
pastorcinco2020@gmail.com
CL: Session Clerk
611 Cheron Road
Madison, TN 37115

Cumberland Valley (4WC)TNNA7307
285 Cumberland Valley Road
Mc Ewen, TN 37101
(931)582-8050 <Houston>
PA: Jesse L Freeman, Jr <M1>
270 Eastside Road
Burns, TN 37029
(615)202-4594
mptc@bellsouth.net

NASHVILLE PRESBYTERY CONTINUED

CL: June R Hicks
1339 Highway 13 S
Waverly, TN 37185
(931)296-4284

_____

Dickson   (4WC)TNNA7308
500 Highway 70 E
Dickson, TN 37055
(615)446-8511   <Dickson>
FAX: (615)446-7827
office@cumberlandpresbyterian.org
PA: Robert D Truitt   <M1>
1238 Old East Side Road
Burns, TN 37029
(615)740-9180
FAX: (615)446-7827
rdtjct@aol.com
AP: Dean Guye   <M1>
2759 Highway 70 E
Dickson, TN 37055
(615)446-7687
deanjoy@att.net
CL: Mark Rolman
102 Charles Court
Dickson, TN 37055
(615)375-7080
mdrolman@gmail.com

_____

Donelson   (4WC)TNNA7327
2914 Lebanon Road
Nashville, TN 37214
(615)516-9427   <Davidson>
email@donelsoncpchurch.com
PA: Michael Bertsch   <M1 RT>
204 Buckleigh Point
Gallatin, TN 37066
(423)763-8314
mikebertsch14@gmail.com
CL: Keith C Vanstone
3803 Plantation Drive
Hermitage, TN 37076
(615)210-5010
clerk@donelsoncpchurch.com

_____

Dry Fork   (4C)TNNA7309
174 Dry Fork Creek Road (mailing)
1050 Dry Fork Creek Road (physical)
Bethpage, TN 37022
(615)841-3169   <Sumner>
PA: Ted Bane   <M1>
903 W Old Hickory Boulevard
Madison, TN 37115
(615)975-9343
tedjan95@aol.com
CL: Sue Carr
174 Dry Fork Creek Road
Bethpage, TN 37022
(615)841-3169
suekencarr@nctc.com

_____

Erin   (4MWC)TNNA7310
PO Box 307 (mailing)
4793 E Main Street (physical)
Erin, TN 37061
( )   <Houston>
erincpchurch@gmail.com
SS: Timothy W Ferrell   <M1>
1850 Dunbar Road
Woodlawn, TN 37191
(931)920-2662
ferrelltw@aol.com

CL: Carolyn Zurawski
978 Scotts Chapel Road
Cumberland City, TN 37050
(931)827-3111

_____

Goodlettsville   (4MWC)TNNA7328
226 South Main Street
Goodlettsville, TN 37072
(615)859-5888   <Davidson>
FAX: (615)859-8820
gcpc@goodlettsvillechurch.com
PA: Tim Stutler   <M1>
1044 Mansker Farm Boulevard
Hendersonville, TN 37075
(615)859-5888
tim@goodletttsvillechurch.com
CL: Dillard Tutor
292 Lake Terrace Drive
Hendersonville, TN 37075

_____

Halls Creek   (4EC)TNNA7313
3650 Perrywinkle Branch Road (mailing)
2803 Halls Creek Road (physical)
Waverly, TN 37185
(931)296-7758   <Humphreys>
SS: Gary Carlton   <M1>
108 Greenbrier Street
Dickson, TN 37055
(615)441-8963
gwcarlton@yahoo.com
CL: Jerry Binkley
3650 Perrywinkle Branch Road
Waverly, TN 37185
(931)296-3154
jerry.sheena@yahoo.com

_____

Hendersonville   (4WC)TNNA7340
453 Walton Ferry Road
Hendersonville, TN 37075
(615)822-6091   <Sumner>
CL: Susan Wyatt
115 Elissa Drive
Hendersonville, TN 37075
(615)948-8242
FAX: (615)824-0195
susandwyatt@comcast.net

_____

Liberty   (4MWC)TNNA7315
725 S Liberty Church Road
Clarksville, TN 37042
( )   <Montgomery>
PA: Rocky Johnson   <M1>
1208 Redwood Drive
Clarksville, TN 37042
(423)620-7753
rockyj1960@gmail.com
CL: Bob Del Giorno
1510 S Freestone Court
Clarksville, TN 37042
(931)647-1086
bodeno@charter.net

_____

Locust Grove   (4WC)TNNA7316
3449 Locust Church Road
Cunningham, TN 37052
( )   <Montgomery>
SS: Timothy W Ferrell   <M1>
1850 Dunbar Road
Woodlawn, TN 37191
(931)920-2662
ferrelltw@aol.com

CL: Lawanda Black
3192 Budds Creek Road
Palmyra, TN 37142
(931)326-5298
jobee39@hughes.net

_____

Madison First   (4MWC)TNNA7329
735 Argyle Avenue
Madison, TN 37115
(615)868-2888   <Davidson>
FAX: (615)868-2888
madisonfirst@yahoo.com
PA: Johnny Parish   <M1>
114 Savo Bay
Hendersonville, TN 37075
(615)824-5842
johnnyparish@bellsouth.net
CL: Edith Marlin
112 Becker Avenue
Old Hickory, TN 37138
(615)847-4148
edithmarlin@outlook.com

_____

Mariah   (4MWC)TNNA7317
43 Mariah Church Lane
Waverly, TN 37185
(931)296-5546   <Humphreys>
SS: Nathaniel Mathews   <M2>
1006 Woodland Drive
New Johnsonville, TN 37134
(931)209-6645
bro.nate-mathews@hotmail.com
CL: Anita Gehring
65 Warden Road
Waverly, TN 37185
(931)296-8059

_____

McAdoo   (4WC)TNNA7318
3724 Ashland City Road
Clarksville, TN 37043
(931)362-3091   <Montgomery>
PA: Joe Vick   <M1>
6064 Old Hickory Boulevard
Whites Creek, TN 37189
(615)519-5249
joervick@gmail.com
CL: Nancy Rhinehart
1601 Harville Road
Clarksville, TN 37043
(931)362-3105
rhinehart.nancy@yahoo.com

_____

Mt Denson   (4MWC)TNNA7319
4558 Highway 161
Springfield, TN 37172
(615)384-3613   <Robertson>
PA: Andrew Ward   <M1>
407 Rose Hill Court
Goodlettsville, TN 37072
(615)456-9136
andrewbward@aol.com
AP: Patricia (Pat) Pickett   <M1 M9>
1460 Cheatham Dam Road
Ashland City, TN 37015
(615)792-4973
tovahtoo@aol.com
CL: Ashley Wilks
4028 Wilks Road
Springfield, TN 37172

NASHVILLE PRESBYTERY CONTINUED

Mt Liberty   (4MWC)TNNA7320
3655 Highway 49 E
Charlotte, TN 37036
(615)789-5916   <Dickson>
SS: Justin Griffin   <M1>
3655 Highway 49 E
Charlotte, TN 37036
(615)969-2426
jjjjgriff@gmail.com
CL: Cindy Simpson
3378 Highway 49 E
Charlotte, TN 37036
(615)945-0010
cindyrsimpson@hotmail.com

Mt Sharon   (4MWC)TNNA7321
4634 Mount Sharon Road
Greenbrier, TN 37073
(615)384-8569   <Robertson>
pastor@mtsharoncpchurch.org
PA: Jason Mikel   <M1>
4630 Mt Sharon Road
Greenbrier, TN 37073
(615)243-8938
jasonemikel@gmail.com
CL: James D Jordan
2100 W End Avenue Ste 1150
Nashville, TN 37203
(615)329-2100
FAX: (615)329-2187
jdjordan@gjplaw.com

Mt Sinai   (4WC)TNNA7330
3738 Hydes Ferry Road
Nashville, TN 37218
(615)586-7886   <Davidson>
OD: David Lomax   <M5>
1501 Robert Cartwright Drive
Goodlettsville, TN 37072
(615)753-2493
lomaxdavid53@yahoo.com
CL: Katherine B Pleas
555 Church Street #801
Nashville, TN 37219
(615)251-4037
pleas5@hotmail.com

Mt View   (4C)TNNA7322
2359 Leatherwood Road (mailing)
Stewart, TN 37175
282 Hickman Creek Road (physical)
Dover, TN 37058
(931)217-0893   <Stewart>
mvcpchurch@gmail.com
PA: Ronald D Burgess   <M1>
116 Harris Ridge Road
Dover, TN 37058
(931)232-5151
revron4@bellsouth.net
CL: Michelle Sills
126 Ralls Road
Dover, TN 37058
(931)305-8893

New Hope   (4C)TNNA7337
c/o Sharon Cook (mailing)
8009 White Oak Road
Stewart, TN 37175
60 New Hope Road (physical)
Stewart, TN 37175
( )   <Houston>
LS: G Ray Mayo
3019 Lights Chapel Road
Clarksville, TN 37040
CL: Sharon E Cook
8009 White Oak Road
Stewart, TN 37175
(931)721-2513
ricsha55@yahoo.com

New Providence   (4MWC)TNNA7305
1307 Fort Campbell Boulevard
Clarksville, TN 37042
(931)647-4455   <Montgomery>
PA: John Adam Smith   <M1 M9>
916 Allen Road
Nashville, TN 37214
(573)453-8455
john.a.smith.81@gmail.com
CL: Toni Boothe
1260 Dotsonville Road
Clarksville, TN 37042
(931)647-8297
alchvic1059@hotmail.com

Shiloh   (4C)TNNA7338
4812 Shiloh-Canaan Road
Palmyra, TN 37142
(931)387-4198   <Montgomery>
greg1013@aol.com
CL: Dianne Harris
400 Attaway Road
Clarksville, TN 37040

St Luke   (4MWC)TNNA7332
901 W Old Hickory Boulevard
Madison, TN 37115
(615)868-1982   <Davidson>
stlukecpchurch@gmail.com
PA: Dwayne Tyus   <M1>
901 W Old Hickory Boulevard
Madison, TN 37115
(615)720-2564
dwayne.tyus@gmail.com
CL: Angie Pinson
901 W Old Hickory Boulevard
Madison, TN 37115
(615)337-7311
stlukecpchurch@gmail.com

Sudanese   (F)TNNA7341
c/o First UMC (mailing)
149 W Main Street
407 Owen Drive (physical)
Gallatin, TN 37066
(615)585-2842   <Sumner>
CL: John Tiang Ping
49 Millwood Drive
Nashville, TN 37217
(615)365-3274

Tusculum   (4MWC)TNNA7333
477 McMurray Drive
Nashville, TN 37211
(615)833-0742   <Davidson>
tusculumchurch@gmail.com
PA: Roger Patton, Jr   <M1>
1534 Eden Rose Place
Nolensville, TN 37135
(615)975-5526
rogerlpatton@att.net
CL: Dawn Gannon
3417 County Hill Road
Antioch, TN 37013
(615)399-2782
dawngannon0317@yahoo.com

Waverly   (4MWC)TNNA7339
109 N Church Street
Waverly, TN 37185
(931)296-3232   <Humphreys>
FAX: (931)296-3232
waverlycpc@att.net
SS: Glenn Warren   <M1>
116 Cedar Hill Drive
Waverly, TN 37185
(931)209-5431
gwarren224@gmail.com
CL: Larry Cochran
581 Wisteria Lane
Waverly, TN 37185
(931)296-4450

West Nashville   (4MWC)TNNA7334
6849 Charlotte Pike
Nashville, TN 37209
(615)352-2800   <Davidson>
FAX: (615)352-2801
info@wncp.org
PA: Rickey Page   <M1>
736 Rodney Drive
Nashville, TN 37205
(615)353-7850
FAX: (615)352-2801
rickey.page@wncp.org
CL: Nancy Crowell
707 Newberry Road
Nashville, TN 37205
nancydcrowell@gmail.com

OTHERS ON MINISTERIAL ROLL:

Acuff, David   <M1 M8>
4969 Quail Lane
Columbia, SC 29206
(803)727-3910
david.acuff@us.army.mil
Barna, Clifton   <M1 WC>
1012 Adam Court
Cottontown, TN 37066
(352)598-3246
cliff.barna@gmail.com
Baranoski, Timothy   <M1 M8>
1205 Tomahawk Drive B
Jber, AK 99505
(615)440-3499
timothy.i.baranoski.mil@mail.mil
Bennett, Alfred J   <M1 HR>
7286 Nolensville Road
Nolensville, TN 37135
(615)776-5181

NASHVILLE PRESBYTERY CONTINUED

Cook, Lisa <M1 M9>
4101 Dalemere Court
Nashville, TN 37207
(615)830-6217
tgoose@comcast.net

Corbin, William <M1 HR>
7300 N Lamar Road
Mount Juliet, TN 37122
(615)459-8998
raven.rest@comcast.net

De Vries, Raymond <M1 HR>
2080 Stanford Village Drive
Antioch, TN 37013
(615)332-3587
ray.devries@comcast.net

Duke, Michael E <M1 WC>
106 Friar Tuck Drive
Dickson, TN 37055
(615)446-6515

Dumas, Byron <M1 OM>
1775 Theresa Drive
Clarksville, TN 37043
(931)552-8772
bdumas7346@aol.com

Earheart-Brown, Daniel <M1 PR>
475 N Highland Street Apt 9L
Memphis, TN 38122
jebrown@memphisseminary.edu
(901)278-0367

Ferguson, E Blant <M1 RT>
704 Bear Run
Hiawassee, GA 30546
(706)896-9296
blantferg@yahoo.com

Goodwill, James L <M1 RT>
205 S English Hill Lane
Hillsborough, NC 27278
(704)526-8729
jim@jimgoodwill.com

Gough, Ernest E <M1 WC>
8366 Highway 70
Nashville, TN 37221
(615)646-4372
eegough@bellsouth.net

Hurley, E C <M1 WC>
221 Fantasia Way
Clarksville, TN 37043
(931)551-6173
hurleyec@gmail.com

Jones, Gregory <M1 WC>
400 Adam Wood Drive Apt D12
Nashville, TN 37211
(931)249-9512
greg1013@aol.com

Miller, Carol <M1 WC>
101 Park Avenue
Dickson, TN 37055
(615)441-6656
lcarolmiller@comcast.net

Norton, Kitty <M1 WC>
251 Westchase Drive
Nashville, TN 37205
(615)584-1464
kitty.a.norton@vanderbilt.edu

Nye, John <M1 WC>
210 Crestview Drive
Mount Juliet, TN 37122

Parrish, Steven <M1 PR>
4610 Dunn Avenue
Memphis, TN 38117
(901)743-9545
sparrish@memphisseminary.edu

Patton, Malcolm <M1 RT>
921 Harris Drive
Gallatin, TN 37066
(615)452-5557
FAX: (615)824-6507
bpatton11@comcast.net

Polacek, Fred E <M1 WC>
907 Graham Drive
Old Hickory, TN 37138
(615)754-5328
revfredp@gmail.com

Rippy, James G <M1 WC>
442 Trina Street
Gallatin, TN 37066
(615)681-7086
lrippy@live.com

Roddy, Lowell G <M1 RT>
2583 Hedgerow Lane
Clarksville, TN 37043
(931)368-1081
FAX: (931)221-1032
lgroddy@yahoo.com

Schott, Fred, Jr <M1 HR>
606 Taylor Trail
Springfield, TN 37172
(615)384-8572
fws195@aol.com

Sims, Edward G <M1 RT>
2161 N Meadow Drive
Clarksville, TN 37043
(931)206-5759
simseg@aol.com

Smith, Billy T <M1 HR>
213 Eller Cove Road
Weaverville, NC 28787
(931)368-0424

Stefan, Gregory <M1 WC>
1917 Birchwood Street
East Pearl, PA 17519
(717)838-1171
pastorstefan@att.net

Stovall, Jeff <M1 WC>
2829 Trelawny Drive
Clarksville, TN 37043
(931)993-6104
jeffstovall@juno.com

Tabor, Don M <M1 RT>
9611 Mitchell Place
Brentwood, TN 37027
(615)776-7292
FAX: (615)373-3356
dontabor@comcast.net

West, David <M1 M9>
2027 Lucille Street
Lebanon, TN 37087
(217)732-7568

Whitworth, Gary W <M1 RT>
1706 Old Hickory Boulevard
Brentwood, TN 37027
(615)915-4180

OTHER LICENTIATES ON ROLL:

Cassell, C J <M2 ST>
825 Aimes Court
Nashville, TN 37221
(615)594-2693
n4cjc@comcast.net

Jones, Steve <M2 ST>
PO Box 368
Burns, TN 37029
(615)441-6159

Young, Taylor <M2>
255 Willard Drive
Nashville, TN 37211
(615)319-8294
brandontayloryoung@yahoo.com

OTHER CANDIDATES ON ROLL:

Chall-Hutchinson, Deborah <M3>
190 Ussery Road
Clarksville, TN 37043
(931)905-1671
challhut@gmail.com

Moore, Kimberly <M3>
1025 Three Island Ford Road
Charlotte, TN 37036
(615)545-1595
kimberly.a.moore@vanderbilt.edu

Norris, Dakota <M3>
4750 Highway 431 N
Springfield, TN 37172
(615)681-6346
volsfan2011@gmail.com

Stevens, Brittany <M3>
606 Huntington Parkway
Nashville, TN 37211
(615)719-3362
bstevens5@my.apsu.edu

Wilkinson, Neal
1174 Tanglewood Street
Memphis, TN 38114
(615)934-7342
nwilkinson@memphisseminary.edu

Wilson, Melissa <M3 ST>
107 Hillwood Drive
Dickson, TN 37055
(615)446-7523
milzwilz@comcast.net

North Central Presbytery
MIDWEST SYNOD

GENERAL		MEMBERSHIP			CHANGES				FINANCES				
	1.Church Number	2.Active	3.Total	4.Church School	5.Prof. of Faith	6.Gains	7.Losses	8.Children Baptized	9. OUR UNITED OUT-REACH	10. Total Out-Reach Giving	11. All Other Expenses	12. Total Income Received	13. Value Church Prop. 1=1000
	1	2	3	4	5	6	7	8	9	10	11	12	13
Bethany	5401	76	336	75	0	0	8	0	11,503	47,526	111,313	137,825	560
Burnt Prairie	5102	16	34	6	No Report Received			0	0	0	0	0	63
Campground	5402	13	15	15	No Report Received			0	650	0	0	0	50
Casey	5201	16	36	15	0	0	0	0	244	1,500	21,440	35,495	50
Christ	5305	8	11	7	No Report Received			0	416	0	0	0	150
Comunidad	5212	25	25	19	No Report Received			0	0	0	0	0	0
Cumb. Chapel	5104	7	7	5	0	0	0	0	0	10,680	9,348	21,730	4
Ebenezer	5203	38	38	30	No Report Received			0	3,780	0	0	0	1,000
Elm River	5107	51	49	71	4	0	1	0	6,790	13,418	53,657	78,085	245
Fairfield	5108	188	327	93	0	6	3	0	0	52,444	189,041	192,581	1,000
Faith	5501	5	13	4	0	0	0	0	5,561	7,079	26,273	55,047	500
Fullerton	5404	27	27	21	0	0	1	0	1,928	4,320	18,227	29,720	50
Georgetown*	5204	19	63	20	1	18	5	0	5,680	10,033	43,747	56,786	113
Good Prospect	5205	90	90	113	2	6	5	0	8,344	28,876	83,062	111,938	1,200
Grace	5502	12	29	16	No Report Received			0	267	0	0	0	245
Knights Chapel	5306	29	36	38	No Report Received			0	0	0	0	0	100
Lebanon North	5113	64	85	65	0	19	0	0	0	11,267	72,673	87,441	200
Lebanon South	5114				No Report Received			0	0	0	0	0	0
Lincoln 1st	5405	39	91	25	No Report Received			0	5,400	0	0	0	575
Monroe City	5307	8	8	0	No Report Received			0	0	0	0	0	200
Morningside	5304	58	80	21	No Report Received			0	2,000	0	0	0	1,600
Mt. Gilead	5406	29	49	42	0	0	0	0	1,000	4,966	26,083	29,018	145
Mt. Olivet	5308	12	26	7	0	0	2	0	247	2,892	22,004	39,404	75
Mt. Oval	5116	6	6	10	CLOSED 2015				0	0	0	0	10
New Hope*	5208	45	108	34	0	1	0	0	7,192	20,476	55,611	76,087	400
Pleasant Grove	5210	20	27	20	0	0	3	0	2,700	19,596	13,540	33,136	175
Shiloh	5409	28	100	23	0	0	0	2	1,000	8,133	16,017	36,247	310
Shinar	5410	31	38	0	No Report Received			0	0	0	0	0	237
Spring Hill	5411	5	5	3	No Report Received			0	0	0	0	0	379
Union North	5124	35	35	20	0	10	0	0	0	6,089	33,227	42,753	120
United*	5119	50	99	20	0	0	7	0	500	500	61,300	58,266	503
Willow Creek	5211	77	100	90	1	0	0	1	10,490	32,660	80,919	104,890	1,000
TOTALS	31	1,124	1,990	926	8	64	35	3	75,692	282,455	937,482	1,226,449	10,992

*Math error corrected. **Purged roll.

NORTH CENTRAL PRESBYTERY CONTINUED

CHURCHES, PASTORS, AND CLERKS:

Bethany (4MWC)MINC5401
PO Box 384 (mailing)
219 S Lincoln Street (physical)
Bethany, IL 61914
(217)665-3034 <Moultrie>
bethanycpc@yahoo.com
CL: Dean McReynolds
399 County Road 1600 N
Bethany, IL 61914
(217)665-3420
wdeanmcreynolds@yahoo.com

Burnt Prairie (4MWC)MINC5102
RR 3 Box 947 (mailing)
Fairfield, IL 62837
Church Street (physical)
Burnt Prairie, IL 62820
(618)925-1185 <White>
LS: Scott D Smothers <M6>
RR 5 Box 573
Fairfield, IL 62837
(618)842-6009
lsmothers@myfrontiermail.com
CL: Andy Pottorff
RR 3 Box 947
Fairfield, IL 62837
(618)925-1185
andypottorff@yahoo.com

Campground (4WEC)MINC5402
1497 Hookdale Avenue (mailing)
Route 4 (physical)
Greenville, IL 62246
(618)664-1547 <Bond>
CL: Rodney Reavis
1497 Hookdale Avenue
Greenville, IL 62246
(618)664-1547
rcreavis@yahoo.com

Casey (4C)MINC5201
PO Box 21 (mailing)
16 N Central (physical)
Casey, IL 62420
(217)932-5404 <Clark>
CL: Mary Gard
7810 N 400th Street
Casey, IL 62420
(217)932-2971
thetoymaker@wildblue.net

Christ (4MC)MINC5305
6140 S Meridian
Indianapolis, IN 46217
(317)787-9585 <Marion>
CL: Paula Price
892 Geagan Street
Greenwood, IN 46143
(317)709-8138

Comunidad Cristina (4F)MINC5212
1714 S 4th Avenue (mailing)
Maywood, IL 60153
15N562 Vista Lane (physical)
Dundee, IL 60118
(708)223-2185 <Cook>
pastorccc@clear.net

CL: Noel Taveras
809 Lexington Circle
Hanover Park, IL 60133
(630)965-7113
cololo809@yahoo.com

Cumberland Chapel (4C)MINC5104
1075 County Road 2400E (mailing)
Route 2 CR 1300 N, CR 1200 E (physical)
Fairfield, IL 62837
( ) <Wayne>
PA: J B Gates <M1>
PO Box 289
Enfield, IL 62835
(618)963-2306
rjjbgate@hamiltoncom.net
CL: Ronald E Huffman
1075 County Road 2400E
Fairfield, IL 62837
(618)842-9518
huffmanrj@hotmail.com

Ebenezer (4WF)MINC5203
1941 W Belmont Avenue
Chicago, IL 60657
(773)528-8218 <Cook>
PA: Eduardo Montoya <M1>
270 Windsor Drive
Roselle, IL 60172
(630)980-1577
edmontoya@hotmail.com
CL: Samuel Alvarez
3740 W Leland Avenue
Chicago, IL 60625
(773)509-9165

Elm River (4EC)MINC5107
2212 County Highway 2 (mailing)
2250 County Highway 2 (physical)
Cisne, IL 62823
( ) <Wayne>
SS: Ralph Blevins <M1>
1623 County Road 2375 E
Geff, IL 62842
(618)854-2494
pastorreblevins@gmail.com
CL: Jack Enlow
2212 County Highway 2
Cisne, IL 62823
(618)854-2492
enlow@wabash.net

Fairfield (4MEWC)MINC5108
1700 W Delaware
Fairfield, IL 62837
(618)847-5281 <Wayne>
FAX: (618)842-2608
PA: Jeff Biggs <M1>
1504 Cumberland Drive
Fairfield, IL 62837
(618)842-2219
jeffbiggsonline@gmail.com
CL: Kevan Stum
15 Brock Lane
Fairfield, IL 62837
(618)842-2705

Faith (4C)MINC5501
20301 E Ten Mile Road
St Clair Shores, MI 48080
(586)775-1524 <Macomb>

CL: Christopher D McMacken
20396 Erben Street
St Clair Shores, MI 48081
(586)771-7855
cmcmacken@itctransco.com

Fullerton (4WC)MINC5404
1105 E Allen Street (mailing)
Route 48 (physical)
Farmer City, IL 61848
( ) <DeWitt>
CL: Duane Runyon
1105 E Allen Street
Farmer City, IL 61848
(309)825-3324
dprunyon@yahoo.com

Georgetown (4EWC)MINC5204
201 Frazier Street
Georgetown, IL 61846
(217)662-6988 <Vermilion>
CL: Stephen K Hughes
1011 E 14th Street
Georgetown, IL 61846
(217)662-6988
hughesst@sbcglobal.net

Good Prospect (4MWC)MINC5205
PO Box 5 (mailing)
301 E Trilla Road (physical)
Trilla, IL 62469
(217)234-8529 <Coles>
trillacp@yahoo.com
CL: Jedd Tolen
PO Box 8
Trilla, IL 62469
trillatolens@gmail.com

Grace (4C)MINC5502
1122 Harrison Boulevard
Lincoln Park, MI 48146
(313)381-3456 <Wayne>
CL: Dorinda Boyer
21625 Knights Lane
Brownstown, MI 48183
(734)675-7322

Knights Chapel (4WC)MINC5306
1285 S County Road 375 W
Petersburg, IN 47567
( ) <Pike>
CL: Janet Church
5541 W County Road 100 S
Petersburg, IN 47567
(812)749-3242

Lebanon North (4C)MINC5113
Route 5
Fairfield, IL 62837
(618)842-5205
FAX: (618)842-5205 <Wayne>
PA: J C McDuffie <M1>
RR 3 Box 574
Fairfield, IL 62837
(618)842-5624
mactrapper4@frontier.com
CL: De Young
107 W King Street
Fairfield, IL 62837
(618)516-1736

NORTH CENTRAL PRESBYTERY CONTINUED

Lebanon South   (4C)MINC5114
  Route 3
  Galatia, IL 62935
  ( )   <Saline>
OD: Robert D Craig   <M5>
  46030 Sunset Drive
  Bay Minette, AL 36507
CL: James Patterson
  RR 2
  Galatia, IL 62935
  (618)268-4471

Lincoln First   (4MEWC)MINC5405
  PO Box 596 (mailing)
  110 Broadway (physical)
  Lincoln, IL 62656
  (217)732-7568   <Logan>
  cumberland@frontier.com
PA: Steven Blaum   <M1>
  184 900 Street
  Middletown, IL 62666
  (217)871-3339
  strab2010@yahoo.com
CL: Ronald (Ron) Hubbard
  330 3rd Street
  Lincoln, IL 62656
  (217)871-5453
  rehubb1@gmail.com

Monroe City   (4MWC)MINC5307
  PO Box 167 (mailing)
  8th & Cleveland Streets (physical)
  Monroe City, IN 47557
  (812)743-5171   <Knox>
  FAX: (812)743-5171
PA: David Parman   <M1>
  5034 S Monroe School Road
  Monroe City, IN 47557
  (812)743-2646
  FAX: (812)743-5171
CL: Marjorie Vories
  PO Box 167
  Monroe City, IN 47557
  (812)743-5286
  FAX: (812)743-5171

Morningside   (4WC)MINC5304
  8419 Newburgh Road
  Evansville, IN 47715
  (812)473-4700   <Vanderburgh>
  FAX: (812)473-4765
  morningsidechurch@sbcglobal.net
PA: James Messer   <M1 M8>
  3653 Old Madisonville Road
  Henderson, KY 42420
  (270)827-0711
  jcmess@hotmail.com
CL: Karen Gossman
  5077 Kenosha Drive
  Newburgh, IN 47630
  (812)490-6522
  km56gossman@yahoo.com

Mt Gilead   (4C)MINC5406
  PO Box 494 (mailing)
  1077 Mt Gilead Road (physical)
  Greenville, IL 62246
  ( )   <Bond>

CL: Elizabeth File
  547 IL Route 140
  Pocahontas, IL 62275
  (618)664-3216

Mt Olivet   (4C)MINC5308
  3153 S State Road 257 (mailing)
  4299 S State Road 57 (physical)
  Washington, IN 47501
  (812)254-4077   <Daviess>
  g9barnard@yahoo.com
CL: Karen Barnard
  3153 S State Road 257
  Washington, IN 47501
  (812)254-4077
  g9barnard@yahoo.com

Mt Oval   (2C)MINC5116
  CLOSED 2015

New Hope   (4EC)MINC5208
  3997 N 100th Street (mailing)
  Casey, IL 62420
  20955 E 2100th Avenue (physical)
  Yale, IL 62481
  ( )   <Jasper>
  royndebbie@hotmail.com
LS: Chris Parr   <M6>
  9956 E 2100th Avenue
  Hidalgo, IL 62438
  (618)793-2704
  parpar62432@yahoo.com
CL: Roy Shanks
  3997 N 100th Street
  Casey, IL 62420
  (217)932-2995
  royndebbie@hotmail.com

Pleasant Grove   (4EC)MINC5210
  6360 E 2100th Avenue (mailing)
  Martinsville, IL 62442
  4125 E 200th Avenue (physical)
  Annapolis, IL 62413
  (618)569-4588   <Crawford>
  donnie.bailey62@yahoo.com
LS: Bill Ulery   <M6>
  10725 E 1500th Road
  Marshall, IL 62441
  (217)382-4593
CL: Donnie B Bailey
  7970 E 1625th Avenue
  Robinson, IL 62454
  (618)569-4588
  donnie.bailey62@yahoo.com

Shiloh   (4MWC)MINC5409
  7722 Shiloh Road
  Virginia, IL 62691
  (217)452-3802   <Cass>
CL: Anna Ruth Long
  6614 IL Route 78
  Virginia, IL 62691
  (217)883-2654
  hjlong@casscomm.com

Shinar   (4WC)MINC5410
  11383 147th Avenue (mailing)
  West Burlington, IA 52655
  19705 185th Avenue (physical)
  New London, IA 52645
  (319)457-2652   <Des Moines>

OD: Shane McCampbell   <M5>
  109 Indian Terrace
  Burlington, IA 52601
  (319)457-2652
  revshane777@yahoo.com
CL: Carolyn Schenk
  11383 147th Avenue
  West Burlington, IA 52655
  (319)754-8274
  carolynschenk@yahoo.com

Spring Hill   (4C)MINC5411
  690 E 1800th Avenue (mailing)
  9 miles SW of Beecher City (physical)
  Beecher City, IL 62414
  ( )   <Fayette>
OD: Donald Ray Miller   <M5>
  Route 2 Box 136C
  Beecher City, IL 62414
  (618)487-5648
CL: Nelda Kline
  690 E 1800th Avenue
  Beecher City, IL 62414
  (618)487-5363

Union North   (4C)MINC5124
  506 Lakeview Drive (mailing)
  635 County Road 2400 E (physical)
  Fairfield, IL 62837
  (618)847-4061   <Wayne>
PA: Ron Fell   <M1>
  PO Box 285
  Fairfield, IL 62837
  (618)638-3744
  r.fell80@gmail.com
CL: Sandra Beckel
  506 W Lakeview Drive
  Fairfield, IL 62837
  (618)842-6400
  gonqwik@fairfieldwireless.net

United   (4MC)MINC5119
  204 S Powell Street
  Norris City, IL 62869
  (618)378-3341   <White>
  FAX: (618)378-3064
  tc_5854@yahoo.com
CL: Nellie Shepard
  206 E Eubanks Street
  Norris City, IL 62869
  (618)378-3997

Willow Creek   (4MWC)MINC5211
  6492 E 400th Road
  Martinsville, IL 62442
  (618)569-4955   <Clark>
PA: Kevin Small   <M1>
  6492 E 400th Road
  Martinsville, IL 62442
  (618)562-1463
  revkev61@gmail.com
CL: Norma Calvert
  6313 E 400th Road
  Martinsville, IL 62442
  (618)569-3035
  norma.calvert@yahoo.com

NORTH CENTRAL PRESBYTERY CONTINUED

OTHERS ON MINISTERIAL ROLL:

Allen, Gail   <M1 WC>
488 County Road 1650 N
Bethany, IL 61914
(217)665-3387
kallen1_61914@yahoo.com

Aros, Jeremias   <M1 RT>
5649 W Roscoe Street
Chicago, IL 60634
(773)685-4395
jeremiasaros@sbcglobal.net

Axton, Durant   <M1 WC>
2441 SE Browning Road
Evansville, IN 47725
(812)459-0089
FAX: (618)842-2608

Barnett, Rudolph   <M1 WC>
RR 5 Box 267
McLeansboro, IL 62859
(618)643-3253

Bender, Richard J   <M1 WC>
5297 Normandy Place
Evansville, IN 47715
(812)983-9597
richardjbenderjr@yahoo.com

Bunting, Geoff   <M1 WC>
9229 Hedgewood Court
Evansville, IN 47725
(812)925-6630
geoff.bunting@yahoo.com

Compton, Marcia   <M1 ST>
6276 Cascade Circle
Indianapolis, IN 46234
(317)209-9798
mcomptonma@yahoo.com

Craig, Robert A   <M1 RT>
1711 Bellevue Avenue Apt D-706
Richmond, VA 23227
(573)219-8051
robertacraig1954@gmail.com

Dallwig, Roger   <M1 WC>
1661 Hickory Lane
Corydon, IN 47112
(812)705-5071
rcd129@hotmail.com

Dill, Diane   <Advisory Mem>
925 Primm Road Apt 113
Lincoln, IL 62656
(217)617-4400
diedremarie@live.com

Furr, Wayne   <M1 WC>
706 E 6th Street
Coal Valley, IL 61240
(309)791-1691
prespreacher@gmail.com

Gross, Ronald   <M1 RT>
2436 N 420th Street
Oblong, IL 62449
(217)932-2788
juneg@eiis.net

Korb, Leon C   <M1 RT>
15360 E 350 North Road
Ridge Farm, IL 61870
(217)662-8398

Lovelace, John G   <M1 RT>
1202 E Cedar Street
New Baden, IL 62265
(812)476-5879
jlove1234@aol.com

Nichols, Oscar Lee   <M1 RT>
1035 N County Road 650E
Trilla, IL 62469
(217)234-6551

Oliveira, Jose   <M1 WC>
7310 Jasmine Drive
Hanover Park, IL 60133
(630)855-0870
valdirsoares@yahoo.com

Richards, Carroll R   <M1 RT M9>
210 Allison Drive
Lincoln, IL 62656
(217)732-7894
FAX: (217)732-7894
dr_cr@comcast.net

Scott, Lisa   <M1 WC>
ADDRESS ON FILE
(816)332-0604
lascott1979@att.net

Shirley, Betty L   <M1 RT>
811 Rotherham Drive
Ballwin, MO 63011
(636)386-3174
therevbls@prodigy.net

Smith, Albert J   <M1 RT>
407 W Main Street Apt 131
Wilkesboro, NC 28697
(217)452-3408
ct_alsmith@casscomm.com

Topar, Shirley   <M1 WC>
2233 Cambridge Drive SE
Grand Rapids, MI 49506
(616)245-0625
s_j_topar@yahoo.com

Wallace, Andrew   <M1 WC>
816 Howard Avenue
Burlingame, CA 94010

Watkins, Robert B   <M1 DE>
235 Misty Drive
Somerset, KY 42503
(319)431-0990
watkr@mac.com

Yarce, Janeth   <M1 WC>
3019 W Calavar Road
Phoenix, AZ 85053
(630)518-0295
janethyarce@yahoo.com

OTHER LICENTIATES ON ROLL:

OTHER CANDIDATES ON ROLL:

Alvarez, Samuel   <M3>
3740 W Leland Avenue
Chicago, IL 60625
(773)509-9165

Sandiford, Holton   <M3>
4227 E 300th Road
Casey, IL 62420
(217)259-3773

Stephenson, Joseph   <M3>
PO Box 129
Bethany, IL 61914
(217)853-7819

Red River Presbytery
MISSION SYNOD

GENERAL		MEMBERSHIP			CHANGES				FINANCES			
	1.Church Number	2.Active 3.Total 4.Church School			5.Prof. of Faith 6.Gains 7.Losses 8.Children Baptized				9. OUR UNITED OUT-REACH	10. Total Out-Reach Giving	11. All Other Expenses	12. Total Income Received	13. Value Church Prop. 1=1000
	1	2	3	4	5	6	7	8	9	10	11	12	13
Burns Flat	6301	90	97	60	8	10	0	1	2,800	35,152	87,767	114,042	1,500
Clinton	6302	120	120	56	1	0	1	0	8,019	14,152	119,992	134,144	1,500
Covenant	6304	84	107	94	2	7	2	0	6,000	34,165	190,837	193,715	1,250
Denton	8404	54	206	34	0	2	0	0	5,500	10,309	56,332	78,344	2,500
Eastlake	6205	61	155	31	16	16	4	0	8,726	14,415	71,935	90,487	1,000
Faith	6201	36	36	0	0	0	2	0	5,160	6,349	114,837	90,184	450
Hubbard*	8410	8	8	0	0	0	5	0	0	0	0	0	200
Lake Highlands+	8411	112	112	68	1	11	48	4	0	1,700	297,820	240,000	3,418
Locust Grove	6203	7	11	5	No Report Received				0	0	0	0	150
Mangum	6306	16	16	11	CLOSED 2015				0	0	0		752
Marlow	6305	35	69	18	0	0	8	0	7,234	17,256	66,542	79,221	690
Mesquite	8412	34	39	15	1	6	14	1	500	4,291	71,915	80,588	1,200
Mt. Zion	8414	5	5	16	0	1	0	0	1,526	0	0	13,071	60
Newberry	8415	16	16	5	0	4	10	0	800	10,750	17,932	26,710	462
Olney	8416	61	91	36	1	1	2	0	9,467	15,085	84,835	95,037	600
Pathway	8418	1,100	2,092	660	39	147	9	3	10,000	291,772	2,264,661	2,803,708	9,420
Sandy Springs	8420	20	35	7	No Report Received				0	0	0	0	200
Shiloh	8421	97	215	56	5	11	1	0	0	59,314	155,395	234,281	950
St. John	8413	30	39	5	0	0	35	0	18,224	9,024	57,668	56,242	916
St. Luke	8407	68	69	49	1	1	18	1	5,833	3,178	203,329	225,132	4,535
St. Mark (TX)	8408	21	21	6	0	0	31	0	520	1,400	47,401	48,801	1,048
St. Timothy*	8419	125	250	117	1	0	1	0	27,147	50,179	225,292	271,921	2,000
Stonegate	6307	48	49	22	1	5	3	2	6,375	8,868	112,255	88,606	748
Trinity	8409	65	89	26	4	12	20	4	12,312	21,422	144,664	164,132	1,300
Whitney	8424	11	11	4	CLOSED 2015				0	0	0		100
Zion Valley	8425	13	13	3	0	0	0	0	0	5,349	10,291	20,046	180
TOTALS	24	2,361	4,010	1,389	81	236	213	16	136,193	617,130	4,401,700	5,148,412	36,979

*Math error corrected. **Purged roll.   +Union church

CHURCHES, PASTORS, AND CLERKS:
_____

Burns Flat   (4WMC)MSRR6301
  PO Box 8 (mailing)
  205 Highway 44 (physical)
  Burns Flat, OK 73624
  (580)562-4706   <Washita>
  burnsflatcpc@windstream.net
PA: Thomas R Spence   <M1>
  PO Box 802
  Burns Flat, OK 73624
  (580)562-4531
  tomspence0302@gmail.com
CL: Gene Reeves
  11649 N 2160 Road
  Dill City, OK 73641
  (580)674-3763
  patsyreeves@windstream.net

_____
Clinton   (4WMC)MSRR6302
  500 S 30th Street
  Clinton, OK 73601
  (580)323-3440
PA: Dale Nease   <Custer>
  500 S 30th Street   <M1>
  Clinton, OK 73601
  (580)323-7557

CL: Dave Felch
  500 S 30th Street
  Clinton, OK 73601
  (580)323-3111

_____
Covenant   (4MEWC)MSRR6304
  15791 State Highway 1W
  Ada, OK 74820
  (580)332-0799   <Pontotoc>
  lindasnelling@covenantcpc.org
PA: Linda Snelling   <M1>
  15791 State Highway 1W
  Ada, OK 74820
  (580)332-0799
  FAX: (580)332-9424
  lindasnelling@covenantcpc.org
CL: Randy C Davidson
  PO Box 880
  Ada, OK 74821
  (580)421-6969
  randy@d-son.com

_____
Denton   (4MWC)MSRR8404
  PO Box 236 (mailing)
  1424 Stuart Road (physical)
  Denton, TX 76202
  (940)387-6811   <Denton>
  gacakee12@verizon.net

CL: Kathy McIntire
  304 Surveyors Road
  Aubrey, TX 76227
  (940)365-2087
  kcm1@att.net

_____
Eastlake   (4C)MSRR6205
  700 SW 134th Street
  Oklahoma City, OK 73170
  (405)799-8987   <Oklahoma>
  eastlakecumberland@att.net
PA: Leslie A Johnson   <M1>
  11716 Price Drive
  Oklahoma City, OK 73170
  (405)248-4232
  ljohnson275@cox.net
CL: Ray Sears
  821 SW 42nd Street
  Moore, OK 73160
  (405)703-0779
  lrsears@cox.net

RED RIVER PRESBYTERY CONTINUED

Faith   (4WC)MSRR6201
    PO Box 690715 (mailing)
    2801 S 129th East Avenue (physical)
    Tulsa, OK 74169
    (918)437-2190   <Tulsa>
    FAX: (918)437-2199
    tulsafaith@att.net
PA: Thomas R Sanders   <M1 DE>
    4201 W Kent Street
    Broken Arrow, OK 74012
    (918)269-0043
    FAX: (918)437-2199
    trsncf@msn.com
CL: Georgia Stevens
    29605 S River Ridge Drive
    Catoosa, OK 74015
    FAX: (918)437-2199
    stevenscabinets@yahoo.com

Hubbard   (4MWC)MSRR8410
    404 N Magnolia
    Hubbard, TX 76648
    (   )   <Hill>
CL: Brenard Nunnelley
    475 H County Road 3350 N
    Hubbard, TX 76648
    (254)576-2468
    bfn76648@aol.com

Lake Highlands   (4WU)MSRR8411
    8525 Audelia Road
    Dallas, TX 75238
    (214)348-2133   <Dallas>
    lhpc@lhpres.org
PA: Perryn Rice   <M1>
    10802 Hayfield Drive
    Dallas, TX 75238
    (931)526-6585
    perryn@lhpres.org
CL: Maureen Ramsay
    8935 Larchwood Drive
    Dallas, TX 75238
    (214)542-6173
    FAX: (214)348-2408
    msramsay@hotmail.com

Locust Grove   (4MWC)MSRR6203
    PO Box 577 (mailing)
    203 E Harriett Avenue (physical)
    Locust Grove, OK 74352
    (918)479-5613   <Mayes>
CL: Mayme Miley
    7847 S 438 Road
    Locust Grove, OK 74352
    (918)479-2575

Mangum   (4MEWC)MSRR6306
    CLOSED 2015

Marlow   (4MWC)MSRR6305
    202 N Sixth
    Marlow, OK 73055
    (580)658-2892   <Stephens>
PA: Terra Sisco   <M1>
    811 W Cheyenne Street
    Marlow, OK 73055
    (618)384-6126
    terrasisco@gmail.com

CL: Faye Kimbrough
    1202 W Randall Court
    Duncan, OK 73533
    (580)786-4434

Mesquite   (4C)MSRR8412
    819 N Town East Boulevard
    Mesquite, TX 75150
    (972)270-6923   <Dallas>
    FAX: (972)270-6923
    mcpchurch@gmail.com
IP: Wesley H Johnson   <M1>
    6222 Crestmoor Lane
    Sachse, TX 75048
    (972)429-6129
    wjohnson@transitionconsulting.com
CL: Joyce Nelson
    4112 Arbor Court
    Mesquite, TX 75150
    (972)226-6425
    ane4112@aol.com

Mt Zion   (2C)MSRR8414
    691 County Road 4108 (mailing)
    Greeneville, TX 75401
    15175 Texas Highway 11 W (physical)
    Cumby, TX 75433
    (903)454-3444   <Hopkins>
    bvwood10@yahoo.com
CL: Virginia Woodworth
    691 County Road 4108
    Greeneville, TX 75401
    (903)454-3444
    bvwood10@yahoo.com

Newberry   (2C)MSRR8415
    PO Box 253 (mailing)
    1301 Newberry Road (physical)
    Millsap, TX 76066
    (   )   <Parker>
SS: Tim Dewhirst   <M3>
    3609 Oakbriar Lane
    Colleyville, TX 76034
    (817)605-8147
    timdew@sbcglobal.net
CL: Joel Young
    2902 Old Milsap Road
    Weatherford, TX 76088
    (817)341-0800
    joelyoung@aol.com

Olney   (4MEWC)MSRR8416
    PO Box 756 (mailing)
    210 S Avenue M (physical)
    Olney, TX 76374
    (940)564-2882   <Young>
    olneycpc@brazosnet.comt
PA: David Carpenter   <M1>
    909 W Elm Street
    Olney, TX 76374
    (940)564-2339
    olneycpc@brazosnet.com
CL: Clifton W Key
    PO Box 615
    Olney, TX 76374
    (940)564-2979
    barkey8@brazosnet.com

Pathway   (4EC)MSRR8418
    (previously named St Matthew)
    PO Box 182 (mailing)
    380 NW Tarrant (physical)
    Burleson, TX 76097
    (817)295-5832   <Johnson>
    FAX: (817)295-2576
    info@pathway.church
PA: Rick Owen   <M1>
    3305 Wild Oaks Court
    Burleson, TX 76028
    (817)295-5832
    FAX: (817)295-2576
    rowen@pathway.church
AP: Josh Fortney   <M1>
    765 Windridge Lane
    Burleson, TX 76028
    (214)794-9912
    jfortney@pathway.church
AP: Jeffrey A Gehle   <M1>
    PO Box 182
    Burleson, TX 76097
    (817)295-5832
    jeff.gehle@pathway.church
AP: R Allan Mink   <M2>
    1113 Hidden Glen Court
    Burleson, TX 76028
    (817)295-5832
    FAX: (817)295-2576
    alan.mink@pathway.church
CL: Kim Perkey
    2600 Embry Lane
    Burleson, TX 76028
    (817)235-9061
    kimberley.k.perkey@wellsfargo.com

Sandy Springs   (4C)MSRR8420
    1865 Bones Chapel Road (mailing)
    Rease Road (physical)
    Whitesboro, TX 76273
    (   )   <Grayson>
CL: Eddie Vidrine
    1865 Bones Chapel Road
    Whitesboro, TX 76273
    (902)584-5148
    eddievid@gmail.com

Shiloh   (4MEWC)MSRR8421
    7810 Shiloh Road
    Midlothian, TX 76065
    (972)723-3758   <Ellis>
    vernon@sansom.us
PA: Vernon Sansom   <M1>
    104 Cockrell Hill Road
    Ovilla, TX 75154
    (972)825-6887
    vernon@sansom.us
CL: Georgia Williams
    1425 Black Champ Road
    Waxahachie, TX 75167
    (214)949-7228
    georgia@reliablegokarts.net

St John   (4WC)MSRR8413
    6007 W Pleasant Ridge Road
    Arlington, TX 76016
    (817)478-6219   <Tarrant>
    FAX: (817)478-8684
    stjohncpc@att.net

RED RIVER PRESBYTERY CONTINUED

CL: Barbara Harrell
6207 W Poly Webb Road
Arlington, TX 76016
(817)229-1796
baharrell@tx.rr.com

_____

St Luke   (4C)MSRR8407
1404 Sycamore School Road
Fort Worth, TX 76134
(817)293-3778   <Tarrant>
FAX: (817)293-2750
office@stlukecpc.org
PA: David Kurtz   <M1>
4700 Elkwood Lane
Arlington, TX 76016
(817)683-4783
davidk36@yahoo.com
CL: Beth McLaughlin
5462 Rutland Avenue
Fort Worth, TX 76133
(817)292-5471
mcbeth1951@att.net

_____

St Mark (TX)   (4MWC)MSRR8408
4101 Hardeman Street
Fort Worth, TX 76119
(817)536-1315   <Tarrant>
PA: Roosevelt Baugh   <M1>
4101 Hardeman Street
Fort Worth, TX 76119
(817)536-1315
gmf1220@charter.net
CL: Hazel F Wilson
2801 Sarah Jane Lane
Fort Worth, TX 76119
(817)536-4892
jesseewilson@charter.net

_____

St Timothy   (4WC)MSRR8419
PO Box 210338 (mailing)
3001 Forest Ridge Drive (physical)
Bedford, TX 76095
(817)571-7474   <Tarrant>
FAX: (817)571-7714
SS: Kevin R Henson   <M1>
1121 Raleigh Path
Denton, TX 76208
(817)354-1182
khenson@servproofheb.com
CL: Danny Washmon
PO Box 210338
Bedford, TX 76095
(817)571-7474
washmon@rocketmail.com

_____

Stonegate   (ARC)MSRR6307
17101 North Western Avenue
Edmond, OK 73012
(405)340-7281   <Oklahoma>
stonegatecpc@gmail.com
PA: Marian Sontowski   <M1>
17101 North Western Avenue
Edmond, OK 73012
(405)340-7281
stonegatecpc@gmail.com
CL: Jeanette Silman
17101 North Western Avenue
Edmond, OK 73012
(405)340-7281
stonegate.clerk@gmail.com

_____

Trinity   (4MEWC)MSRR8409
7120 W Cleburne Road
Fort Worth, TX 76133
(817)292-6149   <Tarrant>
trinitycpc@sbcglobal.net
PA: Randy L Hardisty   <M1>
4908 Redondo Street
Fort Worth, TX 76180
(817)428-3513
rhardisty@sbcglobal.net
CL: Betty Jean Cooper
1108 Trinity Trail
Saginaw, TX 76131
(817)306-4877
bjjacoop@sbcglobal.net

_____

Whitney   (4EC)MSRR8424
CLOSED 2015

_____

Zion Valley   (4C)MSRR8425
2604 South FM 1655
Chico, TX 76431
( )   <Wise>
PA: Barney Hudson   <M1>
10541 Fossil Hill Drive
Fort Worth, TX 76131
(817)851-2960
barneyrev@gmail.com
CL: Priscilla Moreland
1177 N State Highway 101
Chico, TX 76431
(940)644-2462
hdpjmoreland@hotmail.com

_____

OTHERS ON MINISTERIAL ROLL:

Aden, Marty   <M1 M9>
202 Bennington Place
Wilmington, NC 28412
(910)795-1092
maden@ec.rr.com
Baltimore, Claud G   <M1 RT>
PO Box 1358
1430 Lakehurst Drive
Ada, OK 74821
(580)332-2679
baltimorejb@earthlink.net
Brown, Chuck   <M1 DE>
475 N Highland Street
Memphis, TN 38122
(817)915-2907
cbrown@cumberland.org
Brown, Stephanie S   <M1 M9>
475 N Highland Street
Memphis, TN 38122
(901)729-3612
scrudderbrown7@gmail.com
Condon, Jr, Thomas W   <M1 RT>
6508 Victoria Avenue
N Richland Hills, TX 76180
(817)656-9334
Ferrol, Ruben   <M1 M9 RT>
1823 Straford Court
Allentown, PA 18103
(610)966-7289
rubeferrol@msn.com
Gardner, Charles   <M1 RT>
PO Box 1035
Elephant Butte, NM 87035
(719)784-7744

Goodman, Robert   <M1 WC>
604 N 4th Street
Marlow, OK 73055
(580)756-4726
rgoodman4gvn@hotmail.com
Harris, Wendell   <M1 WC>
329 N Louis Tittle Avenue
Mangum, OK 73554
(580)782-2142
wendellharris@itlnet.net
Hendershot, Charles A   <M1 WC>
122 Tree Shadow
Whitney, TX 76692
(254)694-3852
Hong, Soon Gab   <M1 WC>
13600 Doty Avenue Apt 4
Hawthorne, CA 90250
(972)446-0350
lemuelhong@hotmail.com
Howell, Linda   <M1 WC>
PO Box 80050
Keller, TX 76244
(601)942-2015
lshowell1000@yahoo.com
Kays, Michael   <M1 WC>
2505 Canterbury Avenue
Muskogee, OK 74403
(918)577-6255
msppk@suddenlink.net
Lain, Judy   <M1 M9>
1928 Pine Ridge Drive
Bedford, TX 76021
(817)660-8020
judylane5@gmail.com
Lounsbury-Lombard, Kristi <M1 M9>
902 Clearview
Krum, TX 76249
(940)435-5077
kristilounsbury@gmail.com
Madden, Judith Ellen   <M1 WC>
100 SW Brushy Mound
Burleson, TX 76028
(817)295-5832
jmadden@pathway.church
Martinez, Soledad   <M1 WC>
2801 Biway Street
Fort Worth, TX 76114
(817)812-8247
shirleymartinez1252@gmail.com
McGee, Charles Randall   <M1 WC>
9037 Groveland Drive
Dallas, TX 75218
(214)328-2488
randallmcgee@sbcglobal.net
Nelson, Charles E   <M1 WC>
209 Classic Court
Springtown, TX 76082
(903)641-5466
dundeal10@aol.com
Parkhurst, L G, Jr   <M1 WC>
409 Woodhollow Trail
Edmond, OK 73012
(405)341-7477
Petty, Linda Lee   <M1 WC>
4401 W Elgin Street
Broken Arrow, OK 74012
(918)252-4741

RED RIVER PRESBYTERY CONTINUED

Rice, Keith   \<M1 M9\>
PO Box 582
Itasca, TX 76055
(254)087-2418
rsvkeith@yahoo.com

Rivera, Carlos A   \<M1 WC\>
Calle Dr Jose Maria Vertiz 1410
Departmento 202B, Colonia Portales
Delegacion Benito
Juarez, C.P. 03300 MEXICO
(52)1-55-31058377
caralrifra@une.net.co

Ruggia, Mario (Bud)   \<M1 M9 RT\>
603 Rumsey Street
Kiowa, KS 67070
(620)825-4509
ruggia@aol.com

Schmoyer, Donna Marie   \<M1 WC\>
613 Mound Street
Monongahela, PA 15063
(817)266-6572
schmoyerdm@yahoo.com

Scrudder, Norlan   \<M1 RT\>
29688 S 534 Road
Park Hill, OK 74451
(918)949-1326
ndscrudder@gmail.com

Sharpe, Michael G   \<M1 DE\>
3423 Summerdale Drive
Bartlett, TN 38133
(901)276-4572

Shelton, Robert E   \<M1 RT\>
10508 Royalwood Drive
Dallas, TX 75238
(214)349-7162
bshelton67@yahoo.com

Shelton, Robert M   \<M1 RT\>
7128 Lakehurst Avenue
Dallas, TX 75230
(214)696-3237

Shugert, Richard   \<M1 WC\>
5208 Bellis Drive
Fort Worth, TX 76244
(817)913-7211
shugertr@yahoo.com

Smith, Robert H   \<M1 WC\>
5055 S 76th East Avenue Apt D
Tulsa, OK 74145
(918)671-5520
rhsmith@sstelco.com

Thomas, Cassandra   \<M1 RT\>
1920 Dancy Street
Fayetteville, NC 28301
(910)488-4897
chcothomas@yahoo.com

Wagner, Hugh   \<M1 RT\>
12556 Timberline Drive
Garfield, AR 72732
(479)359-0021
hughawagner@gmail.com

Webb, William G   \<M1 OM\>
7926 S 78th East Avenue
Tulsa, OK 74133
(918)294-9117

Youngman, Betty   \<M1 RT\>
1471 Creekview Court
Fort Worth, TX 76112
(817)492-4100
bettyy@swbell.net

Zumbrunnen, Craig H   \<M1 WC\>
1210 Country Club Road Apt 3
Santa Teresa, NM 88008
(580)471-0308
craigzum1@yahoo.com

OTHER LICENIATES ON ROLL:

King, Keith   \<M2 ST\>
3341 S 137th East Avenue
Tulsa, OK 74134
(918)437-5464
cpkking@yahoo.com

OTHER CANDIDATES ON ROLL:

Bohon, Chris Michael   \<M3\>
109 NE McAlister Road
Burleson, TX 76028
(817)228-9494
cbohon@pathway.church

Brown, Houston   \<M3\>
866 N McLean
Memphis, TN 38107
(817)915-9090
hpbrown95@gmail.com

Rosales, David   \<M3\>
101 N Lowe
Hobart, OK 73651
(580)682-0722
sagradalut@gmail.com

Robert Donnell Presbytery
SOUTHEAST SYNOD

GENERAL		MEMBERSHIP			CHANGES				FINANCES				
1.Church Number	2.Active	3.Total	4.Church School	5.Prof. of Faith	6.Gains	7.Losses	8.Children Baptized	9. OUR UNITED OUT-REACH	10. Total Out-Reach Giving	11. All Other Expenses	12. Total Income Received	13. Value Church Prop. 1=1000
1	2	3	4	5	6	7	8	9	10	11	12	13
Alabaster**	0107	192	280	69	2	2	85	1	5,712	21,984	170,442	192,957	2,300
Big Cove*	0801	17	17	11	0	1	15	0	0	230	25,948	22,489	330
Christ Church	0814	77	108	20	0	1	2	1	5,788	21,818	92,420	117,093	650
Concord*	0802	17	78	18	1	0	1	0	1,767	4,061	18,669	19,268	286
East Point	0206	17	19	15	0	2	52	0	625	1,347	29,384	29,858	650
Edgefield	0813	3	3	0	0	0	0	0	0	200	6,216	6,670	127
Eidson Chapel	0207	20	51	17	No Report Received			0	0	0	0	0	140
Goosepond*	0803	27	48	7	0	1	0	0	1,800	7,812	25,940	33,752	250
Gurley**	0804	60	60	25	0	1	21	0	4,369	23,667	110,274	157,609	751
Hope+	0812	38	38	7	1	1	28	0	0	4,517	62,515	67,032	568
Huntsville, 1st	0806	51	112	30	0	1	4	0	1,260	10,255	99,359	99,638	1,500
Meridianville	0808	41	41	20	0	0	0	0	0	1,588	60,401	62,074	1,350
Scottsboro	0809	257	455	115	0	2	9	0	25,670	66,622	200,015	339,765	2,780
Stevenson	0810	46	141	18	0	0	1	0	8,563	21,043	63,498	85,676	1,200
Union Grove	0211	20	27	15	No Report Received			0	0	0	0	0	200
Walnut Grove	0811	10	13	4	0	1	31	0	0	5,151	1,540	6,583	14
TOTALS	16	894	1,537	391	4	13	249	2	55,554	190,653	1,006,222	1,275,216	13,066

*Math error corrected. **Purged roll.   +Union church

CHURCHES, PASTORS, AND CLERKS:

Alabaster   (4WC)SERD0107
  8828 Highway 119
  Alabaster, AL 35007
  (205)663-3152   <Shelby>
  FAX: (205)663-8323
  fpcalabaster@bellsouth.net
PA: Darren Kennemer   <M1>
  8828 Highway 119
  Alabaster, AL 35007
  (205)663-3152
  FAX: (205)663-8323
  dlkennemer@gmail.com
AP: Earl Goodwin   <M1>
  1012 Windsor Parkway
  Moody, AL 35004
  (205)222-1741
  FAX: (205)664-8323
  earlgoodwin@yahoo.com
CL: Margaret Russo
  8828 Highway 119
  Alabaster, AL 35007
  (205)663-3152
  mrusso@harbert.net

Big Cove   (4MWC)SERD0801
  5984 Highway 431 S
  Brownsboro, AL 35741
  (256)518-9657   <Madison>
SS: Donald Reeves   <M1 HR>
  PO Box 528
  Rainsville, AL 35986
  (256)228-4057
  reevesd@nacc.edu

CL: Beryl Tidwell
  680 Old Big Cove Road
  Owens Cross Roads, AL 35763
  (256)518-9977
  beryl.tidwell@gmx.com

Christ Church   (4WC)SERD0814
  1580 Jeff Road
  Huntsville, AL 35806
  (256)837-6014   <Madison>
  christchurch@knology.net
PA: Cardelia Howell Diamond   <M1>
  1580 Jeff Road
  Huntsville, AL 35806
  (256)837-6014
  cpclergymama@gmail.com
CL: Cheryl Caldwell
  1043 Douglass Road
  Huntsville, AL 35806
  (256)837-6014
  sccz4647@att.net

Concord   (4MWC)SERD0802
  1827 Joe Quick Road
  New Market, AL 35761
  (256)828-4503   <Madison>
CL: Richard Dixon
  626 Briar Fork Road
  Hazel Green, AL 35761
  (256)828-0002
\ dixonelec16@gmail.com

East Point   (4WC)SERD0206
  1441 US Highway 278 E
  Cullman, AL 35055
  (256)734-0900   <Cullman>

SS: Philip Nickles   <M1 OP>
  5821 County Road 1114
  Vinemont, AL 35179
  (256)734-9847
  nickles.phil@yahoo.com
CL: Karen Munger
  PO Box 1773
  Cullman, AL 35056
  (256)739-0746
  karenamunger@bellsouth.net

Edgefield   (4UC)SERD0813
  411 McMahan Cove Road (mailing)
  Stevenson, AL 35772
  311 County Road 158 (physical)
  Stevenson, AL 35772
  (   )   <Jackson>
CL: Christie Nunley
  411 McMahan Cove road
  Stevenson, AL 35772
  256-437-9011

Eidson Chapel   (4C)SERD0207
  2680 County Road 1725
  Holly Pond, AL 35083
  (   )   <Cullman>
OD: Floyd Bradford   <M5>
  351 Piney Grove Road W
  Falkville, AL 35622
  (256)784-6510
  FAX: (415)864-1543
CL: Linda Harris
  5910 County Road 747
  Cullman, AL 35058
  (256)734-6697

ROBERT DONNELL PRESBYTERY CONTINUED

Goosepond   (4MWC)SERD0803
1155 East Hancock Drive
Scottsboro, AL 35769
(256)259-4386   <Jackson>
betrich76@gmail.com
CL: Bettie M Jordan
198 County Road 46
Hollywood, AL 35752
(256)437-1546
betrich76@gmail.com

Gurley   (4MEWC)SERD0804
223 Section Line Road
Gurley, AL 35748
(256)776-2331   <Madison>
PA: Toy E Brindley   <M1>
PO Box 335
Gurley, AL 35748
(256)776-2331
gurleycpc@gmail.com
CL: Becky Arnold
423 Sharps Cove Road
Gurley, AL 35748
(256)776-6950
bailey@darnold.net

Hope   (4WU)SERD0812
10001 Bailey Cove Road SE
Huntsville, AL 35803
(256)881-4673   <Madison>
hopepresby@comcast.net
PA: Christie Ashton   <M1>
10001 Bailey Cove Road SE
Huntsville, AL 35803
(256)881-4673
pastorhope@comcast.net
CL: Joanna Sterling-Clutts
10001 Bailey Cove Road SE
Huntsville, AL 35803
(256)479-9899
alabamahoosier@gmail.com

Huntsville First   (4EWC)SERD0806
PO Box 777 (mailing)
1802 Bankhead Parkway (physical)
Huntsville, AL 35804
(256)536-9371   <Madison>
hsvfcpc@att.net
PA: Richard W Hughes   <M1>
2954 Bob Wade Lane
Harvest, AL 35749
(256)859-3178
hughesrichard23@gmail.com
CL: Steve Rowley
PO Box 777
2012 Brandy Court
Huntsville, AL 35811
(256)651-5916
steve.rowley35@gmail.com

Meridianville   (4MWC)SERD0808
PO Box 188 (mailing)
11696 Highway 231/431 N (physical)
Meridianville, AL 35759
(256)828-0160   <Madison>
dptalley@hotmail.com

PA: Keith Lorick   <M1>
127 Chesapeake Boulevard
Madison, AL 35757
(256)325-3865
keithlorick@knology.net
CL: Donna Talley
360 Monroe Road
Meridianville, AL 35759
(256)683-6111
dptalley@hotmail.com

Scottsboro   (4WC)SERD0809
PO Box 639 (mailing)
315 S Kyle Street (physical)
Scottsboro, AL 35768
FAX: (256)259-2809
cumberland@scottsboro.org
(256)574-2575   <Jackson>
PA: Micaiah Thomas Tanck   <M1>
2912 S Broad Street Apt B3
Scottsboro, AL 35769
(205)478-5985
micaiah.thomas@gmail.com
CL: Linda Bray
407 Bynum Street
Scottsboro, AL 35768
(256)574-9791
linda.bray@ymail.com

Stevenson   (4MEWC)SERD0810
112 College Street
Stevenson, AL 35772
(256)437-8632   <Jackson>
PA: Perry Whitaker
202 College Street
Stevenson, AL 35772
(256)437-8632
brotherperry@msn.com
CL: Jen Stewart
112 College Street
Stevenson, AL 35772
(256)437-3116
jstewart306@hotmail.com

Union Grove   (4WC)SERD0211
91 County Road 1734 (mailing)
2760 County Road 1742 (physical)
Holly Pond, AL 35803
(256)796-1023   <Cullman>
johnson9983@att.net
PS: David Hooper   <M6>
115 County Road 682
Cullman, AL 35055
(256)775-2419
davidhoop165@yahoo.com
CL: Glen Johnson
91 County Road 1734
Holly Pond, AL 35083
(256)796-1023
johnson9983@att.net

Walnut Grove   (4WC)SERD0811
PO Box 403 (mailing)
711 New Hope/Cedar Point Road (physical)
New Hope, AL 35760
( )   <Madison>
CL: Kathy Pegues
211 Butler Lane
New Hope, AL 35760
(256)723-8740
mcwoodpeg@nehp.net

OTHERS ON MINISTERIAL ROLL:
Alverson, Elmer L   <M1 HR>
354 Roy Davis Road
New Market, AL 35761
(256)828-4503
bud@alscomputers.com
Babcock, Edward S, Jr   <M1 HR>
1007 San Ramone Avenue
Huntsville, AL 35802
(256)882-9339
ejsb1@aol.com
Bynum, Ronald H   <M1 WC>
121 Sycamore Road
Gurley, AL 35748
(256)776-9313
ronaldbynum@bellsouth.net
Diamond, Steven   <M1 WC>
106 Ultimate Court
Madison, AL 35757
smdiam@hotmail.com
(931)636-7336
Gillis, Aubrey Thomas   <M1 WC>
110 Blue Sky Lane
Alabaster, AL 35007
(251)947-1638
FAX: (205)664-8323
tomgillis63@hotmail.com
Hall, Brad   <M1 WC>
1602 Toll Gate Road SE
Huntsville, AL 35801
(256)533-4845
Hall, John D   <M1 WC>
109 Oddo Lane SE
Huntsville, AL 35802
(256)880-5129
johnhall33@comcast.net
Hall, Roy W   <M1 RT>
87 Lee Hall Street
Scottsboro, AL 35769
(256)259-9340
royhall@scottsboro.org
Herring, C E (Ed) Jr   <M1 RT>
969 Campground Circle
Scottsboro, AL 35769
(256)259-2721
edherring@scottsboro.org
Howton, Orvie Ray   <M1 RT>
4928 Montauk Trail SE
Owens Cross Road, AL 35763
(256)533-9224
orphowton@yahoo.com
Hughes, Charles   <M1 HR>
114 Gaul Street
Estill Springs, TN 37330
(931)649-5189
cphugs@cafes.net
Lambert, James   <M1 RT>
224 Peabody Road
Meridianville, AL 35759
(256)828-6850
Livingston, Ronald L   <M1 HR>
5851 Quantrell Avenue #201
Alexandria, VA 22312
Matthews, James N   <M1 HR>
241 Morning Star Drive
Huntsville, AL 35811
(256)337-2765
brojim10@mediacombb.net

ROBERT DONNELL PRESBYTERY CONTINUED

Murphree, Hughlen <M1 WC>
4298 County Road 1719
Holly Pond, AL 35083
(256)796-5352
hmurph@hiwaay.net

Phillips-Burk, Pam <M1 DE>
3325 Bailey Creek Cove N
Collierville, TN 38017
(256)684-5247
pam@cumberland.org

Smith, James <M1 WC>
1949 Little Cove Road
Owens Cross Roads, AL 35763
dr.james.smith42@gmail.com

OTHER CANDIDATES ON ROLL:

Gilliam, Cody <M3>
2881 Old Big Cove Road SE
Owens Cross Roads, AL 35763
(256)655-7073
roostergilliam@outlook.com

Tennessee-Georgia Presbytery
SOUTHEAST SYNOD

GENERAL		MEMBERSHIP			CHANGES				FINANCES				
	1.Church Number	2.Active	3.Total	4.Church School	5.Prof. of Faith	6.Gains	7.Losses	8.Children Baptized	9. OUR UNITED OUT-REACH	10. Total Out-Reach Giving	11. All Other Expenses	12. Total Income Received	13. Value Church Prop. 1=1000
	1	2	3	4	5	6	7	8	9	10	11	12	13
Bartow	2101	88	153	55	3	4	1	2	5,000	26,337	111,125	139,724	913
Cedar Springs	2119	10	18	0	0	0	1	0	900	1,962	18,223	15,655	323
Charleston	2102	42	54	23	0	3	4	0	4,000	10,494	77,125	58,879	900
Chattanooga 1st	2104	545	545	159	0	8	17	2	5,000	27,105	537,823	498,898	1,250
Cleveland	2108	150	182	67	2	4	1	1	17,227	25,579	261,546	240,105	2,400
Cornerstone Com	2107	12	42	9	No Report Received			0	0	0	0	0	675
Ebenezer*	2110	5	6	0	0	2	0	0	0	1,896	8,790	10,932	75
El Redill	2149	53	53	39	No Report Received			0	3,049	0	0	0	780
Falling Water	2111	56	69	30	2	6	18	0	1,000	37,720	122,257	148,125	890
Flint Springs	2112	24	24	0	0	0	1	0	0	125	23,842	17,946	150
Glory Church*	2144	55	55	7	No Report Received			0	0	0	0	0	2,300
Jasper	2113	30	43	13	0	0	0	0	3,868	3,868	47,909	46,400	750
Kelly's Chapel	2120	11	21	11	2	2	0	0	0	1,382	18,465	14,760	150
Korean Livingsto	2130	30	30	8	Provisional Church			0	150	0	0	0	0
New Hope*	2115	65	78	32	3	3	7	0	0	8,500	87,700	97,100	600
Oak Grove	2121	14	28	0	0	0	0	0	0	1,194	9,692	8,028	110
Pine Hill	2117	13	13	14	No Report Received			0	0	0	0	0	70
Prospect United	2116	72	72	12	0	0	16	0	1,500	4,837	63,725	63,779	1,400
Red Bank**	2105	138	176	68	3	5	94	5	12,240	18,176	0	254,886	1,250
Richard City	2118	25	65	8	0	0	0	0	900	2,240	28,750	36,066	900
Silverdale	2106	124	141	35	2	7	5	0	6,362	10,622	104,952	135,477	1,200
South Pittsburg	2123	19	63	0	1	1	1	0	100	550	22,814	22,796	825
Sumach	2124	110	215	81	4	5	7	2	5,000	11,988	149,452	155,758	680
Whitwell	2122	8	9	10	No Report Received			0	0	0	0	0	25
Tennessee-Georgia Presbytery									250				
TOTALS	25	1,774	2,229	679	22	50	173	11	66,296	194,795	1,694,190	1,965,314	18,467

*Math error corrected. **Purged roll.

TENNESSEE-GEORGIA PRESBYTERY CONTINUED

CHURCHES, PASTORS, AND CLERKS:

Bartow   (4MWEC)SETG2101
   1078 Cassville White Road (mailing)
   Cartersville, GA 30121
   2851 Highway 140 NE (physical)
   Rydal, GA 30171
   (770)382-3896   <Bartow>
   pastormarkbcpcga@gmail.com
PA: Mark Rackley   <M1>
   3060 Highway 140 NE
   Rydal, GA 30171
   (770)382-3790
   pastormarkbcpcga@gmail.com
CL: James Harris Bagwell
   1078 Cassville White Road
   Cartersville, GA 30121
   (770)382-0747
   shadygrovebeef@aol.com

Cedar Springs   (4C)SETG2119
   495 Cedar Springs Loop (mailing)
   6665 Old Dunlap Road (physical)
   Whitwell, TN 37397
   ( )   <Marion>
PA: Kriss McGowan   <M1>
   885 Mount Calvary Road
   Whitwell, TN 37397
   (423)463-8609
   krissmcg658@gmail.com
CL: Sarah Way
   4595 Old Dunlap Road
   Whitwell, TN 37397
   (423)580-7685
   sarahway1958@aol.com

Charleston   (4MEWC)SETG2102
   PO Box 476 (mailing)
   Charleston, TN 37310
   8267 N Lee Highway (physical)
   Cleveland, TN 37312
   (423)336-5004   <Bradley>
PA: Bill Bond   <M1>
   205 Windmere Drive
   Chattanooga, TN 37411
   (423)316-0867
   bill@wcbj.net
CL: Vivian McCormack
   5502 Mouse Creek Road NW
   Cleveland, TN 37312
   (423)479-8230
   mcco6868@bellsouth.net

Chattanooga First   (4WC)SETG2104
   1505 N Moore Road
   Chattanooga, TN 37411
   (423)698-2556   <Hamilton>
   FAX: (423)629-6683
   office@firstcumberland.com
PA: Courtney Krueger   <M2>
   1505 N Moore Road
   Chattanooga, TN 37411
CL: Christy Miller
   7853 Legacy Park Court
   Chattanooga, TN 37421
   (423)894-8220
   christymiller62@epbfi.com

Cleveland   (4WC)SETG2108
   161 2nd Street NE Ste 3 (mailing)
   200 Church Street NE (physical)
   Cleveland, TN 37311
   (423)476-6751   <Bradley>
   FAX: (423)476-6423
   gchudson3@gmail.com
PA: Jennifer Newell   <M1>
   2322 Maraco Circle
   Chattanooga, TN 37421
   (423)892-5834
   FAX: (423)476-6423
   newelljennifer3@gmail.com
CL: Denise Callais
   161 2nd Street NE Suite 3
   Cleveland, TN 37311
   (423)476-6751

Cornerstone Com   (4MWC)SETG2107
   9632 E Brainerd Road
   Chattanooga, TN 37421
   (423)892-3027   <Hamilton>
   cornerstone3cp@gmail.com
SS: Jerry (Butch) Hullander   <M1>
   767 Rifle Range Road
   Ringgold, GA 30736
   (706)935-4878
   jerryihs@catt.com
CL: Session Clerk
   9632 E Brainerd Road
   Chattanooga, TN 37421
   (423)892-3027
   cornerstone3cp@gmail.com

Ebenezer   (4C)SETG2110
   10699 Griffith Highway (mailing)
   2400 Highway 108(physical)
   Whitwell, TN 37397
   (423)942-1939   <Marion>
   cprevinsv@bellsouth.net
PA: Phillip Layne   <M1>
   10699 Griffith Highway
   Whitwell, TN 37397
   (423)658-5849
   44philliplayne@gmail.com
CL: Lloyd Shadrick
   3412 Sequatchie Mountain Road
   Sequatchie, TN 37374
   (423)942-1939

El Redill   (C)SETG2149
   875 Scenic Highway
   Lawrenceville, GA 30045
   (678)698-7971   <Monmouth>
   FAX: (678)225-0127
   mabega@juno.com
PA: Maria (Mabe) Garcia   <M1>
   875 Scenic Highway
   Lawrenceville, GA 30045
   (678)698-7971
   mabega@juno.com
CL: Francia Bryon
   3315 Crooked Stick Drive
   Cumming, GA 30041
   (678)977-8606
   elenabry1@yahoo.com

Falling Water   (4WC)SETG2111
   PO Box 2027 (mailing)
   6534 Old Dayton Pike (physical)
   Hixson, TN 37343
   (423)843-3050   <Hamilton>
   james_barry@bellsouth.net
PA: James C Barry   <M1>
   49 Smitty's Circle
   Chattanooga, TN 37415
   (903)315-7998
   james_barry@bellsouth.net
CL: Diane J Bunch
   8212 Pierpoint Drive
   Harrison, TN 37341
   (423)802-2763
   topdog23@bellsouth.net

Flint Springs   (4WC)SETG2112
   2225 North East Road SE (mailing)
   Flint Springs Road (physical)
   Cleveland, TN 37311
   ( )   <Bradley>
PA: Kevin Wilson   <M1>
   2225 North East Road SE
   Cleveland, TN 37311
   (423)284-6397
   revkev1000@hotmail.com
CL: James F Mitchell, Jr
   517 Mitchell Road SE
   Cleveland, TN 37323
   (423)479-7649

Glory Church of Jesus Christ(C)SETG2144
   3480 Summit Ridge Parkway
   Duluth, GA 30096
   ( )   < >
PA: David Lee   <M1>
   3480 Summit Ridge Parkway
   Duluth, GA 30096
   (404)641-4359
   gcjcatl@gmail.com
CL: Session Clerk Glory Church
   3480 Summit Ridge Parkway
   Duluth, GA 30096

Jasper   (4MWC)SETG2113
   PO Box 877 (mailing)
   148 College Street (physical)
   Jasper, TN 37347
   (423)942-2188   <Marion>
   FAX: (423)942-2188
SS: James H. Patterson   <M1>
   6705 Ballard Drive #211
   Chattanooga, TN 37421
   (423)267-8568
   FAX: (423)942-2188
CL: Dorris G Ross
   214 Hancock Road
   Jasper, TN 37347
   (423)942-5224
   FAX: (423)942-2188
   ross37347@charter.net

Kelly's Chapel   (4MC)SETG2120
   3748 Alvin York Highway (mailing)
   470 Highway 27 (physical)
   Whitwell, TN 37397
   ( )   <Marion>
   carolb8667@bellsouth.net

TENNESSEE-GEORGIA PRESBYTERY CONTINUED

OD: Anthony Tucker   <M5>
209 Rock City Trail
Lookout Mountain, GA 30750
CL: Session Clerk
3748 Alvin York Highway
Whitwell, TN 37397

_____

Korean Livingstone   (P)SETG2130
3340 Bentbill Crossing
Cumming, GA 30041
(770)912-7710
barkmoksa@hanmail.net
PA: Yang Rae Park   <M1>
3340 Bentbill Crossing
Cumming, GA 30041
(770)912-7710
barkmoksa@hanmail.net
CL: Session Clerk Korean Livingstone
3340 Bentbill Crossing
Cumming, GA 30041
(770)912-7710
barkmoksa@hanmail.net

_____

New Hope   (4MWC)SETG2115
176 E Valley Road (mailing)
196 E Valley Road (physical)
Whitwell, TN 37397
(423)949-3951   <Sequatchie>
PA: Jimmy Byrd   <M1>
176 E Valley Road
Whitwell, TN 37397
(615)289-3347
revjimmybyrd@hotmail.com
CL: James Condra
PO Box 1001
Dunlap, TN 37327
(423)447-8126
jwcondra@bledsoe.net

_____

Oak Grove   (4C)SETG2121
872 Alvin York Highway (mailing)
8150 Griffith Highway (physical)
Whitwell, TN 37397
( )   <Marion>
PA: Phillip H Layne   <M1>
10699 Griffith Highway
Whitwell, TN 37397
(423)658-6421
44philliplayne@gmail.com
CL: Martha S Layne
872 Alvin York Highway
Whitwell, TN 37397
(423)658-6421

_____

Pine Hill   (4MC)SETG2117
Rt 2 Box 220 (mailing)
146 Pine Hill Road SW (physical)
McDonald, TN 37353
(423)339-2816   <Bradley>
OD: Russell Maroon   <M5>
7103 Snow Hill Road
Ooltewah, TN 37363
(423)472-1094
CL: Session Clerk
Rt 2 Box 220
McDonald, TN 37353

_____

Prospect United   (4MC)SETG2116
310 New Murraytown Road NW
Cleveland, TN 37312
(423)476-6181   <Bradley>
cloverwreathfarm@hotmail.com
SS: Theresa Martin   <M1>
116 Crisman Street
Chattanooga, TN 37415
(423)903-7260 (cell)
choochootm@usa.net
CL: Betty Brakebill
3512 Windsor Circle NE
Cleveland, TN 37312
(423)479-2731

_____

Red Bank   (4WC)SETG2105
115 Morrison Springs Road
Chattanooga, TN 37415
(423)877-1383   <Hamilton>
rbcpchurch@gmail.com
PA. Jim Duttram   <M1>
5385 Bungalow Circle
Hixson, TN 37343
(865)938-7418
FAX: (865)483-8445
littlejimb@gmail.com
CL: Sylvia Hall
930 Sherry Circle
Hixson, TN 37343
(423)875-3668
hallcad1946@epbfi.com

_____

Richard City   (4MWC)SETG2118
1706 Marion Avenue
South Pittsburg, TN 37380
(423)837-6533   <Marion>
CL: Bill Norman
624 19th Street
South Pittsburg, TN 37380
(423)837-6693
FAX: (423)837-8903
billnorman@catcore.com

_____

Silverdale   (4MEWC)SETG2106
7407 Bonny Oaks Drive
Chattanooga, TN 37421
(423)892-8710   <Hamilton>
FAX: (423)892-7751
PA: George Cliff Hudson   <M1 DE>
4782 Waverly Court
Ooltewah, TN 37363
(423)238-6333
gchudson3@gmail.com
CL: Dotty Manis
7939 Clara Chase Drive
Ooltewah, TN 37363
(423)238-4021
dottmae@centurylink.net

_____

South Pittsburg   (4MWC)SETG2123
PO Box 327 (mailing)
400 Elm Avenue (physical)
South Pittsburg, TN 37380
(423)837-6488   <Marion>
spcpc1@yahoo.com
PA: Kriss McGowan   <M1>
885 Mount Calvary Road
Whitwell, TN 37397
(423)463-8609
krissmcg658@gmail.com

CL: George Holland
214 Dixie Avenue
South Pittsburg, TN 37380
(423)837-7113
georgehollandsp@att.net

_____

Sumach   (4MWC)SETG2124
PO Box 804 (mailing)
9203 Highway 225 N (physical)
Chatsworth, GA 30705
(706)695-4773   <Murray>
FAX: (706)695-4773
sumachcpchurch@windstream.net
PA: Tom Clark   <M1>
2089 Sumach Church Road
Chatsworth, GA 30705
(270)469-4377
CL: Carolyn Luffman
926 Long Avenue
Chatsworth, GA 30705
(706)695-4346
circle11@hotmail.com

_____

Whitwell   (4C)SETG2122
7390 Highway 108
Whitwell, TN 37397
(423)658-5849   <Marion>
PA: Phillip Layne   <M1>
10699 Griffith Highway
Whitwell, TN 37397
(423)658-5849
44philliplayne@gmail.com
CL: Session Clerk
7390 Highway 108
Whitwell, TN 37397
(423)658-5849

_____

OTHERS ON MINISTERIAL ROLL:

Brister, Glenn   <M1 WC>
3004 Delaware Avenue
McComb, MS 39648
(706)934-8629
bearmountainpenworks@gmail.com
Carver, Gary   <M1 WC>
2810 Cabin Road
Chattanooga, TN 37404
(423)698-2556
FAX: (423)629-6683
sandgatthecabin@epbfi.com
Han, Seung Chon   <M0>
3075 Landington Way
Duluth, GA 30096
kpc0191@gmail.com
(678)469-5015
Jackson, Lamar   <M1 HR>
280 Deer Ridge Drive Apt D
Dayton, TN 37321
(423)570-9348
hljaxn@charter.net
Jones, Harold   <M1 WC>
4123 Wilkesview Drive Apt A
Chattanooga, TN 37416
(478)320-4222
harold@personalcharacter.com
Kang, Jin Koo   <M1 OM>
2310 Hisway
Lawrenceville, GA 30044
(678)462-7526
agatopia@hanmail.net

TENNESSEE-GEORGIA PRESBYTERY CONTINUED

Kelso, James H   <M1 HR>
131 Lords Way
Dawsonville, GA 30534
(706)216-7513
elgato@alltel.net

Kim, Mi Young   <M1 WC>
IN KOREA

Kim, Min Soo   <M1 OM>
5350 Taylor Road
Johns Creek, GA 30022
samil2110@yahoo.com
(678)622-2717

Kim, Yoong S   <M1 WC>
225 Bayswater Drive
Suwanee, GA 30024
(678)765-7018
yoongkim1934@yahoo.com

Lee, Sarah   <M1 WC>
(no address on file)

March, Kevin   <M1 HR>
1701 Ray Jo Circle
Chattanooga, TN 37421
(423)499-4180
kmadm1@aol.com

Martin, Tom   <M1 WC>
116 Crisman Street
Chattanooga, TN 37415
(423)903-7260 (cell)
choochootm@usa.net

McCarty, John   <M1 M9 HR>
305 W Martindale Drive
Marshall, TX 75672
(423)650-8788
mtsjohn@gmail.com

McGowan, Rhonda   <M1 WC>
885 Mount Calvary Road
Whitwell, TN 37397
(423)619-5679
pastorrhonda@mcgowanministries.com

Melton, Samuel D   <M1 HR>
2249 Bucks Pocket Road SE
Oldfort, TN 37362
(423)472-8467

Prosser, Forest   <M1 RT>
1157 Mountain Creek Road
Chattanooga, TN 37405
(423)877-4114
forestprosser@comcast.net

Sumrall, Philip (Phil)   <M1 WC>
107 Barnhardt Circle
Fort Oglethorpe, GA 30742
(423)903-1938
phil.sumrall@gmail.com

Tolley, Robert (Butch)   <M1 WC>
1445 New Murraytown Road NW
Cleveland, TN 37312
(423)837-6488
butchtolley@hotmail.com

Turner, Glyn   <M1 M8>
1660 Chattanooga Valley Road
Flintstone, GA 30725
(585)307-7715
glynturner@outlook.com

Wright, B J   <M1 WC>
301 25th Street
Phenix City, AL 36867
(334)298-2896
bojobo3@yahoo.com

OTHER LICENTIATES ON ROLL:

Kennedy, Jim   <M2>
613 English Ivy Way
Aberdeen, MD 21001
jpkak@comcast.net

OTHER CANDIDATES ON ROLL:

Craven, Mark
21 Kingston Street
Chattanooga, TN 37415
(4230618-0169
craven.ma@gmail.com

Garcia, Lucas   <M3>
875 Scenic Highway
Lawrenceville, GA 30045
(678)698-7971
lgvplola@hotmail.com

Hollingshed, Lee   <M3 ST>
3612 Harmony Church Grove Road
Dallas, GA 30132
(770)548-0152
leearmstrong@bellsouth.net

Middleton, Frank, Jr   <M3 ST>
1200 Adele Circle
Slidell, LA 70461
(770)655-0406
fmiddle@bellsouth.net

Park, Young   <M3 ST>
3340 Bentbill Crossing
Cummings, GA 30041
(404)661-6117
barkmogun@gmail.com

Varnell, William   <M3 ST>
6729 Old Dunlop Road
Whitwell, TN 37397
(423)658-0506

Trinity Presbytery
MISSION SYNOD

GENERAL		MEMBERSHIP			CHANGES				FINANCES				
	1.Church Number	2.Active 3.Total	4.Church School	5.Prof. of Faith 6.Gains		7.Losses 8.Children Baptized		9. OUR UNITED OUT-REACH	10. Total Out-Reach Giving	11. All Other Expenses	12. Total Income Received	13. Value Church Prop. 1=1000
	1	2	3	4	5	6	7	8	9	10	11	12	13
Antioch*	8101	14	16	12	0	0	3	0	1,200	19,750	11,575	23,600	325
Austin, First	8601	47	47	8	7	15	2	6	1,200	23,908	148,309	104,202	2,325
Bertram	8605	63	171	21	0	0	1	1	2,100	23,623	98,349	88,008	1,093
Concord*	8104	51	60	35	4	4	40	2	10,904	36,855	69,900	805,000	805
Daingerfield*	8106	8	10	5	0	0	2	0	500	5,899	32,522	31,846	112
Elmira Chapel	8111	64	121	35	0	1	6	0	0	67,829	164,107	176,963	2,500
Freeport	8103	29	29	4	0	0	2	0	1,200	14,150	62,676	65,600	933
Houston, 1st**	8606	64	106	55	5	8	194	3	15,518	123,282	365,630	460,732	2,450
Jefferson**	8109	53	59	38	9	11	13	5	100	10,828	86,630	64,842	360
Longview, 1st	8112	41	163	29	0	0	2	0	8,979	29,100	49,061	89,783	428
Marshall	8115	179	330	102	1	2	5	0	29,879	85,700	347,821	420,384	3,037
Mt. Hope*	8117	1	2	5	0	0	1	0	0	0	5,665	5,681	178
Northminster+	8610	275	275	54	No Report Received			0	0	0	0	0	3,628
Nueva Vida	8612	89	134	26	No Report Received			0	0	0	0	0	0
Oak Grove**	8607	11	11	5	1	0	51	0	0	1,150	8,228	12,901	200
Pine Hill	8122	19	56	15	0	0	3	0	1,000	9,090	24,798	36,524	85
Pine Tree	8113	30	72	22	No Report Received			0	0	0	0	0	800
Progress	8123	6	7	6	No Report Received			0	0	0	0	0	0
Round Rock+	8611	112	113	53	No Report Received			0	0	0	0	0	853
Shepherd/Hills+	8604	441	275	141	1	2	13	2	0	56,497	559,238	671,330	1,100
Shiloh	8125	7	42	0	0	0	0	0	0	2,000	21,268	23,268	66
Stone Oak	8608	115	140	42	No Report Received			0	0	0	0	0	2,200
TOTALS	22	1,722	2,329	702	28	44	299	19	102,610	547,621	2,615,295	2,939,666	23,570

*Math error corrected. **Purged roll. +Union Church

CHURCHES, PASTORS, AND CLERKS:

Antioch   (4MWC)MSTR8101
PO Box 42 (mailing)
518 N Antioch Road (physical)
Quitman, LA 71268
(318)259-7069   <Jackson>
CL: Jerry L Hanes
5104 Beech Springs Road
Quitman, LA 71268
(318)259-4246
lindaameme@hotmail.com

Austin First   (4WC)MSTR8601
6800 Woodrow Avenue
Austin, TX 78757
(512)453-8434   <Travis>
cpaustin@prodigy.net
OD: Ron Stevenson   <M5>
6800 Woodrow Avenue
Austin, TX 78757
(512)453-8434
austinfirstcp@prodigy.net
CL: Session Clerk
6800 Woodrow Avenue
Austin, TX 78757
(512)453-8434
cpaustin@prodigy.net

Bertram   (4MEWC)MSTR8605
PO Box 242 (mailing)
430 Highway 29 (physical)
Bertram, TX 78605
(512)355-2182   <Burnet>
PA: Daryl Johnson   <M1>
425 W Vaughan Street
Bertram, TX 78605
(512)355-2182
djchurch@earthlink.net
CL: Sam Hamilton
8906 N FM 1174
Burnet, TX 78611
(512)788-2020
samandlindaham@yahoo.com

Concord   (4MWC)MSTR8104
212 County Road 4705
Troup, TX 75789
(903)842-4745   <Cherokee>
FAX: (903)842-4745
revdad.duane@gmail.com
PA: Duane A Dougherty Jr   <M1>
212 County Road 4705
Troup, TX 75789
(903)842-4745
revdad.duane@gmail.com
CL: Sandy Mager
356 County Road 4629
Troup, TX 75789
(903)842-3844
stmager@yahoo.com

Daingerfield   (4MC)MSTR8106
PO Box 645 (mailing)
307 Broadnak (physical)
Daingerfield, TX 75638
(903)645-2183   <Morris>
sharjohn@windstream.net
SS: John C Lawson   <M2>
PO Box 645
Daingerfield, TX 75638
(903)645-2183
sharjohn@windstream.net
CL: John C Lawson
PO Box 645
Daingerfield, TX 75638
(903)645-2183
sharjohn@windstream.net

Elmira Chapel   (4MWC)MSTR8111
3501 Elmira Drive
Longview, TX 75605
(903)759-2069   <Gregg>
elmirachapel@aol.com
PA: James M Cantey   <M1>
3505 Elmira Drive
Longview, TX 75605
(903)452-6049
CL: Carol McDowell
3501 Elmira Drive
Longview, TX 75605
(903)759-2069
elmirachapel@aol.com

TRINITY PRESBYTERY CONTINUED

Freeport   (4C)MSTR8103
1402 W Broad Street
Freeport, TX 77541
PA: Lee Attema   <M1>
5 County Road 209
Sargent, TX 77414
(281)728-6263
lattema@icloud.com
AP: Leslie Attema   <M1>
5 County Road 209
Sargent, TX 77414
(281)728-6263
leslieattema@icloud.com
CL: Cathy Bettoney
1149 Ash Street
Clute, TX 77531
(979)265-7630
cathybettoney@yahoo.com

Houston First   (4EWC)MSTR8606
2119 Avalon Place
Houston, TX 77019
(713)522-7821   <Harris>
FAX: (713)522-8869
firstcp@cphouston.org
PA: J Geoffrey Knight   <M1>
2119 Avalon Place
Houston, TX 77019
(713)522-7821
FAX: (713)522-8869
geoff@family.net
AP: Freddy Diaz   <M1>
2425 Holly Hall Apt B42
Houston, TX 77054
(832)305-2379
fredglobeus@yahoo.com
CL: Linda Trajo
2119 Avalon Place
Houston, TX 77019
(713)522-7821
FAX: (713)522-8869
firstcp@cphouston.org

Jefferson   (4EC)MSTR8109
501 E Jefferson Street
Jefferson, TX 75657
(903)665-2883   <Marion>
office@jeffersonpresbyterian.org
PA: Robert (Toby) Davis   <M1>
502 S Alley Street
Jefferson, TX 75657
(901)826-5755
pastortobydavis@gmail.com
CL: Shannon Kuhn
879 Big Cypress Marina Road
Jefferson, TX 75657
(903)407-3409
shannonkuhn1968@gmail.com

Longview First   (4WC)MSTR8112
PO Box 2349 (mailing)
2401 Alpine Street (physical)
Longview, TX 75601
(903)758-5184   <Gregg>
FAX: (903)757-2572
fcpclongview@sbcglobal.net
PA: Donald W Nunn   <M1>
203 Bridgers Hill Road
Longview, TX 75604
(903)297-6074
dwnunn@earthlink.net

CL: Mollie Benson
567 Hidden Forest
Longview, TX 75601
(903)663-0443
FAX: (903)757-2572
fcpclongview@sbcglobal.net

Marshall   (4EWC)MSTR8115
PO Box 1303 (mailing)
501 Indian Spring Road (physical)
Marshall, TX 75671
(903)935-3787   <Harrison>
FAX: (903)935-3193
info@cumberlandofmarshall.org
PA: William Rustenhaven III   <M1>
PO Box 1303
Marshall, TX 75671
(903)935-7275
FAX: (903)935-3193
rusty@cumberlandofmarshall.org
AP: Mary Kathryn Kirkpatrick   <M1>
401 1/2 Henley-Perry Drive
Marshall, TX 75670
(903)930-6236
mkkirpartick@gmail.com
CL: Shirley Jones
104 Hillcrest Terrace
Marshall, TX 75672
(903)938-3980
shopfarm75672@yahoo.com

Mt Hope (CLOSING)   (4MC)MSTR8117
Box 66
Joinerville, TX 75658
(903)847-3451   <Rusk>
CL: Anna J Holman
PO Box 115
Joinerville, TX 75658
(903)847-3801

Northminster   (4U)MSTR8610
6800 Tezel Road
San Antonio, TX 78250
(210)680-4825   <Bexar>
FAX: (210)680-4826
npcoffice@npcsatx.org
PA: Robert E Weston   <M1 HR>
11 Summer Bluff
San Antonio, TX 78254
(210)347-0232
FAX: (210)680-4826
rjaweston@gmail.com
CL: Marsha Schendel
8730 Prince Heights
San Antonio, TX 78254
(210)681-4231

Nueva Vida   (F)MSTR8612
4505 Highway 6 N
Suite 700
Houston, TX 77084
(832)593-8355   <Harris>
PA: Ruben D Albarracin   <M1>
7411 Magnolia Shadows Lane
Houston, TX 77095
(281)463-8617
FAX: (281)463-8617
confiaendios@hotmail.com
CL: Patricia Nunez
7303 Hollow Field W
Cypress, TX 77433
(281)855-1881
FAX: (713)533-9735

Oak Grove   (4C)MSTR8607
12951 Ranch Road 2338
Georgetown, TX 78633
( )   <Williamson>
CL: Wanda Shelton
2355 County Road 226
Florence, TX 76527
(512)579-1325

Pine Hill   (4C)MSTR8122
8236 Farm Road 3019 (mailing)
FM 3019 County Road 3281 (physical)
Winnsboro, TX 75494
( )   <Hopkins>
CL: Elizabeth Aden
404 Yates Street
Mount Vernon, TX 75457
(903)537-7288
libbya1@suddenlink.net

Pine Tree   (4MWC)MSTR8113
PO Box 5340 (mailing)
1805 Pine Tree Road (physical)
Longview, TX 75608
(903)759-2685   <Gregg>
ptcpc@sbcglobal.net
PA: John V Lindsay   <M1>
401 Greenwood Avenue
Marshall, TX 75670
(940)391-1213
CL: Darlynn Jones
1819 Flagstone Drive
Longview, TX 75605
(903)236-7310
darlynnj@att.net

Progress   (4C)MSTR8123
722 Gewin Lane (mailing)
3643 Progress Church Road (physical)
Pleasant Hill, LA 71065
(318)796-3725   <Sabine>
mamacgewin@yahoo.com
CL: Carolyn W Gewin
722 Gewin Lane
Pleasant Hill, LA 71065
(318)796-3703
mamacgewin@yahoo.com

Round Rock   (4U)MSTR8611
4010 Sam Bass Road
Round Rock, TX 78681
(512)544-2152   <Travis>
rrpc_info@roundrockpresbyterian.org
OD: Catherine Craley   <M5>
4010 Sam Bass Road
Round Rock, TX 78681
CL: Elaine B Dodd
1805 Castleguard Way
Cedar Park, TX 78613
(512)260-0310
doddeb@sbcglobal.net

Shepherd of the Hills   (4U)MSTR8604
5226 W William Cannon Drive
Austin, TX 78749
(512)892-3580   <Travis>
FAX: (512)892-6307
church@shpc.org
OD: Jim Capps   <M5>
5226 W William Cannon Drive
Austin, TX 78749
(512)892-3580
FAX: (512)358-0879
jim@shpc.org

TRINITY PRESBYTERY CONTINUED

AP: Michael Killeen   <M1>
   5226 W William Cannon Drive
   Austin, TX 78749
   (512)560-0423
   FAX: (512)358-0879
   mike@shpc.org
AP: Britta Dukes   <M1>
   5226 W William Cannon Drive
   Austin, TX 78749
   (512)892-3580
   FAX: (512)358-0879
   britta@shpc.org
CL: Clift Bowman
   5226 W William Cannon Drive
   Austin, TX 78749
   (512)288-5839
   FAX: (512)358-0879
   cbowman24@austin.rr.com

Shiloh   (4C)MSTR8125
   4928 County Road 3275 (mailing)
   2467 County Road 3205 (physical)
   Clarksville, TX 75426
   (903)427-3785   <Red River>
   shiloh.presbyterian@yahoo.com
PA: Billy Jack Holt   <M1>
   5039 Highway 37 N
   Clarksville, TX 75426
   (903)428-9909
   jackdora@windstream.net
CL: Mary Jo McGill
   4928 County Road 3275
   Clarksville, TX 75426
   (903)427-3785
   hoopnmj@yahoo.com

Stone Oak   (4C)MSTR8608
   20024 Crescent Oaks
   San Antonio, TX 78258
   (210)497-7974   <Bexar>
   FAX: (210)497-8724
   officemanager@satx.rr.com
PA: Kevin Colvard   <M1>
   27027 Harmony Hills
   San Antonio, TX 78260
   (205)267-9372
   FAX: (210)497-8724
   rev_kev@satx.rr.com
CL: Barry Elliott
   2204 Sunderidge
   San Antonio, TX 78260
   (210)884-1749
   FAX: (210)497-8724
   barrydeanelliott@gmail.com

OTHERS ON MINISTERIAL ROLL:

Bone, W Harold   <M1 WC>
   315 Joey Drive
   Bourne, TX 78006
   (210)859-5560
   revdocbone@yahoo.com
Bowers, Sharon G   <M1 M9>
   201 Wild Buffalo Drive
   Kyle, TX 78640
   (512)230-7078
   sharon.bowers@gmail.com

Bozeman, Robert   <M1 HR>
   582 Bozeman Loop
   Belmont, LA 71406
   (318)256-5781
   bo@bozemanengineering.com
Chancellor, Hilton   <M1 HR>
   11905 Preserve Vista
   Austin, TX 78738
   (512)382-1972
   hiltontex@aol.com
Davenport, Mark A   <M1 WC>
   323 Chimney Rock Drive #1314
   Tyler, TX 75703
   (205)427-4941
   hoginbama@yahoo.com
Diaz, Gloria Villa   <M1 OM>
   2425 Holly Hall Apt B42
   Houston, TX 77054
   (832)758-5871
   gloria@newdayinchrist.org
Gonzalez, Nora   <M1 OM>
   2515 Blueberry Lane
   Pasadena, TX 77502
   (832)202-5572
Hannah, Hugh   <M1 HR>
   217 Mitchell Road SE
   Cleveland, TN 37323
   (423)473-7852
   pjhannah23@hotmail.com
Harris, Ernest   <M1 HR>
   610 Turtle Creek Drive
   Reno, TX 75462
   (903)782-9712
   ernie.jeri@yahoo.com
Hoke, Walter   <M1 WC>
   215 Navajo Trail
   Georgetown, TX 78633
   (512)869-1948
Jarnagin, Mary   <M1 WC>
   PO Box 49102
   Austin, TX 78765
   (512)709-4787
   marjar@yahoo.com
Kessie, John Paul   <M1 HR>
   138 Pony Grass Lane
   Bastrop, TX 78602
   (512)585-1617
   jplmkessie@verizon.com
Magrill Jr, J Richard   <M1 HR>
   500 Miller Drive
   Marshall, TX 75672
   (901)685-9454
   rmmagrill@gmail.com
McNeese, Mark   <M1 WC>
   3306 Greenlawn Parkway
   Austin, TX 78757
   (512)517-1042
   2mam53@gmail.com
Mills, David M   <M1 WC>
   60 Huge Oak Street
   Bertram, TX 78605
   (512)355-3511
Park, Sung In   <M1 OM>
   10109 Loxley Lane
   Austin, TX 78717

Parsons, Hugh L   <M1 HR>
   1526 Welch
   Houston, TX 77006
   (713)522-6126
   p-h-parsons@comcast.net
Peters, David J   <M1 IT>
   4010 Sam Bass Road
   Round Rock, TX 78681
   (512)244-2152
Rush, Robert D   <M1 OM>
   12935 Quail Park Drive
   Cypress, TX 77429
   (832-559-1500)
   robertrush832@gmail.com
Rustenhaven, William, Jr   <M1 HR>
   703 W Burleson Street
   Marshall, TX 75670
   (903)935-7056
   rustenhavendolores@yahoo.com
Santillano, Ray Paul   <M1 M8>
   1270 Polo Road Apt 618
   Columbia, SC 29223
   (808)349-3308
   ray.santillano@us.army.mil
Smith, David R   <M1 HR>
   PO Box 892
   Rosepine, LA 70659
   (903)297-6074
   ogreyfox@att.net
Suenram, Timothy   <M1 WC>
   13850 Mizzen Street
   Corpus Christi, TX 78418
   (832)217-6367
   9tdsdt9@gmail.com
Turner, Steven W   <M1 WC>
   7622 Snider Road
   Gilmer, TX 75645
   (903)738-8831
   juxtaposition47@yahoo.com
Wayman, Sam   <M1 HR OM>
   707 High Hill Creek Road
   LaGrange, TX 78945
   (979)968-3734
   samndonnawayman@gmail.com

OTHER LICENTIATES ON ROLL

OTHER CANDIDATES ON ROLL

Montoya, David   <M3>
   20900 FM 1093 Apt 11208
   Richmond, TX 77407
   (823)366-6897
   davinay@hotmail.com

West Tennessee Presbytery
GREAT RIVERS SYNOD

GENERAL		MEMBERSHIP		CHANGES				FINANCES				
1.Church Number	2.Active	3.Total	4.Church School	5.Prof. of Faith	6.Gains	7.Losses	8.Children Baptized	9. OUR UNITED OUT-REACH	10. Total Out-Reach Giving	11. All Other Expenses	12. Total Income Received	13. Value Church Prop. 1=1000
	1	2	3	4	5	6	7	8	9	10	11	12	13

Church	1	2	3	4	5	6	7	8	9	10	11	12	13
Antioch Union*	9401	26	27	21	1	1	5	1	4,670	7,005	37,362	46,703	343
Atwood	9101	5	7	6	0	0	0	0	282	989	7,350	8,427	200
Barren Springs	9102	5	37	4	No Report Received			0	0	0	0	0	25
Beech	9402	66	76	20	1	7	3	0	2,314	6,031	62,809	58,777	400
Bells Chapel*	9403	22	71	20	0	6	0	0	873	1,529	19,339	23,638	500
Bethel (TC)	9301	23	34	15	No Report Received			0	0	0	0	0	300
Bethesda*	9404	40	40	15	8	24	16	0	1,500	1,700	27,285	36,113	350
Bethlehem	9405	11	25	8	No Report Received			0	0	0	0	0	70
Bolivar	9202	30	47	6	No Report Received			0	2,688	0	0	0	350
Bradford	9104	49	131	31	No Report Received			0	2,148	0	0	0	175
Brunswick	9302	28	61	12	0	0	1	0	1,969	3,224	33,159	31,253	418
Camden	9105	55	117	40	No Report Received			0	0	0	0	0	900
Camp Ground	9204	16	29	30	No Report Received			0	0	0	0	0	175
Claybrook	9205	8	8	6	No Report Received			0	150	0	0	0	10
Cloverdale	9407	3	6	5	No Report Received			0	0	0	0	0	5
Colonial*	9305	41	120	25	0	0	14	0	6,935	16,836	78,939	88,284	800
Concord	9106	50	55	19	0	0	1	0	0	2,588	46,033	54,540	500
Cool Springs CC	9107	57	67	35	No Report Received			0	0	0	0	0	150
Cool Springs GC*	9408	61	61	40	0	13	2	0	4,343	11,346	45,423	60,922	300
Davidson Chapel	9108	42	152	41	0	3	2	0	480	7,002	62,997	64,026	450
Double Springs	9109	43	61	41	0	1	4	0	3,575	6,000	31,661	36,276	565
Dresden	9110	31	39	16	0	0	3	0	3,382	5,568	26,113	34,401	315
Dyer	9409	116	116	72	1	2	3	1	10,623	19,466	116,110	106,232	1,085
Dyersburg, 1st**	9410	313	576	100	6	13	83	2	46,924	151,983	507,654	688,750	5,953
Ebenezer (MC)	9206	6	6	7	No Report Received			0	200	0	0	0	50
Ebenezer (TC)	9303	128	128	60	No Report Received			0	3,900	0	0	0	380
Faith	9308	195	338	114	9	12	13	1	21,450	33,247	265,553	298,800	2,575
Fulton*	9412	100	177	50	0	0	4	0	0	14,550	106,559	127,892	850
Germantown	9310	115	156	105	1	6	2	4	17,798	32,451	215,739	248,994	1,000
Gleason*	9111	23	33	15	2	3	0	0	0	0	21,523	22,382	400
Good Springs*	9112	30	30	9	1	1	24	0	0	200	27,199	28,158	266
Holly Grove	9304	204	761	133	18	26	3	4	0	34,642	268,162	306,586	1,300
Hopewell (BC)	9207	35	35	34	1	0	1	0	1,770	242	19,616	17,582	30
Hopewell (WC)	9115	18	14	18	No Report Received			0	2,346	0	0	0	90
Humboldt	9116	71	115	35	1	1	0	1	8,106	19,310	70,623	86,469	1,000
Hurricane Hill	9413	25	52	12	No Report Received			0	0	0	0	0	130
Jackson, 1st	9208	268	439	176	1	4	20	2	10,462	22,768	307,181	329,029	3,000
Kenton*	9414	21	36	21	0	0	10	0	4,072	10,108	30,487	40,723	475
Korean	9322	38	38	14	2	1	8		0	1,508	47,378	59,842	500
Lexington First	9209	65	115	20	0	2	1	1	4,511	5,792	40,052	45,839	900
Maple Springs*	9210	70	145	16	1	3	2	1	0	6,639	84,045	83,905	485
Martin*	9117	42	42	42	1	1	14	0	2,064	3,198	57,000	53,611	175
Mason Hall	9415	7	20	4	No Report Received			0	0	0	0	0	100
McKenzie	9118	307	376	219	6	26	8	4	34,481	63,840	277,213	348,922	3,000
Medina*	9119	13	32	14	0	0	5	0	1,862	3,744	32,421	34,780	161
Meridian	9120	65	141	35	No Report Received			0	0	0	0	0	175
Milan	9121	207	330	80	5	15	9	0	0	12,195	278,616	320,061	2,500
Mill Creek*	9122	21	21	10	0	0	0	0	1,500	6,778	13,391	19,997	50
Morella	9416	6	26	6	No Report Received			0	0	0	0	0	125
Morning Sun	9314	58	81	26	0	0	3	0	3,768	10,338	84,633	99,566	750
Mt. Ararat	9417	87	268	63	1	1	11	0	2,400	21,547	67,068	88,390	500
Mt. Carmel	9315	28	45	15	0	1	0	0	2,255	6,562	15,840	22,402	150
Mt. Olive*	9418	10	25	9	1	1	7	0	300	583	22,779	15,035	205
Mt. Vernon	9213	29	41	18	0	0	6	0	4,439	9,411	32,644	44,748	380
Mt. Zion	9214	101	195	65	3	3	0	1	19,207	35,679	179,216	208,106	2,000
New Beginnings*	9306	68	186	14	31	24	136	8	0	0	0	56,119	124
New Bethel	9215	48	114	19	1	2	0	1	0	1,125	20,377	27,310	90
New Bethlehem	9420	4	4	4	0	0	0	0	1,276	3,411	112	2,300	4
New Ebenezer*	9422	59	63	41	4	6	10	1	3,526	10,054	66,636	71,186	45
New Salem (MC)	9216	9	9	0	No Report Received			0	0	0	0	0	100

West Tennessee Presbytery   (Continued)
GREAT RIVERS SYNOD

| | GENERAL | MEMBERSHIP | | | CHANGES | | | | FINANCES | | | | |
	1.Church Number	2.Active	3.Total	4.Church School	5.Prof. of Faith	6.Gains	7.Losses	8.Children Baptized	9. OUR UNITED OUT-REACH	10. Total Out-Reach Giving	11. All Other Expenses	12. Total Income Received	13. Value Church Prop. 1=1000
	1	2	3	4	5	6	7	8	9	10	11	12	13
New Salem (SC)	9316	44	70	15	1	1	1	1	500	2,603	65,831	81,062	98
New Salem (WC)	9124	17	17	25	0	2	0	0	5,181	30,271	18,498	51,948	75
Newbern	9419	50	61	25	12	15	3	1	8,204	27,282	65,566	146,240	709
Nuevo Empezar	9324	23	25	17	2	0	0	0	1,708	0	30,817	31,718	0
North Union	9423	68	75	40	No Report Received			0	0	0	0	0	360
Oak Grove	9217	32	108	22	No Report Received			0	935	0	0	0	300
Oak Hill	9125	10	10	9	0	0	4	0	544	3,433	3,335	5,435	0
Olive Branch	9312	180	496	130	7	8	13	3	2,749	10,966	200,525	246,107	1,350
Oliver's Chapel	9127	30	74	30	No Report Received			0	1,753	0	0	0	314
Olivet	9220	196	336	100	8	6	7	1	7,425	26,444	245,669	272,113	2,108
Palestine (DC)	9424	5	5	7	No Report Received			0	500	0	0	0	50
Palestine (HC)	9221	51	109	30	0	1	7	0	4,874	10,560	43,630	52,300	150
Parsons, First**	9222	30	49	10	1	1	64	0	0	0	32,141	34,962	550
Pleasant Green	9129	10	20	8	No Report Received			0	0	0	0	0	100
Pleasant Grove	9317	10	22		No Report Received			0	0	0	0	0	32
Pleasant Union	9318	140	140	25	0	0	4	3	0	6,166	92,169	96,807	300
Poplar Grove	9425	40	71	15	0	1	2	1	4,543	9,101	31,940	41,041	350
Protemus	9426	42	51	47	4	12	0	0	6,460	21,143	43,065	64,913	125
Ramer	9223	16	16	12	No Report Received			0	455	0	0	0	100
Roellen	9428	7	7	13	0	1	1	0	500	1,750	8,706	9,342	60
Rutherford	9429	20	28	18	1	1	1	0	4,403	12,453	60,274	57,358	300
Salem	9430	8	17	16	No Report Received			0	0	0	0	0	135
Savannah, 1st	9224	96	143	77	3	12	1	1	0	1,945	155,900	156,000	1,200
Selmer, Ct. Ave.	9225	61	82	16	No Report Received			0	2,415	0	0	0	550
Sharon	9130	17	30	13	0	1	2	0	1,000	6,725	27,114	27,938	589
Shiloh (AC)	9226	35	35	23	0	0	0	0	2,921	10,257	18,856	31,779	95
Shiloh (CC)	9131	31	50	0	0	1	3	0	3,703	9,492	40,098	37,021	175
Trezevant	9132	17	27	17	No Report Received			0	0	0	0	0	150
Troy	9432	17	24	15	No Report Received			0	666	0	0	0	100
Union City	9433	105	203	69	No Report Received			0	0	0	0	0	2,000
Walnut Grove	9320	14	28	18	No Report Received			0	0	0	0	0	300
West Union	9321	104	227	60	No Report Received			0	2,400	0	0	0	1,500
Woodward's Ch	9434	12	12	20	No Report Received			0	0	0	0	0	30
Yorkville	9435	26	59	22	No Report Received			0	500	0	0	0	575
Zion*	9133	4	14	5	0	3	0	0	500	2,620	10,158	11,286	98
TOTALS	95	5,371	9,322	3,219	146	265	434	45	308,888	795,406	4,948,589	5,902,627	54,742

*Math Correction*Math error corrected. **Purged roll.

CHURCHES, PASTORS, AND CLERKS:

Antioch Union   (4C)GRWT9401
   6765 Mount Olive Road (mailing)
   486 W Newman Glover Road (physical)
   Union City, TN 38261
   (731)885-6435   <Obion>
PA: Mitch Boulton   <M1>
   1606 Ebenezer Road
   Troy, TN 38260
   (731)487-2318
   steelermitch@gmail.com
CL: Sharon Barnes
   5765 Mount Olive Road
   Union City, TN 38261
   (731)885-2521

Atwood   (4MWC)GRWT9101
   PO Box 203 (mailing)
   14010 Church Street (physical)
   Atwood, TN 38220
   (731)662-7692   <Carroll>
   rickylong@tennesseetel.net
SS: Richard Reed   <M2>
   236 Madison Street
   Dyer, TN 38330
   (731)692-3604
CL: Ricky Long
   230 Brooks Road
   Atwood, TN 38220
   (731)662-7692
   rickylong@tennesseetel.net

Barren Springs   (4C)GRWT9102
   Box 14 (mailing)
   1860 Barren Spring Church Road (physical)
   Hollow Rock, TN 38342
   ( )   <Carroll>
CL: Cassie Cooper
   Box 14
   Hollow Rock, TN 38342
   (731)586-2167

Beech   (4MEC)GRWT9402
   PO Box 553 (mailing)
   880 Beech Chapel Road (physical)
   Union City, TN 38261
   (731)885-1710   <Obion>
   beth.williams@nwtdd.org

WEST TENNESSEE PRESBYTERY CONTINUED

PA: Bobby D Williams   <M1>
844 W Highway 22
Union City, TN 38261
(731)885-1710
CL: Beth Williams
844 W Highway 22
Union City, TN 38281
(731)885-1710
beth.williams@nwtdd.org

Bells Chapel   (2WC)GRWT9403
309 Bells Chapel Road
Dyer, TN 38330
(731)643-6729   <Gibson>
LS: Dennis Emerson   <M6>
137 Midway Road Apt 25
Dyer, TN 38330
(731)643-6539
dennied53@hotmail.com
CL: Dennis Emerson
137 Midway Road Apt 25
Dyer, TN 38330
(731)643-6539
dennied53@hotmail.com

Bethel (TC)   (1WC)GRWT9301
PO Box 114 (mailing)
Tipton, TN 38071
3406 Tracy Road (physical)
Atoka, TN 38004
(901)837-0343   <Tipton>
SS: Kenneth L McCoy   <M1>
1422 Walton Road
Memphis, TN 38117
(901)682-0891
CL: Cindy Rhodes
PO Box 114
Tipton, TN 38071
(901)837-7793

Bethesda   (4MWC)GRWT9404
10755 State Highway 188 (mailing)
9651 State Highway 188 (physical)
Friendship, TN 38034
( )   <Crockett>
jirvin527@yahoo.com
CL: Jim Irvin
10755 State Highway 188
Friendship, TN 38034
(731)414-7180
jirvin527@yahoo.com

Bethlehem   (4C)GRWT9405
1469 Bethlehem Road
Union City, TN 38261
( )   <Obion>

Bolivar   (4MWC)GRWT9202
PO Box 413 (mailing)
448 Nuckolls Road (physical)
Bolivar, TN 38008
(731)658-5459   <Hardeman>
CL: Faye Cromwell
2995 Naylor Road
Toone, TN 38381
(731)658-5329
cromwellr@bellsouth.net

Bradford   (4MWC)GRWT9104
PO Box 186 (mailing)
117 Highway 45 S (physical)
Bradford, TN 38316
(731)742-3397   <Gibson>
CL: Don Lannom
PO Box 85
Bradford, TN 38316
(731)742-3838

Brunswick   (4MWC)GRWT9302
PO Box 67 (mailing)
4976 Brunswick Road (physical)
Brunswick, TN 38014
(901)386-0105   <Shelby>
CL: Mary Ellen Starks
PO Box 142
Brunswick, TN 38014
(901)388-9862

Camden   (4MWC)GRWT9105
239 W Main Street
Camden, TN 38320
(731)584-7598   <Benton>
FAX: (731)584-7598
camdencpoffice@bellsouth.net
SS: Carey Womack   <M1>
114 Doris Street
Camden, TN 38320
(731)220-3900
FAX: (731)584-7598
camdencppastor@bellsouth.net
CL: Nancy D Arnold
PO Box 214
Camden, TN 38320
(731)441-2778
FAX: (731)584-7598
arnldnnc@aol.com

Camp Ground   (4C)GRWT9204
2535 Middleburg Road
Decaturville, TN 38329
( )   <Decatur>
SS: David Hawley   <M1>
127 John Holt Road
Beech Bluff, TN 38313
(731)427-7284
dhpreach@aol.com
CL: Fred Brasher
771 Middleburg Road
Decaturville, TN 38329
(731)852-4400

Claybrook   (C)GRWT9205
1300 US Highway 412 E (mailing)
1364 US Highway 412 E (physical)
Jackson, TN 38305
( )   <Madison>
SS: Jerald D Smith   <M1>
2625 Beech Bluff Road
Beech Bluff, TN 38313
(731)427-9316
jergensmith@aol.com
CL: Martha Wolfe
1300 US Highway 412 E
Jackson, TN 38305
(731)424-4979
jergensmith@aol.com

Cloverdale   (2C)GRWT9407
3891 S Sellers Road (mailing)
3541 Cloverdale Road (physical)
Obion, TN 38240
( )   <Obion>
FAX: (731)538-2383
CL: Billy J Sellers
3891 S Sellers Road
Obion, TN 38240
(731)538-2986
FAX: (731)538-2383
bsellers@ken-tennwireless.com

Colonial   (4MWC)GRWT9305
1500 S Perkins Road
Memphis, TN 38117
(901)682-4747   <Shelby>
SS: Lisa Anderson   <M1 M9>
1790 Faxon Avenue
Memphis, TN 38112
(901)246-8052
anderli90@gmail.com
CL: George R Marston
1042 LaRue Place
Memphis, TN 38122
(901)685-1488
put11599@bellsouth.net

Concord   (3MWC)GRWT9106
153 Herd Law Road
Trenton, TN 38382
( )   <Gibson>
PA: Don McCurley   <M1>
4036 McAllister Street
Milan, TN 38358
(731)723-3623
dcmccurley@hotmail.com
CL: Don Gibson
4225 Christmasville Road
Medina, TN 38355
(731)783-0992

Cool Springs CC   (4C)GRWT9107
240 Little Grove Road
Lavinia, TN 38348
( )   <Carroll>
LS: Robert Barger   <M6>
7127 Highway 104 W
Lavinia, TN 38348
(731)987-2477
rbarger104@att.net
CL: Ann Hammett
8725 US Highway 70
Cedar Grove, TN 38321
(731)987-2516

Cool Springs GC   (4MWC)GRWT9408
37 Cool Spring Road
Trimble, TN 38259
(731)643-6153   <Gibson>
SS: Steve Rogers   <M3>
119 East Drive
Newbern, TN 38059
(731)882-2229
srtn68@yahoo.com
CL: Mike Pruett
119 Heritage Drive
Rutherford, TN 38369
(731)665-6348
mdpruett@tennesseetel.net

WEST TENNESSEE PRESBYTERY CONTINUED

Davidson Chapel   (4MWC)GRWT9108
  399 Laneview Concord Road
  Trenton, TN 38382
  (731)618-1521
  FAX: (731)664-3735
  dale.cavaness@horne-llp.com <Gibson>
PA: Corey Cummings   <M1>
  1023 W Woodrow Street
  Milan, TN 38358
  (731)686-1851
  corey@milancp.org
CL: Dale Cavaness
  2093 Brentwood Drive
  Milan, TN 38358
  (731)618-1521
  FAX: (731)664-3735
  dale.cavaness@horne-llp.com

Double Springs   (4WC)GRWT9109
  18 Double Springs Road
  Humboldt, TN 38343
  (731)787-6422   <Gibson>
PA: Russell Little   <M1>
  29 Cotton Row
  Medina, TN 38355
  (731)783-3565
  russelllittle@bellsouth.net
CL: Linda Fisher
  65 Spencer Drive
  Medina, TN 38355
  (731)613-8355
  lfisher@eplus.net

Dresden   (4MWC)GRWT9110
  PO Box 131 (mailing)
  121 S Wilson Street (physical)
  Dresden, TN 38225
  ( )   <Weakley>
CL: Martha Killebrew
  PO Box 131
  Dresden, TN 38225
  (731)364-3294
  FAX: (731)364-3500
  killebrewm@frontiernet.net

Dyer   (4MEWC)GRWT9409
  PO Box 181 (mailing)
  256 E College Street (physical)
  Dyer, TN 38330
  (731)692-2594   <Gibson>
  dcpchurch@bellsouth.net
PA: Johnny E Watson   <M1>
  272 Madison Street
  Dyer, TN 38330
  (731)692-3555
  rev.jwatson@bellsouth.net
CL: Johnny Ward
  46 Old Dyer Trenton Road
  Dyer, TN 38330
  (731)692-2594
  ward3363@bellsouth.net

Dyersburg First   (4WC)GRWT9410
  2280 Parr Avenue
  Dyersburg, TN 38024
  (731)285-5703   <Dyer>
  FAX: (731)285-5792
  cpoffice@cumberlandchurch.com

PA: Cory Williams   <M1>
  3148 Long Bridge Lane
  Arlington, TN 38002
  (901)486-5981
  coromis@hotmail.com
AP: Annetta Camp   <M1>
  2303 Mill Creek Road
  Halls, TN 38040
  (731)285-5703
  FAX: (731)285-5792
  annetta@cumberlandchurch.com
CL: William Mallard
  198 Walnut Lane Ext
  Dyersburg, TN 38024
  (731)285-0837
  FAX: (731)287-0873
  wem1950@bellsouth.net

Ebenezer (MC)   (2EWC)GRWT9206
  Main Street
  Mercer, TN 38392
  (731)935-2391   <Madison>
CL: Pope Mulherin
  8 Prestwick Drive
  Jackson, TN 38305
  (731)427-3113

Ebenezer (TC)   (4WC)GRWT9303
  70 Witherington Road
  Mason, TN 38049
  ( )   <Tipton>
CL: Ann Burlison
  564 Baskin Road
  Burlison, TN 38015
  (901)294-3614
  aburlison@tipton-county.com

Faith   (4WC)GRWT9308
  3427 Appling Road
  Bartlett, TN 38133
  (901)377-0526   <Shelby>
  FAX: (901)382-2600
  faithcumberlandp@bellsouth.net
PA: Steven Shelton   <M1>
  7886 Farmhill Cove
  Bartlett, TN 38135
  (901)377-0526
  faithcpcpastor@gmail.com
CL: Karen Patten
  5728 North Street
  Bartlett, TN 38134
  (901)237-0535
  mkpatten@outlook.com

Fulton   (4MWC)GRWT9412
  PO Box 5343 (mailing)
  1159 Parker Road (physical)
  South Fulton, TN 38257
  (731)479-9912   <Obion>
PA: David Bayer   <M1>
  3090 Tom Counce Road
  South Fulton, TN 38257
  (731)479-3060
  dbayer9060@gmail.com
CL: Donald R Moore
  155 Cox Road
  Fulton, KY 42041
  (270)436-2723
  donaldmoore9@aol.com

Germantown   (4EWC)GRWT9310
  2385 Riverdale
  Germantown, TN 38138
  (901)755-3884   <Shelby>
  FAX: (901)759-3653
  cpcgww@aol.com
PA: William Warren   <M1>
  7139 Toro Cove
  Germantown, TN 38138
  (901)755-8058
  cpcgww@aol.com
CL: Iva McCutchen
  1240 Bristol Drive
  Memphis, TN 38119
  (901)761-0575
  ivesmc@att.net

Gleason   (4MC)GRWT9111
  190 David Court (mailing)
  McKenzie, TN 38201
  171 Smyth Lane (physical)
  Gleason, TN 38229
  (731)648-5343   <Weakley>
PA: James (Jim) Pinnell   <M1>
  1525 Parks Well Road
  Gleason, TN 38229
  (731)648-5078
  revpinnell@hotmail.com
CL: Donald Ray Stephens
  190 David Court
  McKenzie, TN 38201
  (731)352-5852
  tuvart@charter.net

Good Springs   (4WC)GRWT9112
  180 Barham Road (mailing)
  Good Springs Road (physical)
  Dukedom, TN 38226
  ( )   <Weakley>
SS: Dennis Weaver   <M2 ST>
  1750 Government Road
  Princeton, KY 42245
  (731)592-9054
  dsweaver@memphisseminary.edu
CL: Loretta Barham
  180 Barham Road
  Dukedom, TN 38226
  (731)469-9555

Holly Grove   (4MWC)GRWT9304
  4538 Holly Grove Road
  Brighton, TN 38011
  (901)476-8379   <Tipton>
  FAX: (901)476-3324
  hollygrovecpchurch@att.net
AP: Debbie Marshall   <M1>
  1494 Bucksnort Road
  Covington, TN 38019
  (901)494-1251
  dsmarshall05@att.net
CL: Donna E Lindley
  4538 Holly Grove Road
  Brighton, TN 38011
  (901)476-8379
  FAX: (901)476-3324
  hollygrovecpchurch@att.net

WEST TENNESSEE PRESBYTERY CONTINUED

Hopewell (BC)   (2EWC)GRWT9207
2309 Saulsbury Road (mailing)
289 Hopewell Road (physical)
Walnut, MS 38683
( )   <Benton>
PA: Byron Forester   <M1>
2376 Eastwood Place
Memphis, TN 38112
(901)324-1707
bforester@bellsouth.net
CL: Kathy D Wilburn
2309 Saulsbury Road
Walnut, MS 38683
(662)223-6447
kwilburn@fareselaw.com

Hopewell (WC)   (2WC)GRWT9115
1061 Gaylord Road (mailing)
Route 1 Box 91 (physical)
Sharon, TN 38255
( )   <Weakley>
CL: Lonnie Hazlewood
1061 Gaylord Road
Sharon, TN 38255
(731)973-2426
lonminh@citlink.net

Humboldt   (4MEWC)GRWT9116
2375 E Mitchell Street
Humboldt, TN 38343
(731)784-2703   <Gibson>
pastor@humboldtcpc.org
PA: Robert Harris   <M1>
619 N 24th Avenue
Humboldt, TN 38343
(731)420-6067
pastor@humboldtcpc.org
CL: Carolyn Hunley
6 Clinton Road
Humboldt, TN 38343
(731)784-2031
carolynhunley16@yahoo.com

Hurricane Hill   (4C)GRWT9413
Newbern, TN 38059
( )   <Dyer>
CL: Holly Powers
684 Hurricane Hill Road
Dyersburg, TN 38024
(731)285-4436

Jackson First   (4WC)GRWT9208
1730 US Highway 45 Bypass
Jackson, TN 38305
(731)664-1632   <Madison>
FAX: (731)664-1633
fcpc1730@bellsouth.net
PA: Terry M Hunley   <M1>
48 Charleston Square
Jackson, TN 38305
(731)660-5685
thunley1@charter.net
CL: Glenn Fesmire
7 Broadfield Drive
Jackson, TN 38301
(731)234-9959
glennfes@aol.com

Kenton   (4MEWC)GRWT9414
301 W College Street
Kenton, TN 38233
( )   <Obion>
LS: Charles McCall   <M6>
549 Mason Hall Road
Trimble, TN 38259
(731)297-3288
cmccall@ycinet.net
CL: Paul E Williams
206 Hillside Street
Kenton, TN 38233
(731)749-5656

Korean   (P)GRWT9322
7565 Macon Road
Cordova, TN 38018
(901)755-9101   <Shelby>
kcomemphis@gmail.com
PA: Ho-Jin Lee   <M1>
7565 Macon Road
Cordova, TN 38018
(901)754-7070
hojin.lee70@gmail.com
CL: Gong Dickens
7565 Macon Road
Cordova, TN 38018
(901)758-1130

Lexington First   (4MWC)GRWT9209
PO Box 11 (mailing)
931 N Broad Street (physical)
Lexington, TN 38351
(731)968-7176   <Henderson>
patfreelandjones@yahoo.com
PA: C William Jones Jr   <M1>
109 Lakewood Drive
Lexington, TN 38351
(731)967-7618
patfreelandjones@yahoo.com
CL: Teresa Ferguson
7747 Middleburg Road
Scotts Hill, TN 38374
(731)968-9079

Maple Springs   (4MWC)GRWT9210
2625 Beech Bluff Road (mailing)
2005 Beech Bluff Road (physical)
Beech Bluff, TN 38313
(731)424-4065   <Henderson>
PA: Jerald D Smith   <M1>
2625 Beech Bluff Road
Beech Bluff, TN 38313
(731)427-9316
jergensmith@aol.com
CL: Tricia Fowler
37 Fowler Cut Off Road
Beech Bluff, TN 38313
(731)423-1255
tfowler@firstbankonline.com

Martin   (4MWC)GRWT9117
312 E Main Street
Martin, TN 38237
(731)587-3222   <Weakley>
FAX: (731)487-6484
cathyjahr@charter.net

PA: Michael T Lavender   (M1)
308 Main Street
Martin, TN 38237
(731)431-9127
mike_lavender@yahoo.com
CL: Cathy Jahr
142 Rolling Meadows
Martin, TN 38237
(731)587-6484
cathyjahr@charter.net

Mason Hall   (2EWC)GRWT9415
549 Mason Hall Road (mailing)
1861 CP Church Road (physical)
Kenton, TN 38233
( )   <Obion>
mccall.cmccall@gmail.com
CL: Charles McCall
549 Mason Hall Road
Trimble, TN 38259
(731)431-8195
mccall.cmccall@gmail.com

McKenzie   (4WC)GRWT9118
PO Box 133 (mailing)
16835 Highland Drive (physical)
McKenzie, TN 38201
(731)352-2440   <Carroll>
FAX: (731)352-3101
church@mckenziecpc.org
PA: Kevin L Wood   <M1>
339 David Street
McKenzie, TN 38201
(865)228-0710
FAX: (865)588-8581
revkevbuford1972@gmail.com
AP: Garrett Burns   <M1>
387 Forrest Avenue
McKenzie. TN 38201
(731)535-3126
gburns2888@gmail.com
CL: June Perritt
PO Box 133
McKenzie, TN 38201
(731)352-2440
FAX: (731)352-3101
church@mckenziecpc.org

Medina   (4EC)GRWT9119
104 Cumberland Street
Medina, TN 38355
(731)618-0192   <Gibson>
PA: Linda H Glenn   <M1>
49 Mason Road
Threeway, TN 38343
(731)618-0192
lindahglenn@click1.net
CL: Kiara Castleman
307 W Main Street
Greenfield, TN 38230
(731)487-3363
kiascham@gmail.com

Meridian   (4C)GRWT9120
1099 Adams Road (mailing)
2590 Meridian Road (physical)
Greenfield, TN 38230
( )   <Weakley>

WEST TENNESSEE PRESBYTERY CONTINUED

CL: David McBride
1099 Adams Road
Greenfield, TN 38230
(731)235-3058

_____

Milan   (4WC)GRWT9121
6083 S First Street
Milan, TN 38358
(731)686-1851   <Gibson>
office@milancp.org
PA: Doy L Daniels Jr   <M1>
1095 Crestview Drive
Milan, TN 38358
(731)686-1851
FAX: (731)723-9324
revdrdoy@gmail.com
CL: Ronnie Parks
62 Hughes Loop
Milan, TN 38358
(731)686-3065
ronnieparks@bellsouth.net

_____

Mill Creek   (4C)GRWT9122
239 Smith Street (mailing)
434 Mill Creek Road (physical)
Puryear, TN 38251
( )   <Henry>
PA: Anne Hames   <M1 M9>
118 Paris Street
McKenzie, TN 38201
(731)352-4066
FAX: (731)352-4069
hamesa@bethelu.edu
CL: Richard E Vincent
239 Smith Street
Puryear, TN 38251
(731)247-5211
richardearlvincent@yahoo.com

_____

Morella   (2EWC)GRWT9416
51 Morella Road
Kenton, TN 38233
( )   <Gibson>
CL: J C Reed
121 Tull Road
Kenton, TN 38233
(731)749-5545

_____

Morning Sun   (4MC)GRWT9314
2682 Morning Sun Road
Cordova, TN 38016
(901)382-3439   <Shelby>
mscpc13@gmail.com
PA: Joey Edwards   <M1>
5279 Ivy Creek Lane
Lakeland, TN 38002
(901)573-7579
edwardsjoey@bellsouth.net
CL: Gwen Hromada
4350 Thorpe Drive
Mason, TN 38049
(901)466-1154
gwen247@aceweb.com

_____

Mt Ararat   (4WC)GRWT9417
1465 Troy-Hickman Road
Union City, TN 38261
(731)536-5406   <Obion>

PA: Robert A Smith   <M1>
PO Box 501
Newbern, TN 38059
(731)627-3332
ras1957@bellsouth.net
CL: Bobby Hall
664 Mill Creek Road
Troy, TN 38260
(731)536-4798

_____

Mt Carmel   (4C)GRWT9315
106 E Marginal Street (mailing)
2355 Union Drive (physical)
Somerville, TN 38068
( )   <Fayette>
PA: Clinton Buck   <M1>
PO Box 770068
Memphis, TN 38117
(901)682-2358
clintonbuck@aol.com
CL: Harry N Wiles
106 E Marginal Street
Somerville, TN 38068
(901)465-9733

_____

Mt Olive   (4MEC)GRWT9418
76 Yorkville Highway (mailing)
42 Mt Olive Road (physical)
Dyer, TN 38330
( )   <Gibson>
PA: Charles Fike   <M1>
2070 N 1st Street
Milan, TN 38358
(731)686-0224
CL: Carolyn Martin
76 Yorkville Highway
Dyer, TN 38330
(731)692-2773

_____

Mt Vernon   (4MC)GRWT9213
3101 Mt Vernon Road
Ramer, TN 38367
(731)645-6420   <McNairy>
CL: Larry Gage
130 Shiloh Terrace Drive
Selmer, TN 38375
(731)645-6828
lgage6828@charter.net

_____

Mt Zion   (4MWC)GRWT9214
480 County Road 401
Falkner, MS 38629
(662)837-7013   <Tippah>
FAX: (662)837-7969
info@mtzioncpc.org
PA: Thomas Richie Lockhart   <M1>
700 County Road 343
Falkner, MS 38629
(662)837-4281
nmsdiamonddawgs@yahoo.com
CL: Dennis Bogue
105 Gowdy Drive
Ripley, MS 38663
(662)837-0265
dennis.bogue@yahoo.com

_____

New Beginnings   (4C)GRWT9306
2300 Frayser Boulevard
Memphis, TN 38127
(901)353-4011

PA: Craig Wilson   <M1>
2300 Frayser Boulevard
Memphis, TN 38127
(901)277-4066
craigwilson2300@yahoo.com
SC: Elnora McKinzie
1111 Holmes Street
Memphis, TN 38122
(870)377-2174

_____

New Bethel   (4C)GRWT9215
3708 New Bethel Road
Selmer, TN 38375
( )   <McNairy>
CL: Preston King
3708 New Bethel Road
Selmer, TN 38375
(731)645-3150
kingpreston2828@yahoo.com

_____

New Bethlehem   (2EWC)GRWT9420
1585 Bethlehem Road (mailing)
825 Bethlehem Road (physical)
Newbern, TN 38059
( )   <Dyer>
CL: Mary Bell Murray
1585 Bethlehem Road
Newbern, TN 38059
(731)627-2332
murrayc2@juno.com

_____

New Ebenezer   (4MEWC)GRWT9422
PO Box 364 (mailing)
1606 Ebenezer Road (physical)
Troy, TN 38260
(731)536-4936   <Obion>
PA: Mitch Boulton   <M1>
1606 Ebenezer Road
Troy, TN 38260
(731)487-2318
steelermitch@gmail.com
CL: Lisa Hamm
656 Ebenezer Road
Troy, TN 38260
lhammnewebenezer@hotmail.com

_____

New Salem (MC)   (4C)GRWT9216
453 New Salem Road
Bethel Springs, TN 38315
( )   <McNairy>
SS: Earl Phelps   <M1>
172 Michie Pebble Hill Road
Stantonville, TN 38379
(731)632-5107
FAX: (901)632-9126
phelps.e@juno.com
CL: Malcolm Dickson
153 Harris Road
Bethel Springs, TN 38315
(731)934-7282
FAX: (731)934-0736
robert.dickson@aol.com

_____

New Salem (SC)   (4MWC)GRWT9316
6813 Salem Road
Lakeland, TN 38002
(901)829-3241   <Shelby>
FAX: (901)829-3241
ptcriss@hotmail.com

WEST TENNESSEE PRESBYTERY CONTINUED

PA: Paul T Criss   <M1>
6831 Salem Road
Lakeland, TN 38002
(901)626-8462
ptcriss@hotmail.com
CL: Patty Butler Little
6909 Salem Road
Lakeland, TN 38002
(901)829-3218

New Salem (WC)   (3C)GRWT9124
3220 Sharon Highway 89 (mailing)
Highway 89 (physical)
Sharon, TN 38255
( )   <Weakley>
SS: Kermit Travis   <M1>
3220 Sharon Highway 89
Dresden, TN 38225
(731)364-2315
CL: John C Clark
215 Rambo Road
Sharon, TN 38255
(731)364-3921
jcjclark@frontiernet.net

Newbern   (4MWC)GRWT9419
310 E Main
Newbern, TN 38059
(731)627-3646   <Dyer>
SS: Steve Rogers   <M3>
119 East Drive
Newbern, TN 38059
(731)882-2229
srtn68@yahoo.com
CL: Jamie Kay Berkley
403 E Main Street
Newbern, TN 38059
(731)676-8626
jamiekayb@hotmail.com

North Union   (4EC)GRWT9423
15 Cardwell Road (mailing)
Dyer, TN 38330
78 Preacher Dowland Road (physical)
Kenton, TN 38233
(731)673-4122   <Gibson>
CL: Chad Murray
2067 Locust Grove Road
Newbern, TN 38059
(731)676-6027
chadgfc@gmail.com

Nuevo Empezar   (4EC)GRWT9324
3442 Tutwiler
Memphis, TN 38122
(901)644-0513
PA: Bertha Davis   <M1>
2242 Slocum Avenue
Memphis, TN 38127
(901)644-0513
CL: Lydia Langbein
4675 Glenmore Lane
Millington, TN 38053
(901)487-6336
lile@rittermail.com

Oak Grove   (4MC)GRWT9217
3655 Talley Store Road
Henderson, TN 38340
(731)989-3825   <Chester>
marcus.hayes@att.net

CL: Don Terry
1450 Braund Road
Henderson, TN 38340
(731)989-7982
FAX: (731)989-7982

Oak Hill   (1C)GRWT9125
5820 Highway 69 N (mailing)
5135 Highway 59 N (physical)
Paris, TN 38242
( )   <Henry>
CL: Theresa Rushing
5820 Highway 69 N
Paris, TN 38242
(731)642-3499
trushing@utm.edu

Olive Branch   (4MWC)GRWT9312
8161 Germantown Road
Olive Branch, MS 38654
(662)893-7347   <Desoto>
FAX: (901)893-7347
officefcpc@yahoo.com
PA: James L Ratliff   <M1>
4027 Club View Drive
Memphis, TN 38125
(901)758-0125
pastorjimfcpc@yahoo.com
CL: Charlie Trapp
4750 Harvest Knoll Cove N
Memphis, TN 38125
(901)626-2952
charliebethtrapp@bellsouth.net

Oliver's Chapel   (4WC)GRWT9127
85 Olivers Chapel Road (mailing)
22 Olivers Chapel Road (physical)
Bradford, TN 38316
(731)742-3559   <Gibson>
FAX: (731)742-3994
mpybas@yahoo.com
PA: Sam Harwell   <M1>
23 Lake Hayes Estates Road
Trenton, TN 38382
(731)414-2153
sambharl@yahoo.com
CL: Marcy Tahmazian
85 Olivers Chapel Road
Bradford, TN 38316
(731)742-3097
FAX: (731)742-3994
mpybas@yahoo.com

Olivet   (4MWC)GRWT9220
6095 Highway 226
Savannah, TN 38372
(731)925-2685   <Hardin>
olivetcp@bellsouth.net
CL: Walton Williams
10875 Highway 64
Savannah, TN 38372
(731)412-7569

Palestine (DC)   (4C)GRWT9424
985 Palestine Road (mailing)
Route 2 (physical)
Newbern, TN 38059
( )   <Dyer>
SS: Donnie Ragsdale   <M1>
915 S Olive Street
Union City, TN 38261
(731)885-0014

CL: Session Clerk Palestine CP Church
985 Palestine Road
Newbern, TN 38059
(731)627-9227

Palestine (HC)   (4MWC)GRWT9221
1010 Nobles Road (mailing)
6835 Highway 22A (physical)
Lexington, TN 38351
( )   <Henderson>
mcadamsjc@bellsouth.net
PA: Wayne Tompkins   <M1>
548 E Columbia Road 23
Emerson, AR 71740
(870)807-2874
waynetompkinsministries@yahoo.com
CL: Cheri McAdams
1010 Nobles Road
Luray, TN 38352
(731)614-0433
mcadamsjc@bellsouth.net

Parsons First   (4MEWC)GRWT9222
PO Box 141 (mailing)
114 Virginia Avenue N (physical)
Parsons, TN 38363
(731)847-7148   <Decatur>
PA: David Hawley   <M1>
127 John Holt Road
Beech Bluff, TN 38313
(731)427-7284
haw177@aol.com
CL: Tony Collett
6636 Rockhouse Road
Linden, TN 37096
(931)589-5103
tacollett@tds.net

Pleasant Green   (4C)GRWT9129
c/o Helen Watkins (mailing)
2776 Highway 105
Trezevant, TN 38258
712 Idlewild-Holly Leaf (physical)
Atwood, TN 38220
( )   <Gibson>
OD: Keith Pence   <M5>
PO Box 703
Gleason, TN 38229
(731)819-2553
CL: Helen Watkins
2776 Highway 105
Trezevant, TN 38258
(731)669-1601
hjoy1@charter.net

Pleasant Grove   (2C)GRWT9317
2320 Pleasant Grove Road
Moscow, TN 38057
(901)877-3287   <Fayette>
CL: Jack Joyner
2320 Pleasant Grove Road
Moscow, TN 38057
(901)877-3287

Pleasant Union   (4MWC)GRWT9318
9251 Brunswick Road
Millington, TN 38053
(901)829-3262   <Shelby>

WEST TENNESSEE PRESBYTERY CONTINUED

PA: Matthew Dean Cunningham   <M1>
1646 Brighton-Clopton Road
Brighton, TN 38011
(901)475-4252
mcunningham0528@comcast.net
CL: Patricia Parks
8995 Mulberry Road
Atoka, TN 38004
(901)829-3012
pittypat28@aol.com

Poplar Grove   (4C)GRWT9425
492 Church Road
Halls, TN 38040
(731)627-2445   <Lauderdale>
2Orrs.mn@charter.net
CL: Larry Keen
323 Pennington Road
Halls, TN 38040
(731)836-5546
lkeen@lctn.com

Protemus   (4EWC)GRWT9426
2372 W Shawtown Road (mailing)
2033 W Shawtown Road (physical)
Troy, TN 38260
( )   <Obion>
LS: James R Gunter   <M6>
6997 Bud Barker Road
Obion, TN 38240
(731)538-9252
CL: Betty Rhamy
2372 W Shawtown Road
Troy, TN 38260
(731)538-9458

Ramer   (4MEWC)GRWT9223
4096 Highway 57 W
Ramer, TN 38367
( )   <McNairy>
OD: Albert Brown   <M5>
1772 Buena Vista Road
Bethel Springs, TN 38315
(731)934-7349
CL: George Armstrong
216 Ballpark Road E
Ramer, TN 38367
(731)645-3987

Roellen   (2C)GRWT9428
6040 Highway 104 E (mailing)
Highway 104 E (physical)
Dyersburg, TN 38024
(731)285-0300   <Dyer>
krector@cableone.net
PA: Dennis Vance   <M1>
1320 Valleywood Drive
Paris, TN 38242
(731)644-3627
rvdvance@hotmail.com
CL: Hal Rector
6040 Highway 104 E
Dyersburg, TN 38024
(731)285-0300
krector@cableone.net

Rutherford   (4MEWC)GRWT9429
945 S Trenton Street (mailing)
113 N Trenton Street (physical)
Rutherford, TN 38369
(731)665-6487   <Gibson>

PA: Hobert Walker   <M1>
PO Box 66
Rutherford, TN 38369
(731)665-7236
rutherfordcpchurch@gmail.com
CL: Joe Bone
945 S Trenton Street
Rutherford, TN 38369
(731)665-7253
jobne@msn.com

Salem   (4MC)GRWT9430
174 Franklin Street (mailing)
184 Franklin Street(physical)
Gadsden, TN 38337
( )   <Crockett>
SS: Karl Schwarz   <M1>
83 W Curtis Street
Bells, TN 38006
(731)663-3987
schw8651@bellsouth.net
CL: Ann Davis
174 Franklin Street
Gadsden, TN 38337
(731)784-4713
cloud31@bellsouth.net

Savannah First   (4WC)GRWT9224
300 Tennessee Street
Savannah, TN 38372
(731)925-4493   <Hardin>
savannah1stcp@hotmail.com
LS: Helen Hamilton   <M3>
245 Elm Street
Savannah, TN 38372
(731)925-7338
helmackham@aol.com
CL: Levin Edwards
300 Tennessee Street
Savannah, TN 38372
(731)925-4493
levinedwards@gmail.com

Selmer Court Ave   (4MWC)GRWT9225
PO Box 741 (mailing)
234 Court Avenue (physical)
Selmer, TN 38375
(731)645-5257   <McNairy>
PA: Richard Reid   <M1>
123 S Fifth Street
Selmer, TN 38375
(731)453-5302
rjreid1964@msn.com
CL: Gwelda W Treece
299 Country Club Lane
Selmer, TN 38375
(731)645-5519
gweldat@bellsouth.net

Sharon   (4MEC)GRWT9130
PO Box 588 (mailing)
5414 US Highway 45 (physical)
Sharon, TN 38255
( )   <Weakley>
SS: David Lancaster   <M1 PR>
426 Fugua Road
Martin, TN 38237
(731)588-5895
lancasterd@bethel-college.edu

CL: Patricia Elam
2275 Mount Vernon Road
Sharon, TN 38255
(731)456-2882
jimelam@frontiernet.net

Shiloh (AC)   (4WC)GRWT9226
c/o Scott Coleman (mailing)
5 County Road 617A
164 County Road 634 (physical)
Corinth, MS 38834
( )   <Alcorn>
CL: LaWanda Burns
37 County Road 750
Corinth, MS 38834
(662)415-1038
ljmburns@gmail.com

Shiloh (CC)   (4C)GRWT9131
2880 Highway 423
McKenzie, TN 38201
( )   <Carroll>
church@shilohcp.org
PA: Melissa Reid Goodloe   <M1>
225 Macedonia Road
McKenzie, TN 38201
(731)412-9657
rev.mgoodloe@shilohcp.org
CL: Vickie Summers
2880 Highway 423
McKenzie, TN 38201
(731)225-6714
vsum1956@gmail.com

Trezevant   (3EC)GRWT9132
PO Box 246 (mailing)
98 Church Street (physical)
Trezevant, TN 38258
(731)669-4525   <Carroll>
CL: James O Hinton
PO Box 246
Trezevant, TN 38258
(731)669-5277
johinton@charter.net

Troy   (4WC)GRWT9432
PO Box 454 (mailing)
308 Main Street (physical)
Troy, TN 38260
( )   <Obion>
PA: Johnnie Welch   <M1>
PO Box 1506
Dyersburg, TN 38025
(731)287-9008
johnniewelch@msn.com
CL: Alan Thompson
171 Country Valley Drive
Troy, TN 38260
(731)536-1107
atthompson2@netzero.com

Union City   (4MW C)GRWT9433
631 E Church Street
Union City, TN 38261
(731)885-9773   <Obion>
FAX: (731)885-9766
uccpc@bellsouth.net

WEST TENNESSEE PRESBYTERY CONTINUED

CL: Pat Wood
822 E Main Street
Union City, TN 38261
(731)885-4489
FAX: (731)885-6500
pat@woodcommunications.com

Walnut Grove   (4MWC)GRWT9320
1383 Walnut Grove Road
Burlison, TN 38015
(901)476-5533   <Tipton>
SS: Christopher Todd   <M1>
3303 Decker Street
Bartlett, TN 38134
(901)848-9*913
catodd1964@gmail.com
CL: Denise Shires
681 Highway 179
Covington, TN 38019
(901)476-4590
billyshires@bellsouth.net

West Union   (4MWC)GRWT9321
3099 W Union Road
Millington, TN 38053
(901)876-5757   <Shelby>
westunionoffice@bigriver.net
PA: James R Hamblin   <M1>
60 Rolling Meadow Drive
Drummonds, TN 38023
(901)840-4747
brojim391@gmail.com
CL: Mary Proctor
3541 Charles Bartlett Road
Millington, TN 38053
(901)872-0109
larry.mary.proctor@gmail.com

Woodward's Chapel   (2C)GRWT9434
1357 Webster Street (mailing)
Union City, TN 38261
3054 Bud O Yates Road (physical)
Obion, TN 38240
(731)431-9127   <Obion>
FAX: (731)623-4226
SS: Mike Lavender   <M3 ST>
308 Main Street
Martin, TN 38237
(731)253-7308
FAX: (731)623-4226
mikelavender@alumni.vanderbilt.edu
CL: Alvin Minnick
1357 Webster Street
Union City, TN 38261
(731)442-1130
alviniraq2004@yahoo.com

Yorkville   (4MEC)GRWT9435
PO Box 156 (mailing)
17 Newbern Highway (physical)
Yorkville, TN 38389
(731)643-6594   <Gibson>
CL: Mike Roberts
PO Box 213
Yorkville, TN 38389
(731)643-6237
roberts8@ycinet.net

Zion   (4C)GRWT9133
8670 Highway 436 (mailing)
3890 New Zion Road (physical)
McKenzie, TN 38201
( )   <Carroll>
SS: Jon T Carlock   <M1>
248 Cherry Avenue
McKenzie, TN 38201
(731)693-0003
carlockj@bethelu.edu
SS: Richard Reed   <M2>
236 Madison Street
Dyer, TN 38330
(731)692-3604
CL: Stan Welch
3670 New Zion Road
McKenzie, TN 38201
(731)358-2238

OTHERS ON MINISTERIAL ROLL:

Akin, Hershel W   <M1 WC>
388 Mysen Drive
Cordova, TN 38018
(901)744-8980
Alexander, Merlyn A   <M1 HR>
80 N Hampton Lane
Jackson, TN 38305
m_j_alexander@eplus.net
(731)668-8185
Anderson, Barry L   <M1 DE>
1790 Faxon Avenue
Memphis, TN 38112
(901)725-0924
wa4mff@aol.com
Bagby, Larry   <M1 WC>
3189 Northwood Drive
Memphis, TN 38111
(901)452-1952
Boatright, William R   <M1 WC>
513 S 6th Street
Murray, KY 42071
(270)761-5052
catfish.boat@gmail.com
Brown, Elinor   <M1 DE>
752 Hawthorne Street
Memphis, TN 38107
(901)274-1474
esb@cumberland.org
Brown, Mark   <M1 M9>
752 Hawthorne Street
Memphis, TN 38107
(901)274-1474
dmbrown@utmem.edu
Burns, J B, Jr   <M1 WC>
1020 Maud Road
Cherokee, AL 35616
(256)360-2252
Caperton, Donald   <M1 RT>
285 Britton Ford Road
Springville, TN 38256
(731)593-5096
dandjcaperton@vol.com
Coleman, Don L   <M1 WC>
85 Orchard Lane
Savannah, TN 38372
(731)925-9710
Condron, Dudley   <M1 RT>
1360 Harbert Avenue
Memphis, TN 38104
(901)726-1488
dudleywcondron@aol.com

Corbin, Eric   <M1 WC>
816 Bluegrass Lane
Champaign, IL 61822
(217)239-9945
eric@corbinzone.com
Crisp, Gregory W   <M1 WC>
635 Eden Brook Lane
Cordova, TN 38018
(901)266-0406
Dyer, Stuart   <M1 WC>
3574 Foxfield Trail
Bartlett, TN 38135
(901)388-0612
Eddleman, Keith   <M1 WC>
2787 Stage Park Drive
Memphis, TN 38134
(901)388-9885
Gam, John   <M1 WC>
1235 Sanders Street
Auburn, AL 36830
Gillock, Ed   <M1 WC>
PO Box 157
Savannah, TN 38372
(731)609-6744
Grimsley, Roger   <M1 WC>
215 N Oak Street
Springfield, TN 37172
Harwell, Keith   <M1 WC>
13132 Stinson Street
Milan, TN 38358
(731)613-3780
Hayes, Drew   <M1 WC>
6322 Labor Lane
Louisville, KY 40291
(731)796-7076
dhayes72@gmail.com
Heflin, Donna S   <M1 WC>
4144 Meadow Court Drive
Bartlett, TN 38135
(901)382-8198
rdheflin@bellsouth.net
Hill, Jody   <M1 WC>
4030 St Andrew Circle
Corinth, MS 38834
(662)512-8226
jody.hill34@gmail.com
Holmes, Aaron G   <M1 WC>
PO Box 171
Atwood, TN 38220
(731)662-7595
agholmes@charter.net
Howe, Francis   <M1 WC>
129 Manley Street
McKenzie, TN 38201
(731)352-5551
Hubbard, Pratt   <M1 WC>
1565 Eli Brown Road
McKenzie, TN 38201
(731)352-9178
Jackson, Terry   <M1 M9>
1461 Mount Pleasant Road
Hernando, MS 38632
(662)429-9741
James, William F   <M1 WC>
2937 Arthur Drive
Murfreesboro, TN 37127
(615)653-1396
wimjim19@gmail.com
Janner, Tony   <M1 WC>
104 Northwood Drive
McKenzie, TN 38201
(731)352-8055
drtonyjanner@yahoo.com

WEST TENNESSEE PRESBYTERY CONTINUED

Jeong, Woo S   \<M1 WC\>
1205 Morganshire Drive
Collierville, TN 38017
(901)302-0558
FAX: (901)854-8185

Jett, Mace T Jr   \<M1 WC\>
109 Park Street
Martin, TN 38237
(731)587-0805

Kleinjan, Lori   \<M1 WC\>
6516 Farnell Avenue
Memphis, TN 38134
(901)372-8413
lkleinj@prodigy.net

Latimer, James M   \<M1 WC\>
7621 Richmond
Memphis, TN 38125
(901)787-7875
jimmylatimer@redeemerevangelical.com

Laurence, Brenda   \<M1 WC\>
2823 Nine Mile Road
Enville, TN 38332
(731)687-2022
southernmoma@hotmail.com

Luttrell, Ben   \<M1 WC\>
262 Main Street
Nettleton, MS 38858
(731)645-5257

Magliolo, Sam   \<M1 WC\>
14352 Fairview
Byhalia, MS 38611
(662)838-7720
samagliolo@fedex.com

Malinoski, Melissa   \<M1 WC\>
9087 Fenmore Cove
Cordova, TN 38016
(420)620-0089
FAX: (423)636-1017
mmalinoski@memphisseminary.edu

Maynard, Geoffery   \<M1 WC\>
1356 Marcia Road
Memphis, TN 38117
(901)409-5269

McClanahan, Jo Ann   \<M1 WC\>
215 White Brothers Road
Humboldt, TN 38343
(731)784-1176
joannmcclanahan@hughes.net

McClanahan, H Walter   \<M1 WC\>
215 White Bros Road
Humboldt, TN 38343
(731)784-1176
waltermac2@hughes.net

McClung, Andy   \<M1 WC\>
919 Dickinson Street
Memphis, TN 38107
(901)606-6615
scubarev@att.net

McClung, Tiffany   \<M1 M9\>
919 Dickinson Street
Memphis, TN 38107
(901)606-6615
tmcclung@memphisseminary.edu

McMillan, L Ronald   \<M1 WC\>
675 Kimberly Drive
Atoka, TN 38004
(901)837-1101
mcmillanron@bellsouth.net

Meeks, Brittany   \<M1 WC\>
1340 Tutwiler Avenue
Memphis, TN 38107
(901)336-9024
bpmeeks@memphisseminary.edu

Minor, Mitzi   \<M1 PR\>
875 S Cox
Memphis, TN 38104
(901)278-6115

Mosley, Karen   \<M1 WC\>
PO Box 172154
Memphis, TN 38187

Nash, Zachary   \<M1 M8\>
(on file in General Assembly Office)
zachary.nash@us.af.mil

Ndoro, Wonder   \<M1 WC\>
111 Roberta Avenue
Memphis, TN 38112
(901)334-5861
gusungo@yahoo.com

Norton, Thomas H   \<M1 RT\>
220 Evergreen Garden Drive
Elizabethtown, KY 42701
(353)584-4695
tnorton16@comcast.net

Orr, Melvin   \<M1 RT\>
806 Washington Street
Newbern, TN 38059
(731)627-2445
2Orrs.mn@charter.net

Perkins, Ed   \<M1 RT\>
721 E Paris Avenue
McKenzie, TN 38201
(731)352-2754

Pinion, Phillip   \<M1 WC\>
PO Box 87
Union City, TN 38281
(731)885-9175

Pounds, James D   \<M1 WC\>
40 Nellie Lane
Savannah, TN 38372
(731)925-2685
olivetcp@bellsouth.net

Powell, Jeff   \<M1 WC\>
547B Fawn Drive
Henderson, TN 38340
(731)608-2040
jfpowell2003@yahoo.com

Prosser, Robert   \<M1 DE\>
1021 Old State Route 76
Henry, TN 38231
(731)243-4467

Qualls, Michael   \<M1 DE\>
5355 June Cove
Horn Lake, MS 38637
(901)377-0526
FAX: (901)382-2600
mqualls1@yahoo.com

Quinton, Noah   \<M1 WC\>
2912 Waller Omer Road
Sturgis, KY 42459
(270)952-3875
noah.quinton@gmail.com

Ridgely, Michael   \<M1 WC\>
5195 Broad Street S
Trezevant, TN 38258
(731)669-3767

Rietz, Allen   \<M1 WC\>
1239 Hopewell Church Road
Finger, TN 38334
(731)989-7872

Rose, Missy   \<M1 DE\>
2986 Ruskin Road
Bartlett, TN 38134
(901)378-1133
missyrose3@yahoo.com

Scrivener, Carol   \<M1 WC\>
746 Willowsprings Boulevard
Franklin, TN 37064
(731)660-6469
csscriv@juno.com

Searcy, James M   \<M1 WC\>
1307 Lucy Way
Knoxville, TN 37912
(817)293-6132
gsearcy@earthlink.net

Smith, James A   \<M1 WC\>
8301 Poplar Pike
Germantown, TN 38138
(901)309-1992
james1493@att.net

Thomas, Don F   \<M1 WC\>
400 Park Hill Road
Collierville, TN 38017
(901)861-6398
thomas63981@comcast.net

Thompson, Tommy   \<M1 WC\>
9160 Tchulahoma Road
Southaven, MS 38671
(662)393-2552

Todd, Laura   \<M1 WC\>
3303 Decker Street
Bartlett, TN 38134
(901)496-1443
littlelaurarose@yahoo.com

Truax, Robert Lee, Jr   \<M1 M9 RT\>
2989 Champions Drive Apt 204
Lakeland, TN 38002
(901)266-5927

Turner, O Gene   \<M1 WC\>
3160 McSpadden Road
Rives, TN 38253
(731)536-0189

Walker, Michael C   \<M1 WC\>
1404 Wilshire Drive
Odessa, TX 79761
(731)643-6730
mworator@gmail.com

Ward, Frank   \<M1 WC\>
46 Henderson Cove
Atoka, TN 38004
(901)837-1972
bamaguy68@xipline.com

Westbrook, James   \<M1 RT\>
1717 Wedgewood Drive
Union City, TN 38261
(731)884-0918
westbrook731@bellsouth.net

Wheeler, Nathan   \<M1 DE\>
1255 Wedgewood Street
Memphis, TN 38111
(901)606-9535
nathantyac@gmail.com

White, Diann   \<M1 WC\>
9394 Alex Dickson Cove
Bartlett, TN 38133
(901)377-7776
diannwhite12@yahoo.com

Williams, Cory   \<M1 WC\>
3148 Long Bridge Lane
Arlington, TN 38002
(901)486-5981
coromis@hotmail.com

Wilson, Thomas   \<M1 WC\>
4543 Lake Vista
Memphis, TN 38128
(901)382-6190
tomjw217@gmail.com

OTHER LICENTIATES ON ROLL:

Harwell, Jacob   \<M2\>
  319 Joy Drive
  McKenzie, TN 38201
  (731)415-1457
  rjharwell@student.memphisseminary.edu
Jett-Rand, Dana   \<M2\>
  78 Lester Lane
  Martin, TN 38237
  (731)587-0805
  msdanajett@yahoo.com
Sims, Joyce   \<M2\>
  6935 Highway 54
  Paris, TN 38242
  (731)364-3537

OTHER CANDIDATES ON ROLL:

Adams, Jamie   \<M3 ST\>
  403 W Washington
  Union City, TN 38261
  (731)885-1217
  adamsj2@k12tn.net
Dimo, Urelia   \<M3\>
  171 Roberta Drive
  Memphis, TN 38112
Earheart-Brown, Paul   \<M3\>
  502 E Lamar Alexander Parkway
  Box 2519
  Maryville, TN 37804
Trapp, Emily   \<M3\>
  4750 Harvest Knoll Cove N
  Memphis, TN 38125
  (901)756-4738

ALPHABETICAL ROLL OF MINISTERS

Symbols in this roll:

(M0) - Mentored Minister
(M1) - Ordained Minister
(M2) - Licentiate
(M3) - Candidate
(M4) - Minister of another denomination who through reciprocal agreement is enrolled as a member of presbytery and has temporarily the rights and privileges of such membership according to the Constitution, Article 5.3.

--==<< A >>==--

Acton, Donald W (M1)
1186 Jenkins Lane
Knoxville, TN 37922
(865)966-5132 SEET#2310

Acton, Donny (M1)
1413 Oak Ridge Drive
Birmingham, AL 35242
FAX: (205)991-5259
donny@newhopecpc.org
(205)991-3204 SEGR#0104

Acton, Mindy (M1)
1413 Oak Ridge Drive
Birmingham, AL 35242
FAX: (205)991-5259
mindy@newhopecpc.org
(205)991-3204 SEGR#0104

Acton, Wade (M1)
1615 Estes Drive
Glencoe, AL 35905
ginnyacton@juno.com
(256)492-8542 SEGR#0406

Acuff, David (M1)
4969 Quail Lane
Columbia, SC 29206
david.acuff@us.army.mil
(803)727-3910 TNNA#7300

Adams, Fred Michael (M1)
42 Julies Way
Somerset, KY 42503
fma46@twc.com
(606)451-9155 MICU#3314

Adams, Jamie (M3)
403 W Washington
Union City, TN 38261
adamsj2@k12tn.net
(731)885-1217 GRWT#9100

Aden, Dare (M1)
1280 Kimber Road
Dongola, IL 62926
FAX: (618)827-4612
dare_aden@hotmail.com
(618)827-3625 MICO#3400

Aden, Marty (M1)
202 Bennington Place
Wilmington, NC 28412
maden@ec.rr.com
(910)795-1092 MSRR#8400

Agudelo, Gildardo (M1)
Cra 73C # 1A-54
Cali, COLOMBIA, SA
( ) MSCA#8223

Aguiar, Neil (M1)
405 E Moulton Street
Decatur, AL 35601
nlajap@yahoo.com
(256)616-1318 SEGR#0214

Ahn, Da-Wit (David) (M1)
1304 Kakyeng-Dong
Sangdang-Gu Cheongju-City
Choongbook, KOREA
(043)235-0219 MMT

Akai, Anum (M1)
458 Dean Taylor Court
Simpsonville, KY 40067
(502)405-3120 MICU#3100

Akin, Hershel W (M1)
388 Mysen Drive
Cordova, TN 38018
(901)744-8980 GRWT#9100

Alas, William (M1)
612 King Valley Circle
Pelham, AL 35124
alas3542085@yahoo.es
(205)966-9411 SEGR#0115

Albarracin, Ruben D (M1)
7411 Magnolia Shadows Lane
Houston, TX 77095
FAX: (281)463-8617
confiaendios@hotmail.com
(281)463-8617 MSTR#8612

Alderson, Cameron (M3)
122 E Cherry Street
Chandler, IN 47610
(812)925-6475 MICO#3400

Alexander, Merlyn A (M1)
80 N Hampton Lane
Jackson, TN 38305
m_j_alexander@eplus.net
(731)668-8185 GRWT#9100

Alhart, Daryl (M1)
2187 Rutledge Ford Road
Decherd, TN 37324
dwalhart@aol.com
(931)349-7104 TNMU#7225

Allen, Gail (M1)
488 County Road 1650 N
Bethany, IL 61914
kallen1_61914@yahoo.com
(217)665-3387 MINC#5200

Alvarez, Samuel (M3)
3740 W Leland Avenue
Chicago, IL 60625
(773)509-9165 MINC#5200

Alverson, Elmer L (M1)
354 Roy Davis Road
New Market, AL 35761
budalv@bellsouth.net
(256)828-4503 SERD#0800

Anderson, Barry L (M1)
1790 Faxon Avenue
Memphis, TN 38112
wa4mff@aol.com
(901)725-0924 GRWT#9100

Anderson, Christopher (M2)
131 Roberta Drive
Memphis, TN 38112
csanderson@memphisseminary.edu
(870)805-0886 GRAR#1100

Anderson, Kyle (M3)
828 E Main Street
Batesville, AR 72501
kanderson@mempisseminary.edu
(870)834-5799

Anderson, Lisa (M1)
1790 Faxon Avenue
Memphis, TN 38112
anderli60@gmail.com
(901)246-8052 GRWT#9305

Ang, John (M1)
5843 S Farm Road 157
Springfield, MO 65810
pastorcares@yahoo.com
(417)886-3487 GRMI#4100

Appling, John (M1)
1722 S Fairway Avenue
Springfield, MO 65804
pegblessings@sbcglobal.net
(417)877-4643 GRMI#4100

Appling, Peggy (M1)
1722 S Fairway Avenue
Springfield, MO 65804
pegblessings@sbcglobal.net
(417)877-4643 GRMI#4100

Arase, Makihiko (M1)
3-355-4 Kamikitadai Higashi
Yamato-shi, Tokyo
207-0023, JAPAN
FAX: (042)567-2977
viator@cb3.so-net.ne.jp
(042)567-2977 MSJA#8309

Arias, John Jairo (M1)
Calle 144 Sur #496-08 / Apto 202
Caldas, Antioquia
COLOMBIA, SA
(57)317-693-1162 MSAN#8900

Ariza, Fabiola (M1)
COLOMBIA, SA
fatvioleta@hotmail.com
(316)419-8414 MSCA#8200

Aros, Jeremias (M1)
5649 W Roscoe Street
Chicago, IL 60634
jeremiasaros@sbcglobal.net
(773)685-4395 MINC#5200

Arteaga, Gilberto (M3)
Aereo 794
Buenaventura, COLOMBIA, SA
pastorgilbertoa@hotmail.com
( )256-4261 MSCA#8210

Asayama, Masaharu (M1)
6-3-2-308 Toyogaoka
Tama-shi, Tokyo
206-0031, JAPAN
asa@ipcc-21.com
(042)373-2710 MSJA#8300

Ashley, Jack (Nick) (M3)
2625A Raleigh Drive
Evansville, IN 47715
edencateringusa@aol.com
(812)204-1422 MICO#3400

MINISTERS CONTINUED

Ashton, Christie (M1)
10001 Bailey Cove Road SE
Huntsville, AL 35803
FAX: (256)881-0031
pastorhope@bellsouth.net
(256)881-4673 SERD#0800

Attema, Lee (M1)
5 County Road 209
Sargent, TX 77414
lattema@icloud.com
(281)728-6263 MSTR#8103

Attena, Leslie (M1)
5 County Road 209
Sargent, TX 77414
leslieattema@icloud.com
(281)728-6263 MSTR#8103

Atwell, Keith G (M1)
7688 Hardyville Road
Hardyville, KY 42746
FAX: (270)524-9100
(270)528-3667 MICU#3102

Axton, Durant (M1)
2441 SE Browning Road
Evansville, IN 47725
(812)459-0089 MINC#5200

--=<< B >>=--

Babcock, Edward S, Jr (M1)
1007 San Ramone Avenue
Huntsville, AL 35802
ejsb1@aol.com
(256)882-9339 SERD#0800

Bagby, Larry (M1)
3189 Northwood Drive
Memphis, TN 38111
(901)452-1952 GRWT#9100

Ballow, Brent (M1)
715 Highland Church Road
Paducah, KY 42001
hcppastor@bellsouth.net
(270)564-8891 MICO#3400

Baltimore, Claud G (M1)
PO Box 1358
1430 Lakehurst Drive
Ada, OK 74821
baltimorejb@earthlink.net
(580)332-2679 MSRR#8400

Bane, Ted (M1)
903 W Old Hickory Boulevard
Madison, TN 37115
tedjan95@aol.com
(615)975-9343 TNNA#7309

Baranoski, Timothy (M1)
1205 Tomahawk Drive B
Jber, AK 99505
timothy.i.baranoski.mil@mail.mil
(615)440-3499 TNNA#7300

Barkley, Daniel (M1)
2732 Rexford Street
Hokes Bluff, AL 35903
daniel@gadsdencp.com
(256)478-0397 SEGR#0402

Barna, Clifton (M1)
1012 Adam Court
Cottontown, tn 37066
cliff.barna@gmail.com
(352)598-3246 TNNA#7300

Barnett, Rudolph (M1)
RR 5 Box 267
McLeansboro, IL 62859
(618)643-3253 MINC#5200

Barnhouse, Donald Grey, Jr (M1)
51 Harristown Road
Paradise, PA 17562
donaldbarnhouse@gmail.com
(610)337-4015 MICU#3131

Barrett, Geoff (M1)
155 Maude Lane
Harrodsburg, KY 40330
FAX: (256)881-0031
glbarrett@live.com
(859)748-8373 MICU#3111

Barrios, Janina (M3)
10090 NW 80th Court
Hialeah Gardens, Fl 33016
janina83@hotmail.com
(786)757-0369 SEGR#0100

Barron, Mark (M1)
836 McArthur Street
Manchester, TN 37355
FAX: (931)728-2975
mbarron@cafes.net
(931)728-2975 TNMU#7224

Barry, James (M1)
49 Smitty's Circle
Chattanooga, TN 37415
jnmcs_barry@bellsouth.net
(903)315-7998 SETG#2111

Barton, Cindy (M2)
83426 Argus Avenue
Trona, CA 93562
cbarton53@hotmail.com
(760)372-4033 MSDC#8700

Barton, Robert (M1)
22460 Klines Resort Road Lot #290
Three Rivers, MI 49093
csm2ndinfbde2002@yahoo.com
(859)613-2686 MICU#3100

Baugh, Roosevelt (M1)
4101 Hademan Street
Fort Worth, TX 76119
FAX: (817)534-1339
gmf1220@charter.net
(817)536-1315 MSRR#8408

Bautista, Juan (M1)
Tranv 30 No 17F-122
Cali
Colombia, South America
( )442-4562 MSCA#8217

Bayer, David (M1)
9060 Tom Counce Road
South Fulton, TN 38257
dbayer9060@gmail.com
(731)479-3060 GRWT#9412

Bell, Marc (M1)
3467 State Route 175 N
Bremen, KY 42325
marcbell@insightbb.com
(270)846-4203 MICU#3503

Bell, Michelle (M2)
8643 Dry Creek Road Unit 1226
Centennial, CO 80112
mabbell@comcast.net
(720)344-4040 MSDC#8700

Benadom, Dennis (M1)
13314 Sage Street
Trona, CA 93562
galerose91@msn.com
(760)372-4536 MSDC#8503

Bender, Richard J (M1)
5297 Normandy Place
Evansville, IN 47715
richardjbenderjr@yahoo.com
(812)983-9597 MINC#5200

Benedict, Mary McCaskey (M1)
892 Pen Oak Drive
Cookeville, TN 38501
marykat_61@hotmail.com
(931)260-1422 TNMU#7200

Bennett, Alfred J (M1)
7286 Nolensville Road
Nolensville, TN 37135
(615)776-5181 TNNA#7300

Benson, William L (M1)
137 W Lowndes Drive
Columbus, MS 39701
willardb715@gmail.com
(662)386-3433 SEGR#0701

Bertsch, Michael (M1)
204 Buckleigh Point
Gallatin, TN 37066
mikebertsch14@gmail.com
(423)763-8314 TNNA#7327

Betancur, Sergio (M1)
Iglesia El Rebano
Calle 128 sur #48-13
Caldas, Antioquia, COLOMBIA, SA
sergiobetancurposada@hotmail.com
(574)278-0787 MSCA#8208

Biggs, Jeff (M1)
1504 Cumberland Drive
Fairfield, IL 62837
jeffbiggsonline@gmail.com
(618)842-2219 MINC#5108

Black, Gary G (M1)
503 S Main Street
Piedmont, AL 36272
(205)447-7142 SEGR#0400

Blackburn, Samuel N (M1)
6706 S 6th Street
Fort Smith, AR 72908
(479)649-9436 GRAR#1100

Blair, Fonda (M1)
2911 Kedzie Drive
Murfreesboro, TN 37130
blairfonda2010@comcast.net
(615)491-2432 TNCO#7145

Blair, John (M1)
108 Cliff Drive
Lawrenceburg, TN 38464
jnbblair@charter.net
(931)766-2480 TNCO#7111

Blakeburn, Larry A (M1)
790 Emory Valley Road Apt 714
Oak Ridge, TN 37830
larry@1stcpc.org
(731)676-2978 SEET#2313

Blandon, Juan Esteban (M1)
Calle 51 #15-32
barrio Los Naranjos
Dosquebradas, Risaralda
COLOMBIA, SA
juanestebanblandon@yahoo.com
57(314)680-2246 MSAN#8907

Blanton, D B (M1)
ADDRESS UNKNOWN
( ) GRAR#1100

Blaum, Steve R (M1)
184 900 Street
Middletown, IL 62666
cumberland@frontier.com
(217)871-3339 MINC#5405

Blevins, Ralph (M1)
1623 County Road 2375 E
Geff, IL 62842
pastorreblevins@gmail.com
(618)854-2494 MINC#5107

MINISTERS CONTINUED

Blevins, Tom (M1)
50 Blevins Road
Center, KY 42214
(270)565-1792   MICU#3100

Board, N Ray (M1)
267 State Route 293 N
Princeton, KY 42445
rayboard@att.net
(270)365-0006   MICO#3400

Boatright, William R (M1)
513 S 6th Street
Murray, KY 42071
catfish.boat@gmail.com
(270)761-5052   GRWT#9100

Boggs, Barry (M1)
1039 Johnnie Bud Lane
Cookeville, TN 38501
boggsone@hotmail.com
(931)979-1701   TNMU#7200

Boggs, Robert (M1)
89 Maple Leaf Lane
Leitchfield, KY 42754
(270)259-5546   MICU#3100

Bohon, Chris Michael (M3)
109 NE McAlister Road
Burleson, TX 76028
cbohon@pathway.church
(817)228-9494   MSRR#8400

Bond, Bill (M1)
205 Windmere Drive
Chattanooga, TN 37411
bill@wcbj.net
(423)316-0867   SETG#2102

Bond, Richard (M1)
2425 Fisk Road Lot 0
Cookeville, TN 38506
erbond@frontier.net
(931)854-0979   TNMU#7213

Bondurant, Lee (M1)
1453 Paseo Del Sur Court
El Paso, TX 79928
leebondurant@yahoo.com
(915)309-7269   MSDC#8700

Bone, Leslie (M1)
16504 George Franklyn Drive
Independence, MO 64055
lesliebone@comcast.net
(816)373-6625   GRMI#4100

Bone, W Harold (M1)
315 Joey Drive
Bourne, TX 78006
ruaha1@sbcglobal.net
(210)859-5560   MSTR#8100

Boulton, Mitch (M1)
1606 Ebenezer Road
Troy, TN 38260
steelermitch@gmail.com
(731)487-2318   GRWT#9422

Bower, Clay (M1)
221 Waterlemon Way
Monroe, NC 28110
cbower@lzbsoutheast.com
(704)575-9497   MSDC#8700

Bowers, Sharon G (M1)
201 Wild Buffalo Drive
Kyle, TX 78640
sharon.bowers@gmail.com
(512)230-7078   MSTR#8100

Bowling, Andrew (M1)
20945 Highway 16 E
Siloam Springs, AR 72761
(479)524-6576   GRAR#1100

Bowman, Greg (M3)
3241 South Fork Road
Glasgow, KY 42141
( )   MICU#3217

Bozeman, Robert (M1)
582 Bozeman Loop
Belmont, LA 71406
bo@bozemanengineering.com
(318)256-5781   MSTR#8100

Bradberry, Jim (M3)
120 Hummingbird Lane
Searcy, AR 72143
(501)278-9750   GRAR#1205

Bradshaw, James (Jim) (M1)
415 S Red Street
Sheridan, AR 72150
(870)942-2525   GRAR#1105

Brantley, Kevin T (M1)
729 Old Hodgenville Road
Greensburg, KY 42743
kbrantley1971@windstream.net
(270)932-3780   MICU#3110

Brasher, Karen (M1)
2931 Barker Cypress Road Apt 415
Houston, TX 77084
ekb077@gmail.com
(205)777-2420   SEGR#0100

Braswell, Jimmy (M1)
1514 E 10th
Odessa, TX 79761
jjcgbraz@cableone.net
(432)335-9346   MSDC#8703

Brewer, Barbara Jean (M1)
1360 White Oak Bluff Road
Rison, AR 71665
(870)325-6449   GRAR#1100

Brindley, Toy (M1)
PO Box 225
Gurley, AL 35748
(256)776-2331   SERD#0804

Brister, Glenn (M1)
3004 Delaware Avenue
McComb, MS 39648
bearmountainpenworks@gmail.com
(706)934-8629   SETG#2100

Brock, Dudley (M1)
490 County Road 1184
Cullman, AL 35057
preacherbrock@att.net
(256)734-0893   SEHO#0213

Brooks, Wayne E (M1)
1505 Parkview Drive
Campbellsville, KY 42718
webrooks@windstream.net
(270)465-9235   MICU#3104

Brown, Amy (M1)
679 Freeze Bend Road
Newport, AR 72112
( )   GRAR#1100

Brown, Charles R (M1)
475 N Highland Street
Memphis, TN 38122
cbrown@cumberland.org
(817)915-2907   MSRR#8400

Brown, Dale M (M1)
HC 61 Box 4740
West Plains, MO 65775
pastorbrown44@yahoo.com
(417)257-0983   GRMI#4304

Brown, Elinor (M1)
752 Hawthorne Street
Memphis, TN 38107
esb@cumberland.org
(901)274-1474   GRWT#9100

Brown, Houston (M3)
866 N McLean
Memphis, TN 38107
hpbrown95@gmail.com
(817)915-9090   MSRR#8400

Brown, Mark (M1)
752 Hawthorne Street
Memphis, TN 38107
dmbrown@utmem.edu
(901)274-1474   GRWT#9100

Brown, Philip (M1)
540 Mt Pisgah Road
Dongola, IL 62926
brownlp75@yahoo.com
(618)827-3516   MICO#5115

Brown, Rex (M1)
134 Everhart Drive
Greeneville, TN 37745
firstcumberland@gmail.com
(423)639-4298   SEET#2205

Brown, Stephanie S (M1)
475 N Highland Street
Memphis, TN 38122
scrudderbrown7@gmail.com
(901)729-3612   MSRR#8400

Brown, Whitney (M3)
137 Roberta Drive
Memphis, TN 38112
(865)387-0002   SEET#2200

Broyles, Byrd (M2)
295 Davy Crockett Road
Limestone, TN 37681
b3broyles@outlook.com
(423)257-4578   SEET#2212

Bruington, Don (M1)
PO Box 105
Falls of Rough, KY 40119
(270)257-2228   MICU#3202

Bryan, Hannah (M1)
32 Trenton Lane
Mead, OK 73449
hbryan@choctawnation.com
(580)775-4955   MSCH#6105

Buchanan, Larry (M1)
720 Shelby Road
Salem, KY 42078
(270)988-1880   MICO#3610

Buck, Clinton (M1)
PO Box 770068
Memphis, TN 38117
clintobuck@aol.com
(901)682-2358   GRWT#9315

Bunnell, Robert (Bob) (M1)
329 Lexington Drive
Glasgow, KY 42141
bob_bunnell@yahoo.com
(270)629-6209   MICU#3312

Bunting, Geoff (M1)
9229 Hedgewood Court
Evansville, IN 47725
geoff.bunting@yahoo.com
(812)925-6630   MINC#5200

Burgess, Ronald D (M1)
116 Harris Ridge Road
Dover, TN 37058
revron4@bellsouth.net
(931)232-5151   TNNA#7322

MINISTERS CONTINUED

Burns, Garrett (M1)
387 Forrest Avenue
McKenzie, TN 38201
gburns2888@gmail.com
(731)535-3126   GRWT#9118

Burns, J B, Jr (M1)
1020 Maud Road
Cherokee, AL 35616
(256)360-2252   GRWT#9100

Burrow, Vernon (M1)
603 Saratoga Drive
Murfreesboro, TN 37130
vernonburrow@comcast.net
(615)406-6385   TNMU#7200

Burrows, Arthur L, Jr (M1)
PO Box 511
Hopkinsville, KY 42241
(270)886-1301   MICU#3505

Butcher, Kenny (M1)
4608 Cather Court
Nashville, TN 37214
bhpastor@birch.net
(615)719-1887   TNNA#7325

Butler, Jim (M1)
507 W Chestnut Street
Leitchfield, KY 42754
jbutler54@insightbb.com
(502)635-8587   MICU#3211

Butler, John (M1)
PO Box 257
Sacramento, KY 42372
jbutler@iccable.com
(270)736-2268   MICU#3512

Butler, Joseph H, Jr (M1)
56 Cline Ridge Road
Winchester, TN 37398
jhbu737@bellsouth.net
(931)224-8423   TNMU#7205

Buttram, Jim (M1)
5385 Bungalow Circle
Hixson, TN 37343
FAX: (865)483-8445
littlejimb@gmail.com
(865)938-7418   TNGA#2105

Byford, Ken (M3)
58 Quincy Lane
Montevallo, AL 35115
kenabyford@gmail.com
(205)665-5753   SEGR#0100

Bynum, Ronald H (M1)
121 Sycamore Road
Gurley, AL 35748
ronaldbynum@bellsouth.net
(256)776-9313   SERD#0800

Byrd, James F (M1)
1158 Cornishville Road
Harrodsburg, KY 40330
jfbyrd@bluezoomwifi.com
(859)734-0534   MICU#3100

Byrd, Jimmy (M1)
176 E Valley Road
Whitwell, TN 37397
FAX: (615)444-6671
revjimmybyrd@gmail.com
(615)289-3347   SETG#2115

--==<< C >>==--

Cadenbach, Mark (M1)
91 Elzadah Lane
Salem, AR 72576
cadenbm@nctc.net
(890)955-9250   GRAR#1100

Caicedo, Efrain (M3)
Aereo 6365
Cali, COLOMBIA, SA
( )   MSCA#8224

Cain, Greg (M2)
2500 Vernon Street Ext B-3
Union City, TN 38261
greg.cain07@gmail.com
(731)445-4446   MICO#3400

Calero, Aldrin (M1)
Cattara 13 3-81
Guacari, COLOMBIA, SA
( )253-0453   MSCA#8212

Camp, Annetta (M1)
2303 Mill Creek Road
Halls, TN 38040
FAX: (731)285-5792
annetta@cumberlandchurch.com
(731)285-5703   GRWT#9410

Campbell, Coyle (M1)
186 Old Limestone Road
New Market, AL 35761
(256)379-4392   TNMU#7215

Campbell, Gordon C (M1)
1469 E Wayland Street
Springfield, MO 65804
gofor12@gmail.com
(417)823-9567   GRMI#4100

Campbell, Thomas D (M1)
PO Box 343
601 Park Street
Calico Rock, AR 72519
FAX: (870)297-3151
tdcampbellar@gmail.com
(870)297-2319   GRAR#1503

Campos, Eva (M3)
PO Box 451405
Miami, FL 33245
(786)426-5997   SEGR#0100

Cantey, James M (M1)
3505 Elmira Drive
Longview, TX 75605
(903)452-6049   MSTR#8111

Caperton, Donald (M1)
285 Britton Ford Road
Springville, TN 38256
dandjcaperton@vol.com
(731)593-5096   GRWT#9100

Cardona, Nancy (M3)
Calle 51 #15-32
Dosquebradas, Risaralda
COLOMBIA, SA
nancycardona10@yahoo.com
(576)322-2938   MSAN#8900

Carlock, Jon T (M1)
248 Cherry Avenue
McKenzie, TN 38201
carlockj@bethel-college.edu
(731)352-0800   GRWT#9133

Carlton, Gary (M1)
108 Greenbrier Street
Dickson, TN 37055
gwcarlton@yahoo.com
(270)965-4358   TNNA#7313

Carpenter, David (M1)
909 W Elm Street
Olney, TX 76374
olneycpc@brazosnet.com
(940)564-2339   MSRR#8416

Carr, Jill (M2)
PO Box 1547
Lebanon, MO 65536
dig.micah.6.8@gmail.com
(417)532-6760   GRMI#4100

Carter, Billy Ray (M1)
33 Mockingbird Drive
Leitchfield, KY 42754
cartercbc@windstream.net
(270)259-3897   MICU#3203

Carter, Gary (M1)
8311 County Road 1082
Vinemont, AL 35179
garycarter51@gmail.com
(256)443-8389   SEHO#0202

Carter, James L (M1)
6155 Hummingbird Lane
Whitesburg, TN 37891
jandjmt@comcast.net
(423)587-8423   SEET#2200

Carter, Patricia (M1)
2509 Decatur Stratton Road
Decatur, MS 39327
revtree@yahoo.com
(601)604-3813   SEGR#0100

Carver, Gary (M1)
2810 Cabin Road
Chattanooga, TN 37411
sandgatthecabin@epbfi.com
(423)698-2556   SETG#2100

Cassell, C J (M2)
825 Aimes Court
Nashville, TN 37221
n4cjc@comcast.net
(615)594-2693   TNNA#7300

Castaneda, Ricardo (M1)
Calle 65 #98-45 (Interior 174)
Altos de la Macarena-Robledo La Campina
Medellin, Antioquia, COLOMBIA, SA
rijcah@gmail.com
(574)577-0717   MSAN#8915

Castano, Juan Alexander (M1)
Calle 127 sur #42-38 Apto 301
Caldas, Antioquia, COLOMBIA, SA
FAX: (574)278-0787
juanalexandercastano@hotmail.com
(574)306-4435   MSAN#8905

Chall-Hutchinson (M3)
190 Ussery Road
Clarksville, TN 37043
challhut@gmail.com
(931)905-1671   TNNA#7300

Chambers, Jason (M1)
131 E Woods Street
Palestine, AR 72372
jmchambers@memphisseminary.edu
(870)807-1930   GRAR#1103

Chambers, Nicholas (M1)
11300 Road 101
Union, MS 39365
nachambrs@hotmail.com
(601)697-4470   SEGR#0608

Chancellor, Hilton (M1)
11905 Preserve Vista
Austin, TX 78738
hiltontex@aol.com
(512)382-1972   MSTR#8100

Chang, Leo (M1)
819 W Division SE
Springfield, MO 65803
(901)287-9901   GRAR#1100

Chapman, Harry W (M1)
4908 El Picador Court
Rio Rancho, NM 87124
wrightrev@gmail.com
(505)620-2427   MSDC#8709

MINISTERS CONTINUED

Chen, Steven (M1)
865 Jackson Street
San Francisco, CA 94133
psalm1305@yahoo.com
(415)421-1624   MSDC#8501

Cheung, Luke (M1)
A-D Flat 3/F 338-340 Castle Peak Road
Cheung Sha Wan
Kowloon HONG KONG
FAX: (852)2706-0114
luke.cheung@cgst.edu
(852)2794-6781   MSHK#8800

Chin, Kwang Sik (M2)
1168 Palisade Avenue
Fort Lee, NJ 07024
(201)220-3390   SECE#2400

Cho, Sangsook (M1)
7 Falmouth Court
Middletown, CT
lovejcamen@yahoo.com
(860)830-6808   SECE#2143

Cho, Sung Wan (M1)
1603 Coolhurst Avenue
Sherwood, AR 72120
swcho100491@gmail.com
(501)247-5953   GRAR#2135

Choe, Byung-Jae (M1)
876-15 Dokok-1dong
Kangnam-Gu, Seoul, KOREA
(023)463-3939   SEET#2222

Choi, Ezra (M1)
605 Arbor Hollow Circle #2103
Cordova, TN 38018
(901)236-8235   SEET#2200

Choi, Hyoung S (M1)
32132 Huntly Circle
Salisbury, MD 21804
pastor0101@naver.com
(443)880-6776   SETG#2138

Choi, Sean (M2)
7565 Macon Road
Cordova, TN 38016
esloveh2@hotmail.com
(901)826-2993   SEET#2200

Chuquimia, Walter (M1)
18240 S US Highway 301
Wimauma, FL 33598
walter@beth-el.info
(813)399-4050   SEGR#0100

Cinco, Carlos (M1)
611 Cheron Road
Madison, TN 37115
pastorcinco2020@gmail.com
(615)586-1269   TNNA#7314

Clark, Amber LaCroix (M1)
80 Bryan Drive
Winchester, TN 37398
revamber@comcast.net
(931)967-2121   TNMU#7249

Clark, J Don (M1)
1601 Lake Ridge Circle
Birmingham, AL 35216
jdsjcl@charter.net
(205)942-4054   SEGR#0100

Clark, Jeff (M1)
327 Haynes Haven Lane
Murfreesboro, TN 37129
jclark7733@aol.com
(615)896-7733   TNMU#7250

Clark, Jonathan (M1)
88 Woodcrest Drive
Winchester, TN 37398
FAX: (931)967-8444
clark3568@bellsouth.net
(931)967-9613   TNMU#7200

Clark, Michael (M1)
80 Bryan Drive
Winchester, TN 37398
michael.clark@winchestercp.org
(931)967-2121   TNMU#7249

Clark, Tom (M1)
2089 Sumach Church Road
Chatsworth, GA 30705
(270)469-5468   TNGA#2124

Clark, Tommy (M1)
124 Roberta Drive
Memphis, TN 37216
fattire77@gmail.com
(615)430-9158   TNCO#7126

Coker, Robert N (M1)
721 Lakeview Drive
Loudon, TN 37774
FAX: (865)458-5360
nickcoker@bellsouth.net
(865)458-8791   SEET#2307

Cole, Dwayne (M1)
6460 Village Parkway
Anchorage, AK 99504
tadpolejr@aol.com
(907)854-5793   TNCO#7100

Coleman, Bobby D (M1)
704 E Webb Street
Mountain View, AR 72560
bobbycoleman@gmail.com
(870)213-5410   GRAR#1514

Coleman, Don L (M1)
85 Orchard Lane
Savannah, TN 38372
(731)925-9710   GRWT#9100

Collins, Paul (M1)
915 Warm Sands Drive SE
Albuquerque, NM 87123
FAX: (505)254-7707
chapp3@comcast.net
(505)294-3842   MSDC#8700

Colvard, Kevin (M1)
20024 Crescent Oaks
San Antonio, TX 78258
FAX: (210)497-8724
rev_kev@satx.rr.com
(205)267-9372   MSTR#8608

Compton, Marcia (M1)
6276 Cascade Circle
Indianapolis, IN 46234
mcomptonma@yahoo.com
(317)209-9798   MINC#5200

Condon, Thomas W, Jr (M1)
6508 Victoria Avenue
N Richland Hills, TX 76180
(817)656-9334   MSRR#8400

Condron, Dudley (M1)
1360 Harbert Avenue
Memphis, TN 38104
dudleywcondron@aol.com
(901)726-1488   GRWT#9100

Contini, John (M1)
4344 Poor Ridge Pike
Lancaster, KY 40444
john@hillsidehritagefarm.com
(859)339-0747   MICU#3103

Cook, Carl (M1)
475 Western Hills Loop
Mountain Home, AR 72653
carlc@suddenlink.net
(870)425-2570   GRAR#1100

Cook, Lisa (M1)
4101 Dalemere Court
Nashville, TN 37207
tgoose@comcast.net
(615)868-4118   TNNA#7300

Corbin, Eric (M1)
816 Bluegrass Lane
Champaign, IL 61822
eric@corbinzone.com
(217)239-9945   GRWT#9100

Corbin, William (M1)
7300 N Lamar Road
Mount Juliet, TN 37122
raven.rest@comcast.net
(615)459-8998   TNNA#7300

Correa, John Jairo (M1)
Calle 2 Norte #16-39
Armenia, Quindio, COLOMBIA, SA
FAX: (576)745-4860
jjcedp07@hotmail.com
(318)285-1209   MSAN#8903

Cottingim, Tom (M1)
353 Atwood Drive
Lexington, KY 40515
FAX: (859)272-4315
t.cottingim@insightbb.com
(859)273-3800   MICU#3100

Coulter, Laurance W (M1)
5226 W William Cannon Drive
Austin, TX 78749
FAX: (512)892-6307
larry@shpc.org
(512)892-3580   MSTR#8604

Cox, Jimmy R (M1)
2250 County Road 156
Anderson, AL 35610
dcox01@msn.com
(256)710-1702   SEHO#0508

Craddock, Barry (M3)
147 Moss Way
Glasgow, KY 42141
( )   MICU#3100

Craig, Aaron (M2)
325 Cherry Avenue
McKenzie, TN 38201
(731)352-6718   SEET#2200

Craig, Peggy Jean (M1)
825 S 13th Street Floor 2
Philadelphia, PA 19147
pjfpeggy@gmail.com
(256)277-1147   SEEC#2300

Craig, Robert A (M1)
1711 Bellevue Avenue Apt D-706
Richmond, VA 23227-5123
robertacraig1954@gmail.com
(573)219-8051   MINC#5200

Craven, Mark
21 Kingston Stret'
Chattanooga, TN 37414
craven.ma@gmail.com
(423)618-0169   SETG#2100

Crawford, Roger B (M1)
541 Highway 25 N
Carthage, MS 39051
(601)298-1899   SEGR#0100

Crawshaw, Randy (M1)
136 NE 1271 Road
Knob Noster, MO 65336
randy_crawshaw@yahoo.com
(660)563-5149 GRMI#4115

Creamer, Jennifer (M1)
22 Oakhurst Avenue
Ipswich, MA 01938
jencreamer@gmail.com
(831)809-9890 SEET#2200

Crisp, Gregory W (M1)
635 Eden Brook Lane
Cordova, TN 38018
(901)266-0406 GRWT#9100

Criss, Paul T (M1)
6831 Salem Road
Lakeland, TN 38002
ptcriss@hotmail.com
(901)626-8462 GRWT#9316

Crosby, Ronald (M3)
407 N "A" Street
Calera, OK 74730
( ) MSCH#6100

Croslin, Dennis (M3)
165 Maple Street
Gordonsville, TN .38563
(615)934-2383 TNMU#7246

Cuartas, Joel (M0)
Calle 34 #24A-36
Cali, COLOMBIA, SA
(000)438-2512 MSCA#8211

Cummings, Corey (M1)
1023 W Woodrow Street
Milan, TN 38358
corey@milancp.org
(731)686-1851 GRWT#9108

Cunningham, Matthew Dean (M1)
1646 Brighton-Clopton Road
Brighton, TN 38011
mcunningham0528@comcast.net
(901)475-4252 GRWT#9318

--==<< **D** >>==--

Dalwig, Roger (M1)
1661 Hickory Lane
Corydon, IN 47112
rcd129@hotmail.com
(812)705-5071 MINC#5200

Dalton, Frank (M2)
1606 Ebenezer Road
Troy, TN 38260
(731)536-4553 GRWT#9100

Daniels, Doy L, Jr (M1)
1095 Crestview Drive
Milan, TN 38358
revdrdoy@gmail.com
(731)686-1851 GRWT#9121

Darland, Chris (M1)
582 Ada Drive
Harrodsburg, KY 40330
(859)734-2254 MICU#3303

Davenport, Donna (M1)
PO Box 234
Wingo, KY 42088
chamberdonna@yahoo.com
(270)376-5488 MICO#3400

Davenport, Mark A (M1)
323 Chimney Rock Drive #1314
Tyler, TX 75703
hoginbama@yahoo.com
(205)427-4941 MSTR#8100

Davenport, Vondal (M1)
PO Box 823
Lavaca, AR 72941
(479)965-2036 GRAR#1408

Davis, C Timothy (M1)
8880 Childress Road
West Paducah, KY 42086
FAX: (904)994-6003
charles0828@earthlink.net
(850)995-8383 SEGR#0100

Davis, Robert (Toby) (M1)
502 S Alley Street
Jefferson, TX 75657
pastortobydavis@gmail.com
(901)826-5755 MSTR#8109

Daza, Edilberto (M1)
Cra 12 #8-47
Cartago, Valle
Colombia, South America
presbicartago@gmail.com
57(314)794-1905 MSAN#8900

Daza, Johan (M1)
8148 Yellow Stone Drive
Cordova, TN 38016
jdaza@cumberland.org
(281)793-3869 MSAN#8900

De Jimenez, Luciria Aguirre (M1)
AA6365
COLOMBIA, SA
pastorluciana50@yahoo.com.co
(300)686-9161 MSCA#8200

De Vries, Raymond (M1)
2080 Stanford Village Drive
Antioch, TN 37013
ray.devries@comcast.net
(615)332-3587 TNNA#7300

De Wees, Jeff (M1)
116 Lancaster Court
Gallatin, TN 37066
pastorjeff@beechcp.com
(931)209-3331 TNNA#7301

Deaton, John (M1)
277 School Lanet
Springfield, PA 19064
deatonjr11@gmail.com
(215)906-7067 SEHO#0500

Deere, Thomas (Tom) (M1)
460 Yukon Drive
Russellville, AR 72802
tdeere@suddenlinkmail.com
(479)498-0318 GRAR#1100

Delashmit, Steve (M1)
2705 Garrett Drive
Bowling Green, KY 42104
FAX: (270)781-2368
(270)796-8822 MICU#3304

Dewhirst, Tim (M3)
3609 Oakbriar Lane
Colleyville, TX 76034
timdew@sbcglobal.net
(817)605-8147 MSRR#8415

Diamond, Cardelia Howell (M1)
1580 Jeff Road
Huntsville, AL 35806
cpclergymama@gmail.com
(256)837-6014 SERD#0814

Diamond, James (M1)
214 Falmouth Drive
Georgetown, KY 40324
james.diamond007@comcast.net
(615)220-2341 MICU#3100

Diamond, Steven (M1)
106 Ultimate Court
Madison, AL 35757
smdiam@hotmail.com
(931)636-7336 SERD#0800

Diaz, Esperanza (M1)
Calle 2 Norte #16-19
Armenia, Quindio, COLOMBIA, SA
jjcedp07@hotmail.com
(576)745-0496 MSAN#8903

Diaz, Freddy (M1)
2425 Holly Hall Apt B42
Houston, TX 77054
fredglobeus@yahoo.com
(832)305-2379 MSTR#8606

Diaz, Gloria Villa (M1)
2425 Holly Hall Apt B42
Houston, TX 77054
gloria@newdayinchrist.org
(832)758-5871 MSTR#8100

Diaz, William (M1)
Calle 5 Con Cra 89
Cali, COLOMBIA, SA
nuevaesperanza1983@hotmail.com
( )332-5849 MSCA#8221

Diego, Aida Melendez (M2)
412 SW 87 Place
Miami, FL 33174
revaidamd@yahoo.com
(305)815-1197 SEGR#0100

Dimo, Urelia (M3)
171 Roberta Drive
Memphis, TN 38112
( ) GRWT#9100

Doles, Steve (M1)
7702 Indiana Avenue
Lubbock, TX 79423
steve@cpclubbock.com
(806)787-7551 MSDC#8702

Dougherty, Duane A, Jr (M1)
212 County Road 4705
Troup, TX 75789
revdad.duane@gmail.com
(903)842-474 MSTR#8104

Driskell, James P (M1)
154 Mountain Way
Anderson, AL 35610
FAX: (256)247-3339
patprespax@yahoo.com
(256)648-6758 SEHO#0517

Duke, Michael E (M1)
106 Friar Tuck Drive
Dickson, TN 37055
(615)446-6515 TNNA#7300

Dukes, Britta (M1)
5226 W William Cannon Drive
Austin, TX 78749
FAX: (512)892-6307
britta@shpc.org
(512)892-3580 MSTR#8604

Dumas, Byron (M1)
1775 Theresa Drive
Clarksville, TN 37043
bdumas7346@aol.com
(931)552-8772 TNNA#3302

Duncan, Ronnie (M1)
146 Deseree Broyles Road
Chuckey, TN 37641
ronkduncan@icloud.com
(423)552-0321 SEET#2204

MINISTERS CONTINUED

Dyer, Stuart (M1)
3574 Foxfield Trail
Bartlett, TN 38135
(901)388-0612   GRWT#9100

--==<< E >>==--

Earheart-Brown, Daniel J (Jay) (M1)
475 N Highland Street Apt 9L
Memphis, TN 38122
jebrown@memphisseminary.edu
(901)278-0367   TNNA#7300

Earheart-Brown, Paul (M3)
502 E Lamar Alexander Parkway
Box 2519
Maryville, TN 37804
( )   GRWT#9100

Eatherly, John (M1)
1377 Moss Road
Chapel Hill, TN 37034
jrev@united.net
(931)364-2087   TNCO#7127

Eddleman, Keith (M1)
2787 Stage Park Drive
Memphis, TN 38134
(901)388-9885   GRWT#9100

Edmonds, Wayne (M1)
112 Dogwood Trail
Eclectic, AL 36024
sweetpea@comlinkinc.net
(334)857-2202   SEGR#0100

Edwards, James Scott (M3)
226 Jasmine Drive
Alabaster, AL 35007
jedwards53163@bellsouth.net
(205)529-4507   SEGR#0101

Edwards, Joey (M1)
5279 Ivy Creek Lane
Lakeland, TN 38002
edwardsjoey@bellsouth.net
(901)573-7579   GRWT#9314

Emsinger, Mike (M3)
4910 Cox Cove
Helena, AL 35080
me0573@att.com
(205)620-4699   SEGR#0108

English, Don W (M1)
4311 Guys Court
Bessemer, AL 35022
(205)428-4790   SEGR#0100

Eppard, Andrew (M1)
1427 W McGee Street
Springfield, MO 65807
reformedminister@yahoo.com
(417)862-6434   GRMI#4314

Espinoza, Virginia (M1)
PO Box 132
Boswell, OK 74727
vespinoza@choctawnation.com
(580)434-7971   MSCH#6109

Estep, William (M1)
239 Skyline Drive
Harriman, TN 37748
(865)882-5114   TNMU#7200

Estes, George R (M1)
7910 Cloverbrook Lane
Germantown, TN 38138
geoestes@gmail.com
(901)755-6673   MSDC#8700

Estes, Sam R, Jr (M1)
3026 54th Street
Lubbock, TX 79413
(806)748-6116   MSDC#8700

--==<< F >>==--

Fackler, David (M1)
3409 Benton Road
Paducah, KY 42003
woodlawnpastor@live.com
(270)442-7713   MICO#3417

Fahl, D Frederick (Fred) (M1)
500 3rd Street
Fulton, KY 42041
dffahl@gmail.com
(270)472-1476   MICO#3419

Fancher, Michael E (M3)
356 Breeding Road
Edmonton, KY 42129
princo1975@live.com
(270)579-3139   MICU#3101

Fell, Ron (M1)
PO Box 285
Fairfield, IL 62837
r.fell80@gmail.com
(618)638-3744   MINC#5124

Ferguson, David (M2)
1841 Pebble Lake Drive
Birmingham, AL 35232
fergusondavid15@yahoo.com
(205)200-9205   SEGR#0105

Ferguson, E Blant (M1)
704 Bear Run
Hiawassee, GA 30546
blantferg@yahoo.com
(706)896-9296   TNNA#7300

Ferguson, Elizabeth (M1)
PO Box 839
Sewanee, TN 37375
ferguea9@gmail.com
(931)636-8076   TNMU#7200

Ferree, Carole (M1)
2475 Fallen Timber Road
Campbellsville, KY 42718
ferree047@windstream.net
(270)789-4339   MICU#3100

Ferrell, Timothy W (M1)
1850 Dunbar Road
Woodlawn, TN 37191
ferrelltw@aol.com
(931)920-2662   TNNA#7310

Ferrol, Ruben (M1)
1823 Straford Court
Allentown, PA 18103
rubeferrol@msn.com
(610)966-7289   MSRR#8400

Fife, Patric (M1)
73 Jordan Road
Lawrenceburg, TN 38464
pnlfifernak@gmail.com
(931)629-8146   TNCO#7130

Fike, Charles (M1)
2070 N 1st Street
Milan, TN 38358
(731)686-0224   GRWT#9418

Fisk, James R (M1)
1 Webb Lane
Bella Vista, AR 72714
jimfisk95@yahoo.com
(479)886-1216   GRAR#1100

Fleming, Christopher (M1)
133 Minerva Place
Paducah, KY 42001
holyday@vci.net
(615)424-8561   MICO#3415

Fleming, Patrick T (M1)
616 N Border Street
Benton, AR 72015
ptfleming@live.com
(501)944-4678   GRAR#1100

Flores, Fabian (M3)
Aereo 6365, Cali Valle
COLOMBIA, SA
( )   MSCA#8222

Fly, William (M1)
3002 Trowbridge Drive
Paragould, AR 72450
billyfly3@gmail.com
(865)938-6273   SEET#2200

Fong, Danny (M1)
1224 Fairfax Avenue
San Francisco, CA 94124
dfong@redeemersf.org
(415)671-2194   MSDC#8512

Fonseca, Roberto (M1)
Cll 46 A No 4N 25
Colombia, South America
( )446-3311   MSCA#8218

Foreman, Samuel L (M1)
2811 Laredo Drive
Hattiesburg, MS 39402
slfcpc@yahoo.com
(601)562-1415   SEGR#0100

Forester, Byron (M1)
2376 Eastwood Place
Memphis, TN 38112
bforester@bellsouth.net
(901)324-1707   GRWT#9207

Fortner, Terry (M1)
1079 Luzerne Depoy Road
Greenville, KY 42345
terryfortner@att.net
(270)821-6541   MICU#3508

Fortney, Josh (M1)
765 Windridge Lane
Burleson, TX 76028
jfortney@pathway.church
(214)794-9912   MSRR#8418

Fossey, Donald, II (M3)
328 Waterloo Road
Cookeville, TN 38506
dfossey@twlakes.net
(931)498-2149   TNMU#7223

Fowler, Scott (M1)
1900 Alex Mill Road
Montevallo, AL 35115
springcreekcp@aol.com
(205)901-8478   SEGR#0113

Franco, Ricardo (M1)
7 Hancock Street
Melrose, MA 02176
casadefericardo@verizon.net
(781)662-0267   SEET#2200

Franklin, Chris (M1)
310 Yellow Springs Road
Midway, TN 37809
chrisfranklin104@comcast.net
(423)972-3609   SEET#2208

Franklin, Curtis (M1)
7620 Cross Mill Road
Paducah, KY 42001
brocurtis@fredonia.biz
(270)545-3481   MICO#3410

Freeman, A Daniel (M1)
210 Dogwood Drive
Greeneville, TN 37743
(423)638-5925   SEET#2200

MINISTERS CONTINUED

Freeman, Jesse L, Jr (M1)
270 Eastside Road
Burns, TN 37029
mptc@bellsouth.net
(615)202-4594 TNNA#7307

French, Jeff (M1)
5 Rose Petal Lane
Dawson Springs, KY 42408
brojeff7@bellsouth.net
(270)993-0855 MICO#3400

Freund, Henry O (M1)
913 Sam Houston Drive
Dyersburg, TN 38024
freundly@att.net
(731)285-1744 MSDC#8700

Frost, Sherrlyn (M1)
5557 Surrey Lane
Birmingham, AL 35242
FAX: (205)991-5259
sherrlyn@newhopecpc.org
(205)408-0729 SEGR#0104

Fulton, James (M1)
1520 Oak Grove Road
Benton, KY 42025
(270)437-4320 MICO#3619

Fung, David (M1)
1846 Gunston Way
San Jose, CA 95124
(408)266-3398 MSDC#8700

Fung, Lawrence (M1)
367 El Dorado Drive
Daly City, CA 94015
revfung@yahoo.com
(650)756-1702 MSDC#8700

Furr, Wayne (M1)
706 E 6th Street
Coal Valley, IL 61240
prespreacher@gmail.com
(309)791-1691 MINC#5200

Furuhata, Kazuhiko (M1)
#310, 9-41-15 Kamitsurumahoncho
Minamiku Sagamihara-shi
Kanagawa-ken
cpc.furuhata@gmail.com
252-0318, JAPAN
(501)430-8885 MSJA#8310

--==<< G >>==--

Gaither, Randy (M1)
No 3 Pacific Street
Belmopan City
BELIZE, CENTRAL AMERICA
rgaither@valuelinx.net
( ) SEGR#0100

Galvis, Alexander (M1)
Calle 76 #87-14
Medellin, Antioquia, COLOMBIA, SA
alexgt7@hotmail.com
(300)778-4354 MSAN#8906

Gam, John (M1)
1235 Sanders Street
Auburn, AL 36830
( ) GRWT#9100

Garcia, Lucas (M3)
875 Scenic Highway
Lawrenceville, GA 30045
(678)698-7971 SETG#2100

Garcia, Maria (Mabe) (M1)
875 Scenic Highway
Lawrenceville, GA 30045
FAX: (678)225-0127
mabega@juno.com
(678)698-7971 SETG#2149

Garcia, Ramon (M1)
2714 Callista Court Apt 104
Naples, FL 34114
revga@hotmail.com
(239)200-5714 SEGR#0100

Gardner, Charles (M1)
PO Box 1035
Elephant Butte, NM 87935
(719)784-7744 MSRR#8400

Gary, Brian (M1)
105 Wilma Avenue
Radcliff, KY 40160
(502)351-6938 MICU#3100

Gaskill, Todd (M1)
430 Haysland Road
Petersburg, TN 37144
tgaskill@pens.com
(931)580-2708 TNCO#7121

Gaskin, Tony (M1)
1414 Saint Joseph Street NW
Cullman, AL 35055
tgaskin46@hotmail.com
(256)338-7893 TNCO#7100

Gates, J B (M1)
PO Box 289
Enfield, IL 62835
rjjbgate@hamiltoncom.net
(618)963-2306 MINC#5104

Gaviria, Mario (M1)
Cra 27 #7-48
Cali, COLOMBIA, SA
pastormariogaviria@hotmail.com
(314)773-2601 MSCA#8201

Gehle, Jeffrey A (M1)
PO Box 182
Burleson, TX 76097
FAX: (817)295-2576
jeff.gehle@pathway.church
(817)295-5832 MSRR#8418

Gentry, Michele (M1)
Urb San Jorge casa 28
Km 8 via a La Tebaida
Armenia, Quindio, COLOMBIA, SA
gentry.andes@yahoo.com
(318)285-1161 MSAN#8900

George, Thomas (M2)
908 N Brown Avenue
Casa Grande, AZ 85222
tgeorge@aerogram.net
(640)447-2676 MSDC#8700

Gerard, Eugene S (M1)
615 N 42nd Street
Paducah, KY 42001
(270)443-2889 MICO#3400

Gilliam, Cody (M3)
2881 Old Big Cove Road SE
Owens Cross Roads, AL 35763
roostergilliam@outlook.com
(256)655-7073 SERD#0800

Gillis, Aubrey Thomas (M1)
110 Blue Sky Lane
Alabaster, AL 35007
FAX: (205)664-8323
tomgillis63@hotmail.com
(251)947-1638 SERD#0800

Gillis, Ernest H (M1)
3273 Bruckner Boulevard
Snellville, GA 30078
professorgil64@hotmail.com
(770)982-6587 SEET#2200

Gillock, Ed (M1)
PO Box 157
Savannah, TN 38372
(731)609-6744 GRWT#9100

Giraldo, Andres (M2)
Calle 76 #87-14 Apto 202
Medellin, Antioquia, COLOMBIA, SA
andresgiraldo@une.net.co
(574)422-6669 MSAN#8911

Giraldo, Marcela (M3)
Calle 68 D #40-15
Manizales, Caldas, COLOMBIA, SA
(576)878-5412 MSAN#8900

Giraldo, William (M1)
CLL 62 No 18 11
Cali, COLOMBIA, SA
( )439-5436 MSCA#8200

Giron, Francisco (M1)
3451 Los Mochis Way
Oceanside, CA 92056
FAX: (760)414-1236
thegirons@cox.net
(760)203-0381 MSDC#8700

Glenn, Linda H (M1)
49 Mason Road
Threeway, TN 38343
lindahglenn@click1.net
(731)618-0192 GRWT#9119

Goehring, Marty (M1)
8600 Academy NE
Albuquerque, NM 87111
FAX: (505)797-8599
mgoehring@heightscpc.org
(505)821-3628 MSDC#8701

Gonzales, Homer (M1)
8924 Armistice NE
Albuquerque, NM 87109
FAX: (505)841-4267
hgabq1985@gmail.com
(505)821-4376 MSDC#8700

Gonzales, Miguel (M1)
200 Bethel Drive
Lenoir City, TN 37772
(865)988-4238 SEET#2320

Gonzalez, Nora (M1)
2515 Blueberry Lane
Pasadena, TX 77052
(832)202-5572 MSTR#8100

Goodloe, Melissa Reid (M1)
225 Macedonia Road
McKenzie, TN 38201
rev.mgoodloe@shilohcp.org
(731)412-9657 GRWT#9131

Goodman, Robert (M1)
604 N Fourth Street
Marlow, OK 73055
rgoodman4gvn@hotmail.com
(580)756-4726 MSRR#8400

Goodwill, James L (M1)
205 S English Hill Lane
Hillsborough, NC 27278
jim@jimgoodwill.com
(704)526-8729 TNNA#7300

Goodwin, Earl (M1)
1012 Windsor Parkway
Moody, AL 35004
FAX: (205)664-8323
earlgoodwin@yahoo.com
(205)222-1741 SERD#0107

Gough, Ernest E (M1)
8366 Highway 70
Nashville, TN 37221
eegough@bellsouth.net
(615)646-4372 TNNA#7300

MINISTERS CONTINUED

Graham, Steve (M1)
11108 Thornton Drive
Knoxville, TN 37934
(865)206-0012   SEET#2316

Gray, Brad (M3)
6378 Highway 59 S
Mason, TN 38049
dgray@aol.com
(901)475-6140   GRWT#9100

Gray, Drew (M1)
8220 Timberland Drive
West Paducah, KY 42086
drewgray01@gmail.com
(615)332-8360   MICO#3222

Gray, Isaac (M1)
512 Ed Taft Road
Smithville, TN 37166
revgray08@gmail.com
(870)373-4731   TNMU#7243

Gray, Randall (M1)
1230 New Liberty Big Meadow Road
Knob Lick, KY 42154
(270)432-5322   MICU#3120

Green, Harry N (M1)
45 Wood Way
McMinnville, TN 37110
(931)815-9190   TNMU#7200

Green, Larry (M1)
525 Dearman Street
Smithville, TN 37166
larrylgreen24@aol.com
(615)597-5832   TNMU#7244

Green, Paul (M1)
5228 Anchorage Avenue
El Paso, TX 79924
(915)751-7960   MSDC#8700

Green, Troy (M1)
105 Cobb Hollow Lane
Petersburg, TN 37144
thegreens101@att.net
(931)659-6627   TNCO#7135

Greene, Tammy L (M1)
109 Armitage Drive
Greeneville, TN 37745
tg6386@aol.com
(423)972-5525   SEET#2217

Greenwell, James C (M1)
7165 Wind Whisper Boulevard
Knoxville, TN 37924
FAX: (865)742-1653
greenwelljc@comcast.net
(865)742-1653   SEET#2200

Griffin, Adam (M3)
23502 Clinton Road
Lebanon, MO 65536
plowboy3500@hotmail.com
(417)588-2522   GRMI#4100

Griffin, Justin (M1)
3655 Highway 49 E
Charlotte, TN 37036
jjjjgriff@gmail.com
(615)969-2426   TNNA#7320

Grimsley, Roger (M1)
215 N Oak Street
Springfield, TN 37172
( )   GRWT#9100

Gross, Ronald (M1)
2436 N 420th Street
Oblong, IL 62449
juneg@eiis.net
(217)932-2788   MINC#5200

Guarneros, Stephen H (M1)
506 Clifton Court
Hopkinsville, KY 42240
pastorsteve88@yahoo.com
(270)869-7544   MICO#3400

Guasaquillo, Samuel (M3)
Aereo 10701, Cali
COLOMBIA, SA
FAX: (408)255-5938
( )   MSCA#8204

Guerrero, Cruzana (M1)
Calle 83 #74-179
Medellin, Antioguia, COLOMBIA, SA
(574)257-0613   MSAN#8919

Guerrero, Josue (M1)
Calle 76 #88-65
Medellin, Antioquia, COLOMBIA, SA
josueggutierrez@yahoo.es
(574)412-3504   MSAN#8919

Guerrero, Luz Dary (M1)
Calle 22 #25-33
Manizales, Caldas, COLOMBIA, SA
clementinajacobo7@hotmail.com
(576)888-4203   MSAN#8900

Guin, Larry (M1)
125 Glider Loop
Eagleville, TN 37060
lguin43@hotmail.com
(615)668-5236   TNCO#7123

Guthrie, William (M1)
11130 Frenchmen Loop Apt B
Maumelle, AR 72113
billybarloe@yahoo.com
(501)584-0019   GRAR#1100

Guye, Dean (M1)
2759 Highway 70 E
Dickson, TN 37055
deanjoy@att.net
(615)446-7687   TNNA#7303

--=＝<< H >>＝=--

Ha, Ting Bong (M2)
3/F 338-340 Castle Peak Road
Kowloon, HONG KONG
FAX: (852)3020-0365
tingbongha@yahoo.com.hk
(852)2386-6563   MSHK#8803

Hackman-Truhan, Deborah (M1)
7314 N Miramar Drive
Peoria, IL 61614
cprevdeb@hotmail.com
(931)537-9040   TNMU#7200

Hagelin, Gerald (M1)
10851 E Old Spanish Trail
Tucson, AZ 85712
azcef@cs.com
(520)275-8110   MSDC#8705

Haire, Shelby O (M1)
3179 Meeting Creek Road
Eastview, KY 42732
(270)862-3887   MICU#3219

Halford, Angela (M1)
PO Box 404
Sebastopol, MS 39359
revhalford@gmail.com
(501)251-4668   GRAR#0607

Hall, Brad (M1)
1602 Toll Gate Road SE
Huntsville, AL 35801
(256)533-4845   SERD#0800

Hall, John D (M1)
109 Oddo Lane SE
Huntsville, AL 35802
johnhall33@comcast.net
(256)880-5129   SERD#0800

Hall, Roy W (M1)
87 Lee Hall Street
Scottsboro, AL 35769
royhall@scottsboro.org
(256)259-9340   SERD#0809

Hamazaki, Takashi (M1)
1551-1-202 Inokuchi Nakai-cho
Ashigarakami-gun
Kanagawa-ken
259-0151, JAPAN
gen22-14@qf7.so-net.ne.jp
(046)543-8550   MSJA#8300

Hamblin, James R (M1)
60 Rolling Meadow Drive
Drummonds, TN 38023
brojim391@gmail.com
(901)840-4747   GRWT#9321

Hamelink, Ronald L (M1)
5045 Starlite Court
Las Cruces, NM 88012
hamronelink@yahoo.com
(575)640-4341   GRAR#1100

Hames, Anne (M1)
118 Paris Street
McKenzie, TN 38201
hamesa@bethelu.edu
(731)352-4066   GRWT#9122

Hamilton, Bruce (M1)
1037 Binns Drive
Monticello, AR 71655
bruce@hamiltonnet.org
(870)224-5007   GRAR#1106

Hamilton, Helen (M3)
300 Tennessee Street
Savannah, TN 38372
helmackham@aol.com
(731)925-4493   GRWT#9224

Han, Seung Chon (M0)
3075 Landington Way
Duluth, GA 30096
kpc0191@gmail.com
(678)469-5015   SETG#2100

Hancock, B J (M1)
103 W Cowan Street
Cowan, TN 37318
(931)967-8491   TNMU#7200

Hancock, Paul (M1)
107 Highland Ridge
Hendersonville, TN 37075
paul.hancock6@comcast.net
(615)4269-4331   TNMU#7233

Hannah, Hugh (M1)
217 Mitchell Road SE
Cleveland, TN 37323
pjhannah23@hotmail.com
(423)473-7852   MSTR#8100

Hansen, Terry (M1)
16549 Highway 5
Lebanon, MO 65536
(417)533-8106   GRMI#4315

Harbour, Ethan (M2)
77 Burton Road
Booneville, AR 72927
ethanharbour@gmail.com
(479)849-6329   GRAR#1100

MINISTERS CONTINUED

Hardisty, Randy (M1)
4908 Redondo Street
Fort Worth, TX 76180
rhardisty@sbcglobal.net
(817)428-3513 MSRR#8409

Harper, Carlton (M1)
255 Glenview Cove
Lenoir City, TN 37771
carltonharperone@gmail.com
(865)317-1296 SEET#2200

Harper, Josh (M1)
227 LaCroix Drive #1
Collierville, TN 38017
jdharperministry@hotmail.com
(615)934-7940 TNMU#7200

Harris, Anthony (M2)
1604 Parkview Drive
Campbellsville, KY 42718
aharris044@gmail.com
(270)403-1126 MICU#3214

Harris, Edward (M1)
10000 Wornall Road Apt 2315
Kansas City, MO 64114
ed121@kcrr.com
(816)214-8977 GRMI#4100

Harris, Ernest (M1)
610 Turtle Creek Drive
Reno, TX 75462
ernie.jeri@yahoo.com
(903)782-9712 MSTR#8100

Harris, Robert (M1)
619 N 24th Avenue
Humboldt, TN 38343
pastor@humboldtcpc.org
(731)420-6067 GRWT#9116

Harris, Rodney E (M1)
7420 Conjar Court
Louisville, KY 40214
rodneypat@insightbb.com
(502)368-5501 MICU#3212

Harris, Wendell (M1)
329 N Louis Tittle Avenue
Mangum, OK 73554
wendellharris@itlnet.net
(580)782-2142 MSRR#8400

Harrison, Richard (M3)
93 Earl Jones Road
Hodgenville, KY 42748
( ) MICU#3119

Hartman, Gary (M1)
3001 Hines Valley Road
Lenoir City, TN 37771
g37771@att.net
(865)986-4949 SEET#2200

Hartung, J Thomas (M1)
2291 Americus Boulevard W Apt 1
Clearwater, FL 33763
revtom6@aol.com
(727)797-2882 SEGR#0100

Harwell, Jacob (M2)
319 Joy Drive
McKenzie, TN 38201
rjharwell@student.memphisseminary.edu
(731)415-1457 GRWT#9100

Harwell, Keith (M1)
13132 Stinson Street
Milan, TN 38358
(731)613-3780 GRWT#9100

Harwell, Sam (M1)
23 Lake Hayes Estates Road
Trenton, TN 38382
sambharl@yahoo.com
(731)414-2153 GRWT#9127

Hassell, Samantha (M3)
510 N Main Street
Sturgis, KY 42459
FAX: (270)333-3118
hassell_samantha@hotmail.com
(270)333-9170 MICO#3400

Hassell, Victor (M1)
510 N Main Street
Sturgis, KY 42459
FAX: (270)333-3118
hassellvictor@hotmail.com
(270)333-9170 MICO#3625

Hawley, David R (M1)
127 John Holt Road
Beech Bluff, TN 38313
haw177@aol.com
(731)427-7284 GRWT#9204

Hayes, Brian (M1)
69 Cactus Drive
Benton, KY 42025
cprevbhayes@gmail.com
(270)210-8165 MICO#3422

Hayes, Drew (M1)
6322 Labor Lane
Louisville, KY 40291
dhayes72@gmail.com
(731)796-7076 GRWT#9100

Hayes, Jennifer (M1)
102 River Drive
McMinnville, TN 37110
hayesj712@gmail.com
(205)533-1018 TNMU#7222

Hayes, Marcus (M1)
102 River Drive
McMinnville, TN 37110
marcus.hayes@att.net
(270)841-7576 TNMU#7222

Headrick, Anthony (M1)
3327 N Eagle Road Ste 110-132
Meridian, ID 83646
chaps2a@yahoo.com
(619)524-8821 SEGR#0100

Headrick, Christopher (M1)
1913 Vestavia Court Apt B
Vestavia Hills, AL 35216
bravespop@gmail.com
(205)240-0979 SEGR#0100

Headrick, Jerry (M1)
9950 Old Stage Road
Stockton, AL 36579
willjheadrick@gmail.com
(251)377-9744 SEGR#0100

Heflin, Donna S (M1)
4144 Meadow Court Drive
Bartlett, TN 38135
rdheflin@bellsouth.net
(901)382-8198 GRWT#9100

Heflin, Robert (M1)
4144 Meadow Court Drive
Bartlett, TN 38135
rdheflin@bellsouth.net
(901)382-8198 TNCO#7100

Heidel, Jason (M1)
218 Morningside Drive
Hopkinsville, KY 42240
heidelj@hotmail.com
(270)498-7380 MICO#3400

Heilbron, Luz Maria (M1)
Cra 12 bis #11-51
Pereira, Risaralda, COLOMBIA, SA
pastorapresbi@hotmail.com
(576)333-9295 MSAN#8916

Hendershot, Charles A (M1)
122 Tree Shadow
Whitney, TX 76692
(254)694-3852 MSRR#8400

Henson, Kevin R (M1)
1121 Raleigh Path
Denton, TX 76208
khenson@servproofheb.com
(817)354-1182 MSRR#8419

Heo, Mu Sak (M1)
170 Applewood Drive #210
Lawrenceville, GA 30046
drhou@hanmail.net
(404)644-6514 SETG#2100

Hernandez, Jhonathan (M3)
10090 NW 80th Court
Hialeah Gardens, FL 33016
jhoto2006@hotmail.com
(786)508-8578 SEGR#0100

Hernden, Matthew (M3)
206 Smith Lane
Brighton, TN 38011
mhernden023@gmail.com
(901)484-7661 GRWT#9100

Herring, C F (Ed), Jr (M1)
969 Campground Circle
Scottsboro, AL 35769
edherring@scottsboro.org
(256)259-2721 SERD#0800

Herston, Terry (M1)
390 County Road 95
Rogersville, AL 35652
tpaw51@gmail.com
(256)247-3004 SEHO#0513

Hess, Jean (M1)
2200 E Dartmouth Circle
Englewood, CO 80113
jeanhess@316denver.com
(303)504-0275 MSDC#8700

Hess, Rick (M1)
2200 E Dartmouth Circle
Englewood, CO 80113
rick@densem.edu
(303)504-0275 MSDC#8700

Hester, Mark S (M1)
763 Finn Long Road
Friendsville, TN 37737
markshester@att.net
(865)995-1541 SEET#2200

Hill, Jody (M1)
4030 St Andrew Circle
Corinth, MS 38834
jody.hill34@gmail.com
(662)512-8226 GRWT#9100

Ho, Carmen (M2)
Tin Yuet Estate
Tin Shui Wai NT, HONG KONG
FAX: (852)2617-0287
ho_carcar@yahoo.com.hk
(852)2617-7872 MSHK#8801
ho_carcar@yahoo.com.hk

Ho, Kelvin (M2)
11 On Wing Centre, 2/F
Pak She Back Street
Cheung Chau, HONG KONG
kelvinskho@gmail.com
(852)2981-4933 MSHK#8801

Hocker, David (M3)
309 N Taylor Street
Morgantown, KY 42261
davidhocker@hockerins.com
(270)526-6027 MICU#3311

MINISTERS CONTINUED

Hoke, Walter   (M1)
215 Navajo Trail
Georgetown, TX 78633
(512)869-1948   MSTR#8100

Holley, Ann   (M1)
PO Box 345
Lockesburg, AR 71846
ladyrev1115@yahoo.com
(870)289-3421   GRAR#1310

Hollingshed, Lee   (M3)
3612 Harmony Church Grove Road
Dallas, GA 30132
leearmstrong@bellsouth.net
(770)548-0152   SETG#2100

Holmes, Aaron G   (M1)
PO Box 171
Atwood, TN 38220
agholmes@charter.net
(731)662-7595   GRWT#9100

Holt, Billy Jack   (M1)
5039 Highway 37 N
Clarksville, TX 75426
jackdora@windstream.net
(903)428-9909   MSTR#8125

Hom, Patti   (M3)
811 Faxon Avenue
San Francisco, CA 94112
phom@gfccsf.org
(415)486-5998   MSDC#8700

Hom, Paul   (M1)
722 24th Avenue
San Francisco, CA 94121
FAX: (415)386-8423
(415)751-9766   MSDC#8700

Hong, Soon Gab   (M1)
13600 Doty Avenue Apt 4
Hawthorne, CA 90250
lemuelhong@hotmail.com
(972)446-0350   MSRR#8400

Hood, Charles   (M1)
6535 Bailey Road
Anderson, AL 35610
hooddad11@gmail.com
(256)229-6251   SEHO#0516

Hopkins, Daniel   (M2)
1608 Oak Park Boulevard
Calvert City, KY 42029
danielhopkins2469@yahoo.com
(270)205-1847   MICO#3400

Hopkins, Wayne   (M3)
1413 E Unity Church Road
Hardin, KY 42048
(270)437-4481   MICO#3400

Howe, Francis   (M1)
129 Manley Street
McKenzie, TN 38201
(731)352-5551   GRWT#9100

Howell, Linda   (M1)
PO Box 80050
Keller, TX 76244
lshowell1000@yahoo.com
(601)942-2015   MSRR#8400

Howton, Orvie Ray   (M1)
4928 Montauk Trail SE
Owens Cross Road, AL 35763
orphowton@yahoo.com
(256)533-9224   SERD#0800

Hoyos, Javier   (M3)
Calle 34 24A-36
Cali, COLOMBIA, SA
(   )445-5556   MSCA#8200

Hubbard, Donald   (M1)
2128 N Campbell Station Road
Knoxville, TN 37932
djhubbard@mindspring.com
(865)693-0264   SEET#2200

Hubbard, Pratt   (M1)
1565 Eli Brown Road
McKenzie, TN 38201
(731)352-9178   GRWT#9100

Hudson, Barney   (M1)
10541 Fossil Hill Drive
Fort Worth, TX 76131
barneyrev@gmail.com
(817)851-2960   MSRR#8425

Hudson, George Cliff   (M1)
4782 Waverly Court
Ooltewah, TN 37363
gchudson3@gmail.com
(423)238-6333   SETG#2106

Hudson, Jennifer   (M3)
716 Apache Drive
Marshall, MO 65340
(660)631-3893   GRMI#4100

Huey, Sharon   (M1)
3265 16th Street
San Francisco, CA 94103
sharon_huey@yahoo.com
(415)703-6090   MSDC#8510

Hughes, Charles   (M1)
114 Gaul Street
Estill Springs, TN 37330
cphugs@cafes.net
(931)649-5189   SERD#0800

Hughes, Douglas   (M1)
5545 Hocker Road
Paducah, KY 42001
milburnchapel@gmail.com
(270)488-2588   MICO#3400

Hughes, Richard W   (M1)
2954 Bob Wade Lane
Harvest, AL 35749
hughesrichard23@gmail.com
(256)859-3178   SERD#0806

Hullander, Jerry (Butch)   (M1)
767 Rifle Range Road
Greeneville, TN 37743
jerryihs@catt.com
(706)935-4878   SETG#2107

Hung, Ella Siu Kei   (M1)
2/F Welland Plaza
188 Nam Cheong Street
Sham Shui Po, Kowloon, HONG KONG
FAX: (852)2771-2726
siukee@taohsien.org.hk
(852)2794-2382   MSHK#8800

Hunley, Jearl   (M1)
2618 Canterbury Road
Columbus, MS 39705
jdhunley@cableone.net
(662)329-1516   SEGR#0100

Hunley, Terry M   (M1)
48 Charleston Square
Jackson, TN 38305
thunley1@charter.net
(731)660-5685   GRWT#9208

Hunt, Shelley   (M2)
6035 State Route 506
Marion, KY 42064
sheljean@kynet.biz
(270)704-2189   MICO#3615

Hurley, E C   (M1)
221 Fantasia Way
Clarksville, TN 37043
hurleyec@gmail.com
(931)551-6173   TNNA#7300

Hyden, John   (M1)
6525 Peytonsville Arno Road
College Grove, TN 37046
cp1876@hotmail.com
(615)975-9584   TNCO#7116

--==<< I >>==--

Ikushima, Michinobu   (M1)
2074 Nakashinden
Ebina-Shi Kanagawa-Ken
243-0422 JAPAN
m.ikushima@tbz.t-com.ne.jp
(046)232-9888   MSJA#8300

Impastato, Paulino   (M3)
1547 Mt Zion Church Road
Marion, KY 42064
(270)965-9528   MICO#3400

Ingram, Matthew   (M3)
29 Quincy Lane
Montevallo, AL 35115
mbingram80@gmail.com
(205)914-0829   SEGR#0100

Inoh, Yuki   (M3)
Tokyo Christian University
3-301-5 Uchino Inzai-shi, Chiba
270-1347 JAPAN
yuki_inoh0615@yahoo.co.jp
(047)646-1141   MSJA#8300

Ishitsuka, Keishi   (M1)
Nucleo Colonial JK
Lote 56 Mata De Sao Joao
48280-000, Bahia, BRAZIL
FAX: (5571)3664-1019
kishitsuka@hotmail.com
(5571)3664-1019   MSJA#8313

Ivey, Billy F   (M1)
409 Rodeo Drive
Knoxville, TN 37922
iveybe@tds.net
(865)966-5946   SEET#2200

--==<< J >>==--

Jacks, Mathew Derek   (M1)
341 Shadeswood Drive
Hoover, AL 35226
pastorderek@homewoodcpc.com
(205)903-8469   SEGR#0111

Jackson, Lamar   (M1)
280 Deer Ridge Drive Apt D
Dayton, TN 37321
hljaxn@charter.net
(423)570-9348   SETG#2100

Jackson, Terry   (M1)
1461 Mount Pleasant Road
Hernando, MS 38632
(662)429-9741   GRWT#9100

Jacob, Randy   (M1)
PO Box 158
Broken Bow, OK 74728
FAX: (580)584-2099
chocpres@pine-net.com
(580)584-2099   MSCH#6106

James, William F   (M1)
2937 Arthur Drive
Murfreesboro, TN 37127
wimjim19@gmail.com
(615)653-1396   GRWT#9100

MINISTERS CONTINUED

Jang, Won Jeon (M1)
Lot2-C Teresa Subdivision
Tabucan Mandurriao
Iloilo City 5000, Phillippine
( ) SEET#2200

Janner, R Tony (M1)
104 Northwood Drive
McKenzie, TN 38201
FAX: (731)352-3101
drtonyjanner@yahoo.com
(731)352-8055 GRWT#9100

Jaramillo, Luciano (M1)
6248 SW 14th Street
West Miami, FL 33144
ljara@aol.com
(305)264-1074 SEGR#0310

Jarnagin, Mary L (M1)
PO Box 49102
Austin, TX 78765
marjar27@yahoo.com
(512)367-9922 MSTR#8100

Jeffrey, Peter (M1)
61 Northwood Drive
McKenzie, TN 38201
jeffreyp@bethelu.edu
(731)352-0792 TNMU#7200

Jeffrey, Sarah Ann (M1)
5271 Highway 202 E
Yellville, AR 72687
FAX: (870)715-9229
annjeffrey2001@yahoo.com
(870)453-7076 GRAR#1100

Jenkins, Henry (M1)
PO Box 148
Magazine, AR 72943
henryj@magtel.com
(479)969-8352 GRAR#1401

Jenkins, William E (M1)
1836 S Ridge Drive
Valrico, FL 33594
hopechurch4@aol.com
(813)651-3802 SEGR#0308

Jeong, Woo S (M1)
1205 Morganshire Drive
Collierville, TN 38017
(901)302-0558 GRWT#9100

Jett, Mace, Jr (M1)
109 Park Street
Martin, TN 38237
(731)587-0805 GRWT#9117

Jett-Rand, Dana (M2)
78 Lester Lane
Martin, TN 38237
msdanajett@yahoo.com
(731)587-0805 GRWT#9100

Jimenez, Jacqueline (M3)
11161 San Ysidro
Socorro, TX 79927
jjimenez2228@gmail.com
(915)252-8395 MSDC#8700

Jimenez, Jorge Enrique (M2)
Urb Manantiales MzC Casa 6
Armenia, Quindio, COLOMBIA, SA
joenjimu@yahoo.es
(576)749-1166 MSAN#8900

Jobe, J Tommy (M1)
PO Box 8
Eagleville, TN 37060
cppreacher@united.net
(615)776-7755 TNMU#7240

Johnson, Beverly B (M1)
801 Riverhill Drive Apt 308
Athens, GA 30606
bevloujohnson@aol.com
(865)977-0405 SEET#2200

Johnson, Daryl (M1)
425 W Vaughan Street
Bertram, TX 78605
djchurch@earthlink.net
(512)355-2182 MSTR#8605

Johnson, Ken (M1)
122 Ridge Lane
Clinton, TN 37716
kenjoxav122@bellsouth.net
(865)463-7090 SEET#2314

Johnson, Lanny (M1)
120 S Mill Street
Morrison, TN 37357
ljohnson37357@gmail.com
(931)212-1658 TNMU#7200

Johnson, Leslie A (M1)
11716 Price Drive
Oklahoma City, OK 73170
ljohnson275@cox.net
(405)759-3189 MSRR#6205

Johnson, Roberta Smith (M1)
397 Ouachita 54
Camden, AR 71701
(870)231-5827 GRAR#1309

Johnson, Rocky L (M1)
1208 Redwood Drive
Clarksville, TN 37042
jjjjgriff@gmail.com
(423)620-7753 TNNA#9300

Johnson, Thomas C (M1)
PO Box 566
Helena, AL 35080
revtomjohnson@aol.com
(205)936-1350 SEGR#0100

Johnson, Wesley H (M1)
6222 Crestmoor Lane
Sachse, TX 75048
wjohnson@transitionconsulting.com
(972)270-6923 MSRR#8412

Jones, Gregory (M1)
400 Adam Wood Drive Apt D12
Nashville, TN 37211
greg1013@aol.com
(931)249-9512 TNNA#7300

Jones, Harold (M1)
4123 Wilkesview Drive Apt A
Chattanooga, TN 37416
harold@personalcharacter.com
(478)320-4222 SETG#2100

Jones, Joseph M (M1)
405 Lakeview Drive
Campbellsville, KY 42718
joepegjones@windstream.net
( ) MICU#3100

Jones, Michael (M1)
120 Jennifer Lane
Branson, MO 65616
(417)334-2058 GRAR#1100

Jones, Steve (M2)
PO Box 368
Burns, TN 37029
(615)441-6159 TNNA#7300

Jones, Victor (M1)
7017 Highway 177 S
Jordan, AR 72519
mommom@centurytel.net
(870)499-5882 GRAR#1100

Jones, C William, Jr (M1)
109 Lakewood Drive
Lexington, TN 38351
patfreelandjones@yahoo.com
(731)967-7618 GRWT#9209

Justice, Michael (M1)
250 W 5th Street #B
Russellville, KY 42276
(270)726-6673 MICU#3501

--==<< K >>==--

Kang, Eun Hee (M3)
147-15 46th Avenue
Flushing, NY 11355
(718)762-0778 SECE#2400

Kang, Jin Koo (M1)
2310 Hisway
Lawrenceville, GA 30044
agatopia@hanmail.net
(678)462-7526 SETG#2100

Karasawa, Kenta (M1)
3-15-10 Higashi
Kunitachi-shi, Tokyo
186-0002 JAPAN
FAX: (042)575-5549
smbno6@gmail.com
(042)575-5549 MSJA#8306

Katsuki, Shigeru (M1)
2-14-16 Higashi-cho
Koganei-shi, Tokyo
184-0011 JAPAN
shigeru.katsuki@nifty.com
(042)231-1279 MSJA#8301

Kays, Michael (M1)
2505 Canterbury Avenue
Muskogee, OK 74403
msppk@suddenlink.net
(918)577-6255 MSRR#8400

Keller, Abby Cole (M1)
4415 Fieldstone Drive
Kingsport, TN 37664
colekeller@yahoo.com
(423)863-6565 SEET#2206

Kelly, Lawrence (M1)
77 Stonewall Court
Mount Juliet, TN 37122
(615)934-1517 TNCO#7100

Kelly, Patrick L (M1)
1449 Rainbow Road
Limestone, TN 37681
(423)727-4067 SEET#2200

Kelso, James H (M1)
131 Lords Way
Dawsonville, GA 30534
elgato@alltel.net
(706)216-7513 SETG#2100

Kennedy, Don (M3)
5335 Dizzy Dean Road
Booneville, AR 72927
donkennedy@centurytel.net
(479)675-4418 GRAR#1414

Kennedy, Jim (M2)
613 English Ivy Way
Aberdeen, MD 21001
jpkak@comcast.net
( ) SETG#2100

Kennemer, Darren (M1)
8828 Highway 119
Alabaster, AL 35007
dlkennemer@gmail.com
(205)663-3152 SERD#0107

MINISTERS CONTINUED

Keown, Gale J (M1)
2130 Cason Lane
Murfreesboro, TN 37128
galeesther@aol.com
(865)805-5451 SEET#2200

Kerner, Leanne (M2)
156 State Route 348 W
Symsonia, KY 42082
cooldoll@bellsouth.net
(270)851-9709 MICO#3400

Kessie, John Paul (M1)
138 Pony Grass Lane
Bastrop, TX 78628
jplmkessie@verizon.com
(512)585-1617 MSTR#8100

Keung Yung, Amos Chung (M3)
28 Hong Yip Street
Yuen Long, NT, HONG KONG
FAX: (522)639-5620
amos@xilincpc.org.hk
(522)639-9176 MSHK#8809

Killeen, Michael (M1)
5226 W William Cannon Drive
Austin, TX 78749
FAX: (512)892-6307
mike@shpc.org
(512)892-3580 MSTR#8604

Kim, Byong Sam (M1)
6290 Dawnridge Court
Paradise, CA 95969
(530)877-4651 MSDC#8700

Kim, Kio Seob (M1)
14430 35th Avenue Apt A62
Flushing, NY 11354
(718)539-3476 SECE#2400

Kim, Mi Young (M1)
(IN KOREA)
( ) SETG#2100

Kim, Min Soo (M1)
5350 Taylor Road
Johns Creek, GA 30022
samil2110@yahoo.com
(678)622-2717 SETG#2100

Kim, Yoong S (M1)
225 Bayswater Drive
Suwanee, GA 30024
yoongkim1934@yahoo.com
(678)765-7018 SETG#2100

Kim, YoungHo (Steve) (M1)
B02 Hyundai I-Space 1608-2
Burim Dong, Dong An Gu
AnYang City, Kyunggi Do, S KOREA
paidion4377@naver.com
(231)348-8033 MMT

King, Keith (M2)
3341 S 137th E Avenue
Tulsa, OK 74134
(918)437-5464 MSRR#8400

King, Mark (M3)
717 Big Swan Creek Road
Hampshire, TN 38461
(931)626-6915 TNCO#7100

Kinnaman, Richard T (M1)
2018 Spring Meadow Circle
Spring Hill, TN 37174
kinnaman91@att.net
(615)302-3321 TNCO#7100

Kirkpatrick, Mary Kathryn (M1)
401 1/2 Henley-Perry Drive
Marshall, TX 75670
mkkirkpatrick@gmail.com
(903)930-6236 MSTR#8115

Kleinjan, Lori (M1)
6516 Farnell Avenue
Memphis, TN 38134
lkleinj@prodigy.net
(901)372-8413 GRWT#9100

Knight, J Geoffrey (M1)
2119 Avalon Place
Houston, TX 77019
geoff@cphouston.org
(713)522-7821 MSTR#8606

Knight, Melissa (M1)
5730 Haley Road
Meridian, MS 39305
revlissa@gmail.com
(530)632-6472 MSDC#8700

Ko, John Jae (M1)
13955 35th Avenue #5A
Flushing, NY 11354
spcko@hanmail.net
(718)762-4348 SECE#2141

Koopman, David L (M1)
5606 Brandon Park Drive
Maryville, TN 37804
racewthrev@aol.com
(865)660-2440 SEET#2311

Korb, Leon C (M1)
15360 E 350 North Road
Ridge Farm, IL 61870
(217)662-8398 MINC#5200

Krueger, Courtney (M2)
1505 N Moore Road
Chattanooga, TN 37411
( ) SETG#2104

Kurtz, David (M1)
4700 Elkwood Lane
Arlington, TX 76016
davidk36@yahoo.com
(817)683-4783 MSRR#8407

--==<< L >>==--

Labrada, Hector (M1)
74 Cumberland Drive
McMinnville, TN 37110
( ) TNMU#7200

Ladd, Sherry (M1)
4521 Turkey Creek Road
Williamsport, TN 38487
revsherryladd@gmail.com
(931)682-2263 TNCO#7138

Lain, Judy (M1)
1928 Pine Ridge Drive
Bedford, TX 76021
judylane5@gmail.com
(817)660-8020 MSRR#8400

Lam, Janice (M2)
G/F & 1/F 251 Tin Sum Village
Tai Wai, Shatin NT, HONG KONG
FAX: (852)2607-2245
janiceyeung929@gmail.com
(852)2693-3444 MSHK#8800

Lambert, James (M1)
224 Peabody Road
Meridianville, AL 35759
(256)828-6850 SERD#0800

Lancaster, David (M1)
426 Fugua Road
Martin, TN 38237
lancasterd@bethel-college.edu
(731)588-5895 GRWT#9130

LaPerche, Michael (M1)
9317 Moondancer Circle
Roseville, CA 95747
pastor-mike@earthlink.net
(727)859-3998 SEGR#0303

Lathem, W Ray (M1)
452 County Road 1462
Cullman, AL 35055
lathemray@bellsouth.net
(256)734-7146 SEGR#0100

Latimer, James M (M1)
7621 Richmond
Memphis, TN 38125
jimmylatimer@redeemerevangelical.com
(901)787-7875 GRWT#9100

Lau, Walter (M1)
865 Jackson Street
San Francisco, CA 94133
FAX: (415)421-1874
walter@cumberlandsf.org
(650)583-7878 MSDC#8501

Laurence, Brenda (M1)
2823 Nine Mile Road
Enville, TN 38332
southernmoma@hotmail.com
(731)687-2022 GRWT#9100

Lavender, Michael T (M1)
308 Main Street
Martin, TN 38237
mike_lavender@yahoo.com
(731)253-7308 GRWT#9117

Lawson, James (M1)
1003 W 3rd Street
Fulton, KY 42041
(270)472-5272 MICO#3400

Lawson, Jerry L (M1)
6039 MS Highway 415
Ackerman, MS 39735
lawson@dtcweb.net
(662)285-8295 SEGR#0707

Lawson, John C (M2)
PO Box 645
Daingerfield, TX 75638
sharjohn@windstream.net
(903)645-2183 MSTR#8106

Lawson, Luke (M1)
270 N Ridgeland Circle
Columbus, MS 39705
luke_lawson03@hotmail.com
(662)295-9322 SEGR#0706

Layne, Phillip (M1)
10699 Griffith Highway
Whitwell, TN 37397
44philliplayne@gmail.com
(423)658-6421 SETG#2110

LeNeave, David (M1)
8725 Hamletsburg Road
Brookport, IL 62910
mscpchurch_bd@yahoo.com
(618)564-2437 MICO#5117

Lee, David (M1)
3480 Summit Ridge Parkway
Duluth, GA 30096
gcjcatl@gmail.com
(404)641-4359 SETG#2100

Lee, Douglas (M1)
3265 16th Street
San Francisco, CA 94103
dlee@gum.org
(415)703-6090 MSDC#8510

MINISTERS CONTINUED

Lee, George (M1)
104 Parc Circle
Florence, AL 35630
butchleeautos@yahoo.com
(256)740-0809 SEHO#0514

Lee, Ho-Jin (M1)
7565 Macon Road
Cordova, TN 38018
hojin.lee70@gmail.com
(901)754-7070 GRWT#9322

Lee, Priscilla (M2)
Tin Yuet Estate
Tin Shui Wai NT, HONG KONG
FAX: (852)2617-0287
wai_yung_lee@yahoo.com.hk
(852)2617-7872 MSHK#8800

Lee, Sang-Do (M1)
1342 Seocho-2dong, Seocho-Gu
Seoul, KOREA
(023)474-8405 MMT

Lee, Sarah (M1)
( ) SETG#2100

Lee, Ted Shu Tak (M1)
2/F Welland Plaza
188 Nam Cheong Street
Sham Shui Po, Kowloon, HONG KONG
FAX: (852)2771-2726
tedlee@taohsien.org.hk
(852)2783-8923 MSHK#8800

Lee, Timothy Daniel (M1)
186 Blasingame Drive
Columbus, MS 39702
eelmit@bellsouth.net
(601)433-3714 SEGR#0702

Lefavor, David (M1)
414 S Monroe Siding Road
Xenia, OH 45385
david.lefavor@med.va.gov
(813)613-4133 SEGR#0100

Li, Chun Wai (M2)
1/F Block B
14 Tsat Tsz Mui Road
North Point, Hong Kong
FAX: (852)2564-2898
cwli2000hk@yahoo.com.hk
(852)2562-2148 MSHK#8800

Liles, Dwight (M1)
8467 Joy Road
Mount Pleasant, TN 38474
dwightliles@att.net
(931)379-0326 TNCO#7100

Lim, Keum-Taek (M1)
1342 Seocho-2dong, Seocho-Gu
Seoul, KOREA
limkt114@hanmail.net
(023)474-8405 MMT

Lindsay, John V (M1)
401 Greenwood Avenue
Marshall, TX 75670
(940)391-1213 MSTR#8113

Linski, David (M2)
1060 Alpine Way
Indian Springs, AL 35124
david.linski@gmail.com
(205)677-8163 SEGR#0100

Little, Russell (M1)
29 Cotton Row
Medina, TN 38355
russelllittle@bellsouth.net
(731)783-3565 GRWT#9109

Liu, Lai Yuet (M2)
2/F Fu Tung Shopping Center
Tung Chung
Lantau Island, HONG KONG
FAX: (852)2109-1737
(852)2109-1738 MSHK#8800

Lively, James W (M1)
906 Lyle Circle
Greeneville, TN 37745
FAX: (423)636-1017
jlively@gcpchurch.org
(423)798-1959 SEET#2206

Lively, Louella (M1)
196 Vicksburg Estate Road
Benton, KY 42025
(270)527-3776 MICO#3400

Livingston, Ronald L (M1)
5851 Quantrell Ave #201
Alexandria, VA 22312
( ) SERD#0800

Lockhart, Thomas Richie (M1)
700 County Road 343
Falkner, MS 38629
nmsdiamonddawgs@yahoo.com
(662)837-7281 GRWT#9214

Lockmiller, Lem Jr (M1)
PO Box 348
Leesburg, AL 35983
(256)490-3021 SEGR#0403

Logan, Jason (M1)
212 Saddlebag Court
Rineyville, KY 40162
jason.b.logan.mil@mail.mil
(502)626-0722 TNMU#7200

Longmire, Ronald L (M1)
2041 Eckles Drive
Maryville, TN 37804
ronaldlongmire@charter.net
(865)984-1647 SEET#2309

Lopez, Wilson (M3)
Diag 26M #73A-69
Cali, COLOMBIA, SA
( )422-3940 MSCA#8225

Lorick, Keith (M1)
127 Chesapeake Boulevard
Madison, AL 35757
keithlorick@knology.net
(256)325-3865 SERD#0808

Louder, Paula (M1)
98 Gallant Court
Clarksville, TN 37043
paula@clarksvillecpc.com
(615)804-4809 TNNA#7304

Louder, Stephen L (M1)
98 Gallant Court
Clarksville, TN 37043
pastorsteve@clarksvillecpc.com
(931)217-0369 TNNA#7304

Lounsbury-Lombard, Kristi (M1)
902 Clearview
Krum, TX 76249
kristilounsbury@gmail.com
(940)435-5077 MSRR#8400

Love, James R (M1)
14382 Sonora Hardin Springs Road
Eastview, KY 42732
(502)862-4119 MICU#3100

Lovelace, John G (M1)
1202 E Cedar Street
New Baden, IL 62265
jlove1234@aol.com
(812)476-5879 MINC#5200

Lowe, Randy (M1)
222 McDougal Drive
Murray, KY 42071
loweshodle@aol.com
(270)753-8255 MICO#3412

Lubo, Jaime (M3)
AA 6365
Montebello, COLOMBIA, SA
( ) MSCA#8223

Lui, Stephen (M1)
512 16th Avenue
San Francisco, CA 94118
FAX: (415)386-2302
(415)386-2302 MSDC#8700

Lunn, Calvin (M1)
859 Cranford Hollow Road
Columbia, TN 38401
pastor@fcpccolumbia.com
(931)381-2397 TNCO#7110

Luo, Tian-en (M1)
87 Berta Circle
Daly City, CA 94015
FAX: (650)754-9885
tianenyang555@gmail.com
(650)754-9885 MSDC#8700

Luthy, Dusty (M3)
400 S Friendship Road Apt G
Paducah, KY 42003
dustyluthy@gmail.com
(270)933-2722 MICO#3400

Luttrell, Ben (M1)
262 Main Street
Nettleton, MS 38858
(731)645-5257 GRWT#9225

--==<< M >>==--

Ma, Choil (M1)
300 Ringgold Road Apt 503
Clarksville, TN 37042
choilma@yahoo.com
(931)824-2443 TNNA#7342

Macy, William M (M1)
1358 Ephesus Church Road
Harned, KY 40144
(270)756-2775 MICU#3218

Madden, Judith Ellen (M1)
100 SW Brushy Mound
Burleson, TX 76028
jmadden@pathway.church
FAX: (512)258-7325
(817)295-5832 MSRR#8400

Maddux, Cynthia (M1)
5735 Timber Creek Place Drive Apt 212
Houston, TX 77084
cmaddux1962@gmail.com
(823)343-8867 MSDC#8700

Magliolo, Sam (M2)
14352 Fairview
Byhalia, MS 38611
samagliolo@fedex.com
(662)838-7720 GRWT#9100

Magrill, J Richard, Jr (M1)
500 Miller Drive
Marshall, TX 75672
rmmagrill@gmail.com
(901)685-9454 MSTR#8100

MINISTERS CONTINUED

Mak, Daphne Suet Chung (M2)
2/F Welland Plaza
188 Nam Cheong Street
Sham Shui Po, Kowloon, HONG KONG
FAX: (852)2771-2726
daphne@taohsien.org.hk
(852)2783-8923 MSHK#8800

Malinoski, Melissa (M1)
9087 Fenmore Cove
Cordova, TN 38016
FAX: (423)636-1017
mmalinoski@memphisseminary.edu
(420)620-0089 GRWT#9100

Malinoski, T J (M1)
9087 Fenmore Cove
Cordova, TN 38016
mlmalinoski@comcast.net
(423)972-1239 SEET#2200

Malone, John W (M1)
3693 Highway 67 South
Sommerville, AL 35670
(256)778-8237 SEHO#0500

Malone, Michael (M1)
1229 Farrish Drive
Fredericksburg, VA 22401
(865)692-2415 TNMU#7200

March, Kevin (M1)
1701 Ray Jo Circle
Chattanooga, TN 37421
kmadm1@aol.com
(423)499-4180 SETG#2100

Mariott, Keith L (M1)
155 Ridgewood Lane
Odenville, AL 35120
kjmariott@windstream.net
(205)903-5251 SEGR#0106

Marquez, Alfonso (M1)
389 Bethel Drive
Lenoir City, TN 37772
amarquez61@bellsouth.net
(865)660-7579 SEET#2320

Marquez, Jose Ignacio (M3)
8976 W Flagler Street
Miami, FL 33174
jimarquez.aviation@gmail.com
( ) SEGR#0100

Marquez, Martha (M1)
389 Bethel Drive
Lenoir City, TN 37772
amarquez61@bellsouth.net
(865)660-7579 SEET#2320

Mars, Stan (M1)
PO Box 274
Mt Pleasant, AR 72561
smars2@liberty.edu
(217)254-5120 GRAR#1100

Marshall, Debbie (M1)
1494 Bucksnort Road
Covington, TN 38019
dsmarshall05@att.net
(901)494-1251 GRWT#9304

Martin, Theresa (M1)
116 Crisman Street
Chattanooga, TN 37415
choochootm@usa.net
(423)903-7260 SETG#2116

Martin, Tom (M1)
116 Crisman Street
Chattanooga, TN 37415
choochootm@usa.net
(423)903-7260 (cell) SETG#2100

Martin, William E, Jr (M1)
741 Chapel Hill Road
Marion, KY 42064
juniormartin@yahoo.com
(870)270-3344 MICO#3620

Martinez, Dagoberto (M1)
Cra 62D #71-113
Bello, Antioquia
COLOMBIA, SA
(574)452-3466 MSAN#8900

Martinez, Rodrigo (M1)
Mz2 Casa 21 Urb Casas De Milan
Dosquebradas, Risaralda
COLOMBIA, SA
oikoinonia@gmail.com
(576)322-2177 MSAN#8916

Martinez, Soledad (M1)
2801 Biway Street
Ft Worth, TX 76114
shirleymartinez1252@gmail.com
(817)812-8247 MSRR#8400

Masuda, Yasuo (M1)
1-11-20 Kokubu
Ichikawa-shi, Chiba-ken
272-0834 JAPAN
FAX: (047)369-7540
fwgc6854@mb.infoweb.ne.jp
(047)369-7540 MSJA#8314

Mata, Elizabeth (M1)
PO Box 1040
San Elizario, TX 79849
hectoryliz@att.net
(915)851-5354 MSDC#8706

Mata, Hector (M1)
PO Box 1040
San Elizario, TX 79849
hectoryliz@att.net
(915)851-5354 MSDC#8706

Mata, Isaac (M1)
PO Box 1040
San Elizario, TX 79849
isaacmata96@yahoo.com
(915)851-5354 MSDC#8706

Mata, Pablo (M1)
230 Flor Blanca
El Paso, TX 79927
pablomata@yahoo.com
(915)319-8407 MSDC#8700

Mathews, Nathaniel (M2)
755 Cherokee Road
New Johnsonville, TN 37134
bro.nate-mathews@hotmail.com
(931)209-6645 TNNA#7300

Matlock, Robert (M1)
156 Dovenshire Drive
Fairfield Glade, TN 38558
revbobm@msn.com
(931)210-0614 TNMU#7200

Matsumoto, Masahiro (M1)
2-14-1 Minami Rinkan
Yamato-shi, Kanagawa-ken
242-0006 JAPAN
matsumoto@koza-church.jp
(046)275-2767 MSJA#8313

Matsuya, Ryuzo (M1)
72-2 Naka Kibogaoka Asahi-ku
Yokohama, Kanagawa-ken
241-0825 JAPAN
matsuya.r@woody.ocn.ne.jp
(045)364-8297 MSJA#8302

Matthews, James N (M1)
241 Morning Star Drive
Huntsville, AL 35811
brojim10@mediacombb.net
(256)337-2765 SERD#0800

Mayfield, Randall (M1)
12470 Daisywood Drive
Knoxville, TN 37932
FAX: (865)769-4756
mayfield07@comcast.net
(865)769-4756 SEET#2308

Maynard, Geoffery (M1)
1356 Marcia Road
Memphis, TN 38117
(901)409-5269 GRWT#9100

Maynard, Terrell D (M1)
3 Nelson Cove
Milan, TN 38358
terrellmaynard@bellsouth.net
(731)437-0056 SEGR#0100

Mays, Ronald B (M1)
1100 Cindy Lane
Mayfield, KY 42066
rbmays@wk.net
(270)247-0070 MICO#3400

McCallum, Frank (M1)
PO Box 56
Garfield, KY 40140
mccallum@bbtel.com
(270)580-4796 MICU#3208

McCarty, John (M1)
305 W Martindale Drive
Marshall, TX 75672
mtsjohn@gmail.com
(423)650-8788 SETG#2100

McCaskey, Charles (M1)
679 Canter Lane
Cookeville, TN 38501
charles@cookevillecpchurch.org
(931)526-4885 TNMU#7210

McClanahan, H Walter (M1)
215 White Bros Road
Humboldt, TN 38343
waltermac2@hughes.net
(731)784-1176 GRWT#9110

McClanahan, Jo Ann (M1)
215 White Bros Road
Humboldt, TN 38343
joannmcclanahan@hughes.net
(731)784-1176 GRWT#9100

McClung, Andy (M1)
919 Dickinson Street
Memphis, TN 38107
scubarev@att.net
(901)606-6615 GRWT#9100

McClung, Tiffany (M1)
919 Dickinson Street
Memphis, TN 38107
tmcclung@memphisseminary.edu
(901)606-6615 GRWT#9100

McConnell, Donald R (M1)
147 Confederacy Circle
Knoxville, TN 37934
donjoyce515@hotmail.com
(865)288-0230 SEET#2200

McCoy, Kenneth L (M1)
1422 Walton Road
Memphis, TN 38117
(901)682-0891 GRWT#9301

MINISTERS CONTINUED

McCurley, Don (M1)
4036 McAllister Street
Milan, TN 38358
dcmccurley@hotmail.com
(731)723-3623 GRWT#9106

McDuff, Dwayne (M1)
9770 County Road 5
Florence, AL 35633
fcpdmcduff@comcast.net
FAX: (256)766-0736
(256)764-6354 SEHO#0506

McDuffie, J C (M1)
RR 3 Box 574
Fairfield, IL 62837
mactrapper4@frontier.com
(618)842-5624 MINC#5113

McGee, Charles Randall (M1)
9037 Groveland Drive
Dallas, TX 75218
randallmcgee@sbcglobal.net
(214)328-2488 MSRR#8400

McGill, James A (M1)
433 S Walnut Avenue
Cookeville, TN 38501
jam7235@frontiernet.net
(931)526-6936 TNMU#7234

McGowan, Kriss (M1)
885 Mount Calvary Road
Whitwell, TN 37397
krissmcg658@gmail.com
(423)463-8609 SETG#2119

McGowan, Rhonda (M1)
885 Mount Calvary Road
Whitwell, TN 37379
pastorrhonda@mcgowanministries.com
(423)619-5679 SETG#2100

McGuire, James D (M1)
220 Southwind Circle #2
Greenville, TN 37745
jmcguire915@comcast.net
(423)638-6380 SEET#2200

McGuire, Timothy (M1)
PO Box 42
Mt Sherman, KY 42764
brotim.cpc@gmail.com
(270)766-9027 MICU#3509

McInnis, Rodney (M1)
6589 Harbor Place
Gadsden, AL 35907
mcinnisrodneyand@bellsouth.net
(256)454-2399 SEGR#0404

McMichael, Jeff (M1)
224 John Drane Lane
Harned, KY 40144
revmcmichael@outlook.com
(270)617-4016 MICU#3207

McMillan, L Ronald (M1)
675 Kimberly Drive
Atoka, TN 38004
mcmillanron@bellsouth.net
(901)837-1101 GRWT#9100

McMillan, Lloyd Aaron (M1)
8600 Academy Road NE
Albuquerque, NM 87111
FAX: (505)797-8599
mcmillanaaron@hotmail.com
(505)503-0714 MSDC#8700

McNeese, Mark (M1)
3306 Greenlawn Parkway
Austin, TX 78757
2mam53@gmail.com
(512)517-1042 MSTR#8100

McNeese, Michael C (M1)
16410 Wesley Evans Road
Prairieville, LA 70769
mcneesemc@cox.net
(520)722-1350 MSDC#8700

McSpadden, Nancy (M1)
120 Roberta Drive
Memphis, TN 38112
revnancy77@gmail.com
(870)612-0067 GRAR#1100

Mearns, Duawn (M1)
107 Westoak Place
Hot Springs, AR 71913
duawn@lakehamiltonchurch.com
(501)276-1266 GRAR#1221

Medlin, Kevin (M1)
316 Dandelion Drive
Lebanon, TN 37087
FAX: (615)444-6671
kmedlin12@hotmail.com
(615)444-7453 TNMU#7220

Meeks, Brittany (M1)
1340 Tutwiler Avenue
Memphis, TN 38107
bpmeeks@memphisseminary.edu
(901)336-9024 GRWT#9100

Meinzer, Alan (M1)
780 Barren Fork Road
Mt. Pleasant, AR 72561
brotheralan@centurylink.net
(870)612-3936 GRAR#1515

Melson, Glenda (M1)
331 Tickle Weed Road
Swansea, SC 29160
gmelson@fidnet.com
(417)588-2758 GRMI#4100

Melton, Samuel D (M1)
2249 Bucks Pocket Road SE
Oldfort, TN 37362
(423)472-8467 SETG#2100

Meredith, Charles (M1)
144 Barbara Circle
Elizabethtown, KY 42701
(270)307-0607 MICU#3210

Merritt, Joyce (M1)
3929 Snail Shell Cave Road
Rockvale, TN 37153
(615)574-3047 TNMU#7200

Messer, James (M1)
3653 Old Madisonville Road
Henderson, KY 42420
jcmess@hotmail.com
(270)827-0711 MINC#5304

Middleton, Bill S (M1)
12826 Union Road
Knoxville, TN 37922
revbill@charter.net
(865)966-1706 SEET#2304

Middleton, Frank, Jr (M3)
1200 Adele Circle
Slidell, LA 70461
fmiddle@bellsouth.net
(770)655-0406 SETG#2100

Middleton, Todd (M3)
PO Box 1913
Russellville, AR 72811
(479)748-4613 GRAR#1100

Mikel, Jason (M1)
4630 Mt Sharon Road
Greenbrier, TN 37073
jasonemikel@gmail.com
(615)243-8938 TNNA#7321

Milby, Elizabeth L (M1)
207 Summersville Road
Greensburg, KY 42743
(270)932-5659 MICU#3100

Miller, Carol (M1)
101 Park Avenue
Dickson, TN 37055
lcarolmiller@comcast.net
(615)411-6656 TNNA#7300

Miller, James R (M1)
1214 Whitney Drive
Columbia, TN 38401
rev.james.miller@charter.net
(931)381-3367 TNCO#7101

Mills, David M (M1)
60 Huge Oak Street
Bertram, TX 78605
(512)355-3511 MSTR#8100

Mink, R Allan (M2)
1113 Hidden Glen Court
Burleson, TX 76028
FAX: (817)295-2576
alan.mink@pathway.church
(817)295-5832 MSRR#8418

Minor, Mitzi (M1)
875 S Cox
Memphis, TN 38104
(901)278-6115 GRWT#9100

Minton, Grant (M1)
PO Box 270
Auburn, KY 42206
FAX: (270)271-4603
gminton@logantele.com
(270)542-7991 MICU#3301

Miyai, Takehiko (M1)
A-201 2-2-48 Higashihara Zama-shi
Kanagawa-ken
228-0004 JAPAN
FAX: (046)256-3212
tacke.m@gmail.com
(046)207-6558 MSJA#8304

Miyajima, Atsushi (M2)
Rua Araja
58 Paraiso Sao Joa
48280-000, Bahia, BRAZIL
ariel.atsushi@gmail.com
(5571)3664-1037 MSJA#8313

Montano, Jhony (M1)
Cra 9 No 6 6N 87 Bello Horizonte
Popayan
Colombia, South America
(092)823-8988 MSCA#8227

Montoya, David (M1)
Cra 12 bis #11-69
Pereira, Risaralda, COLOMBIA, SA
FAX: (576)324-4110
adamonva@gmail.com
(576)324-4109 MSAN#8916

Montoya, David (M3)
20900 FM 1093 Apt 11208
Richmond, TX 77407
davinay@hotmail.com
(823)366-6897 MSTR#8100

Montoya, Eduardo (M1)
270 Windsor Drive
Roselle, IL 60172
edmontoya@hotmail.com
(630)980-1577 MINC#5203

Moore, Angela (M1)
3756 Douglass Avenue
Memphis, TN 38111
(870)581-2509 GRAR#1100

MINISTERS CONTINUED

Moore, Hillman C   (M1)
300 Medical Parkway Ste 2320
Lakeway, TX 78738
hillmancm@att.net
(731)537-9561   MICO#3400

Moore, James R, Sr   (M1)
2778 Marguerite Street S
Hokes Bluff, AL 35903
jmoore@microxl.com
(256)494-9030   SEGR#0100

Moore, Kimberly   (M3)
1025 Three Island Ford Road
Charlotte, TN 37036
kimberly.a.moore@vanderbilt.edu
(615)545-1595   TNNA#7300

Mora, Wilfredo   (M2)
17512 SW 153rd Court
Miami, FL 33187
moraw68@gmail.com
(786)554-1478   SEGR#0100

Morgan, Kenneth P   (M1)
5400 Highway 101
Rogersville, AL 35652
FAX: (256)247-1424
kennymorgan330@hotmail.com
(256)247-3890   SEHO#0515

Morgan, Richard   (M1)
1468 Williams Cove Road
Winchester, TN 37398
icthuse3@gmail.com
(931)349-4474   TNMU#7214

Morris, Carey   (M3)
2167 W Shawtown Road
Troy, TN 38260
carey@cyberianwolf.net
(731)538-9477   GRWT#9100

Morrow, Charles   (M1)
5032 Pine Grove Road
Union, MS 39365
morrowp7@yahoo.com
(601)479-0288   SEGR#0100

Mosley, Karen   (M1)
PO Box 172154
Memphis, TN 38187
( )   GRWT#9100

Mosley, Steve   (M1)
1200 N Arkansas Avenue
Russellville, AR 72801
FAX: (479)880-0071
stevemosley@hotmail.com
(479)968-1061   GRAR#1216

Mullenix, Robert   (M1)
1408 Azalee Lane
Chapel Hill, TN 37034
glonix@live.comt
(931)379-3617   TNCO#7133

Murphree, Hughlen   (M1)
4298 County Road 1719
Holly Pond, AL 35083
hmurph@hiwaay.net
(256)796-5352   SERD#0800

Murray, Joshua   (M1)
3714 Landings Way Drive Apt 305
Tampa, FL 33624
jdm4428@yahoo.com
(870)723-3286   GRAR#0303

Murrie, Willard   (M1)
506 11th Street
Vienna, IL 62995
(618)658-2430   MICO#3400

--==<< N >>==--

Nash, Zachary   (M1)
(on file in General Assembly Office)
( )   GRWT#9100

Nave, Steve   (M1)
5172 Fall River Road
Leoma, TN 38468
thenaves@wildblue.net
(931)424-0020   TNCO#7131

Navrkal, Amy   (M3)
302 W 3rd Street
Brookport, IL 62910
brinkleydanne2@gmail.com
(618)638-4218   MICO#3400

Ndoro, Wonder   (M1)
111 Roberta Avenue
Memphis, TN 38112
gusungo@yahoo.com
(901)334-5861   GRWT#9100

Neafus, Kenneth R   (M1)
237 Richland Church Road
Morgantown, KY 42261
(270)526-6835   MICU#3100

Nease, Dale   (M1)
500 S 30th Street
Clinton, OK 73601
(580)323-7557   MSRR#6302

Nelson, Charles E   (M1)
209 Classic Court
Springtown, TX 76082
dundeal10@aol.com
(903)641-5466   MSRR#8410

Newcomb, Troy   (M3)
PO Box 858
Salem, KY 42078
( )   MICO#3610

Newell, Jennifer   (M1)
2322 Maraco Circle
Chattanooga, TN 37421
newelljennifer3@gmail.com
(423)892-5834   SETG#2108

Nichols, Oscar Lee   (M1)
1035 N County Road 650E
Trilla, IL 62469
(217)234-6551   MINC#5200

Nicholson, Casey   (M1)
1020 Tusculum Boulevard
Greeneville, TN 37745
caseynicholson@mac.com
(423)638-4504   SEET#2200

Nickles, Philip   (M1)
5821 County Road 1114
Vinemont, AL 35179
nickles.phil@yahoo.com
(256)734-9847   SEHO#0206

Niswonger, Richard   (M1)
20941 Highway 16 E
Siloam Springs, AR 72761
rniswonger@cox.net
(479)524-4081   GRAR#1100

Niwa, Yoshimasa   (M1)
15-402 Narakita Danchi
2913 Naramachi Aoba-ku
Yokohama, Kanagawa-ken
227-0036 JAPAN
FAX: (042)725-9909
rsb09335@nifty.com
(045)961-1540   MSJA#8310

Norman, Maury A   (M1)
1750 Shipley Road
Cookeville, TN 38501
maurynorman@yahoo.com
(931)526-1644   TNNA#7229

Norris, Dakota   (M3)
4750 Highway 431 N
Springfield, TN 37172
volsfan2011@gmail.com
(615)681-6346   TNNA#7300

Norris, Freddie   (M1)
330 Lexington Drive
Glasgow, KY 42141
(270)651-7932   MICU#3100

Norton, Kitty   (M1)
251 Westchase Drive
Nashville, TN 37205
kitty.a.norton@vanderbilt.edu
(615)584-1464   TNNA#7300

Norton, Thomas H   (M1)
220 Evergreen Garden Drive
Elizabethtown, KY 42701
tnorton16@comcast.net
(353)584-4695   GRWT#9100

Notley, Sharon   (M1)
16500 S Grey Wolf Apt 5
Odessa, TX 79766
sharon_standrewcp@sbcglobal.net
(432)210-9059   MSDC#8703

Nunn, Donald W   (M1)
203 Bridgers Hill Road
Longview, TX 75604
dwnunn@earthlink.net
(903)297-6074   MSTR#8113

Nye, John   (M1)
210 Crestview Drive
Mount Juliet, TN 37122
( )   TNNA#7300

--==<< O >>==--

O'Neal Danhof, Claire   (M1)
301 Whispering Hills Street
Hot Springs, AR 71901
acglenn@aol.com
( )   GRAR#1100

Oh, Taeho   (M1)
42-40 2908th Street #1
Bayside, NY 11361   SETG#2100

Ohi, Keitaro   (M1)
2-14-21 Minami Rinkan
Yamato-shi Kanagawa-ken
242-0006 JAPAN
keitaro_o@hotmail.com
(046)275-9616   MSJA#8303

Okala, Achile   (M2)
5887 Newcombe Court
Arvada, CO 80004
archileok@me.com
(720)820-8511   MSDC#8700

Oliveira, Jose   (M1)
7310 Jasmine Drive
Hanover Park, IL 60133
valdirsoares@yahoo.com
(630)855-0870   MSDC#8700

Oliver, Lisa   (M1)
110 Allen Drive
Hendersonville, TN 37075
lisa.oliver316@gmail.com
(615)319-6466   TNNA#7300

MINISTERS CONTINUED

O'Mara, Shelia (M1)
533 Loughton Lane
Arnold, MD 21012
chaplainshelia@aol.com
(410)757-5713 MSDC#8700

Ordway, Wendell (M1)
4775 Calvert City Road
Calvert City, KY 42029
(270)395-7318 MICO#3423

Orozco, Joaquin (M1)
Cra 3 #7-14
Aguadas, Caldas, COLOMBIA, SA
jeob40@hotmail.com
(576)851-4773 MSAN#8900

Orozeo Ariza, Juan Carlos (M2)
Aereo 6365
Cali Vale, COLOMBIA, SA
( ) MSCA#8200

Orr, Melvin (M1)
806 Washington Street
Newbern, TN 38059
2Orrs.mn@charter.net
(731)627-2445 GRWT#9100

Ortega, Juan (M3)
COLOMBIA, SA
jortegaus@yahoo.com
(574)323-9305 MSAN#8900

Ortiz, Milton (M1)
8846 N Cortona Circle
Cordova, TN 38018
mortiz@cumberland.org
(901)486-6679 SEET#2200

Osorio, Fernando (M3)
Aereo 329
Palmira, COLOMBIA, SA
( )272-7584 MSCA#8215

Ostander, Shirley (M1)
210 Glen Park Drive #3
Cordova, TN 38018
(901)827-4830 GRAR#1104

Overton, Janice M (M1)
3320 Pipeline Road
Birmingham, AL 35243
FAX: (205)968-8105
jan@crestlinechurch.org
(205)281-6819 SEGR#0102

Owen, Rick (M1)
3305 Wild Oaks Court
Burleson, TX 76028
FAX: (817)295-2576
rowen@pathway.church
(817)295-5832 MSRR#8418

--==<< P >>==--

Page, Rickey (M1)
736 Rodney Drive
Nashville, TN 37205
FAX: (615)352-2801
rickey.page@wncp.org
(615)353-7850 TNNA#7334

Paredes, Fabio (M3)
Carerra 7 # 1-76
La Cruztala, Ipiales, COLOMBIA, SA
(092)773-1036 MSCA#8200

Park, Bo-Seong (M1)
304-28 Sinlim-Dong, Kwanak-Gu
Seoul, KOREA
(002)884-3474 SEET#2200

Park, Jin Soo (M1)
21155 45th Drive
Bayside, NY 11361
jpkorea@daum.net
(516)558-7298 SECE#2137

Park, Sang Hoon (M1)
3504 W Shawnee Drive
Springfield, MO 65810
hesed-park@hanmail.net
(417)888-0442 GRMI#4100

Park, Si Hoon (M1)
511 4th Street #B
Palisades Park, NJ 07650
(201)944-7913 SECE#2137

Park, Sung In (M1)
12320 Alameda Trace Circle #1309
Austin, TX 78727
( ) MSTR#8100

Park, Yang Rae (M1)
4175 Buford Highway
Duluth, GA 30096
barkmoksa@hanmail.net
(770)912-7710 SETG#2130

Park, Young (M3)
3340 Bentbill Crossing
Cummings, GA 30041
barkmogun@gmail.com
(404)661-6117 SETG#2100

Parker, Susan (M1)
655 York Drive
Rogersville, AL 35652
park9301@bellsouth.net
(256)247-3877 SEHO#0500

Parkhurst, L G, Jr (M1)
409 Woodhollow Trail
Edmond, OK 73012
(405)341-7477 MSRR#8400

Parks, Sam (M1)
10 Lila Way
Cartersville, GA 60120
wsamparks@aol.com
(615)529-2465 TNMU#7200

Parman, David (M1)
5034 S Monroe School Road
Monroe City, IN 47557
FAX: (812)743-5171
(812)743-2646 MINC#5307

Parish, Johnny (M1)
114 Savo Bay
Hendersonville, TN 37075
johnnyparish@bellsouth.net
(615)824-5842 TNNA#7329

Parrish, Steven (M1)
4610 Dunn Avenue
Memphis, TN 38117
sparrish@memphisseminary.edu
(901)743-9545 TNNA#7300

Parsons, Hugh L (M1)
1526 Welch
Houston, TX 77006
p-h-parsons@comcast.net
(713)522-6126 MSTR#8100

Patterson, James H (M1)
6705 Ballard Drive #211
Chattanooga, TN 37421
FAX: (423)942-2188
(423)267-8568 SETG#2113

Patterson, Jerry (M1)
7007 Whitaker Avenue
Van Nuys, CA 91406
(818)994-5828 MSDC#8700

Patton, Malcolm (M1)
921 Harris Drive
Gallatin, TN 37066
FAX: (615)824-6507
bpatton11@comcast.net
(615)452-5557 TNNA#7300

Patton, Roger, Jr (M1)
1534 Eden Rose Place
Nolensville, TN 37135
rogerlpatton@att.net
(615)975-5526 TNNA#7333

Payne, Robert (Bob) (M1)
1660 3rd Street NW
Birmingham, AL 35215
payne.bob.emmet@gmail.com
(205)856-2427 SEGR#0100

Peach, John (M3)
221 Geronimo Road
Knoxville, TN 37934
peachroot@aol.com
(865)675-5956 SEET#2200

Pedigo, Russell (M1)
1002 Haney Avenue
El Dorado, AR 71730
russell_pedigo@hotmail.com
(870)862-4689 GRAR#1100

Peery, Terry (M1)
1431 Spainwood Street
Columbia, TN 38401
coppreacher@gmail.com
(931)381-6871 TNCO#7143

Pejendino, Fhanor (M1)
Cra 26 #36-40
Tulua, COLOMBIA, SA
(317)654-5750 MSCA#8226

Pejendino, Socorro (M1)
Cra 26 #36-40
Tulua, COLOMBIA, SA
(317)654-5750 MSCA#8200

Perez, Jose (M1)
3512 Chesnut Ridge Lane
Birmingham, AL 35216
(205)663-3110 TNMU#7200

Perkins, Ed (M1)
721 E Paris Avenue
McKenzie, TN 38201
(731)352-2754 GRWT#9100

Perkins, William H (M1)
PO Box 632
Central City, KY 42330
(270)754-5333 MICU#3100

Peters, David J (M1)
4010 Sam Bass Road
Round Rock, TX 78681
(512)244-2152 MSTR#8100

Peterson, Lisa (M1)
7778 Cedar Creek Road
Townsend, TN 37882
petersonli@aol.com
(901)604-0737 GRWT#9100

Petty, Linda Lee (M3)
4401 W Elgin Street
Broken Arrow, OK 74012
(918)252-4741 MSRR#8400

Peyton, James L (M1)
1455 County Road 643
Cullman, AL 35055
jakjpeyton@att.net
(256)734-6001 SEHO#0212

MINISTERS CONTINUED

Phelps, Earl   (M1)
172 Michie Pebble Hill Road
Stanntonville, TN 38379
FAX: (901)632-9126
phelps.e@juno.com
(731)632-5107   GRWT#9216

Phillips, Kenneth P   (M1)
6419 Town Creek Road East
Lenoir City, TN 37772
(865)986-7344   SEET#2306

Phillips-Burk, Pam   (M1)
3325 Bailey Creek Cove N
Collierville, TN 38017
pam@cumberland.org
(256)684-5247   SERD#0800

Piamba, Juan Carlos   (M3)
Cra 7 #21N-35
Popayan, COLOMBIA, SA
(092)838-5761   MSCA#8200

Pickard, Ronald   (M1)
6292 Golden Drive
Morristown, TN 37814
(423)587-9735   SEET#2200

Pickett, Darrell   (M1)
113 Woods Drive
Glasgow, KY 42141
dpickett@glasgow-ky.com
(270)834-6102   MICU#3107

Pickett, Patricia   (M1)
1460 Cheatham Dam Road
Ashland City, TN 37015
tovahtoo@aol.com
(615)792-4973   TNNA#7319

Pinion, Phillip   (M1)
PO Box 87
Union City, TN 38281
(731)885-9175   GRWT#9432

Pinnell, James (Jim)   (M1)
1525 Parks Well Road
Gleason, TN 38229
revpinnell@hotmail.com
(731)648-5078   GRWT#9111

Pittenger, Ronnie M   (M1)
207 Cowan Street W
Cowan, TN 37318
(615)832-8832   TNMU#7211

Plachte, Richard   (M1)
615 Grover Street
Warrensburg, MO 64093
rap@aerobiz.org
(660)441-4427   GRMI#4100

Polacek, Fred E   (M1)
907 Graham Drive
Old Hickory, TN 37138
revfredp@gmail.com
(615)754-5328   TNNA#7300

Pope, Charles (Buddy)   (M1)
2391 Fairfield Pike
Shelbyville, TN 37160
pope6897@yahoo.com
(931)205-6897   TNCO#7137

Porras, Rene Wilgen   (M3)
Cra 4 bis #10-51
La Virginia, Risaralda
COLOMBIA, SA
renewilgen@hotmail.com
(576)367-9529   MSAN#8900

Potts, Danny   (M1)
418 Eddings Street Apt 2
Fulton , KY 42041
(270)355-2264   MICO#3400

Pounds, James D   (M1)
40 Nellie Lane
Savannah, TN 38372
olivetcp@bellsouth.net
(731)925-2685   SEET#0105

Powell, Jeff   (M1)
547B Fawn Drive
Henderson, TN 38340
jfpowell2003@yahoo.com
(731)608-2040   GRWT#9100

Powell, Omer T   (M1)
11856 Sonora Hardin Springs Road
Eastview, KY 42732
(270)862-4720   MICU#3100

Prenshaw, Rebecca   (M1)
1100 Albermarie Lane
Knoxville, TN 37923
bprenshaw@yahoo.com
(865)531-1954   SEET#2307

Preston, Dennis   (M1)
7447 Knottsville Mount Zion Road
Philpot, KY 42366
dennis.preston@daviess.kyschools.us
(270)925-8144   MICU#3507

Prevost, Abigail   (M3)
4731 Lafayette Road
Hopkinsville, KY 42240
abbyprevost@gmail.com
(731)343-5386   SEGR#0100

Prosser, Forest   (M1)
1157 Mountain Creek Road
Chattanooga, TN 37405
forestprosser@comcast.net
(423)877-4114   SETG#2100

Prosser, Robert   (M1)
1021 Old State Route 76
Henry, TN 38231
(731)243-4467   GRWT#9100

Puckett, Rian   (M3)
3784 Harrison Street
Batesville, AR 72501
rppuckett@memphisseminary.edu
(731)288-7742   GRAR#1510

--==<< Q >>==--

Qualls, Michael   (M1)
5355 June Cove
Horn Lake, MS 38637
mqualls1@yahoo.com
(901)377-0526   GRWT#9100

Quevedo, Mariano   (M3)
289 Golf Club Lane
McMinnville, TN 37110
( )   TNMU#7200

Quinonez, Wilfrido   (M1)
Cra 3 No 36-29, Juan XXIII
BuenaventurValle, COLOMBIA, SA
ipc.divinoredentor@gmail.com
(310)412-1711   MSCA#8206

Quintero, Alexander   (M3)
Carrera 13 #3-81
Guacari, COLOMBIA, SA
( )   MSCA#8212

Quinton, Noah   (M1)
2912 Waller Omer Road
Sturgis, KY 42459
noah.quinton@gmail.com
(270)952-3875   GRWT#9100

--==<< R >>==--

Racines, Jairo   (M1)
CLL 39 No 13-40
Cali, COLOMBIA, SA
(311)385-6546   MSCA#8200

Rackley, Mark   (M1)
3060 Highway 140 NE
Rydal, GA 30171
pastormarkbcpcga@gmail.com
(770)382-3790   SETG#2101

Ragsdale, Donnie   (M1)
915 S Olive Street
Union City, TN 38261
(731)885-0014   GRWT#9424

Ralph, Brian   (M2)
6419 S Vinewood Street Apt 205
Littleton, CO 80120
ralph1970@gmail.com
(312)315-6915   MSDC#8700

Ramiriz, Araceli   (M3)
235 Vinewood Road Apt DG
McMinnville, TN 37090
( )   TNMU#7200

Ranson, Doris   (M1)
9440 Fenwick Road
Owensboro, KY 42301
dorisranson@bellsouth.net
(270)229-2875   MICU#3100

Ratliff, James L   (M1)
4027 Club View Drive
Memphis, TN 38125
pastorjimfcpc@yahoo.com
(901)758-0125   GRWT#9312

Reed, Charles   (M1)
10235 Highway 301
Dade City, FL 33525
instchuck12@centurylink.net
(352)567-7427   SEGR#0311

Reed, Richard   (M2)
236 Madison Street
Dyer, TN 38330
richardcplist@hotmail.com
(731)692-3604   GRWT#9101

Reese, Michael   (M1)
404 Five Oaks Boulevard
Lebanon, TN 37087
michaelhreese@bellsouth.net
(615)443-0457   TNMU#7208

Reeves, Donald   (M1)
PO Box 528
Rainsville, AL 35986
reevesd@nacc.edu
(256)228-4057   SERD#801

Reid, Richard   (M1)
123 S Fifth Street
Selmer, TN 38375
rjreid1964@msn.com
(731)453-5302   GRWT#9225

Reid, Roger   (M1)
1505 Experiment Farm Road
Lewisburg, TN 37091
drrtr@yahoo.com
(931)422-5257   TNCO#7125

Renner, Wallace   (M1)
1648 Griffith Avenue
Owensboro, KY 42303
pwrenner@adelphia.net
(270)685-4359   MICU#3100

MINISTERS CONTINUED

Reno, Michael (M3)
52 Rolla Gardens
Rolla, MO 65401
rollarenomike@gmail.com
(573)578-5321 GRMI#4309

Rice, Keith (M1)
PO Box 582
Itasca, TX 76055
rsvkeith@yahoo.com
(254)087-2418 MSRR#8400

Rice, Perryn (M1)
10802 Hayfield Drive
Dallas, TX 75238
perryn@lhpres.org
(931)526-6585 MSRR#8411

Richards, Carroll R (M1)
210 Allison Drive
Lincoln, IL 62656
FAX: (217)732-7894
dr_cr@comcast.net
(217)732-7894 MINC#5200

Richardson, W Jean (M1)
7533 Lancashire Boulevard
Powell, TN 37849
jeanandregena@frontier.com
(865)947-3111 SEET#2200

Richter, Justin (M1)
8600 Academy Road NE
Albuquerque, NM 87111
richteryp@gmail.com
(505)363-8738 MSDC#8701

Ricketts, Roger (M1)
205 Contantz Drive
Canton, MO 63435
( ) MICU#3100

Ridgely, Michael (M1)
5195 Broad Street S
Trezevant, TN 38258
(731)669-3767 GRWT#9100

Rietz, Allen (M1)
1239 Hopewell Church Road
Finger, TN 38334
(731)989-7872 GRWT#9100

Rincon, Alfredo (M1)
12008 Fred Carter
El Paso, TX 79936
yaanaivitaly@yahoo.com
(915)857-1343 MSDC#8704

Rincon, Lyvia (M1)
12008 Fred Carter
El Paso, TX 79936
yaanaivitaly@yahoo.com
(915)857-1343 MSDC#8706

Rippy, James G (M1)
442 Trina Street
Gallatin, TN 37066
lgrippy@live.com
(615)681-7086 TNNA#7300

Rivera, Carlos A (M1)
Calle Dr Jose Maria Vertiz 1410
Departmento 202B, Colonia Portales
Delegacion Benito
Juarez, C.P. 03300 MEXICO
caralrifra@une.net.co
(52)1-55-31058377 MSRR#8400

Rivera, Zenobia (M1)
Cra 12 #8-47
Cartago, Valle, COLOMBIA, SA
zenobiadedaza@yahoo.com.mx
(572)214-5060 MSAN#8900

Rodden, Linda (M1)
363 Cornelison Street
Lebanon, MO 65536
linda.rodden@mercy.net
(417)588-2207 GRMI#4100

Roddy, Lowell G (M1)
2583 Hedgerow Lane
Clarksville, TN 37043
lgroddy@yahoo.com
(931)368-1081 TNNA#7300

Rodgers, Howard (M1)
336 County Road 1216
Vinemont, AL 35179
djbr421@yahoo.com
(256)739-6296 SEHO#0500

Rodriguez, Jairo Hernan (M1)
Cll 42 No 80B 64
Barrio Versalles
Cali-Valle, COLOMBIA, SA
jairo.hrodriguez@hotmail.com
(572)377-8741 MSCA#8200

Roedder, Unhui Grace (M1)
419 S Jonathan Avenue
Springfield, MO 65802
kimroedder@hotmail.com
(417)494-6491 GRMI#4100

Rogers, Steve (M3)
37 Cool Spring Road
Trimble, TN 38259
(731)882-2229 GRWT#9408

Rojas, Antonio Mena (M1)
1421 1st Street NW
Cullman, AL 35055
antonio.mena.7@facebook.com
(256)531-8193 SEGR#0100

Rolman, William L, Jr (M1)
602 Canyon Drive
Columbia, TN 38401
wmrolmanjr@att.net
(931)388-2611 TNCO#7136

Romines, Sam (M1)
PO Box 127
Lewisburg, KY 42256
sam60romines@hotmail.com
(270)755-4282 MICU#3307

Ros, Ramiro (M1)
107 Bracken Lane
Brandon, FL 33511
bethel@gte.net
(813)633-1548 SEGR#0100

Rosales, David (M3)
101 N Lowe
Hobart, OK 73651
sagradalut@gmail.com
(580)682-0722 MSRR#8400

Rose, Missy (M1)
2986 Ruskin Road
Bartlett, TN 38134
missyrose3@yahoo.com
(901)378-1133 GRWT#9100

Rowlett, Ron (M1)
22 Diana Drive
Savannah, GA 31406
(912)351-0736 SEGR#0100

Rudolph, Allie D (M1)
855 Old Rosebower Church Road
Paducah, KY 42003
rallie307@aol.com
(270)898-4903 MICO#3400

Ruggia, Mario (Bud) (M1)
603 Rumsey Street
Kiowa, KS 67070
ruggia@aol.com
(620)825-4509 MSRR#8400

Rush, Kip John (M1)
513 Meadowlark Lane
Brentwood, TN 37027
pastor@brenthaven.org
(615)376-4563 TNNA#7331

Rush, Robert D (M1)
12935 Quail Park Drive
Cypress, TX 77429
robertrush832@gmail.com
(832)559-1500 MSTR#8100

Russell, Albert (M2)
375 Ashton Park Drive
Millbrook, AL 36054
chemistry.russell@gmail.com
(334)290-0399 SEGR#0407

Russell, Olen (Bud) (M1)
9595 Wickliffe Road
Wickliffe, KY 42087
olen552@aol.com
(270)562-1096 MICO#3414

Rustenhaven, William, III (M1)
PO Box 1303
Marshall, TX 75671
FAX: (903)935-3193
rusty@cumberlandofmarshall.org
(903)935-6609 MSTR#8115

Rustenhaven, William, Jr (M1)
703 W Burleson Street
Marshall, TX 75670
rustenhavendolores@yahoo.com
(903)935-7056 MSTR#8100

Ryan, Jack (M1)
8806 Kennesaw Mountain Drive
Mabelvale, AR 72103
(501)749-8572 GRAR#1100

Ryoo, Hwa Chang (M1)
450 Island Road Unit 146
Ramsey, NJ 07446 SECE#2400

--==<< S >>==--

Saldana, Manuel (Alex) (M1)
536 Telop
El Paso, TX 79927
campe13@yahoo.com
(915)317-9349 MSDC#8706

Salisbury, Rebecca (M1)
1033 Twin Oaks Drive
Murfreesboro, TN 37130
rebsalisbury@yahoo.com
(615)410-7801 TNMU#7200

Salyer, Stewart (M1)
2211 Foxfire Road
Clarksville, TN 37040
stewart.salyer@gmail.com
(931)980-2829 TNNA#7302

Sanchez, Josefina (M1)
7 Hancock Street
Melrose, MA 02176
fsfamily64@gmail.com
(479)970-8654 SEET#2220

Sanchez, Sol Maria (M1)
Av Americas 19 N - 18
Cali Valle
Colombia, South America
solmarias@starmedia.com
( ) MSCA#8200

MINISTERS CONTINUED

Sanders, Thomas R   (M1)
4201 W Kent Street
Broken Arrow, OK 74012
FAX: (918)437-2199
trsncf@msn.com
(918)269-0043   MSRR#6201

Sandiford, Holton   (M3)
4227 E 300th Road
Casey, IL 62420
(217)259-3773   MINC#5200

Sansom, Vernon   (M1)
7810 Shiloh Road
Midlothian, TX 76065
vernon@sansom.us
(972)825-6887   MSRR#8421

Santillano, Ray Paul   (M1)
1270 Polo Road
Columbia, SC 29223
ramon.santillano@us.army.mil
(915)500-4928   MSTR#8100

Satoh, Iwao   (M1)
8710 Hickory Falls Lane
Pewee Valley, KY 40056
iwaosatoh@gmail.com
(502)657-9643   MSJA#8300

Schmoyer, Donna Marie   (M1)
613 Mound Street
Monongahela, PA 15063
schmoyerdm@yahoo.com
(817)266-6572   MSRR#8400

Schott, Fred, Jr   (M1)
606 Taylor Trail
Springfield, TN 37172
(615)384-8572   TNNA#7321

Schultz, Don   (M1)
708 Gateway Lane
Tampa, FL 33613
(813)960-1473   SEGR#0100

Schwarz, Karl   (M1)
83 W Curtis Street
Bells, TN 38006
schw8651@bellsouth.net
(731)663-3987   GRWT#9430

Scott, Jerry   (M1)
2310 Sentell Drive
Maryville, TN 37803
dmjlscott@yahoo.com
(865)809-2621   SEET#2200

Scott, Linda   (M3)
960 S Katy Road
Atoka, OK 74525
(580)889-2292   MSCH#6100

Scott, Lisa   (M1)
(On File in General Assembly Office)
lascott1979@att.net
(816)332-0604   MINC#5200

Scott, Nathan   (M1)
960 S Katy Road
Atoka, OK 74525
(580)364-6155   MSCH#6102

Scrivener, Carol   (M1)
746 Willowsprings Boulevard
Franklin, TN 37064
csscriv@juno.com
(731)660-6469   GRWT#9100

Scrudder, Norlan   (M1)
29688 S 534 Road
Park Hill, OK 74451
ndscrudder@gmail.com
(918)949-1326   MSRR#8400

Searcy, James M   (M1)
1307 Lucy Way
Knoxville, TN 37912
gsearcy@earthlink.net
(817)293-6132   GRWT#9100

Seki, Nobuko   (M1)
4-12-42-403 Shimorenjyaku
Mitaka-shi
242-0004 JAPAN
seki@koza-church.jp
(042)248-5379   MSJA#8300

Seva, Judith   (M3)
7685 Tara Circle Apt 204
Naples, FL 34104
jclthgirl12@gmail.com
(239)269-3917   SEGR#0100

Shanley, Dwight   (M1)
16904 Old Mill Road
Little Rock, AR 72206
dwightshanley@att.net
(501)888-4190   GRAR#1100

Shannon, Randy   (M1)
30282 Highway H
Marshall, MO 65340
pastor_randy_shannon@yahoo.com
(660)886-9545   GRMI#4210

Sharpe, Michael G   (M1)
3423 Summerdale Drive
Bartlett, TN 38133
(901)276-4572   MSRR#8400

Shauf, Steve   (M1)
3032 Monroe Street
Paducah, KY 42001
sshauf@hotmail.com
(870)291-2046   MICO#3400

Shauf, Teresa   (M1)
3032 Monroe Street
Paducah, KY 42001
theshaufs@hotmail.com
(870)291-2938   MICO#3400

Shelton, Robert E   (M1)
10508 Royalwood Drive
Dallas, TX 75238
bshelton67@yahoo.com
(214)349-7162   MSRR#8400

Shelton, Robert M   (M1)
7128 Lakehurst Avenue
Dallas, TX 75230
(214)696-3237   MSRR#8400

Shelton, Steven   (M1)
7886 Farmhill Cove
Bartlett, TN 38135
faithcpcpastor@gmail.com
(901)377-0526   GRWT#9308

Shepard, Denny C   (M1)
8514 Newsom Station Road
Nashville, TN 37221
(615)662-1114   TNMU#7209

Shepherd, Sandra   (M1)
525 Summitt Oaks Court
Nashville, TN 37221
woolywagon@gmail.com
(615)772-5358   TNNA#7331

Shin, Kyung I   (M1)
1805 Gallinas Road NE
Rio Rancho, NM 87144
pastorkshin@gmail.com
(505)453-5461   MSDC#8700

Shipley, Howard E   (M1)
3800 Dan Drive
Morristown, TN 37814
hshipley@charter.net
(423)581-1092   SEET#2207

Shirey, John   (M1)
10181 State Route 56 W
Sturgis, KY 42459
amshirey7@ips.com
(270)389-3562   MICO#3400

Shirley, Betty L   (M1)
811 Rotherham Drive
Ballwin, MO 63011
therevbls@prodigy.net
(636)386-3174   MINC#5200

Shoulta, John R   (M1)
1154 Mount Carmel Road
White Plains, KY 42464
johnshoulta@bellsouth.net
(270)676-3563   MICO#3613

Shugert, Rich   (M1)
5208 Bellis Drive
Fort Worth, TX 76244
shugertr@yahoo.com
(817)913-7211   MSRR#8400

Sides, Judy Taylor   (M1)
534 Bethany Circle
Murfreesboro, TN 37128
(615)895-1627   TNMU#7231

Sims, Edward G   (M1)
2161 N Meadow Drive
Clarksville, TN 37043
simseg@aol.com
(931)206-5759   TNNA#7300

Sims, Jacob   (M1)
23716 Alabama Highway 9 N
Piedmont, AL 36272
jacobdsims@gmail.com
(205)907-8273   SEGR#0406

Sims, Joyce   (M2)
5935 Paris Highway 54
Paris, TN 38242
(731)364-3537   GRWT#9100

Sisco, Terra   (M1)
811 W Cheyenne Street
Marlow, OK 73055
terrasisco@gmail.com
(618)384-6126   MSRR#6305

Siu, Jonathan Chor K   (M1)
251 Tin Sam Estate
Shatin, HONG KONG
FAX: (852)2607-2245
cpccksiu@yahoo.com.hk
(852)2693-3444   MSHK#8807

Skidmore, Garland   (M1)
2083 US Highway 278 E
Hampton, AR 71744
(870)798-4634   GRAR#1101

Sledge, Jeff   (M1)
241 Long Bow Road
Knoxville, TN 37934
jeffsledge@charter.net
(865)318-5565   SEET#2200

Small, Kevin   (M1)
6492 E 400th Road
Martinsville, IL 62442
revkev61@gmail.com
(618)562-1463   MINC#5211

Smith, Albert J   (M1)
407 W Main Street Apt 131
Wilkesboro, NC 28697
ct_alsmith@casscomm.com
(217)452-3408   MINC#5200

Smith, Billy T   (M1)
213 Eller Cove Road
Weaverville, NC 28787
(931)368-0424   TNNA#7300

MINISTERS CONTINUED

Smith, Christian (M1)
2017 Grademere Drive
Cookeville, TN 38501
csmith2490@gmail.com
(931)265-8896   TNMU#7210

Smith, David R (M1)
PO Box 892
Rosepine, LA 70659
ogreyfox@att.net
(903)297-6074   MSTR#8100

Smith, James A (M1)
8301 Poplar Pike
Germantown, TN 38138
james1493@att.net
(901)309-1992   GRWT#9100

Smith, James (M3)
222 Southcrest Drive SW
Huntsville, AL 35802
dr.james.smith@netzero.com
(256)655-6541   SERD#0800

Smith, Jerald D (M1)
2625 Beech Bluff Road
Beech Bluff, TN 38313
jergensmith@aol.com
(731)427-9316   GRWT#9205

Smith, John Adam (M1)
916 Allen Road
Nashville, TN 37214
john.a.smith.81@gmail.com
(573)453-8455   TNNA#7305

Smith, Kirk (M1)
813 1st Avenue
Fayetteville, TN 37334
FAX: (931)438-8649
kirks37334@att.net
(931)438-8649   TNCO#7100

Smith, Nicholas (M2)
101 Cumberland Street
Glasgow, KY 42141
pastornic@gcpchurch.tv
(270)651-3308   MICU#3100

Smith, Robert A (M1)
PO Box 501
Newbern, TN 38059
ras1957@bellsouth.net
(731)627-3332   GRWT#9417

Smith, Robert H (M1)
5055 S 76th East Avenue Apt D
Tulsa, OK 74145
rhsmith@sstelco.com
(918)671-5520   MSRR#8400

Smith, Steven (M3)
100 Valleyview Drive
Leitchfield, KY 42754
( )   MICU#3201

Smith, Timothy (M1)
712 Morningside Drive
Fayetteville, TN 37334
FAX: (931)433-0056
tims38@hotmail.com
(931)438-2820   TNCO#7112

Smyrl, Jerry (M1)
3421 Montreal Street NE
Albuquerque, NM 87111
jwsmyrl@hotmail.com
(505)293-0108   MSDC#8701

Snelling, Linda (M1)
15791 State Highway 1W
Ada, OK 74820
FAX: (580)332-9424
lindasnelling@covenantcpc.org
(580)332-0799   MSRR#6304

Snyder, Joel (M1)
224 Lord Lane
Mountain View, AR 72560
snyder.joel@ymail.com
(870)269-9743   GRAR#1504

So, Lai Yuet (M3)
2/F Fu Tung Shopping Centre
Tung Chung
Lantau Island NT, HONG KONG
FAX: (852)2109-1737
laiyuet0914@gmail.com
(852)2109-1738   MSHK#8800

So, Patrick (M1)
2/F Fu Tung Shopping Center
Tung Chung
Lantau Island, HONG KONG
FAX: (852)2109-1737
pattwso@gmail.com
(852)2109-1738   MSHK#8810

Solis, Arcadio (M1)
Crr 42 D1 No 55-69
Guapi, COLOMBIA, SA
( )328-5486   MSCA#8200

Solito, Carlos (M3)
106 Highway 63
Caleru, AL 35040
fcg9700@gmail.com
(205)329-8514   SEGR#0100

Sontowski, Marian (M1)
17101 N Western Avenue
Edmond, OK 73012
stonegatecpc@gmail.com
(405)340-7281   MSRR#6307

Sosa, Alexandri (M1)
2828 W Kirby Street
Tampa, FL 33614
FAX: (813)932-9700
sosapcus@gmail.com
(813)960-1473   SEGR#0307

Spence, Thomas R (M1)
PO Box 809
Burns Flat, OK 73624
tomspence0302@gmail.com
(580)562-4531   MSRR#6301

Spurling, Robert T, Jr (M1)
305 Wayne Drive
Hopkinsville, KY 42240
(865)803-8582   MICO#3611

Steeley, Tim (M3)
PO Box 281
Mt Vernon, MO 65712
tsteeley@swr5.k12.mo.us
(417)466-4345   GRMI#4102

Stefan, Gregory (M1)
1917 Birchwood Street
East Pearl, PA 17519
pastorstefan@att.net
(931)296-5291   GRWT#7300

Stephens, Blake (M1)
2559 Holders Cove Road
Winchester, TN 37398
blsteph@edge.net
(931)939-2628   TNMU#7235

Stephenson, Joseph (M3)
PO Box 129
Bethany, IL 61914
(217)853-7819   MINC#5200

Stevens, Brittany (M3
606 Huntington Parkway
Nashville, TN 37211
bstevens5@my.apsu.edu
(615)719-3362   TNNA#7300

Stone, Paul (M1)
3490 State Route 2837
Clay, KY 42404
stonepstc@aol.com
(270)664-6244   MICO#3621

Stovall, Jeff (M1)
2829 Trelawny Drive
Clarksville, TN 37043
jeffstovall@juno.com
(931)993-6104   TNNA#7300

Stutler, Tim (M1)
1044 Mansker Farm Boulevard
Hendersonville, TN 37075
tim@goodlettsvillechurch.com
(615)859-5888   TNNA#7328

Suenram, Timothy (M1)
13850 Mizzen Street
Corpus Christi, TX 78418
9tdsdt9@gmail.com
(832)217-6367   MSTR#8100

Sumerlin, Larkin (M2)
174 Brookgreen Lane
Indian Springs, AL 35124
larkin_sumerlin72@hotmail.com
(334)357-0007   SEGR#0100

Sumrall, Phil (M1)
107 Barnhardt Circle
Fort Oglethorpe, GA 30742
phil.sumrall@gmail.com
(423)903-1938   SETG#2100

Sung, John (M2)
26 Old Orchard Road
Cherry Hill, NJ 08003
(856)751-0227   SETG#2100

Suttle, Michael (M1)
507 Ouachita 18
Camden, AR 71701
m_s_suttle@msn.com
(870)836-0008   GRAR#1303

Suzuki, Atsushi (M1)
53-17 Higashi Kibogaoka
Asahi-ku Yokohama Kanagawa-ken
241-0826 JAPAN
asyuwa98@m10.alpha-net.ne.jp
FAX: (045)362-2603
(045)362-2603   MSJA#8315

Suzuki, Temote (M2)
9-14-15-310 Honcho Kamitsuruma
Sagamihara-shi, Kanagawa-ken
228-0818 JAPAN
temo_suzuki@hotmail.com
( )   MSJA#8300

Sweet-Brockman, Anna (M2)
210 E Main Street Apt B
Greenfield, TN 38230
amsweet@memphisseminary.edu
(865)803-8582   SEET#2200

Sweet, Don (M1)
3008 Shropshire Boulevard
Powell, TN 37849
mariondon77@netscape.com
(865)938-7435   SEET#2200

Sweet, Thomas (M1)
2711 Windemere Lane
Powell, TN 37849
tsweet1@comcast.net
(865)938-0508   SEET#2301

Sweigart, John M (M1)
PO Box 876
Dover, AL 72837
(479)229-4041   GRAR#1100

MINISTERS CONTINUED

Sze, Joseph (M1)
Rau Sao Joaquim, 382
Liberdale, Sao Paulo, SP
CEP 015068-000, BRAZIL
pastorsze@yahoo.com
( ) MSDC#8700

--=≪ T ≫=--

Tabor, Don M (M1)
9611 Mitchell Place
Brentwood, TN 37027
FAX: (615)373-3356
dontabor@comcast.net
(615)776-7292 TNNA#7300
Taborda, Arturo (M1)
Cra 43 #20D-46
Zamora, Medellin
Antioquia, COLOMBIA, SA
chilalu1147@hotmail.com
(574)267-1351 MSAN#8900
Talley, Edward (M1)
404 Serenity Circle
Walland, TN 37886
(205)854-1886 SEGR#0100
Tamai, Yukio (M1)
3-17-57 Nakashinden
Ebina-shi Kanagawa-ken
243-0422 JAPAN
yukiotamai@icloud.com
(046)234-3426 MSJA#8311
Tan, Pek Hua (M1)
7 Belhaven Avenue
Daly City, CA 94015
ptan27@yahoo.com
(415)515-0076 MSDC#8700
Tanck, Brian (M2)
64 Mercer Street
Princeton, NJ 08540
brian.tanck@gmail.com
(630)730-1577 SEGR#0100
Tanck, Micaiah Thomas (M1)
2912 S Broad Street Apt B3
Scottsboro, AL 35769
micaiah.thomas@gmail.com
(205)478-5985 SERD#0809
Terrell, Elizabeth (M1)
2073 Vinton Avenue
Memphis, TN 38104
(901)647-2788 GRAR#1220
Thomas, Cassandra (M1)
1920 Dancy Street
Fayetteville, NC 28301
chcothomas@yahoo.com
(910)488-4897 MSRR#8400
Thomas, Don F (M1)
400 Park Hill Road
Collierville, TN 38017
thomas63981@comcast.net
(901)861-6398 GRWT#0501
Thomas, Don H (M1)
4829 Caldwell Mill Road
Birmingham, AL 35242
dhtatn4ybc@cs.com
(205)742-0785 SEGR#0105
Thomas, Lynn (M1)
4833 Caldwell Mill Lane
Birmingham, AL 35242
lynndont@gmail.com
(205)601-5770 SEGR#0100

Thompson, Dee Ann (M1)
226 W Bellville Street
Marion, KY 42064
deethomp5@hotmail.com
(270)445-0310 MICO#3207
Thompson, Eugene (M1)
2825 Albatross Road
Del Ray Beach, FL 33444
( ) MICU#3100
Thompson, Tommy (M1)
9160 Tchulahoma Road
Southaven, MS 38671
(662)393-2552 GRWT#9100
Thompson, W Fay (M1)
210 Macbeth Lane
Glasgow, KY 42141
(270)646-2218 MICU#3100
Thornton, Jesse (M1)
122 E Cherry Street
Chandler, IN 47610
jessthornton@msn.com
(812)925-6475 MINC#5302
Tobler, Garth (M1)
136 Boat Landing Road
Oneonta, AL 35121
gatobler@gmail.com
(205)683-0298 SEGR#0100
Todd, Christopher (M1)
3303 Decker Street
Bartlett, TN 38134
catodd1964@gmail.com
(901)848-9913 GRWT#9320
Todd, Laura (M1)
3303 Decker Street
Bartlett, TN 38134
littlelaurarose@yahoo.com
(901)496-1443 GRWT#9100
Tolley, Robert (Butch) (M1)
1445 New Murraytown Road NW
Cleveland, TN 37312
butchtolley@hotmail.com
(423)837-6488 SETG#2100
Tompkins, Wayne (M1)
548 E Columbia Road 23
Emerson, AR 71740
waynetompkinsministries@yahoo.com
(870)807-2874 GRWT#9221
Topar, Shirley (M1)
2233 Cambridge Drive SE
Grand Rapids, MI 49506
s_j_topar@yahoo.com
(616)245-0625 MINC#5200
Torres, Rodrigo (M3)
Aereo 6365
Cali, COLOMBIA, SA
(011)882-8372 MSCA#8205
Townsend, Mary Anna (M3)
1123 Tyler
Warrensburg, MO 64093
wrenhse1123@gmail.com
(660)909-5966 GRMI#4111
Trapp, Emily (M3)
4750 Harvest Knoll Cove N
Memphis, TN 38125
(901)756-4738 GRWT#9100
Travieso, Julio (M1)
15910 Countrybrook Street
Tampa, FL 33624
jutra98@aol.com
(813)963-3727 SEGR#0100

Travis, Kermit (M1)
3220 Sharon Highway 89
Dresden, TN 38225
(731)364-2315 GRWT#9124
Treadaway, Kenneth A (M1)
172 Miller County 494
Texarkana, AR 71854
treadaways@ark.net
(870)574-1609 GRAR#1100
Trotter, Wendell (M1)
1516 Fell Avenue NE
Huntsville, AL 35811
wendelltrotter@knology.net
(256)519-6571 TNCO#7100
Truax, Robert Lee, Jr (M1)
2989 Champions Drive Apt 204
Lakeland, TN 38002
(901)266-5927 GRWT#9100
Truitt, Robert D (M1)
1238 Old East Side Road
Burns, TN 37029
FAX: (615)446-7827
rdtjct@aol.com
(615)740-9180 TNNA#7308
Tsui, Jackson (M2)
258 Carlos D'Assumpcao
Ed Kin Heng Long 4 Andar LMN
Macau
FAX: (852)2771-2726
(853)2892-1702 MSHK#8800
Tsujimoto, Mark (M1)
88 S Broadway Unit 3210
Millbrae, CA 94030
mltsuijimoto@gmail.com
(650)697-6901 MSDC#8700
Tubb, Gary Robert (M1)
103 Forest Drive
Mountain Home, AR 72653
grtubb@yahoo.com
(870)424-0603 GRAR#1505
Tucker, Greg (M2)
612A Idlewood Lane
Knoxville, TN 37923
greg.tucker311@outlook.comt
(865)242-4086 SEET#2319
Tucker, James D (M1)
PO Box 34
Mc Daniels, KY 40152
(270)257-8971 MICU#3100
Tucker, Paul (M1)
3801 Brush Hill Pike
Nashville, TN 37216
paultucker@gmail.com
(615)430-9158 TNNA#7325
Turner, Glyn (M1)
1660 Chattanooga Valley Road
Flintstone, GA 30725
glynturner@outlook.com
(585)307-7715 SETG#2100
Turner, O Gene (M1)
5160 McSpadden Road
Rives, TN 38253
(731)536-0189 GRWT#9100
Turner, Leonard E, Jr (M1)
12651 Wagon Wheel Circle
Knoxville, TN 37934
pastor@unioncpchurch.com
FAX: (865)675-3787
(865)966-8262 SEET#2315

MINISTERS CONTINUED

Turner, Steven W   (M1)
7622 Snider Road
Gilmer, TX 75645
FAX: (903)757-2572
fcpclongview@sbcglobal.net
(903)758-5184   MSTR#8112

Twilla, Kevin   (M3)
287 Owl Circle
Lebanon, TN 37087
( )   TNMU#7200

Tyus, Dwayne   (M1)
901 W Old Hickory Boulevard
Madison, TN 37115
dwayne.tyus@gmail.com
(615)862-0431   TNNA#7332

--==<< U >>==--

Underwood, Jerrell M   (M1)
PO Box 9
Garfield, KY 40140
(270)536-3706   MICU#3100

Ushioda, Kenji   (M1)
2-47-3 Akuwa-higashi Seya-ku
Yokohama, Kanagawa-ken
246-0023 JAPAN
ushioda@jc.ejnet.ne.jp
(046)361-4351   MSJA#8312

--==<< V >>==--

Vacca, Gary   (M1)
2203 Creekwood Drive
Murray, KY 42071
(270)978-0818   MICO#3406

Valdez, Diana   (M1)
Cra 50 D#62-69
Medellin, Antioquia, COLOMBIA, SA
dianamariavaldezduque@gmail.com
(574)263-2154   MSAN#8915

Valencia, Jorge   (M1)
Aereo 4290
Cali, COLOMBIA, SA
( )332-5840   MSCA#8200

Valencia, Nulbel   (M1)
Diag 11D Casa 11 urbGemelas
Dosquebradas
Risaralda, COLOMBIA, SA
(576)330-7704   MSAN#8900

Van Meter, Bill   (M1)
10626 Highway 41
Charleston, AR 72933
revbill46@gmail.com
(479)965-2998   GRAR#1402

Vance, Dennis   (M1)
1320 Valleywood Drive
Paris, TN 38242
rvdvance@hotmail.com
(731)420-4261   GRWT#9428

Vanderlaan, D Kevin   (M1)
17246 Highway K
Aurora, MO 65605
pastorkevin2@gmail.com
(217)620-2723   GRMI#5401

Varilla, Adan Manuel   (M3)
Calle 48 D E #96A-30
Medellin, Antioquia
COLOMBIA, SA   MSAN#8900

Varnell, William   (M3)
6729 Old Dunlop Road
Whitwell, TN 37397
billvatagts@hotmail.com
(423)658-0506   SETG#2100

Varner, Susan   (M1)
14709 Glisten Lane
Little Rock, AR 72223
smvarner76@yahoo.com
(901)371-1249   GRAR#1100

Vasquez, Alejandro   (M1)
Cra 58 #32A-41 Apt 420
Bello, Antioquia, COLOMBIA, SA
almaesda@une.net.co
(574)451-4816   MSAN#8918

Vasseur, Terry   (M1)
121 Crossland Road
Murray, KY 42071
tvasseur@bellsouth.net
(270)876-8083   MICO#3400

Vaught, Joseph R   (M1)
7424 Highland Lick Road
Lewisburg, KY 42256
brojoe2@logantele.com
(270)726-8497   MICU#3308

Velez, Gabriel   (M1)
CL 8A #16A-26
Dosquebradas
Risaralda, COLOMBIA, SA
(576)330-1168   MSAN#8900

Velez, Gloria Patricia   (M3)
Cra 4 bis #10-51
LaVirginia, Risaralda
COLOMBIA, SA
renewilgen@hotmail.com
(576)385-4517   MSAN#8900

Vick, Joe   (M1)
6064 Old Hickory Boulevard
Whites Creek, TN 37189
joervick@gmail.com
(615)519-5249   TNNA#7318

Vickers, Fran   (M1)
7225 Old Clinton Pike
Knoxville, TN 37921
franv3@comcast.net
(865)859-0805   SEET#2301

--==<< W >>==--

Wada, Ichiro   (M3)
Tokyo Christian University
3-301-5 Uchino Inzai-shi, Chiba
270-1347 JAPAN
ichirowada@gmail.com
(047)646-1141   MSJA#8300

Wagner, Hugh   (M1)
12556 Timberline Drive
Garfield, AR 72732
hughawagner@gmail.com
(479)359-0021   MSRR#8400

Walker, Hobert   (M1)
PO Box 66
Rutherford, TN 38369
rutherfordcpchurch@gmail.com
(731)665-7236   GRWT#9429

Walker, Michael C   (M1)
1404 Wilshire Drive
Odessa, TX 79761
mworator@gmail.com
(731)643-6730   GRWT#9100

Walkup, Lyon   (M1)
225 Bertha Owen Road
Morrison, TN 37357
dirtroad@blomand.net
(931)604-3233   TNMU#7207

Wallace, Andrew   (M1)
816 Howard Avenue
Burlingame, CA 94010
( )   MINC#5200

Wallace, Boyce   (M1)
Cra 101 No 15-93
Cali, COLOMBIA, SA
hbwcali@yahoo.com
( )339-1579   MSCA#8200

Walsh, Devin   (M3)
801 East "M" Street
Russellville, AR 72801
(479)890-6716   GRAR#1100

Wan, Sonny   (M1)
13 Wexford Place
Aladema, CA 94502
sonny@cumberlandsf.org
(415)421-1874   MSDC#8700

Wang, Huiling   (M2)
5562 S Yank Court
Littleton, CO 80127
whuiling88@yahoo.com
(303)330-3929   MSDC#8700

Ward, Andrew   (M1)
407 Rose Hill Court
Goodlettsville, TN 37072
andrewbward@aol.com
(615)456-9136   TNNA#7319

Ward, Frank   (M1)
46 Henderson Cove
Atoka, TN 38004
bamaguy68@xipline.com
(901)837-1972   GRWT#9100

Warren, Christopher   (M1)
906 Prince Lane
Murfreesboro, TN 37129
chris@murfreesborocpc.org
(615)828-8719   TNMU#7232

Warren, Elizabeth   (M3)
811 W Wall Street
Morrilton, AR 72110
(501)354-4139   GRAR#1100

Warren, Glenn   (M1)
116 Cedar Hill Drive
Waverly, TN 37185
gwarren224@gmail.com
(931)209-5431   TNNA#7339

Warren, Gordon   (M1)
811 Wall Street
Morrilton, AR 72110
jogordonwarren@suddenlink.net
(501)208-1120   GRAR#1219

Warren, Jo   (M1)
811 Wall Street
Morrilton, AR 72110
pastorjo47@ymail.com
(501)354-4139   GRAR#1211

Warren, Joy   (M1)
907 W Main Street
Murfreesboro, TN 37129
revjoywarren@gmail.com
(615)828-8719   TNMU#7232

Warren, William   (M1)
7139 Toro Cove
Germantown, TN 38138
FAX: (901)759-3653
cpcgww@aol.com
(901)755-8058   GRWT#9310

Washburn, Gloria   (M2)
PO Box 2484
Jordan, AR 72519
grwashburn07@gmail.com
(870)321-3539   GRAR#1100

MINISTERS CONTINUED

Watkins, Robert B (M1)
235 Misty Drive
Somerset, KY 42503
watkr@mac.com
(319)431-0990   MINC#5200

Watson, April (M1)
529 W Bellville
Marion, KY 42064
aprilwatson@hotmail.com
(270)965-2850   MICO#3411

Watson, Dale (M1)
1705 Lawnville Road
Kingston, TN 37763
revdwatson@comcast.net
(865)376-2192   SEET#2317

Watson, Johnny E (M1)
272 Madison Street
Dyer, TN 38330
rev.jwatson@bellsouth.net
(731)692-3555   GRWT#9409

Watson, Jonathan (M1)
4017 Claude Drive
Smyrna, TN 37167
watsonjonathan@bellsouth.net
(615)630-9153   TNCO#7100

Watson, Micah (M3)
2529 Middle Tennessee Boulevard
Murfreesboro, TN 37130
mwatson4289@gmail.com
(615)692-2742   TNMU#7200

Watt, Eva (M3)
258 Carlos D'Assumpcao
Ed Kin Heng Long 4 Andar LMN
MACAU
FAX: (852)2892-1702
eva6e@hotmail.com
(853)2892-1702   MSHK#8804

Watts, Glenn David (M2)
7400 Willowbend Drive
Crestwood, KY 40014
hongkongbrother@hotmail.com
(502)241-0436   MICU#3100

Wayman, Sam (M1)
707 High Hill Creek Road
LaGrange, TX 78945
samndonnawayman@gmail.com
(979)968-3734   MSTR#8100

Weaver, Dennis (M1)
1750 Government Road
Princeton, KY 42245
dsweaver@memphisseminary.edu
(731)592-9054   MICO#3614

Webb, William G (M1)
7926 S 78th E Avenue
Tulsa, OK 74133
(918)294-9117   MSRR#8400

Welch, Johnie (M1)
PO Box 1506
Dyersburg, TN 38025
johniewelch@msn.com
(731)287-9008   GRWT#9100

Weldon, Mark (M1)
1515 Chambliss Drive
Birmingham, AL 35226
weldonm@bellsouth.net
(205)330-8580   SEGR#0100

West, David (M1)
2027 Lucille Street
Lebanon, TN 37087
(217)732-7568   TNNA#7300

West, Earl (M1)
246 Maple Avenue
Greensburg, KY 42743
west5010@windstream.net
(207)932-5010   MICU#3116

West, Fred E, Jr (M1)
510 Cedaredge Drive
New Smyrna, FL 32168
jwest616@earthlink.net
(206)409-8321   SEET#2200

Westbrook, James (M1)
1717 Wedgewood Drive
Union City, TN 38261
westbrook731@bellsouth.net
(731)884-0918   GRWT#9100

Westfall, Charles K (M1)
94 Honeysuckle Drive
Gilbertsville, KY 42044
(270)362-0816   MICO#3400

Weston, Robert E (M1)
11 Summer Bluff
San Antonio, TX 78254
rjaweston@gmail.com
(210)347-0232   MSTR#8610

Whaley, Greg (M2)
4970 Comstock Road
Chapel Hill, TN 37034
grewha@mail.com
(931)364-7637   TNMU#7202

Wheeler, Nathan (M1)
1255 Wedgewood Street
Nashville, TN 38111
nathantyac@gmail.com
(901)606-9535   GRWT#9100

Whitaker, Perry Eugene (M1)
235 Sykes Road
Brush Creek, TN 38547
brotherperry@msn.com
(615)631-1844   SERD#0810

White, Diann (M1)
9394 Alex Dickson Cove
Bartlett, TN 38133
diannwhite12@yahoo.com
(901)377-7776   GRWT#9110

White, Mack (M2)
408 W Main Street
Smithville, TN 37166
wnax408@yahoo.com
(615)318-9863   TNMU#7200

Whitworth, Gary W (M1)
1706 Old Hickory Boulevard
Brentwood, TN 37027
(615)915-4180   TNNA#7300

Whray, Richard "Rocky" (M1)
201 8th Avenue SE
Winchester, TN 37398
rocklex1017@att.net
(931)636-4844   TNMU#7228

Wieland, Jack G Jr (M1)
PO Box 116
Napoleon, MO 64074
jgwieland@hotmail.com
(217)823-4331   GRMI#4100

Wiggins, Joe (M1)
2734 US Highway 41A S
Eagleville, TN 37060
jwigginz@aol.com
(615)274-2011   TNCO#7109

Wilborn, Kimberley (M3)
4743 Happy Hollow Road
Hawesville, KY 42348
(270)927-9577   MICU#3204

Wilkerson, Patrick (M1)
7719 S Whispering Oak Circle
Powell, TN 37849
patrickwilkerson3@gmail.com
(865)617-9126   SEET#2301

Wilkinson, Michael (M1)
1174 Tanglewood Street
Memphis, TN 38114
pastormike@kfcpc.comcastbiz.net
(205)533-2001   SEET#2305

Wilkinson, Neal (M3)
1174 Tanglewood Street
Memphis, TN 38114
(615)934-7382   TNNA#7300

Williams, Bobby D (M1)
844 W Highway 22
Union City, TN 38261
(731)885-1710   GRWT#9402

Williams, Cory (M1)
3148 Long Bridge Lane
Arlington, TN 38002
coromis@hotmail.com
(901)486-5981   GRWT#9100

Williams, Dale (M1)
3156 State Route 2837
Clay, KY 42404
dalewilliams@roadrunner.com
(270)664-2044   MICO#3618

Williams, David J (M1)
20 Acorn Drive
Harrisburg, IL 629463790
(618)252-1851   MICO#3400

Williamson, Dave (M1)
PO Box 67
Dolph, AR 72528
(870)499-7448   GRAR#1513

Wills, Brent (M1)
4607 E Richmond Shop Road
Lebanon, TN 37090
bwills9185@yahoo.com
(615)449-3258   TNMU#7218

Wills, Robin (M3)
4607 E Richmond Shop Road
Lebanon, TN 37090
robinrush24@aol.com
(615-870-4773)   TNMU#7200

Wilson, Brenda (M1)
35 Collins Drive
Elizabethtown, KY 42701
susieq2007@windstream.net
(270)249-3835   MICU#3100

Wilson, Craig (M1)
2300 Frayser Boulevard
Memphis, TN 38127
craigwilson2300@yahoo.com
(901)277-4066   GRWT#9306

Wilson, Don (M1)
7300 Calle Montana NE
Albuquerque, NM 87113
don-wilson07@comcast.net
(505)823-2594   MSDC#8700

Wilson, Kevin (M1)
2225 North East Road SE
Cleveland, TN 37311
revkev1000@hotmail.com
(423)284-6397   SETG#2112

Wilson, Melissa (M3)
107 Hillwood Drive
Dickson, TN 37055
milzwilz@comcast.net
(615)446-7523   TNNA#7300

Wilson, Thomas (M1)
4543 Lake Vista
Memphis, TN 38128
tomjw217@gmail.com
(901)382-6190   GRWT#9100

Wing So, Patrick Tat (M1)
2/F Fu Tung Shopping Centre
Tung Chung
Lantau Island, HONG KONG
FAX: (852)2109-1737
cpctwso@yahoo.com.hk
(522)109-1738   MSHK#8810

Winn, Don (M1)
375 Cumberland Mountain Circle
Sunbright, TN 37872
dwinn_ky@yahoo.com
(615)478-9910   SEET#2200

Wolf, Matthew (M3)
1178 S Salt Pond
Marshall, MO 65340
cleanwolf77@yahoo.com
(660)202-3762   GRMI#4100

Womack, Carey (M1)
114 Doris Street
Camden, TN 38320
camdencppastor@bellsouth.net
(731)220-3900   GRWT#9105

Wong, Bruce (M1)
716 Duncanville Court
Campbell, CA 95008
revbwong@gmail.com
(408)628-1723   MSDC#8700

Wong, Samson (M2)
CPC Yao Dao Primary School
Tin Yuet Estate
Tin Shui Wai, NT, HONG KONG
FAX: (852)2617-0287
wongchishui@yahoo.com.hk
(852)2617-7872   MSHK#8800

Wong, So Li (M1)
2/F Fu Tung Shopping Centre
Tung Chung, Lantau Island
HONG KONG
FAX: (852)2109-1737
soliwong@gmail.com
(852)2109-1738   MSHK#8800

Wong, Yim Ngar (M2)
Wing B&C, G/F, Ming Wik House
Kin Ming Estate
Tseung Kwan O,NT, HONG KONG
FAX: (852)2706-0114
yimngar@yahoo.com.hk
(852)2706-0111   MSHK#8808

Wood, Kevin L (M1)
339 David Street
McKenzie, TN 38201
FAX: (865)588-8581
revkevbuford1972@gmail.com
(865)228-0710   GRWT#9100

Wood, Wayne (M1)
HC 61 Box 600
Calico Rock, AR 72519
FAX: (870)297-3151
bexarwood@centurytel.net
(870)297-2205   GRAR#1100

Woodliff, George (M1)
310 W Cleveland Street Apt A3
Prairie Grove, AR 72956
mwoodliff@kih.net
(479)410-1933   GRAR#1100

Wooten, Wallace (M1)
1152 Melrose Road
Lockesburg, AR 71846
(870)289-2224   GRAR#1100

Wright, B J (M1)
301 25th Street
Phenix City, AL 36867
bojobo3@yahoo.com
(334)298-2896   SETG#2100

Wright, John (M3)
( )   TNMU#7200

--==<< X >>==--

--==<< Y >>==--

Yang, Buhwan (M1)
19 Taylors Run
Tinton Falls, NJ 07712
yangmoksa@gmail.com
(732)458-2203   SECE#2131

Yano, Fumitsuta (M1)
424-4 Kamide, Fjinomiya-shi
Shuizuika-ken JAPAN
(054)454-0313   MSJA#8300

Yaple, George H (M1)
2051 Lost Creek Road
Carbon Hill, AL 35549
(205)924-9921   SEHO#0500

Yarce, Janeth (M1)
3019 W Calavar Road
Phoenix, AZ 85053
janethyarce@yahoo.com
(630)518-0295   MINC#5200

Yarce, Omar (M1)
10925 Neptune Drive
Cooper City, FL 33026
alphavida@gmail.com
(205)919-9685   SEGR#0100

Yarce, Virginia (M3)
10925 Neptune Drive
Cooper City, FL 33026
ginnyyarce@gmail.com
(954)850-7111   SEGR#0100

Yates, Scott (M1)
8818 New Town Road
Rockvale, TN 37153
scott@scottyates.net
(615)274-3000   TNCO#7141

Yau, Chat Ming (M2)
G/F 251 Tin Sam Village
Shatin, NT, HONG KONG
FAX: (852)2607-2245
summerycm@yahoo.com.hk
(852)2693-3444   MSHK#8800

Yau, Eliza Yuk Lan Chui (M2)
14-16 TsatTsz Mui Road
1/Fl Block B North Point
HONG KONG
FAX: (852)2564-2898
elizaylyau@yahoo.com.hk
(852)2562-2148   MSHK#8805

Yeung, William Kin Keung (M1)
28 Hong Yip Street
Yuen Long, HONG KONG
FAX: (852)263-9562
william@xilincpc.org.hk
(852)2639-9176   MSHK#8809

York, Danny (M1)
5420 State Route 902
Fredonia, KY 42411
nonnieyork@yahoo.com
(270)350-7262   MICO#3413

Young, Taylor (M2)
255 Willard Drive
Nashville, TN 37211
brandontayloryoung@yahoo.com
(615)319-8294   TNNA#7300

Youngman, Betty (M1)
1471 Creekview Court
Fort Worth, TX 76112
bettyy@swbell.net
(817)492-4100   MSRR#8400

Yu, Alexis (M1)
1761 Willow Way
San Bruno, CA 94066
alexis.yu.k@gmail.com
(415)421-1624   MSDC#8501

Yu, Carver Tat Sum (M1)
2/F Welland Plaza
188 Nam Cheong Street
Sham Shui Po, Kowloon, HONG KONG
FAX: (852)2771-2726
carver.yu@cgst.edu
(852)2794-2382   MSHK#8800

Yu, Grace Siu Tim (M1)
2/F Welland Plaza
188 Nam Cheong Street
Sham Shui Po, Kowloon, HONG KONG
FAX: (852)2771-2726
yuleungsiutim@netvigator.com
(852)2783-8923   MSHK#8800

Yu, Pyong San (Sonny) (M1)
139 Silverado Drive
Santa Teresa, NM 88008
pyongsanyu@hotmail.com
(915)329-3451   MSDC#8700

Yu, Wn-yong (M1)
325-1 DongHyen-Dong
Jecheon-city, Choongbuk, KOREA
lifeyu@hanmail.net
(043)652-0540   MMT

Yuen, Amos Pui Chung (M1)
2/F Welland Plaza
188 Nam Cheong Street
Sham Shui Po, Kowloon, HONG KONG
FAX: (852)2771-2726
revyuen@taohsien.org.hk
(852)2783-8923   MSHK#8806

Yuen, Susanna (M2)
28 Hong Yip Street
28 Hong Yip Street
Yuen Long, NT, HONG KONG
FAX: (522)639-5620
susanna@yuenlongcpc.org
(522)639-9176   MSHK#8800

Yung, Karen (M2)
Flat D, 2/F
338-340 Castle Peak Road
Kowloon, HONG KONG
FAX: (852)3020-0365
(852)2386-6563   MSHK#8800

--==<< Z >>==--

Zumbrunnen, Craig (M1)
1210 Country Club Road Apt 3
Santa Teresa, NM 88008
craigzum1@yahoo.com
(580)471-0308   MSRR#8400

ALPHABETICAL INDEX OF CHURCHES

The four letter abbreviation indicates the synod and presbytery of which the congregation
is a member. The four digit number indicates the church number.
(See pages 10-12 for abbreviations of presbyteries.)

--=<<A>>==--

Alabaster
   AL Alabaster .... SERD#0107
Algood
   TN Algood......................TNMU#7201
Allsboro
   AL Cherokee .... SEHO#0501
Antioch
   AL Reform .... .SEGR#0701
   KY Knob Lick.................. MICU#3101
   LA Quitman .... MSTR#8101
Antioch Union
   TN Union City .... GRWT#9401
Appleton
   AR Atkins........................ .GRAR#1202
Arkansas Loving
   AR Little Rock .... GRAR#2135
Arlington
   TN Erin ....TNNA#7311
Armenia
   CO Quindio.....................MSAN#8903
Asahi Mission Point
   JA 241-0021 .... MSJA#8315
Ash Hill
   TN Spring Hill ....TNCO#7101
Atwood
   TN Atwood......................GRWT#9101
Auburn
   KY Auburn......................MICU#3301
Austin, First
   TX Austin.........................MSTR#8601

--=<<B>>==--

Bald Knob
   KY Russellville................. MICU#3302
Baldwin Chapel
   AL Cullman...................... SEHO#0202
Banks
   TN Smithville...................TNMU#7202
Barren Fork
   AR Mount Pleasant .... GRAR#1501
Barren Springs
   TN Hollow Rock...............GRWT#9102
Bartow
   GA Rydal........................SETG#2101
Bates Hill
   TN McMinnville ....TNMU#7203
Bayou de Chien
   KY Water Valley .... MICO#3401
Beaver Creek
   TN Knoxville .... SEET#2301
Beech
   TN Hendersonville............ TNNA#7301
   TN Union City .... GRWT#9402
Beech Grove
   TN Beechgrove ....TNMU#7204
Beersheba
   MS Columbus .... SEGR#0702
Belleview
   TN Franklin......................TNCO#7104
Bells Chapel
   TN Dyer ....GRWT#9403
Belvidere
   TN Belvidere....................TNMU#7205

Ben Lomond
   AR Ben Lomond .... GRAR#1301
Benton
   KY Benton ....MICO#3403
Bertram
   TX Bertram ....MSTR#8605
Betania Mission
   CO Cali ....MSCA#8204
Bethany
   IL Bethany......................MINC#5401
Bethel
   CO Cali ....MSCA#8205
   KY Center ....MICU#3102
   KY Kevil ....MICO#3404
   MO Wentworth ....GRMI#4102
   TN Atoka........................GRWT#9301
   TN Clarksville................... TNNA#7302
Bethel #1
   KY Harrodsburg................MICU#3103
Bethesda
   AR Camden.................... .GRAR#1302
   TN Fall Branch..................SEET#2201
   TN Friendship ....GRWT#9404
Bethlehem
   TN Union City .... GRWT#9405
Beulah
   KY Hartford .... MICU#3501
Big Cove
   AL Brownsboro................. SERD#0801
Blues Hill
   TN McMinnville ....TNMU#7207
Boiling Springs
   TN Portland.....................MICU#3303
Bolivar
   TN Bolivar ....GRWT#9202
Booneville
   AR Booneville.................. GRAR#1401
Boonshill
   TN Boonshill....................TNCO#7106
Bowling Green
   KY Bowling Green .... MICU#3304
Bradford
   TN Bradford....................GRWT#9104
Branchville
   AL Odenville..................... SEGR#0106
Brenthaven
   TN Brentwood.................. TNNA#7331
Bridgeport 1st
   PA Bridgeport....................MICU#3131
Brier Creek
   KY Bremen ....MICU#3503
Brunswick
   TN Brunswick...................GRWT#9302
Brush Hill
   TN Nashville..................... TNNA#7325
Burns Flat
   OK Burns Flat...................MSRR#6301
Burnt Prairie
   IL Burnt Prairie ....MINC#5102
Byron
   AR Calico Rock .... GRAR#1508

--=<<C>>==--

Cairo
   MS Cedarbluff............ SEGR#0704

Caleb Mission
   CO Montebello.................. MSCA#8223
Calico Rock
   AR Calico Rock .... GRAR#1503
Calvary
   KY Mayfield .... MICO#3405
   TN Clarksville.................. TNNA#7342
Camden
   AR Camden..................... GRAR#1303
   TN Camden....................GRWT#9105
Camp Ground
   AR Hampton ....GRAR#1101
   IL Anna ....MICO#5103
   TN Decaturville................GRWT#9204
   TN Erin .... TNNA#7312
Campbellsville
   KY Campbellsville.............MICU#3104
Campground
   IL Greenville ....MINC#5402
Cane Ridge
   TN Cane Ridge................. TNNA#7326
Caneyville
   KY Caneyville..................MICU#3201
Cartago
   CO Valle.........................MSAN#8906
Casa De Fe
   MA Malden .... SEET#2220
Casey
   IL Casey ....MINC#5201
Casey's Fork
   KY Marrowbone ....MICU#3105
Caulksville
   AR Ratcliff...................... GRAR#1402
Cedar Flat
   KY Edmonton .... MICU#3106
Cedar Hill
   TN Greeneville................... SEET#2202
Cedar Springs
   TN Whitwell ....SETG#2119
Central
   CO Cali .... MSCA#8208
Champ
   TN Mulberry ....TNCO#7108
Chandler
   IN Chandler......................MICO#5302
Chapel Hill
   TN Chapel Hill..................TNCO#7109
Charleston
   TN Cleveland ....SETG#2102
Charlotte
   TN Charlotte .... TNNA#7303
Chattanooga 1st
   TN Chattanooga ....SETG#2104
Cheung Chau
   HO Cheung Chau.............MSHK#8801
Chinese
   CA San Francisco.............MSDC#8501
Christ
   FL Lutz............................SEGR#0303
   IN Indianapolis.................MINC#5305
Christ Church
   AL Huntsville................... SERD#0814
Clark's Grove
   TN Maryville....................SEET#2302
Clarksville
   TN Clarksville .... TNNA#7304

ALPHABETICAL INDEX OF CHURCHES CONTINUED

Claybrook
  TN Jackson......................GRWT#9205
Clear Point
  KY Horse Cave ....MICU#3107
Cleveland
  TN Cleveland.....................SETG#2108
Clifton Mills
  KY Irvington ....MICU#3202
Clinton
  OK Clinton........................MSRR#6302
Cloverdale
  TN Obion ....GRWT#9407
Cloyd's
  TN Mt Juliet......................TNMU#7208
Coal Creek
  OK Coalgate.....................MSCH#6102
Coker
  AL Coker.......................... SEGR#0705
Colonial
  TN Memphis ....GRWT#9305
Columbia 1st
  TN Columbia.....................TNCO#7110
Columbus
  MS Columbus .... SEGR#0706
Commerce
  TN Watertown..................TNMU#7209
Comunidad Cristiana
  IL Dundee ....MINC#5212
Concord
  AL New Market .... SERD#0802
  TN Trenton.......................GRWT#9106
  TN Waverly .... TNNA#7306
  TX Troup...........................MSTR#8104
Cookeville 1st
  TN Cookeville....................TNMU#7210
Cool Springs CC
  TN Lavinia........................GRWT#9107
Cool Springs GC
  TN Trimble........................GRWT#9408
Cornerstone Community
  TN Chattanooga.................SETG#2107
Corntassel
  TN Madisonville .... SEET#2304
Covenant
  OK Ada .... MSRR#6304
Cowan
  TN Cowan.........................TNMU#7211
Coyle
  KY Hudson ....MICU#3203
Crestline
  AL Birmingham .... SEGR#0102
Cristo Vive
  TN Madison .... TNNA#7314
Cumberland Chapel
  IL Fairfield ....MINC#5104
Cumberland Valley
  TN McEwen...................... TNNA#7307

--==<<D>>==--

Daingerfield
  TX Daingerfield ....MSTR#8106
Davidson Chapel
  TN Trenton.......................GRWT#9108
Den-en Mission
  JA 228-0818 .... MSJA#8310
Denton
  TX Denton.........................MSRR#8404
Desert Gardens
  AZ Tucson.........................MSDC#8705
Dibrell
  TN McMinnville ....TNMU#7212

Dickson
  TN Dickson .... TNNA#7308
Dilworth
  AR Horatio .... GRAR#1304
Divino Redentor
  CO Buenaventura.............. MSCA#8206
Donelson
  TN Nashville..................... TNNA#7327
Dosquebradas
  CO Risaralda..................... MSAN#8907
Double Springs
  TN Humboldt ....GRWT#9109
Dover
  AR Dover .... GRAR#1203
  TN Morristown .... SEET#2203
Dresden
  TN Dresden ....GRWT#9110
Dry Fork
  TN Bethpage .... TNNA#7309
Dry Valley
  TN Cookeville....................TNMU#7213
Dukes
  KY Hawesville...................MICU#3204
Dyer
  TN Dyer ....GRWT#9409
Dyersburg 1st
  TN Dyersburg ....GRWT#9410

--==<<E>>==--

E T Allen
  AR Ashdown .... GRAR#1307
East Point
  AL Cullman....................... SERD#0206
Eastlake
  OK Oklahoma City .... MSRR#6205
Ebenezer
  IL Chicago........................MINC#5203
  IL Thompsonville..............MICO#5105
  TN Mason ....GRWT#9303
  TN Mercer........................GRWT#9206
  TN Whitwell ....SETG#2110
Ebenezer Hall
  IL Buncombe....................MICO#5106
Ebina Shion No Oka
  JA 243-0422 .... MSJA#8311
Edgefield
  AL Stevenson .... SERD#0813
Eidson Chapel
  AL Holly Pond .... SERD#0207
El Camino
  FL Miami ....SEGR#0310
El Paso 1st
  TX El Paso ....MSDC#8704
El Rebano
  CO Antioquia ....MSAN#8905
El Redil
  GA Lawrenceville ....SETG#2149
Elk Creek
  MO West Plains ....GRMI#4304
Elm River
  IL Cisne............................MINC#5107
Elmira Chapel
  TX Longview ....MSTR#8111
Elora
  TN Elora...........................TNCO#7111
Emaus
  CO Buenaventura.............. MSCA#8219
Enon
  MS Ackerman .... SEGR#0707
Ephesus
  KY Harned ....MICU#3205

Erin
  MS Union..........................SEGR#0601
  TN Erin .... TNNA#7310

--==<<F>>==--

Fairfield
  IL Fairfield ....MINC#5108
Fairview
  KY Bremen ....MICU#3504
  TN Afton .... SEET#2204
Faith
  AL Cullman.......................SEHO#0213
  MI St Clair Shores ....MINC#5501
  OK Tulsa ....MSRR#6201
  TN Bartlett ....GRWT#9308
Faith Fellowship
  TN Lenoir City................... SEET#2319
Faith-Hopewell
  AR Batesville .... GRAR#1502
Falling Water
  TN Hixson.........................SETG#2111
Falls Chapel
  AR Lockesburg .... GRAR#1308
Fayetteville
  TN Fayetteville ....TNCO#7112
Fellowship
  AR Camden....................... GRAR#1309
  AR Mountain Home.......... GRAR#1505
Fiducia
  TN Prospect......................TNCO#7113
Filipos
  CO Cali .... MSCA#8211
First Hispanic
  FL Tampa .... SEGR#0307
Flat Lick
  KY Herndon ....MICO#3606
Flint Springs
  TN Cleveland ....SETG#2112
Flintville
  TN Flintville......................TNCO#7115
Florence 1st
  AL Florence.......................SEHO#0506
Fomby
  AR Ashdown .... GRAR#1310
Forrest Avenue
  AL Gadsden.......................SEGR#0403
Fort Smith
  AR Fort Smith .... GRAR#1406
Franklin
  TN Franklin.......................TNCO#7116
Fredonia
  KY Fredonia......................MICO#3608
Freeport
  TX Freeport......................MSTR#8103
Freedom
  KY Harned ....MICU#3207
Fullerton
  IL Farmer City ....MINC#5404
Fulton
  TN South Fulton...............GRWT#9412

--==<<G>>==--

Gadsden
  AL Gadsden.......................SEGR#0402
Garfield
  KY Garfield.......................MICU#3208
Gasper River
  KY Auburn ....MICU#3306
Gass Memorial
  TN Greeneville...................SEET#2205

ALPHABETICAL INDEX OF CHURCHES CONTINUED

Georgetown
  IL Georgetown .... MINC#5204
Germantown
  TN Germantown .... GRWT#9310
Getsemani
  CO El Cerrito .... MSCA#8210
Gilead
  IL Simpson .... MICO#5110
Gill's Chapel
  KY Guthrie...................... MICU#3307
Glasgow
  KY Glasgow.................... MICU#3108
Gleason
  TN Gleason .... GRWT#9111
Glencoe
  AL Glencoe .... SEGR#0404
Glory Church of Jesus Christ
  GA Duluth....................SETG#2144
God's Grace
  MO Greenfield .... GRMI#4104
Good Hope
  KY Campbellsville............ MICU#3109
Good Prospect
  IL Trilla .... MINC#5205
Good Spring
  KY Fredonia...................... MICO#3609
  TN Dukedom.................... GRWT#9112
Goodlettsville
  TN Goodlettsville.............. TNNA#7328
Goosepond
  AL Scottsboro .... SERD#0803
Goshen
  TN Winchester .... TNMU#7214
Grace
  AR Fayetteville .... GRAR#1405
  CA San Francisco.............. MSDC#8510
  MI Lincoln Park .... MINC#5502
  TN Franklin.....................TNCO#7145
Grace Community
  AL Millbrook .... SEGR#0407
Green Hill
  TN Bell Buckle .... TNCO#7118
Green Ridge
  KY Lewisburg................... MICU#3308
Greeneville
  TN Greeneville.................. SEET#2206
Greens Chapel
  AL Cleveland .... SEGR#0208
Greensburg
  KY Greensburg .... MICU#3110
Greenville
  KY Greenville................... MICU#3505
Groverton
  MS Morton........................ SEGR#0602
Gum Creek
  TN Winchester .... TNMU#7215
Gum Springs
  AR Searcy .... GRAR#1205
Gurley
  AL Gurley .... SERD#0804

--==<<H>>==--

Halls Creek
  TN Waverly...................... TNNA#7313
Happy Home
  MO Conway....................... GRMI#4306
Harmony
  MO San Antonio .... GRMI#4203
  TN Winchester .... TNMU#7216
Harpeth Lick
  TN College Grove.............. TNCO#7119

Harrodsburg
  KY Harrodsburg................. MICU#3111
Heartland
  Lenoir City .... SEET#2306
Heartsong
  KY Louisville.................... MICU#3222
Hector
  AR Hector .... GRAR#1207
Heights
  NM Albuquerque .... MSDC#8701
Helena
  AL Helena .... SEGR#0108
Hendersonville
  TN Hendersonville............ TNNA#7340
Hickory Grove
  AL Moulton .... SEHO#0507
Hickory Valley
  TN Sparta ....TNMU#7251
Higashi Koganei
  JA 184-0011 .... MSJA#8301
High Point Community
  KY West Somerset .... MICU#3314
Highland
  KY Paducah .... MICO#3414
Hillsboro
  TN Hillsboro .... TNMU#7217
Hohenwald
  TN Hohenwald................... TNCO#7120
Holly Grove
  TN Brighton .... GRWT#9304
Homewood
  AL Homewood...................SEGR#0111
Hope
  AL Huntsville.................... SERD#0812
  FL Valrico......................... SEGR#0308
Hope Korean
  NJ Tinton Falls...................SECE#2131
Hopewell
  AL Bessemer .... SEGR#0101
  KY Canmer .... MICU#3112
  KY Salem .... MICO#3610
  MS Walnut .... GRWT#9207
  MO Lamar......................... GRMI#4105
  TN Sharon .... GRWT#9115
Hopkinsville
  KY Hopkinsville .... MICU#3611
Horeb-Central
  CO Antioquia .... MSAN#8915
House of Prayer
  AL Decatur........................ SEGR#0214
Houston 1st
  TX Houston....................... MSTR#8606
Howell
  TN Fayetteville .... TNCO#7121
Hubbard
  TX Hubbard .... MSRR#8410
Hueytown 1st
  AL Hueytown .... SEGR#0109
Humboldt
  TN Humboldt.................... GRWT#9116
Huntsville 1st
  AL Huntsville.................... SERD#0806
Hurricane
  AL Rogersville .... SEHO#0508
Hurricane Hill
  TN Newburn .... GRWT#9413

--==<<I>>==--

Ichikawa Grace Mission Point
  JA 272-0834 .... MSJA#8314
Immanuel

FL Dade City..................... SEGR#0311
Irvington
  KY Irvington .... MICU#3210
Izumi Mission
  JA 245-0016 .... MSJA#8312

--==<<J>>==--

Jackson 1st
  TN Jackson........................ GRWT#9208
Jasper
  TN Jasper ....SETG#2113
Jefferson
  TX Jefferson......................MSTR#8109
Jenkins
  TN Nolensville...................TNCO#7144
Jerusalem
  TN Murfreesboro ....TNMU#7218
Joywood
  TN Murfreesboro ....TNMU#7250

--==<<K>>==--

Kelly's Chapel
  TN Whitwell ....SETG#2120
Kelso
  TN Kelso...........................TNCO#7122
Kenton
  TN Kenton......................... GRWT#9414
Kibougaoka
  JA 241-0825 .... MSJA#8302
Kingdom
  TN Unionville .... TNCO#7123
Knights Chapel
  IN Petersburg .... MINC#5306
Knoxville
  TN Knoxville .... SEET#2305
Korea 1st
  KO South Korea................. SEET#2221
Korean
  TN Cordova....................... GRWT#9322
Korean Livingstone
  GA Cumming ....SETG#2130
Kowloon
  HO Kowloon..................... MSHK#8803
Koza
  JA 242-0006 .... MSJA#8303
Kunitachi Nozomi
  JA 186-0002 .... MSJA#8306

--==<<L>>==--

La Rosa De Saron
  CO Antioquia .... MSAN#8911
La Virginia
  CO Risaralda..................... MSAN#8913
LaGuardo
  TN Lebanon ....TNMU#7219
Lake Hamilton
  AR Hot Springs................ GRAR#1221
Lake Highlands
  TX Dallas...........................MSRR#8411
Lawrenceburg
  TN Lawrenceburg .... TNCO#7124
Lebanon
  TN Jefferson City...............SEET#2207
  TN Lebanon ....TNMU#7220
Lebanon North
  IL Fairfield .... MINC#5113
Lebanon South
  IL Galatia .... MINC#5114
Leitchfield

ALPHABETICAL INDEX OF CHURCHES CONTINUED

ALPHABETICAL INDEX OF CHURCHES CONTINUED

Nebo
AL Lexington .... SEHO#0512
Needham
KY Eastview .... MICU#3219
New Beginnings
TN Memphis .... GRWT#9306
New Bethel
TN Columbia..................... TNCO#7134
TN Greeneville................... SEET#2210
TN Selmer....................... GRWT#9215
New Bethlehem
TN Newbern................... GRWT#9420
New Cypress
KY Rumsey..................... MICU#3508
New Ebenezer
TN Troy....................... GRWT#9422
New Hope
AL Birmingham .... SEGR#0104
AR Batesville .... GRAR#1510
IL Yale......................... MINC#5208
KY Paducah .... MICO#3410
MO Salem .... GRMI#4309
TN Lebanon .... TNMU#7233
TN Madisonville .... SEET#2311
TN Stewart .... TNNA#7337
TN Whitwell .... SETG#2115
New Providence
TN Clarksville.................. TNNA#7305
New Salem
TN Bethel Springs............. GRWT#9216
TN Lakeland .... GRWT#9316
TN Sharon .... GRWT#9124
Newbern
TN Newbern................... GRWT#9419
Newberry
TX Millsap .... MSRR#8415
North Pleasant Grove
KY Murray .... MICO#3411
North Point
HO North Point .... MSHK#8805
North Union
TN Kenton........................ GRWT#9423
Northminster
TX San Antonio .... MSTR#8610
Nueva Esperanza
CO Cali .... MSCA#8221
Nueva Jerusalen
CO Cali .... MSCA#8222
Nueva Vida
TX Houston....................... MSTR#8612
Nuevo Empezar................... GRWT#9324
TN Memphis

--==<<O>>==--

Oak Forest
KY Summersville............... MICU#3123
Oak Grove
KY Benton .... MICO#3412
MO Springfield .... GRMI#4310
TN Henderson .... GRWT#9217
TN Whitwell .... SETG#2121
TX Georgetown................... MSTR#8607
Oak Grove Union
KY Clay .... MICO#3619
Oak Hill
TN Paris .... GRWT#9125
Oak Ridge
TN Oak Ridge .... SEET#2313
Oakland
KY Calvert City .... MICO#3413
TN Telford....................... SEET#2211

Old Mt Bethel
AL Rogersville .... SEHO#0513
Old Union
AR Magazine .... GRAR#1409
Old Zion
TN Sparta .... TNMU#7234
Olive Branch
MS Olive Branch .... GRWT#9312
Oliver Springs
TN Oliver Springs.............. SEET#2314
Oliver's Chapel
TN Bradford.................... GRWT#9127
Olivet
TN Savannah................... GRWT#9220
Olney
TX Olney .... MSRR#8416
One Way
NY Flushing..................... SECE#2137
Orange
MO Aurora .... GRMI#4108
Our Good
MD Salisbury .... SETG#2138
Owens Chapel
TN Winchester .... TNMU#7235
Owensboro
KY Owensboro .... MICU#3509
Oxford
AR Oxford......................... GRAR#1511

--==<<P>>==--

Palestine
AR Palestine...................... GRAR#1103
TN Lexington................... GRWT#9221
TN Newbern.................... GRWT#9424
Panki Bok
OK Eagletown.................. MSCH#6108
Park Terrace
AL Sheffield .... SEHO#0514
Parsons 1st
TN Parsons....................... GRWT#9222
Pathway
TX Burleson..................... MSRR#8418
Pereira
CO Risaralda.................... MSAN#8916
Petersburg
TN Petersburg .... TNCO#7135
Philadelphia
TN Limestone .... SEET#2212
Phillipsburg
MO Phillipsburg................ GRMI#4311
Piedmont
AL Piedmont .... SEGR#0406
Pierson
MO Martinville .... GRMI#4312
Pigeon Roost
OK Atoka .... MSCH#6109
Pilot Knob
TN Bulls Gap .... SEET#2213
Pine Bluff 1st
AR Pine Bluff.................... GRAR#1104
Pine Hill
TN McDonald .... SETG#2117
TX Winnsboro.................. MSTR#8122
Pine Ridge
AR Grapevine................... GRAR#1105
Pine Tree
TX Longview .... MSTR#8113
Pineville
AR Pineville .... GRAR#1512
Piney Fork
KY Marion .... MICO#3620

Pleasant Green
TN Atwood....................... GRWT#9129
Pleasant Grove
AR Searcy .... GRAR#1214
IL Annapolis..................... MINC#5210
MO Knob Noster............... GRMI#4109
TN Moscow...................... GRWT#9317
Pleasant Hill
AL Bessember .... SEGR#0710
KY Owensboro .... MICU#3510
TN Chuckey .... SEET#2214
Pleasant Mount
TN Columbia.................... TNCO#7136
Pleasant Union
TN Millington .... GRWT#9318
Pleasant Vale
TN Chuckey .... SEET#2215
Pleasant Valley
KY Kevil .... MICO#3418
Po Lam
HO Tseung Kwan O,NT.... MSHK#8808
Point Pleasant
KY Beaver Dam................. MICU#3313
Popayan
CO Popayan .... MSCA#8227
Poplar Grove
KY Sacramento .... MICU#3511
TN Halls.......................... GRWT#9425
Principe De Paz
CO Cali .... MSCA#8201
Progress
LA Pleasant Hill................ MSTR#8123
Prospect United
TN Cleveland .... SETG#2116
Protemus
TN Troy........................... GRWT#9426
Providence
TN Hartsville.................... TNMU#7238
Providence 1st
KY Providence.................. MICO#3621

--==<<Q>>==--

--==<<R>>==--

Radcliff
KY Radcliff....................... MICU#3220
Ramer
TN Ramer......................... GRWT#9223
Red Bank
TN Chattanooga................. SETG#2105
Redeemer
CA San Francisco.............. MSDC#8512
Renacer
CO Cali .... MSCA#8225
Richard City
TN South Pittsburg............. SETG#2118
Richland
TN Lewisburg .... TNCO#7137
Roca De Salvacion
AL Birmingham .... SEGR#0115
Rock Creek
OK Honobia...................... MSCH#6111
Rockvale
TN Rockvale .... TNMU#7239
Rocky Glade
TN Eagleville................... TNMU#7240
Rocky Ridge
AL Birmingham .... SEGR#0105
Rodney
AR Jordan......................... GRAR#1513
Roellen

ALPHABETICAL INDEX OF CHURCHES CONTINUED

ALPHABETICAL INDEX OF CHURCHES CONTINUED

--==<<**X**>>==--

--==<<**Y**>>==--

--==<<**Z**>>==--

LOCATION INDEX OF CHURCHES

The four letter abbreviation indicates the synod and presbytery of which the congregation
is a member. The four digit number indicates the church number.
(See pages 10-13 for abbreviations of presbyteries.)

ALABAMA

AL Alabaster
    Alabaster .... SERD#0107
AL Anderson
    Union Hill .... SEHO#0516
AL Bessemer
    Hopewell...................... SEGR#0101
    Pleasant Hill.................. SEGR#0710
AL Birmingham
    Crestline...................... SEGR#0102
    New Hope .... SEGR#0104
    Roca De Salvacion........ SEGR#0115
    Rocky Ridge.................. SEGR#0105
AL Brownsboro
    Big Cove .... SERD#0801
AL Cherokee
    Allsboro......................... SEHO#0501
    Maud .... SEHO#0509
    Mt. Hester .... SEHO#0510
AL Cleveland
    Greens Chapel............... SEGR#0208
AL Coker
    Coker............................ SEGR#0705
AL Cullman
    Baldwin Chapel.............. SEHO#0202
    East Point .... SERD#0206
    Faith .... SEHO#0213
    Welti .... SEHO#0212
AL Decatur
    House of Prayer............. SEGR#0214
AL Florence
    Florence 1st................... SEHO#0506
AL Gadsden
    Gadsden......................... SEGR#0402
    Forrest Avenue .... SEGR#0403
AL Glencoe
    Glencoe .... SEGR#0404
AL Gurley
    Gurley .... SERD#0804
AL Helena
    Helena .... SEGR#0108
AL Holly Pond
    Eidson Chapel............... SERD#0207
    Union Grove.................. SERD#0211
AL Homewood
    Homewood....................SEGR#0111
AL Hueytown
    Hueytown 1st .... SEGR#0109
AL Huntsville
    Christ Church................ SERD#0814
    Hope............................. SERD#0812
    Huntsville 1st .... SERD#0806
AL Lexington
    Nebo............................. SEHO#0512
AL Meridianville
    Meridianville................. SERD#0808
AL Millbrook
    Grace Community.......... SEGR#0407
AL Montevallo
    Spring Creek .... SEGR#0113
AL Moulton
    Hickory Grove .... SEHO#0507
AL Muscle Shoals
    Mt. Pleasant.................. SEHO#0511
AL New Hope
    Walnut Grove .... SERD#0811
AL New Market

AL Concord.......................... SERD#0802
AL Odenville
    Branchville.................... SEGR#0106
AL Piedmont
    Piedmont .... SEGR#0406
AL Reform
    Antioch......................... SEGR#0701
AL Rogersville
    Hurricane...................... SEHO#0508
    Old Mt Bethel .... SEHO#0513
    Rogersville 1st ... SEHO#0517
    Springfield.................... SEHO#0515
AL Scottsboro
    Goosepond .... SERD#0803
    Scottsboro .... SERD#0809
AL Sheffield
    Park Terrace .... SEHO#0514
AL Stevenson
    Edgefield .... SERD#0813
    Stevenson .... SERD#0810
AL Vance
    Union............................ SEGR#0114

ARIZONA

AZ Tucson
    Desert Gardens.............. MIDC#8705

ARKANSAS

AR Ashdown
    E T Allen .... GRAR#1307
    Fomby .... GRAR#1310
AR Atkins
    Appleton....................... GRAR#1202
AR Batesville
    Faith-Hopewell .... GRAR#1502
    New Hope .... GRAR#1510
    Sidney .... GRAR#1515
AR Ben Lomond
    Ben Lomond.................. GRAR#1301
AR Booneville
    Booneville..................... GRAR#1401
AR Calico Rock
    Byron............................ GRAR#1508
    Calico Rock................... GRAR#1503
AR Camden
    Bethesda....................... GRAR#1302
    Camden .... GRAR#1303
    Fellowship.................... GRAR#1309
AR Charleston
    Marietta........................ GRAR#1408
AR Dolph
    Trimble Camp Ground .. GRAR#1504
AR Dover
    Dover............................ GRAR#1203
AR Fayetteville
    Grace .... GRAR#1405
AR Fort Smith
    Fort Smith .... GRAR#1406
AR Grapevine
    Pine Ridge....................GRAR#1105
AR Hampton
    Camp Ground...............GRAR#1101
AR Hector
    Hector.......................... GRAR#1207
AR Horatio
    Dilworth .... GRAR#1304

AR Hot Springs
    Lake Hamilton .... GRAR#1221
AR Jordan
    Rodney .... GRAR#1513
AR Little Rock
    Arkansas Loving .... GRAR#2135
AR Lockesburg
    Falls Chapel .... GRAR#1308
    Lockesburg....................GRAR#1311
AR London
    Mt Carmel .... GRAR#1212
AR Louann
    Sulphur Springs............. GRAR#1315
AR Magazine
    Old Union..................... GRAR#1409
    Walnut Grove .... GRAR#1414
AR Magnolia
    Walkerville .... GRAR#1317
AR Melbourne
    Mt Olive....................... GRAR#1517
AR Monticello
    Rose Hill ....GRAR#1106
AR Morrilton
    Trinity.......................... GRAR#1219
AR Mount Pleasant
    Barren Fork .... GRAR#1501
AR Mountain Home
    Fellowship.................... GRAR#1505
AR Oxford
    Oxford..........................GRAR#1511
AR Palestine
    Palestine ....GRAR#1103
AR Paris
    Shaver .... GRAR#1413
AR Pine Bluff
    Pine Bluff 1st ....GRAR#1104
    Shell Chapel..................GRAR#1108
AR Pineville
    Pineville .... GRAR#1512
AR Pottsville
    Mars Hill ....GRAR#1211
AR Ratcliff
    Caulksville .... GRAR#1402
AR Russellville
    Russellville................... GRAR#1216
AR Salem
    Salem........................... GRAR#1514
AR Searcy
    Gum Springs .... GRAR#1205
    Pleasant Grove .... GRAR#1214
    Searcy.......................... GRAR#1218
AR Sherwood
    Sherwood .... GRAR#1220

BRAZIL

BR Bahia
    Mata de Sao Joao .... GRAR#8313

CALIFORNIA

CA San Francisco
    Chinese.........................MSDC#8501
    Grace............................ MSDC#8510
    Redeemer .... MSDC#8512
CA Trona
    Trona .... MSDC#8503

LOCATION INDEX OF CHURCHES CONTINUED

COLOMBIA

CO Antioquia
    Horeb-Central .... MSAN#8915
    El Rebano..................... MSAN#8905
    La Rosa De Saron .... MSAN#8911
    Senta de Libertad .... MSAN#8919
    Zamora .... MSAN#8918
CO Buenaventura
    Divino Redentor............ MSAN#8206
    Emaus......................... MSCA#8219
CO Caldas
    Manizales .... MSAN#8914
CO Cali
    Betania Mission .... MSAN#8204
    Bethel .... MSCA#8205
    Central......................... MSCA#8208
    Filipos .... MSCA#8211
    Nueva Esperanza........... MSCA#8221
    Nueva Jerusalen .... MSCA#8222
    Principe De Paz............. MSCA#8201
    Renacer .... MSCA#8225
    Samaria .... MSCA#0217
    San Marcos................... MSCA#8218
CO El Cerrito
    Getsemani .... MSCA#8210
CO Guacari
    San Pablo .... MSCA#8212
CO Guapi
    Maranatha .... MSCA#8220
CO Montebello
    Caleb Mission .... MSCA#8223
CO Palmira
    San Lucas..................... MSCA#8215
CO Popayan
    Popayan....................... MSCA#8227
CO Quindio
    Armenia....................... MSAN#8903
CO Risaralda
    Dosquebradas................ MSAN#8907
    La Virginia .... MSCA#8913
    Pereira .... MSAN#8916
CO Tulua
    Tulua Mission................ MSCA#8226
CO Valle
    Cartago........................ MSAN#8906

FLORIDA

FL Dade City
    Immanuel .... SEGR#0311
FL Lutz
    Christ........................... SEGR#0303
FL Miami
    El Camino .... SEGR#0310
FL Tampa
    First Hispanic................. SEGR#0307
FL Valrico
    Hope............................ SEGR#0308
FL Wimauma

GEORGIA

GA Chatsworth
    Sumach.......................... SETG#2124
GA Cumming
    Korean Livingstone.......... SETG#2130
GA Duluth
    Glory Church of Jesus..... SETG#2144
GA Lawrenceville
    El Redil .... SETG#2149
GA Rydal

Bartow............................ SETG#2101

HONG KONG

HO Cheung Chau
    Cheung Chau................. MSHK#8801
HO Kowloon
    Kowloon...................... MSHK#8803
    Tao Hsien .... MSHK#8806
HO Landau Island
    Mu Min .... MSHK#8810
HO NT
    Yao Dao...................... MSHK#8811
HO North Point
    North Point................... MSHK#8805
HO Shatin NT
    Shatin .... MSHK#8807
HO Tseung Kwan O NT
    Po Lam .... MSHK#8808
HO Yuen Long
    Xi Lin .... MSHK#8809

ILLINOIS

IL Anna
    Camp Ground.................. MICO#5103
IL Annapolis
    Pleasant Grove .... MICO#5210
IL Beecher City
    Spring Hill..................... MINC#5411
IL Bethany
    Bethany .... MINC#5401
IL Brookport
    Mt. Sterling .... MICO#5117
IL Buncombe
    Ebenezer Hall................. MICO#5106
IL Burnt Prairie
    Burnt Prairie .... MINC#5102
IL Casey
    Casey........................... MINC#5201
IL Chicago
    Ebenezer....................... MINC#5203
IL Cisne
    Elm River .... MINC#5107
IL Dongola
    Mt Zion .... MICO#5118
IL Dundee
    Comunidad Cristiana ...... MINC#5212
IL Fairfield
    Cumberland Chapel .... MINC#5104
    Fairfield .... MINC#5108
    Lebanon North .... MINC#5113
    Union North .... MINC#5124
IL Farmer City
    Fullerton....................... MINC#5404
IL Galatia
    Lebanon South .... MINC#5114
    Union Chapel .... MICO#5123
IL Georgetown
    Georgetown.................... MINC#5204
IL Greenville
    Campground.................... MINC#5402
    Mt. Gilead .... MINC#5406
IL Lincoln
    Lincoln 1st .... MINC#5405
IL Martinsville
    Willow Creek .... MINC#5211
IL Norris City
    United........................... MINC#5119
    Village .... MICO#5125
IL Petersburg
    Petersburg...................... MINC#5408

IL Simpson
    Gilead .... MICO#5110
IL Thompsonville
    Ebenezer....................... MICO#5105
IL Trilla
    Good Prospect................. MINC#5205
IL Virginia
    Shiloh .... MINC#5409
IL Yale
    New Hope .... MINC#5208

INDIANA

IN Chandler
    Chandler .... MICO#5302
IN Evansville
    Morningside .... MINC#5304
IN Indianapolis
    Christ........................... MINC#5305
IN Monroe City
    Monroe City .... MINC#5307
IN Petersburg
    Knights Chapel............... MINC#5306
IN Washington
    Mt Olivet...................... MINC#5308

IOWA

IA New London
    Shinar .... MINC#5410

JAPAN

JA 184-0011
    Higashi Koganei............. MSJA#8301
JA 186-0002
    Kunitachi Nozomi........... MSJA#8306
JA 194-0041
    Naruse .... MSJA#8305
JA 207-0023
    Megumi .... MSJA#8309
JA 228-0004
    Sagamino...................... MSJA#8304
JA 228-0818
    Den-en Mission.............. MSJA#8310
JA 241-0021
    Asahi Mission Point .... MSJA#8315
JA 241-0825
    Kibougaoka.................... MSJA#8302
JA 242-0006
    Koza .... MSJA#8303
JA 243-0422
    Ebina Shion No .... MSJA#8311
JA 245-0016
    Izumi Mission .... MSJA#8312
JA 259-1321
    Sibusawa .... MSJA#8307
JA 272-0834
    Ichikawa Grace Mission . MSJA#8314

KENTUCKY

KY Auburn
    Auburn......................... MICU#3301
    Gasper River .... MICU#3306
KY Beaver Dam
    Point Pleasant................. MICU#3313
KY Benton
    Benton.......................... MICO#3403
    Oak Grove..................... MICO#3412
KY Big Clifty
    Mt Olive....................... MICU#3216

LOCATION INDEX OF CHURCHES CONTINUED

LOCATION INDEX OF CHURCHES CONTINUED

MS Walnut Grove
    Salem............................ SEGR#0607

MISSOURI

MO Aurora
    Orange.......................... GRMI#4108
MO Chilhowee
    Shawnee Mound............. GRMI#4111
MO Conway
    Happy Home .... GRMI#4306
MO Dunnegan
    Spring Creek .... GRMI#4113
MO Greenfield
    God's Grace .... GRMI#4104
MO Independence
    Lobb .... GRMI#4209
MO Knob Noster
    Pleasant Grove .... GRMI#4109
MO Lamar
    Hopewell .... GRMI#4105
MO Lebanon
    White Oak Pond............. GRMI#4315
MO Mansfield
    Mansfield....................... GRMI#4308
MO Marshall
    Marshall .... GRMI#4210
MO Martinville
    Pierson.......................... GRMI#4312
MO Phillipsburg
    Phillipsburg .... GRMI#4311
MO Salem
    New Hope .... GRMI#4309
MO San Antonio
    Harmony .... GRMI#4203
MO Seymour
    Seymour .... GRMI#4313
MO Springfield
    Oak Grove .... GRMI#4310
    Springfield 1st .... GRMI#4314
MO Warrensburg
    Salem............................ GRMI#4216
    Warrensburg .... GRMI#4115
MO Wentworth
    Bethel .... GRMI#4102
MO West Plains
    Elk Creek .... GRMI#4304

NEW JERSEY

NJ Tinton Falls
    Hope Korean .... SECE#2131

NEW MEXICO

NM Albuquerque
    Heights .... MSDC#8701
NM Rio Rancho
    Westside .... MSDC#8709

NEW YORK

NY Flushing
    One Way......................... SECE#2137
    Sharing .... SECE#2141

OKLAHOMA

OK Ada
    Covenant .... MSRR#6304
OK Atoka
    Pigeon Roost .... MSCH#6109

OK Broken Bow
    McGee Chapel .... MSCH#6106
OK Burns Flat
    Burns Flat...................... MSRR#6301
OK Clinton
    Clinton.......................... MSRR#6302
OK Coalgate
    Coal Creek .... MSCH#6102
    Lone Star....................... MSCH#6105
OK Eagletown
    Panki Bok..................... MSCH#6108
OK Edmond
    Stone Gate .... MSRR#6307
OK Honobia
    Rock Creek.................... MSCH#6111
OK Locust Grove
    Locust Grove................. MSRR#6203
OK Marlow
    Marlow.......................... MSRR#6305
OK Oklahoma City
    Eastlake .... MSRR#6205
OK Tulsa
    Faith .... MSRR#6201
OK Tupelo
    Round Lake .... MSCH#6112

PENNSYLVANIA

PA Bridgeport
    Bridgeport .... MICU#3131

TENNESSEE

TN Afton
    Fairview .... SEET#2204
    Mt Pleasant................... SEET#2209
TN Algood
    Algood..........................TNMU#7201
TN Atoka
    Bethel ....GRWT#9301
TN Atwood
    Atwood..........................GRWT#9101
    Pleasant Green ....GRWT#9129
TN Bartlett
    Faith ....GRWT#9308
TN Beech Bluff
    Maple Springs ....GRWT#9210
TN Beechgrove
    Beech Grove..................TNMU#7204
TN Bell Buckle
    Green Hill......................TNCO#7118
TN Belvidere
    Belvidere ....TNMU#7205
TN Bethel Springs
    New Salem....................GRWT#9216
TN Bethpage
    Dry Fork .... TNNA#7309
TN Bolivar
    Bolivar..........................GRWT#9202
TN Boonshill
    Boonshill......................TNCO#7106
TN Bradford
    Bradford ....GRWT#9104
    Oliver's Chapel.............GRWT#9127
TN Brentwood
    Brenthaven .... TNNA#7331
TN Brighton
    Holly Grove ....GRWT#9304
TN Brunswick
    Brunswick ....GRWT#9302
TN Brush Creek
    Union Hill ....TNMU#7246

TN Bulls Gap
    Pilot Knob .... SEET#2213
    Willoughby.................... SEET#2219
TN Burlison
    Walnut Grove ....GRWT#9320
TN Camden
    Camden ....GRWT#9105
TN Cane Ridge
    Cane Ridge.................... TNNA#7326
TN Centerville
    Swan.............................TNCO#7140
TN Chapel Hill
    Chapel Hill ....TNCO#7109
TN Charlotte
    Charlotte....................... TNNA#7303
    Mt Liberty .... TNNA#7320
TN Chattanooga
    Chattanooga 1st.............SETG#2104
    Cornerstone CommunityTNNA#2107
    Red Bank.......................SETG#2105
    Silverdale ....SETG#2106
TN Chuckey
    Pleasant Hill.................. SEET#2214
    Pleasant Vale .... SEET#2215
TN Clarksville
    Bethel .... TNNA#7302
    Calvary .... TNNA#7342
    Clarksville .... TNNA#7304
    Liberty.......................... TNNA#7315
    McAdoo .... TNNA#7318
    New Providence .... TNNA#7305
TN Cleveland
    Charleston ....SETG#2102
    Cleveland ....SETG#2108
    Flint Springs.................SETG#2112
    Prospect United.............SETG#2116
TN College Grove
    Harpeth Lick ....TNCO#7119
TN Columbia
    Columbia 1st.................TNCO#7110
    McCains ....TNCO#7126
    New Bethel....................TNCO#7134
    Pleasant Mount..............TNCO#7136
    Union Grove..................TNCO#7141
    West Point ....TNCO#7143
TN Cookeville
    Cookeville 1st ....TNMU#7210
    Dry Valley ....TNMU#7213
    Mt Hermon...................TNMU#7229
TN Cordova
    Korean..........................GRWT#9322
    Morning Sun ....GRWT#9314
TN Cowan
    Cowan...........................TNMU#7211
TN Cunningham
    Locust Grove................. TNNA#7316
TN Decaturville
    Camp Ground................GRWT#9204
TN Dickson
    Dickson .... TNNA#7308
TN Dover
    Mt View........................ TNNA#7322
TN Dresden
    Dresden ....GRWT#9110
TN Dukedom
    Good Springs ....GRWT#9112
TN Dyer
    Bells Chapel.................GRWT#9403
    Dyer..............................GRWT#9409
    Mt Olive.......................GRWT#9418
TN Dyersburg
    Dyersburg 1st................GRWT#9410

LOCATION INDEX OF CHURCHES CONTINUED

CUMBERLAND PRESBYTERIAN CHURCH IN AMERICA
Denominational Center
226 Church Street, NW, Huntsville, AL 35801
(256)536-7481 OR FAX (256)536-7482
cpcaga@aol.com

Moderator of the General Assembly:
Elder Lewis Leon Cole, Jr., PO Box 335, Warren, MI 48090
(248)770-1540   llcole1951@yahoo.com

Vice-Moderator of the General Assembly:
Reverend Anthony Hollis, 1100 Gateway Avenue, Apt 200, Chattanooga, TN 37402 (resigned)
(423)645-3277   anthony_hollis@att.net

Administrative Director of the Cumberland Presbyterian Church in America:
Reverend Doctor G. Lynne Herring, 3244 Vicksburg SW, Decatur, AL 35603
(256)536-7481(w)   (256)355-7677(h)   cpcaga@aol.com   johneherring@aol.com

Stated Clerk of the General Assembly:
Elder Craig A. White, 134 McEntire Lane SW A36, Decatur, AL 35603
(256)565-5751   white8@bellsouth.net

Engrossing Clerk of the General Assembly:
Reverend Lela Fencher, 620 Live Oak Circle, Fairfield, AL 35064, (205)780-4913
(205)789-3913

Church Paper: *THE CUMBERLAND FLAG*
Editor: Reverend Doctor G. Lynne Herring, 3244 Vicksburg SW, Decatur, AL 35603
(256)536-7481(w)   (256)355-7677(h)   cpcaga@aol.com

SYNODS - PRESBYTERIES - STATED CLERKS

Alabama Synod - Elder Vanessa Midgett, 118 Thunderbird Drive, Harvest, AL 35749
1. Birmingham Presbytery - Rev. Teresa Paige, 228 S Park Road, Birmingham, AL 35211
   (205)706-9057   tcpaige12@yahoo.com
2. Florence Presbytery - Rev. Dr. Nancy Fuqua, 1963 County Road 406, Town Creek, AL 35672
   (256)685-0218   fuq23@bellsouth.net
3. Huntsville Presbytery - Rev. Dr. Theodis Acklin, 3415 Mastin Lake Road, Huntsville, AL 35810
   (256)945-7216
4. South Alabama Presbytery - Elder Minnie McMillan, 54 Riverview Avenue, Selma, AL 36701
   (334)875-9617   mmcmillan@ccal.edu
5. Tennessee Valley Presbytery - Rev. Critis Fletcher, 68 Mattie Street, Russellville, AL 35654
   (256)332-6325   gepolar@bellsouth.net
6. Tuscaloosa Presbytery - Rev. Jacqueline Lang, 904 35th Avenue, Tuscaloosa, AL 35401
   (205)292-1048

Kentucky Synod - Elder Leon Cole, Jr., PO Box 335, Warren, MI 48090
1. Cleveland, Ohio Presbytery - Elder Greg Scruggs, 1117 Mt Vernon Blvd, Cleveland Heights, OH 44112
   (216)645-9584   gsagi57@yahoo.com
2. Ohio Valley Presbytery - Elder Sharon Combs, PO Box 122, Sturgis, KY 42459
   (270)860-4175   scombs1@bellsouth.net
3. Purchase Presbytery - Elder Sherell Sparks, 79 Paraadise Lane, Metropolis, IL 62960
   (618)203-2799   relld2000@yahoo.com

Tennessee Synod - Elder Roy Innman, 190 Latham Loop, Sweetwater, TN 37874
1. Elk River Presbytery - Elder Jacquelyn Cooper, 4705 Indian Summer Drive, Nashville, TN 37207
   (615)440-3010   jmcooper12@comcast.net
2. Hiwassee Presbytery - Elder Stephine Martin, 205 North Point Road, Sweetwater, TN 37874
   (423)486-7633   stephanie.nicole@yahoo.com
3. New Hope Presbytery - Elder Cecelia Bowden, PO Box 661, Huntington, TN 38344
   (731)9864266

Texas Synod - Elder Gladys Brandon, 719 Olive Street, Waco, TX 76704
1. Angelina Presbytery - Elder Tom Jones, 739 County Road 4720, Troup, TX 75789
   (972)285-0642   tjones1239@aol.com
2. Brazos River Presbytery - Elder Joy Wallace, 541 Glen Arbor Drive, Dallas, TX 75241
   (214)415-8734
3. East Texas Presbytery - Rev. Kay Ward Creed, PO Box 1316, Henderson, TX 75653
   (903)657-7169